MBA: The First Century

For Beth, Carl, and David

MBA: The First Century

Carter A. Daniel

Lewisburg
Bucknell University Press
London: Associated University Presses

Associated University Presses
440 Forsgate Drive
Cranbury, NJ 08512

Associated University Presses
16 Barter Street
London WC1A 2AH, England

Associated University Presses
P.O. Box 338, Port Credit
Mississauga, Ontario
Canada L5G 4L8

The paper used in this publication meets the requirements
of the American National Standard for Permanence of Paper
for Printed Library Materials Z39.48–1984.

Library of Congress Cataloging-in-Publication Data

Daniel, Carter A., 1938–
    MBA : the first century / Carter A. Daniel.
        p.   cm.
    Includes bibliographical references and index.
    ISBN 0-8387-5362-0 (alk. paper)
    1. Master of business administration degree—United States—
History.   2. Business education—United States—History.
3. Business schools—United States—History.   I. Title.
HF1111.D36   1998
650′.071′173—dc21   97-25110
                                                                         CIP

PRINTED IN THE UNITED STATES OF AMERICA

Contents

Illustrations

9

Preface

GRADUATE business education has gone through important changes in its first century of existence. The challenges that confront today's MBA students bear only a few resemblances to those that confronted the first seven graduates of Dartmouth's program in 1902.

This book traces the development of the curriculum, the objectives, the popularity, and the reputation of graduate business programs during this eventful century.

My aim has been to establish a general framework for discussion and analysis of this neglected subject, so that other people can assist me in making additions and elaborations. Every faculty member and every alumnus of graduate business schools will have had personal encounters with the problems and trends described here, and I hope that many of them will want to provide augmentations or corrections to the account presented. With their help, subsequent editions of this book may become, in effect, an encyclopedia of the history of management education.

In the process of locating, sifting through, selecting from, and interpreting the massive information on my subject, I have incurred many debts.

At Rutgers I have benefited from the advice of James Bailey, George Benson, Michael Crew, Nancy DiTomaso, Hal Eastman, Wayne Eastman, Bernice Fair, George Farris, Larry Fisher, Richard Hoffman, Farrokh Langdana, Donald McCabe, Giles Mellon, Paul Nadler, dt ogilvie, Jerry Rosenberg, Daniel Rosenblum, Allan Roth, Robert Rothberg, Robert Schlosser, J.-C. Spender, Dorothy Torres, and George Walters.

People from other universities and organizations who have helped me include Charles Hickman, Sharon Barber, Karen Martinez, and Janet Lipkind (AACSB); David Blake (Southern Methodist University); Tim Brennan (University of Maryland/Baltimore County); Lori Breslow (MIT); Nick Didow (University of North Carolina); Stan Finkelstein (MIT); Ann Fischer (University of North Carolina); Janis Forman (UCLA); Maxine Freed (New York University); Joel Haefner (Illinois State University); Ellen Herman (Harvard University); Jim Hickman (University of Michigan); Christine Kelly (New York University); Judy Lease (University of Utah); John Leland (Purdue University); John Miller (Bucknell University); Mary Munter (Dartmouth College); Martha Nord (Nord Consultants and Vanderbilt University); Priscilla Rogers (University of Michigan); Charlotte Rosen (Cornell University); Lynn Russell (Columbia University); Gary Shaw (University of North Carolina); Annette Shelby (Georgetown University); Kathy Slaughter (University of Western Ontario); David Wolford (University of Pennsylvania); JoAnne Yates (MIT); and Michelle Zak (Stanford University).

In addition to the endless demands I have made on the marvelous staff of Dana Library here at Rutgers, I have received special help from librarians at Boston University, the University of Chicago, Columbia University, Drexel University, Harvard University, the University of Illinois, Indiana University, the University of Iowa, the University of Kansas, the University of Michigan, New York University, the University of Oklahoma, Princeton University, the Wharton School Library at the University of Pennsylvania, the University of Wisconsin, and Yale University.

One further debt deserves special mention. Teachers College Library at Columbia University has preserved what is undoubtedly the greatest collection of college-related materials in the world. It includes, among many other resources, a complete collection of the catalogs of virtually every college in the United States, dating well back into the nineteenth century. For three years, Dr. David Ment, Director of Special Collections, and Mrs. Kathleen Murphy and her courteous circulation staff have granted me unrestricted access to roam freely through this remarkable archive. Had it been otherwise, this book simply could not have been written.

To all these, as well as to Rutgers University, to Mills F. Edgerton Jr. of the Bucknell University Press, and to the staff of Associated University Presses, my thanks.

MBA: The First Century

1

Getting Started: Before 1910

Few events in the history of the master's degree in business can have been as insignificant as the awarding of the first diplomas. President William Jewett Tucker of Dartmouth College, noticing the rising tide of interest in collegiate business education, wanted to get in on it. At the same time, however, neither he nor anyone else wanted to do away with the traditional liberal arts curriculum that the college had cherished over so many years. The solution they arrived at was to teach business in what we now call a 3–2 program: after finishing three years of college in any field of study, students could be admitted into a two-year business program, and at the end of the fifth year they would receive both the bachelor's and the master's degrees. President Jewett obtained a generous gift from prominent financier Edward Tuck, who incidentally had been his old roommate, and the program got started in 1900.

Thus it was that, in the spring of 1902, seven young men (out of the eight who started) marched down the aisle in Hanover, New Hampshire, and received their M.C.S. (Master of Commercial Science) diplomas, thereby becoming the first graduate-degreed businessmen in all the world. They all went on to have quite adequately successful careers, in the hotel, railroad, banking, import-export, manufacturing, retailing, and leather businesses. Perhaps their extended training contributed something to their success. There is no doubt that they knew they held the first M.C.S. degrees Dartmouth had ever awarded. They may even have known that they held the first master's degrees in business in the whole world.[1]

What they never could have known about, however, was the avalanche that eventually would follow them. Today about nine hundred universities in the United States award about ninety thousand MBAs each year, making business the second most popular graduate subject (after education). A modest estimate would put the number of MBA holders in American society at well over a million, or an incredible 1 out of every 250 people. The portion of corporation chief executives with MBAs has climbed steadily and is now probably around 30 percent. Of course these figures do not include any of the other nations of the world, where graduate business education, after a slow start, is now catching on fast.

So great now is the business of business education that a full-scale attempt to size it up—where it came from, how it has changed, what the heck it is anyway—is thoroughly warranted. Vast misconceptions, both in and out of universities, have always existed about the purposes and accomplishments of business education, and public perceptions of its worth have followed up and down cycles ever since its beginnings. At almost the same time that a major newspaper was recently dismissing graduate management education as "something very close to a confidence trick," a major journal was solemnly proclaiming that the schools are doing a great job: "Those who carry the burdens of leadership today can rest easy knowing that a tested cadre of young leaders stands ready to assume the load."[2] Moreover, even though MBA enrollments are at an all-time peak, so are predictions of an imminent decline: every year for the past twenty, somebody has proclaimed a forthcoming "MBA glut" because employers have supposedly grown disenchanted with the results.

Yet despite the criticisms, despite the dire economic forecasts, MBA enrollment has inexorably risen each year. At one time scorned by classics and humanities departments, the degree has come to be envied and emulated by them. Once derided as narrow and vocational, it has come to be probably the broadest and most interdisciplinary of all graduate degrees. Although ostensibly practical and career-oriented, it is probably more undefined in its nature and more flexible in its applications than a master's degree in English, geology, or math.

ANTECEDENTS IN HISTORY

Whatever business education is, and however popular it has become, it was not always so. Unclear in its content from the first and confronted with strong opposition from all sides, the degree got off to a slow start and did not really catch on for over fifty years after that spring day at Dartmouth.

Apprenticeship and Texts

Historians can find precedents for business education as far back as four thousand years, but these were mainly just variations on the apprenticeship principle: a young person who wanted to learn a trade would, quite logically, sign on with a tradesman for a period of time. Such arrangements, however, were appropriate mainly for crafts or manual trades, where the master would teach the pupil all the details of silversmithing, carpentry, or milling and baking. What the apprenticeship system did not touch on, generally, was the business side of an operation, such as the keeping of accounts. Accordingly, other arrangements—such as teach-yourself textbooks—occasionally emerged to fill in that gap. Five hundred years ago an Italian mathematician, Fra Luca Paciolo, wrote what was apparently the first such textbook, *Summa de Arithmetica,* which included instruction in bookkeeping principles.

Even that left many aspects of a business operation untouched. Some four hundred years ago England's amazing Sir Francis Bacon issued, typically, a call for the systematic study of business. Noting that "the wisdom touching negotiation or business hath not been collected in to writing," he went on to lament that "there be no books of it, except for some scattered advertisements that have no proportion to the magnitude of this subject." And then, anticipating by four centuries the ideas of today—that there are principles that can be learned and that learning them in school is far more efficient and effective than learning them on the job by trial and error—he concluded that the person who has education, even though lacking in experience, "would far excel men of long experience without learning, and outshoot them in their own bow."[3]

Political Economy vs. Private Economy

Since there did exist books on economics at the time, some of them written by people whom Bacon no doubt knew personally, such as Thomas Wilson and Edward Misselden, what he meant by saying "there be no books of it" was clearly something different from the works they had written. The distinction was between what later came to be called "private economy," or one's personal financial affairs, and "political economy," or the financial affairs of a nation. Except for Bacon, not many people saw a need for systematic study of personal business affairs.

As for the second, "political economy," however, it was already thriving by Bacon's time. It continued thereafter to grow and grow and served for two centuries or so as the closest thing a person could find to instruction in the ways of business. Generations of people who wanted to sharpen their commercial instincts found nowhere else to turn but to the works of such political economists as François Quesnay (1694–1774) and Adam Smith (1723–1790), even though the applicability of their lofty economic theories to daily commerce was slight.

During the nineteenth century political economy became established and accepted as part of the curriculum at most universities, perhaps a little more quickly in Europe than in America. When Thomas Cooper came from England to become president of the University of South Carolina in 1824, he sought and received permission to teach political economy, the subject he was most interested in, rather than metaphysics, as the trustees wanted.[4] Other American colleges followed—for example Brown in the 1830s, Kansas in 1866, Tulane in 1867—until departments of political economy, or just of "economics," were already elder statesmen of just about every campus by the end of the century.

A look at a typical textbook sheds light on the nature of the instruction. Charles Gide's *Principles of Political Economy,* widely used in all its many editions, was an imposing volume (six hundred pages, weighing about three pounds). Clearly written and organized, it laid out its subject before the reader in meticulous detail. With every new topic and subtopic and sub-subtopic, first is presented a detailed definition accounting for every aspect of its nature, followed by an inquiry into its history and then by a classification of all the various kinds, again with definition and history.

For example book 3 (out of five), "The Circulation of Wealth," contains five chapters—on exchange, metallic money, paper money, international trade, and credit. The chapter on exchange tells of the history of exchange, the two theories of the value of exchange, how value is measured by exchange, the advantages of exchange, the means of facilitating exchange, the history of the part played by merchants, the means of transportation, and the division of barter into sale and purchase. The forty-five-page chapter on metallic money begins with the history of money and goes on to consider, among other things, the varieties of disturbance caused by fluctuations in the value of money, the conditions which should be fulfilled by all good money, and the relative merits of bimetallism and monometallism. Even the chapter on credit (forty-nine pages) begins with a formal definition and then a history of credit. Throughout, the treatment is always historical, classificatory, and theoretical. Gide's book is never pompous or uninteresting, but its subject clearly has almost no application at all to the concerns of someone who has to run a business.

The Elements of Political Economy, by Brown University president Francis Wayland, illustrates the problem even better. Even though this very widely used book, first published in 1837, repeatedly reveals the author's concern for practical, applicable principles a businessperson could use, it still is not the long-missing book, such as Francis Bacon was looking for, that would tell a proprietor how to run a business. Wayland shows awareness of this problem from the very beginning by wondering if people might think that "the author, having had no experience in mercantile business, should have left this subject to be treated of by practical men." His three very reasonable defenses are that such a book is necessary, that active businessmen do not seem to be writing anything on the subject, and that they still certainly can if they want to.

Concern for the applicability of theoretical knowledge permeates the book. "How groundless is the opinion," he says, that education and science are without *practical* benefit, and that philosophers and students are merely a useless burthen upon the community; since it is *knowledge* which has given to us all the advantages which we possess over savages, and it is the *application* of that knowledge, which furnishes employment for nine-tenths of the whole community.

Yet even with this concern for practicality, the book is organized along strictly classical lines in its four parts—production, exchange, distribution, and consumption—with sub- and sub-sub-divisions as neat, precise, and remote from daily concern as in Gide's book. The chapter on exchange, for example, is divided into sections on barter, metallic, and paper. The chasm between such a presentation and the daily conduct of a business is, obviously, vast.

It was not just textbook writers who were dealing with ideas and principles remote from the daily affairs of business. The few other attempts at giving business advice came no closer than these to being practical and applicable. Since businesses were still mostly local, owner-operated, one-location establishments, there was simply no necessity to train people to be "managers," either of a branch office or of a function such as marketing. Thus when the editor of *Hunt's Merchants' Magazine* wrote an article called "The Education of a Man of Business" shortly before the middle of the nineteenth century, his list of four "necessary qualities" never mentioned anything about what and how to sell, or about when and how to borrow money, or about how to keep records. The first quality that education must instill was simply "love of truth." The second was moral principles, a calm temperament, and the habit of thinking for oneself. Specific skills needed were the "technical" ones, which apparently meant knowledge of the line of work (such as blacksmithing), as well as extensive reading of classics such as Bacon, the making of "digests," practice in arranging and classifying materials, and fluency in writing. Finally, a properly educated businessman will be able to fix attention on details, to hear every kind of argument, to be courageous, and to have a sense of responsibility. Matters of money, inventory control, customer relations, keeping of accounts, and the like never enter the discussion; character and work habits are almost the only things. Since this was the prevailing view of "private economy," or what we would now call business administration, it actually isn't surprising that no attempt was made to teach it in school.[5]

The Private Business College Movement

There was, moreover, still another reason why the movement toward collegiate business education as we know it thus did not even get started before midcentury, nor in fact had any reason to. Employee training, which had been satisfactorily handled for centuries by the apprenticeship method, was now being taken over by private business schools, also known as business colleges, business academies, or even business universities. Because of the industrial revolution, which made possible vast quantities of production by machine, the business side of an operation was now requiring far more worker input than ever before and sometimes even more than the production side itself. To train these clerical workers, private business colleges began springing up in the 1820s, mainly in areas near Boston and New York City, and after 1850 they grew rapidly all over the country until by 1893 over five hundred existed.

A look at the typical curriculum reveals which subjects were considered important for a career in business. Three—bookkeeping, arithmetic, and penmanship—dominated in all the schools for several decades, with stenography making its way in slowly beginning in the 1860s, and typewriting doing likewise beginning in the 1870s. Commercial geography and commercial law were introduced still later.

From the present-day perspective, the inclusion of bookkeeping and arithmetic seems quite normal. Penmanship, however, requires a bit of comment. Since all business correspondence, both internal and external, had to be written in longhand, the clarity and neatness of the writing assumed great importance, both because of communication needs and because it was the writing that conveyed the firm's image to the customers. It was not unusual for professionals in either business or business education to go on at length about this subject, stressing for example the importance of a plain and bold "business hand" without traces of ornateness. At least one school had both a "Normal Penmanship Department" and a "Plain Penmanship Department," and the distinction was considered obvious enough that it required no explanation.

It is interesting to note that the emphasis on these three subjects—bookkeeping, arithmetic, and penmanship—had remained pretty much unchanged for at least a century. Historians have uncovered a little book written in 1716 by Boston schoolmaster Thomas Watts, *An Essay on the Proper Method for Forming the Man of Business*. The first of his five requirements is "correspondence," by which he means "plain, strong, and neat" penmanship: "The motion of the joints and position of the hand determine the black and fine strokes and give the same indication and likeness in the standing and turn of the letters." Arithmetic is "the next necessary qualification," followed by "Merchants Accounts," "Mathematics and Sciences," and, last, "Propriety of Expression," or style in speaking and writing, including modern foreign languages. Watts's ideas, rudimentary as they were, were nonetheless far ahead of the time, and no other schools or books took them up. Not until a century and a half later did the business college movement get started.[6]

Some of these schools were apparently quite good at what they did. S. S. Packard's Business College in New York, Harvey G. Eastman's in Poughkeepsie, and the Bryant and Stratton chain of business schools that were established in 1853 and lasted until the 1890s were widely and favorably remembered. Prof. F. G. Nichols (1878–1954), who taught business education at Harvard University for many years, remembered with admiration his training in 1895 at Rochester Business University, which had originally been a Bryant and Stratton school. Besides its large and airy classrooms outfitted with mahogany, brass, and plate glass, the school had a practice "bank" and six practice "offices" where students received "business practice" training under very realistic conditions. Most instruction, he recalled, took the form of rote memorization, exact copying, and repetitive drill, in either bookkeeping or stenography, the two programs available to students. The former consisted of bookkeeping, business writing, business arithmetic, business English, business correspondence, business practice, and rapid calculations; and the latter (mostly taken by young women) of shorthand, typewriting, business English, business correspondence, and spelling. These were perceived to be the skills that businesses needed, Nichols noted, and no regular college provided them anywhere near as well.[7]

In general, however, the whole private business college movement did not have a good reputation at all. For one thing the schools, having no admissions requirements, attracted low-quality students. For another, the teaching was often poor, since the schools had no certification requirements to contend with and could hire, at pitifully small pay, inexperienced and otherwise inappropriate instructors. (Scholfield's Commercial Academy in Providence listed one instructor whose expertise was in "lunar observation.")

But there was still a more basic flaw. Even where the students and the instructors were of satisfactory quality, the whole conception of this kind of schooling was impossibly narrow from every point of view. The young man or woman trained to be a bookkeeper or stenographer was forever trapped in that one job, lacking any broader knowledge of the business as well as any kind of intellectual development. Businesses themselves were often impatient with the products of such training. "Initiative, originality, and judgment," rather than bookkeeping, arithmetic, and penmanship, were the qualities one business owner said he wanted in young men. For women it was virtually the same:

> If a girl comes into the office as a stenographer, it is of little importance to us whether she can write sixty words per minute on the typewriter, and take down her notes at one hundred words per minute and transcribe everything you dictate, and transcribe it exactly as you dictate it. It is far more important if she has a capacity for quick comprehension about our business, gathering the essential elements of our business, and whether she has good judgment of the construction of a letter, so that by and by, as she gets worked into the organization and some man dictates a letter hurriedly, she can at the right time suggest that the letter is not clear and should be rephrased in certain particulars.[8]

As a result of the reputation for low quality and narrowness of training, business college graduates often had trouble getting even the jobs they were trained for, a situation that led Harvard's president, Charles W. Eliot, to call such schools worse than useless: they not only do not help the student get a job, he said, but they displace the subjects that would have developed knowledge and thinking ability.[9] Calls for reform were frequently heard—to stop using copy books and to teach the students how to think, to replace the cheap and poorly trained teachers with highly qualified ones, to set sights on a broad view of business rather than on narrow utility, and to replace the "quickie" training with a longer and more sustained course. But the schools were prospering to such an extent—from none at all in 1843 to over five hundred by 1893—that nobody wanted to risk changing the formula. Whenever they appear, one observer noted, they fill up.[10]

The Growth of Practical Education in General

The growth of business colleges should be seen as part of an international movement toward greater practicality in education. In the United States, colleges of medicine, law, and engineering had all developed during the nineteenth century, and calls for secondary-level "trade schools" and "manual schools" were widely heard. The main theme of a massive 1885 Senate committee report was that American education was useless, obsolete, and far behind that in other countries. "Our college system certainly does not train our youth in habits of useful industry," newspaper owner Joseph Medill testified.

> Its purpose is not to increase the effectiveness of labor, to make two blades of grass grow where only one grew before; it does not show the pupil how, by acquiring a manual art, he can double or treble the value of his labor. It does not teach a science in a practical form. On the contrary, college education is conducted with a view to imparting a knowledge of dead languages and the higher mathematics to the pupils, which is all well enough for the wealthy and leisure classes, but is not best suited for bread-winners.

Others went even further and found the traditional curriculum positively harmful. Carriagemaker John W. Cooper of New York testified that "the average boy who is sent to acquire a classical education is ruined by the time he gets through with it. If he has any good horsesense in him it is educated out of him." Then, in order to emphasize his contempt, he added, "Whenever I find a rich man dying and leaving a large amount of money to found a college, I say to myself, 'It is a pity he had not died while he was poor.'"[11]

Most of the witnesses before the committee believed the consequences for society to be alarming. While Germany and Austria were developing a highly skilled workforce through their practical school systems, America's schools, according to sculptor Wilson McDonald, were producing only "briefless lawyers, bad doctors, worse preachers, half-educated engineers, untrained business men, speculators; and the large crop of the new specimen of the *genus homo*, the 'Dude,' the output of our rich society families." Maverick physician and writer Joseph Rodes Buchanan made the additional observation that placing emphasis instead on practical education could have "a still greater effect in increasing the productive power and national wealth, and giving to our country by superior skill the command of all the markets of the world." Finally, anticipating arguments to be heard aplenty forty years later, he noted that education in the practical affairs of our lives could also be a service to an orderly society: "A right industrial education puts an end to the commercial convulsions which throw thousands out of employment, and, by keeping all in steady occupation, will add not less than from 10 to 20 per cent to the prosperity of producers."[12]

The Call for Business Education in Particular

There can be no dispute that this clamor for a new paradigm in education was in fact long overdue. Colleges trained people, much as they had for the past century and a half, for the ministry and now for law, medicine, or engineering. Even at its most inclusive, the list of college-trained professions included only three other groups—artists, architects, and various kinds of scientists. Yet people in these seven professions together made up just a small portion of the workforce. Massachusetts in 1875, for example, had only 23,403 such "professionals," as compared with 104,935 people working in trade, transportation, banking, and insurance. The president of the Boston Board of Trade pointed out the absurdity:

> You put a man into the pulpit or at the bar or in the school room without any training, and let him undertake to preach or practice or teach, and he will prove a miserable failure. . . . Into business life, however, men rush with no certificate and nothing in the way of qualification for the calling on which a certificate could be based. Without any business talent or training or foresight they buy and sell, but get no gain. Only failure can be looked for in such cases.[13]

The situation was serious, and it presented problems for the nation, for business, for the colleges, and for individuals.

Noncompetitive Nation. The belief that the United States was falling behind other countries, especially Germany, in mechanical and technical fields, was very widely held. "With the exception of a few special branches of industry," Joseph Medill told the Senate committee, "Americans have surrendered the mechanical fields to foreigners, and when more artisans are needed they are not trained here but are imported, as we import our merchandise. This is all wrong. It is a cruel injustice to the rising generation of Americans and a source of weakness to the body politic." A *New York Times* article the same year called the need for technical education "one of the most important social problems of the times," as "thoughtful far-seeing men and women" were looking to the schools as a way "to increase the standard value of the national production."[14]

Poorly Managed Businesses. Even without international comparisons, such a need should have been apparent. American business was, beyond question, in a constantly chaotic state. Dr. Edmund J. James, a Wharton School professor who went on to become president of both the University of Illinois and Northwestern University, observed that American banks, widely called "the greatest banks in the world," existed in a chronic state of fear bordering on panic; that three-fourths of the mileage of American railways, "the greatest railways in the world," had passed through bankruptcy; and that a majority of people who took up a business career failed. "Business," Horace Greeley noted, "multiplies and extends itself on every hand, and calls for new brains and new minds on every side"—but, he continued, to the detriment of everyone no such new brains and new minds were forthcoming from the nation's schools and colleges.[15]

Underenrolled Colleges. Colleges themselves had strong reasons to be interested in teaching business, although some of them were slow to recognize it. It is hard to realize from the present-day vantage point that, for many decades, colleges played only a tiny part in American society: in 1870 only one and one-tenth percent of American young people were enrolled in college, as compared to over seven percent by 1920 and over thirty percent today. A day-to-day struggle for survival characterized most of the smaller colleges, since the loss of tuition fees from just a few students could have put them out of business. In fact twenty-one colleges closed their doors between 1890 and 1900, and more than twenty-six additional ones between 1900 and 1910.

Any alert observer should have been able to see that the traditional market for college graduates—church, law, and medicine—was not large enough or growing fast enough to support all the colleges that had sprung up and that business—which was already employing a third or more of the graduates—offered a new and almost untapped source of vitality. Even though, as will be seen, some parts of the college community fought hard against the teaching of business, it was plainly and unmistakably in the economic interest of higher education to give heed to the rising call for collegiate business education.

Neglected Students. Yet the most serious consequences of the outdated education system may have been felt not by the nation, not by the business community, and not by the colleges, but by individual young men and women. There is no way of determining the number who did not go to college at all because college as it existed had nothing to offer them, but it must have been very large. Families who wanted their sons and daughters to become more educated and cultured, and who had the means to pay for it, had no place to send them unless they were going to become ministers, doctors, lawyers, or engineers. Many of them thus simply discontinued their education after high school. Young people who made such a decision were often stigmatized as ignorant, lazy, or indifferent, and their parents were criticized as being too short-sighted to see the immense advantage of college. But, as Edmund J. James pointed out, these families were making a decision that was in actuality entirely rational:

> This so-called higher education appears to bear but little relation to their future work. It may all be very nice. It may belong to the accomplishments of life. It doubtless makes a fine dessert: but it is in all probability a pure article of luxury which no energetic and vigorous person who is determined to succeed in the fierce conflict of competitive business can afford to acquire at the cost of years of effort.[16]

Families who had made their fortunes through commerce felt the problem especially keenly, because they found no educational program designed to train their children to take over the family business. Fathers who had climbed to positions of power by initially working sixteen-hour days of drudgery for poor pay may have been proud of their accomplishment, but they would not have wished the same thing on their sons. Yet universities not only provided no relevant training the fathers could call on to replace such experience, but often did (or at least were believed to do) even worse by cultivating habits and tastes inimical to the business life. Many academic traditionalists continued to argue enthusiastically that "general" university studies would lead to general mental agility that would lead to success in life, but such a theory usually proved untrue in practice: young people trained in Latin poetry, moral philosophy, and higher mathematics generally were not interested in spending their lives on the factory floor or in the counting room. Several whole generations of fathers were disappointed when the sons they had proudly sent to the universities did not want to come home and run the factory.

People who challenged the traditional curriculum's usefulness were very sensitive to the charge that they were advocating a narrow utilitarian kind of education. Attempting to head off such an accusation, Edmund James willingly conceded that "we should be human beings before we are bankers, or manufacturers, or lawyers, or physicians." But, he added forcefully, "all this has reached its limit when the educational process itself has so warped individual development as to turn aside the individual from a calling for which he has special aptitude."[17]

So common was this state of affairs that colleges and their graduates developed a poor reputation in the business world. The most ringing denunciation came from the colorful Andrew Carnegie, proudly and unequivocally

a "self-made man," who, in an 1899 *New York Tribune* article, asked the
telling question "Where is the *college*-made man?" Noting the near absence
of college graduates among contemporary business leaders, he concluded
that, in business at least, "college education as it exists seems almost fatal
to success."

> Nor is this surprising . . . While the college student has been learning a little
> about the barbarous and petty squabbles of a far-distant past, or trying to master
> languages which are dead, such knowledge as seems adapted for life upon another
> planet than this, as far as business affairs are concerned—the future captain of
> industry is hotly engaged in the school of experience, obtaining the very knowl-
> edge required for his future triumphs. . . . The graduate has little chance, entering
> at twenty, against the boy who swept the office, or who begins as shipping clerk
> at fourteen.[18]

Others expressed the same contempt. The famed financier Henry Clews
answered a survey, around 1899 or 1900, with this flat declaration of scorn:

> I do not employ college men in my banking office, none need apply. I don't want
> them, for I think they have been spoiled for a business life. The college man is
> not willing to begin at the bottom. He looks down on the humble places, which
> he is fitted to fill. And, indeed, he looks down on all business as dull and unattrac-
> tive. . . . His thoughts are not with his business, but with his books, literature,
> philosophy, Latin. Now no man can approach the exacting business life in that
> half-hearted way. Business requires the undivided mind. . . . [The successful man]
> is the man who has started in as an office boy and who gets the education of
> keenness and practical knowledge that comes from early contact with business-
> men. He has his natural sharpness and originality, and the edge of it is not dulled
> by ideas and theories of life entirely out of harmony with his occupation.[19]

A more reasonable and humane perspective on the problem would have
led people to view college graduates as objects of compassion rather than
derision. It was, after all, their desire to improve themselves that had led
them to attend college, and the fact that college had failed to serve them
well was hardly their fault. Such was the view of Horace Greeley as far
back as 1867. "Our old fashioned colleges," he lamented, "are practical with
reference to two or three pursuits, but . . . the demands of the time require
nine-tenths of our young men in other pursuits than those. . . . This has
often saddened me."

> There are today one thousand college graduates . . . who are walking the stony
> streets of this New York, and know not how to earn a living. This is a condemna-
> tion of our university system. . . . When I see, as I do, so many men whose
> education has cost so much, find themselves totally unable, with all that, to earn
> a living, . . . when I see this, I am moved to protest against a system of education
> which seems to me so narrow and so partial.[20]

A quarter century later Professor James was saying the same thing: "Of the successful business men in this country," he told the American Bankers' Association in 1892, "but very few are college graduates. . . . Our colleges are not educating our business men."[21]

Resistance against Collegiate Business Education

The obvious question, then, is *why not?* Since the absence of business subjects from college curricula was felt as a hardship for the nation, for business, for colleges, and for all young people whether or not they went to college, some powerful inhibitors clearly must have been at work to prevent these subjects from making their way into colleges. And indeed they were. It is hard to realize today how absolute was the dichotomy between the perception of college and the perception of business; they were truly regarded, from both sides, as polar opposites. The intense resistance that colleges put up against the admission of business subjects into their curricula seems to have derived from three beliefs—about the nature of business, the mission of colleges, and the absence of a curriculum.

The Low-Class Reputation of Commerce. Prejudice against the commercial life has a history extending back into antiquity, for both monetary and social reasons. Anything involving money has always had sinister overtones of course; "the love of money is the root of all evil" was already an ancient proverb by King Solomon's time, and new life had been breathed into the adage by the resentment and suspicions surrounding the unprecedentedly huge fortunes amassed by American businessmen in the 1880s and 1890s. It was at exactly this time that the now-familiar phrase "tainted money" was coined, with reference to a Rockefeller gift to the Congregational Church.

Even where no corruption was suspected, moreover, resentment could exist for social reasons. In addition to the attitudes engendered by mere envy, there was the general contempt reserved for those who, unable to enter one of the traditional professions, had to resort to mere shopkeeping for a livelihood. Tradition held that in England a wealthy man had five sons, the oldest of whom inherited the land, the second, third, and fourth of whom went into the ministry, the law, and the army, and the last of whom, alas, went into "the countinghouse." In the family's portrait gallery the portrait of the youngest was turned face against the wall, and on the back was written the simple but devastating caption, "Gone Into the Trade."[22]

In fairness, one has to acknowledge that the life of a merchant in the preceding centuries had in truth been a thoroughly unglamorous one. The proprietor of a one-shop establishment led a constricted and monotonous existence with no similarities to that of today's tycoons in their plush and computerized skyscraper offices. Their work was hard, and everything they dealt with was unbeautiful—"seared with trade; bleared, smeared with toil," the poet Hopkins said. Thus when a merchant who had grown wealthy made motions toward acquiring social stature as well, he was likely to be met with ridicule and scorn. It was so in 1870 just as it had been in 1600, when a mercenary merchant in an English play was laughed at for claiming that he should be called a gentleman. Puzzled and hurt, he asked "Do you judge no merchants gentlemen?," only to be given an emphatically negative answer.[23] And it was at least equally so outside the Anglo-American sphere. In Chile, for example, as recently as 1900 it was considered absolutely inappropriate, practically forbidden, for sons of well-to-do families to be in trade. The aristocracy, in agriculture, looked down on the merchant classes with contempt; such work, in fact, was generally reserved for foreigners.[24]

The Dignity of Universities. Partly, no doubt, for these reasons, traditional colleges reacted in horror to any suggestion that they should allow commercial subjects to intrude into the classical curriculum. Colleges were for learning, not for earning; colleges were to teach how to think, not how to do; colleges were sanctuaries of peace and tranquility, not centers for commercial bustle and turmoil; colleges were guardians of the accumulated wisdom of the centuries, not training grounds for new skills. Moreover, commerce was not merely demeaning but very possibly corrupting. When the University of Pennsylvania opened its Wharton School of Finance and Economy in 1881, according to Professor Edmund J. James,

> the other departments in the University and most of the other members of the faculty were bitterly opposed to the whole project. And even if they did not actually interfere to prevent the progress of the work, they stood with watchful, jealous eyes to see that no concession of any sort should be made to these new subjects which, in their opinion, might in any way lower the level of scholarship as the ideal had been accepted by the upholders of the traditional course.[25]

Later, when James mentioned his ideas on collegiate business education to Princeton University president Woodrow Wilson, Wilson gasped in shock and astonishment, "Why, you wouldn't have the *colleges* teach *business,* would you?" To such people, steeped in the traditional subjects—Latin, Greek, and ancient history—the importation of commerce into the college curriculum was, simply and truly, unthinkable.

The Lack of a Defined Curriculum. Finally, another, but sharply different, reason was widely invoked to keep business out of colleges: that there was not anything to teach. The skills required in running a business were considered so ordinary that no education was needed or appropriate. All that a merchant has to do, William Hazlitt had written early in the nineteenth century, "is let things take their course. Keep what you have, take what you can get, seize every opportunity for promoting your own interest, and you will become a first class merchant." Arithmetic, bookkeeping, and penmanship were still the only subjects people thought of in connection with business, and these were the province of nonacademic organizations, such as the Bryant and Stratton schools. Education in more advanced areas, such as in management principles, was uncharted territory. "There were no models we could follow," Professor James wrote; "there was no experience from which we could profit." The suspicion was widespread that departments and schools of business were not really teaching anything, because there was nothing to be taught. Concerning the newly formed Wharton School, the student yearbook at the University of Pennsylvania said "It is a 'School of Commerce and Economy.' If you know what that means, good for you—we don't." All they did know was that, since it lacked a recognizable discipline, it must be pretty easy. The 1885 yearbook sneered, "Wharton— for those who find the arts too severe."[26]

Advocates of Collegiate Business Education

As for what a "school of commerce and economy" really did mean, nobody else knew for sure any more than the Wharton yearbook writer did, but a few far-sighted and highly articulate people believed strongly that such a thing was possible, worthwhile, and in fact necessary. The opposition views that Carnegie and Clews had expressed, although they were colorful and made good headlines, were coming to be less and less widely accepted as the nineteenth century drew to its close.

As far back as the 1860s Horace Greeley, in the address quoted earlier, advocated education for "developing a larger capacity to apprehend and to seize the opportunities that so abundantly exist on every side, for giving new activity and new power to the creation of material wealth."[27] Cornell University's distinguished president Andrew D. White had argued eloquently in 1866 for a department of bookkeeping and commerce, and the University of Illinois actually had, for a brief time, such a department, for "young men who wish to fit themselves for the arduous and riskful responsibilities of the merchant and the businessman." A distinguished engineer, Henry R. Towne of the Yale and Towne Manufacturing Company, argued fervently that training for engineers should include not just mechanical subjects but "Shop Management" and "Shop Accounting" as well. And finally, another early voice raised in advocacy of this kind of education was that of Robert E. Lee, newly appointed president of what subsequently became Washington and Lee University. He called for a program of college studies "not merely to give instruction in bookkeeping and the forms and details of business but to teach the principles of commerce, economy, trade, and mercantile law."[28]

Joseph Wharton. One of the most remarkable, and certainly ultimately the most influential, of these pioneer spokespersons for college business education was Joseph Wharton (1826–1909), founder of the University of Pennsylvania's famous Wharton School. Everything in his life converged to lead him to do what he did. Although he was from a prominent and prosperous family and would normally have gone to Harvard for a traditional education, a bout of bad health forced him to stay in Philadelphia, where he became apprenticed to a "counting-house," predecessor of today's accounting firms. There he not only learned the financial side of business operation but also became aware that the real power in a business lies in the control of the finances rather than on the factory floor.

Yet Wharton was also of scientific persuasion, and he learned the technical operations of businesses as thoroughly as any shop foreman ever did. Beginning in the zinc business, he built it into a huge success through his joint knowledge of both finance and industrial technology. When his partners refused him the freedom to develop the business as he wanted, he started over in the nickel business and again, through fiercely hard work and despite many obstacles, became enormously successful in it. Finally, when nickel appeared to have reached its maximum growth, he started a third time, this time in iron, and again mastered the technical as well as the financial sides of the industry. In each of these ventures, he not only helped in forming the partnerships but designed the facilities, raised the capital, supervised the technology, and assessed the markets and the competition. Doing all these things just once would have convinced anyone that business had grown too complex to be treated as a one-person operation; doing them three times was enough to persuade Wharton that he should do something about it.

In addition to his abilities in business and technology, Wharton was also a highly cultured man, and he knew that commercial, trade, and technical schools did not provide the kind of mind-expanding education that truly effective management required. He spoke and read several languages, an ability that gave him access to technical publications from Europe and enabled him to converse with (and employ) leading foreign experts on metals. He also was constantly increasing his store of knowledge and cultivating an active imagination by reading widely and even by writing verse. Thus, in assessing the "commercial colleges" and schools of technology that were growing across America, he recognized that no matter how well they did their work they still were training only clerks, not business leaders. "However valuable may be the knowledge which they impart," he wrote, "it does not suffice to fit a young man for the struggle of commercial life, for wise management of a private estate, or for efficient public service." He therefore concluded that the valuable parts of university training should be joined with the kind of commercial training that modern industrial administration demanded. And because of his hard-earned fortune, he, unlike all the other people who championed the same cause, could do it.

In his proposal letter to the University of Pennsylvania, he pointed out that America had an increasing number of young men of "wealth, keenness of intellect, and latent power of command or organization," who were being denied the opportunity to develop their abilities because colleges as presently constituted offered education only for the three traditional professions. "No country," he wrote, "can afford to have this inherited wealth and capacity wasted for want of that fundamental knowledge which would enable the possessors to employ them with advantage to themselves and to the community." And then, sounding a note that would be heard again and again in coming decades, he added, "Nor can any country long afford to have its laws made and its government administered by men who lack such training as would suffice to rid the mind of fallacies and qualify them for the solution of the social problems incident to our civilization." To correct this deficiency, he bestowed on the University the substantial amount of one hundred thousand dollars to establish "The Wharton School of Finance and Economy," with this declared "object":

> To provide for young men special means of training and of correct instruction in the knowledge and in the art of modern Finance and Economy, both public and private, in order that, being well informed and free from delusions upon these important subjects, they may either serve the community skillfully as well as faithfully in offices of trust, or, remaining in private life, may prudently manage their own affairs and aid in maintaining sound financial morality; in short, to establish means for imparting a liberal education in all matters concerning Finance and Economy.

But, as noted earlier, many people remained unconvinced by Wharton's arguments, and the school met with overt hostility from some. Such criticism could have been expected, since this—the first collegiate school of business—was something new. But the important thing is that it was done, and once in place it was never removed.[29]

The Senate committee hearings previously referred to were occurring about this same time, and they elicited the same sentiments that Wharton expressed, and more. The need for practical education of all descriptions was thoroughly impressed on the committee by the parade of witnesses who cited the damage being done, under the present educational system, to individuals, to the business community, to society, and to the nation. Thus the idea was no longer new or shocking after the mid-1880s, and by the 1890s some prominent advocates were making their voices heard across the land.

Edmund James. The comments of one of them, Edmund J. James (1855–1925), have already graced these pages several times. Approaching the question of business education from the academic side, he came to exactly the same conclusions that businessman Wharton had reached—that collegiate education in business is not only feasible but imperative for the prosperity of the business community and the well-being of the nation. He was a pioneer in nearly everything he touched. One of the first professors at the new Wharton School, he helped organize the American Economic Association and served as one its two first vice presidents, and he later almost single-handedly founded the still prestigious American Academy of Political and Social Science, which he served as the first editor of its Annals. Before he

retired in 1919, he had served as president of both Northwestern University
and the University of Illinois and had been an advocate of business education
at both.

Although trained in classical economics, with a doctorate from the University of Halle, Germany, he was impatient with the remoteness of economics from contemporary affairs. In 1887 he characterized the study of
economics in America as "pure and unadulterated teaching of dogma" and
accused it of producing "not merely superficiality, but an extreme form of
doctrinaireism and *a priori*-ism." The consequence of this miseducation, he
went on to say, was the frequently heard opinion, thoroughly wrong and
exasperating, that economic doctrines "may be true in theory, but they will
not work in practice."[30]

The quest for practicality consumed his energies for twenty years. As a
professor at the new Wharton School he not only did his part as a teacher
of business subjects but went outside the university to proselytize others to
the cause. His address to the American Bankers' Association (ABA) in 1890
was so persuasive it brought a large number of letters expressing interest in
the subject, not just from bankers but from educators all over the country,
including the presidents even of liberal arts colleges such as Earlham, Emory, Trinity (North Carolina), Trinity (Texas), Bryn Mawr, Gallaudet, Drake,
Brown, Hampden-Sidney, Adrian, Carleton, Lawrence, and Wooster, as well
as the Universities of Wisconsin, Iowa, Ohio, and Nebraska.[31]

As a result, the ABA sent him to Europe in 1891–92 to study methods of
business education there, a project that resulted in the publication of *Education of Business Men in Europe* (1893), a widely noted book. In it he meticu-
lously detailed the history, curricula, and administrative arrangements of
commercial schools in Austria, France, Germany, Belgium, Italy, and England. Yet instead of simply reporting he constantly interpolated editorial
comments extolling the kind of education that dared come down from its
theoretical heights long enough to show students some of the knowledge
and skills they would need in the real world. After detailing the archaic
curricula he found in French schools, for example, he wrote,

> Without contesting then the utility of courses in political economy, which contain,
> so to speak, the general philosophy of commercial instruction, we should like to
> see in the programs of our schools of commerce a course in commercial and
> industrial economy, from which the pupils would derive great professional gain.

He then went on to list nine subjects that might constitute this "course in
commercial and industrial economy":

> First, of the various kinds of commercial and industrial classifications;
>   second, the capital necessary for various enterprises; the necessity of deter-
> mining this exactly; the establishment of the business; the study of the laws;
>   third, of merchandise; of the raw materials; of the margin of the markets;

fourth, of the workmanship; of general costs; of gains and losses;

fifth, commercial and industrial organization and administration;

sixth, the importance of accounting in methods of control; the exact determination of the selling price; the keeping of inventories;

seventh, of the conduct of the business; of the material and moral conditions necessary to its success; of credit; of the general methods of conducting it; of the means of getting rid of middle-men;

eighth, corporations—the great branches of administration; methods of liquidation, etc;

ninth, of the duties of the employee; of the merchant; of the agent; of the shareholder; of the manager, etc.[32]

He also ruefully noted the existence in Europe of exactly the same objections, from both sides, that were delaying the acceptance of higher business education in America. "Of what use is it to train shopkeepers?" sneered a Belgian trained in the classics, while from the other side a merchant snorted "Did we learn commerce in school? Practice has made us what we are; practice alone can do it."[33]

Back home, in speeches from Toronto to Cincinnati to San Francisco, he made the same forceful points over and over—that colleges, students, businesses, society, and the whole nation would benefit from the introduction of business studies into the higher education curriculum; that business is just as legitimate a subject as law, medicine, and engineering, all of which had been introduced within the past seventy-five years; that a science of business, which he called "commercial and industrial economy" to distinguish it from political economy, does exist; and that people who have studied this science will become better business men and women than those who have not. By 1902, when James began refocusing his attention from business education to broader questions of university administration, he could look with satisfaction on the newly burgeoning field of collegiate education for business that his own efforts had done so much to foster.[34]

Frank Vanderlip. An equally powerful spokesman, but from the financial rather than the manufacturing or academic community, was Frank A. Vanderlip (1864–1937). An Illinois farmboy, he took a few night courses at a college and then became, in rapid succession, city editor of a local paper, financial reporter and then financial columnist for the *Chicago Tribune,* associate editor of a Chicago-based magazine called *The Economist,* private secretary to the U.S. secretary of the treasury, assistant secretary of the treasury, and finally vice president and then president (for ten years) of the National City Bank of New York. From his triple perspective—as journalist, government official, and banker—he had plenty of opportunity to view the growth of American business during the astonishing period from the 1880s to the 1920s, and he recognized quite early the urgent need for trained leaders in business. In a profusion of speeches and articles he outlined again and again the new needs of people in business, the inadequacies of school

curricula as they existed, the superiority of some European countries' education systems, and the obligation of the business community to step in and
design a program of business education, which, he specified far ahead of
everyone else, should ideally be at the master's level.

Changes in the world of business over the prior twenty years, Vanderlip
repeatedly pointed out, required a corresponding change in the way the
nation prepared its future business people. "We have," he wrote, "seen the
capital employed in business enterprises jump from millions to billions. That
change is significant of something much more than mere growth in the magnitude of commercial operations. It is significant of fundamental alteration
in conditions and methods."

> We have seen struggling lines of railways united into systems and systems into
> vast nets, all operated under a single management. We have seen whole industries
> concentrated in a few combinations, and those combinations dominating their
> especial markets throughout the world. These new conditions have surrounded
> us with problems for the solution of which experience furnishes neither rule nor
> precedent. To solve them we need a grounding in principles, an understanding of
> broad underlying laws.

Although he constantly chastised business leaders for not showing much
interest in developing a system of education that could help people address
these changes, he heaped most of the blame not on business leaders but on
intransigent educators. While the industrial world had been rapidly going
through a process of unprecedented and revolutionary "combinations"—in
labor, in capital, in the control of whole industries—the school curriculum,
Vanderlip noted, had been left in the hands of "teachers whose lives have
been largely in the classroom [and who] are not likely to have comprehended
fully the true significance of the development of the forces of combination."[35] Thus one main reason the nation was so slow to respond to the
challenge was that "the solution of the problem has been left too largely in
the hands of professional educators," and such people are "quite as likely
to become narrow and provincial as any other specialist." "Book covers,"
he added, "contain much knowledge but may also shut out from a too close
student much wisdom—much of that sort of wisdom which is gained by
experience in the world."[36]

By contrast, he said, Germany had made wise use of its schools and could
attribute much of its industrial and commercial superiority to its excellently
trained corps of young people. Whereas America had always thought of
education as a means of the "proper political development of the republic,"
Germany believed its schools' main purpose was "to turn out the most
efficient economic units," which would then be sent on to industry where
they would be turned into "the most effective economic corps possible."[37]
Vanderlip praised the German system over and over, without reservation:

Today we find in that nation, in spite of its lack of natural resources, pre-eminence in many industrial fields, a striking pre-eminence in foreign commerce and a superior intelligence in the administration of finance. Those successes can all be, in the greatest measure, traced back to the schoolmaster.[38]

To business groups everywhere, he stressed that they had a duty to "identify and scientifically clarify the principles and underlying laws of commerce and finance," so that these laws and principles can be communicated to educators and taught in the nation's schools and colleges. "I can think of no more fruitful field of inquiry for this Commercial Club," he told assembled business men of Boston in 1903, "than that of the need of a school for training young men for international commerce."

> I believe if you would make a study of that question and would come to realize what a great impetus could be given our foreign trade by a school which would turn out young men thoroughly equipped to enter such a field of activity, you would find yourselves enthusiastic advocates of some radical departures in education.

Moreover, he wrote, if this enthusiastic advocacy could result in persuading some of America's great universities to offer such a course, "you would not only be offering golden opportunities to your young men, but you would be placing the whole commercial country under another debt of obligation to you."[39]

But he was also careful to insist that commercial subjects should supplement, not replace, traditional ones. One danger brought on by the new complexity of the commercial and industrial world was that employees might become "automatic workers," without active intelligence, intellectual interest, understanding of principles, or ambition. Thus, what he sought was a means of providing education to intellectuals, and the solution he advocated was a postbaccalaureate degree in business. Addressing the University of the State of New York in 1905, he fervently argued that such a business degree would broaden and ennoble society:

> When we have reached a point of really making a scientific classification of the principles of finance and commerce, . . . and when we have developed a class of teachers capable of giving adequate instruction, . . . we will then have taken a long step in the direction of creating that respect for law of which we are now in need. There will be a greater respect for legislative laws because, with wiser legislators, those laws will more surely be based on correct economic principles.

And then he concluded with a resounding call for a specifically postgraduate program in business:

> Whatever your ideals of education may be, cannot you all unite in helping to evolve a college course which will be worthy of upholding a degree of Master of Commerce?[40]

He was part persuader, part prophet. Just three years later, Harvard University established its graduate-level business school, fulfilling all Vanderlip's requirements and setting off a new era in American education.

Harlow Person. Still another perspective was provided by Harlow Stafford Person (1875–1955), the Amos Tuck School's first real dean. The absolute epitome of an orderly minded engineer, he brought a systematic approach, with charts and diagrams, to each educational decision he had to make as dean, while at the same time remaining flexible enough to modify his systems when practical experience showed a better way.

A Nebraskan by birth, he attended the University of Michigan, where he earned a bachelor's degree in engineering and master's and doctoral degrees in economics. From the first he allied himself with the movement that soon came to be called "scientific management," and thus he became, as *The New York Times* later said, one of the early experts in "a field where economics, engineering, and managing merge." The Amos Tuck School hired him as its tentative director—"acting secretary" was his actual title—just one year after he finished his Ph.D., and he set himself to work immediately on the task of bringing organization and rationality into what was still a nebulous field of study. Although Wharton, James, and Vanderlip had argued forcefully, and successfully, to have business taught in college, there still was little agreement about what was to be taught, or how it should be taught, or who should teach it, or to whom, and even where and when: in place of regular college courses, or in addition to, or afterwards. These were the issues that Harlow Person brought his engineering perspective to—and ended up establishing directions that business education has followed ever since.

The questions of when and where were already settled for him by the Dartmouth trustees, who, eager to preserve the liberal arts character of the college, insisted from the first that education in business should take place only after the traditional basics had been learned. The business curriculum was thus grafted onto the standard undergraduate years as a "3–2" program, in which students could combine their fourth year of college with their first year of business studies and then receive both the bachelor's and the master's degrees after the fifth year. This arrangement prevailed for years: not until the mid-1950s did students from colleges other than Dartmouth constitute the majority at the Amos Tuck School.

As for the other questions, however, Person had little or no guidance in seeking answers. Applying his systematic training, he drew diagrams to show what levels and kinds of subjects could be taught and what category of businessman he was trying to produce. He divided business employees into three "zones"—administration, management, and operations—and noted the kind of training needed for each (Illustration 1–1). The third zone, operations, consisted of workers and clerks whose contributions to the firm were obviously indispensable but who required no advanced education to perform their duties. Every worker, he said, should start at this bottom level, but since six weeks on the job will teach more than two years at school it would not be reasonable to aim a program of higher business education at them. At the opposite end, zone one, are the president and directors, whose positions require "ripe judgment" rather than specific skills. For that reason, and because few workers will ever rise to that level, it would again not be appropriate to aim higher business education at that zone. It is, therefore, the members of the middle group, management, which consists of people whose task is the supervision of finance and accounts, design, works management, personnel, and sales, whom the collegiate business school should teach.[41]

The next step, then, was to identify the kinds of skill and knowledge needed by such managers. They required, he observed, a suitable personality or "motor temperament," appropriate mental characteristics or "ability to adjust," and finally extensive knowledge of the field, or "information and experience." Since personality is innate and mental characteristics are acquired in the first sixteen years of education, it is this remaining area, knowledge of the field, that is the business school's domain.[42]

Such knowledge he divided into seven areas—elements common to all business and elements peculiar to accountancy, manufacturing and mercantilism, foreign trade, transportation, banking, and insurance. This division of the field corresponds closely to what later became the standard "core" and "electives" of the business administration curriculum.

Yet despite his reliance on such deductive declarations, Person was quite open to learning from experience and modifying his practices when he found reason to. Thus when he observed that "students who had taken a certain grouping of courses showed the largest grasp of general fundamental business problems," he had the school make these general courses required rather than elective. Similarly, he noted with satisfaction that the students' master's theses—which he regarded as essential both as a part of their training as well as because they marked the beginning of the systematic accumulation of knowledge so important in the development of business education—were becoming more practical and less descriptive. Whereas a typical early one was "Trade Opportunities in South America," after only ten years they were more likely to be "The Cost Problems of a Shoe Factory."

Finally, when Person saw a need he moved to fill it. He was one of the founders of the concept of executive education—advanced training for practicing executives already in senior positions—and he seems to have been just about the first to see the importance of having what is now called the placement office, which brings together potential employers and potential employees. Except for such "a clearinghouse, a labor intelligence bureau," he said, students would have to walk along the streets looking for a "Boy Wanted" sign.[43]

Illustration 1-1:

HARLOW PERSON'S THREE ZONES
OF BUSINESS ACTIVITY
(AROUND 1910)

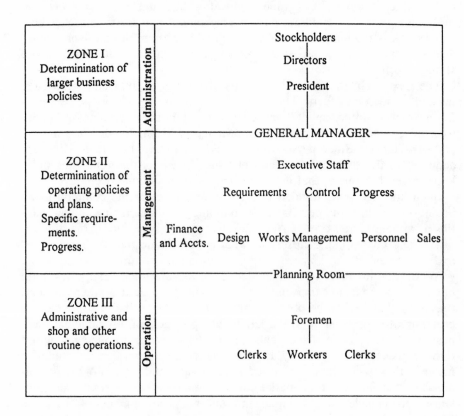

Source: <u>Journal of Political Economy</u>, 28 (Feb. 1920), 110.

The limitations of parts of his vision are plain, but what he accomplished in his fifteen years in the field far outweighs them. After World War I he went on to other areas of activity—water resources management, analysis of petroleum economies, and environmental conservation—and never returned to academic work, but by the time of his death in 1955 he could look on a vastly developed field of study that bore his clear imprint at every level.

Harvard University. But the biggest single boost to the movement to get business programs introduced in colleges was not the actions of individual spokesmen. It was the creation of the Harvard Business School in 1908. A dozen other universities had taken the step first, but when an institution of Harvard's prestige did so it conferred a dignity and legitimacy that broke down the last barriers of resistance. After Harvard, university schools of business came in a deluge.

The route to the founding was circuitous rather than direct. Although some prominent alumni had urged the establishment of studies in business areas, notably railroad management, Harvard's revered president, Charles W. Eliot, was not enthusiastic about the idea. He did, however, favor creation of a school of diplomatic service—presumably because such a subject seemed more dignified and more within the traditional domain of a university.

Although Eliot is known now as a strong and innovative leader who revolutionized Harvard during his forty-year presidency, and although he came to prominence by publishing two articles in the *Atlantic Monthly* advocating "a practical education" that could not be found in the colleges of the day, he was slow to support business education. For many years he was as conservative as anybody when confronted with the prospect of allowing any commercial subjects into the college curriculum. Even as late as 1905, in the thirty-sixth year of his presidency, he was holding the line by arguing that the object of education should be not to teach students how to earn a living but to show them how to live happy and worthy lives inspired by ideals that exalt both labor and pleasure. He even called it "monstrous" that some schools had begun teaching compound numbers and bank discounting. Although he acknowledged that business now required greater intellectual skills than ever before, he continued to insist that the traditional academic curriculum was the way to develop them. "A young man who is going into business had better take an academic course," he wrote in that same year. "That is an indisputable proposition, and there is no use discussing it."[44]

What happened to his opinions between 1905 and 1908, the year of the founding, was more practical than intellectual. The idea for a school of diplomatic service, which he strongly espoused, proved impractical (too little demand) at just the same time as the pressures for a business school were mounting, and business just sort of slid into the place that had been vacated. Two prominent faculty members—economics professor F. W. Taussig and government professor (and later president) A. Lawrence Lowell—

helped, through their advocacy, to smooth the transition in Eliot's mind. And thus, as almost the last act of his long term of office, the classically trained Eliot oversaw the opening of what has become the incredibly influential Harvard Business School.

Conceived of as a five-year experiment, the school was provisionally housed in the Graduate School of Arts and Sciences while the university watched to see if it would survive. Its three required courses—Principles of Accounting, Commercial Contracts, and Economic Resources of the United States—were essentially just shifted from an old department into the new school, as was the elective, Banking and Finance. Other electives, such as Railway Accounting, seem to have been new.

One unusual and unexpected development in this, the first purely graduate-level business program ever established, was the high attrition. Although enrollment was always strong, for nearly a decade fewer than half the students who completed the first year returned for the second. The degree itself, being a novelty, had no particular market value, and most students easily calculated that their earnings from one extra year of working would more than equal any advantage of actually completing the degree. Employers seem to have placed a value on the fact that someone had "studied business at Harvard," even though they didn't attach much value to the actual degree that might have been earned.

The Market Demand for Business Education

Yet it was not, after all, the influence of a few prominent spokespeople, or even the example of a major university, that broke the dam of resistance. It was the overpowering force of the market. Business had undergone a revolution in the span of just one lifetime, and education, slow to respond at first, finally could hold out no longer. The number of middle-level managers in the United States, which was probably around a million in 1926, the year Charles W. Eliot died, had been exactly zero in 1834, when Eliot was born.[45]

These managers—who both supervise lower-level workers and report to higher-level administrators—are the ones who make up the second "zone" of Harlow Person's diagram referred to earlier, the zone with which collegiate business education must be concerned. Before the Civil War, businesses had been one-shop and owner-managed; when the owner died, they went out of existence. In the four decades afterwards, however, everything changed in a way that was visible almost daily. Both the gross national product and the gross domestic product multiplied fivefold, while manufacturing was up sixfold and mining eightfold. Agricultural employees, nearly half the workforce in 1870, were less than a third by 1910, while workers in manufacturing, trade, and finance grew from a fourth of the workforce to a third. The number of production workers grew 300 percent and manufacturing production an astonishing 660 percent. What enabled all this to happen was the combination of capital, whereby production could take place on an unprecedented scale and with an unprecedented division of responsibility among the many managers required to operate an enterprise. Thus, over the second half of the nineteenth century an entire category of employment—the "middle management ranks"—rose from nonexistence to ubiquitousness. Impossible to explain in 1850, it was too obvious to require explanation by 1900.

Universities everywhere cited this development as the single major reason for having a school of business. "Commercial organization on a large scale is the order of the day," the University of California catalog said in 1897,

> and the successful administration of the vast aggregations of capital, the buying and selling of goods in the world's markets under the conditions of world-wide competition, require the broadest mental training and the widest knowledge that can possibly be obtained.

The University of Nebraska's 1913 catalog added a note of status and importance:

> Business is now, in its higher forms, as much a learned profession as theology, law, medicine, engineering, agriculture, and other difficult and complicated arts, and demands of those who would rise from the ranks a thorough, scientific, and practical training.

The aim of Nebraska's College of Business, therefore, was to provide "a supply of officers for the industrial army." "Those who aspire to places of trust," the statement pompously concluded, "must first go through a long and arduous training."

Other schools stressed the same points. In 1900 the University of Oregon stated the purpose of its business school as being "intended to fit young men more thoroughly and definitely for the successful management of large manufacturing and commercial enterprises" and the next year added that "civil and consular service, banking, transportation, domestic and foreign commerce . . . are rapidly approximating the character of professions."

The catalog of the University of Georgia stressed the local aspect of the argument: because Georgia and other southern states were taking the lead in American manufacturing and textile industries, the university must train business promoters, organizers, financiers, and general administrators. "A president of an Atlanta corporation," it went on ominously, "states that several times in the history of his company men have been obtained from other states to accept salaries that ranged from $3,000 to $5,000 because capable men could not be obtained in Georgia." Ohio State University's president had said much the same thing in 1898: "Today as never before business has become one of the leading professions. . . . Ohio cannot afford to lag behind in such a movement, in this industrial age."[46]

As much as these statements may sound like advertising, they should be seen as efforts to explain to the universities' conservative governing constituencies the changes that the institutions had already been forced to make. A much-cited study showed in 1904 that more Yale graduates were going into business than into any other field, and a study commissioned by the Georgia General Assembly the same year reported that business occupations claimed no fewer than sixty percent of the University of Georgia's graduates. Even when an institution tried to hold out against such a tide, as the University of Wisconsin did, by insisting that a liberal arts training was perfectly suited for future business people, the students circumvented (and finally forced a change in) official policy by registering as "special students" and taking every related course they could find, in the Colleges of Agriculture and Engineering as well as Arts and Sciences.[47] No organization can long afford to ignore its customers, and when American society demanded that its universities train their students in business, the universities, ultimately, had no choice but to comply.

Thus by 1910 business studies in college, and even in two graduate schools, were a fact of life in the United States. That year the president of the University of Cincinnati summed up the reasons in a report to its board of trustees. Such schools, he said, were springing up all over the country, even at Harvard; business was becoming so complex it required highly trained managers; among the university's graduates, fewer were going into the "literary professions" and more into business; and Germany and Great Britain were already teaching such subjects. Faced with such strong arguments, no one could resist, and the scientific study of the principles of business in college was firmly established.

*   *   *

At an educators' meeting in Boston toward the end of the nineteenth century, Mr. Eustace Fitz, president of the Boston Board of Trade, spoke eloquently about the importance of teaching the laws of business in school. After the address, according to the minutes, a Mr. Huling of Fitchburg rose and asked, "How can a teacher become acquainted with the 'laws of business,' alluded to by you, so that he may effectively impart them to the boys in his school?"

His question was on the mark. The struggle to get business into the university was won, and now the people whose job it was to teach these subjects had to grapple with the fact that nobody knew exactly what "business" was or how it was to be taught. Coming up with a curriculum was the challenge of the next three decades.

2

1910–1918:
Searching for a Curriculum

By the end of the first decade of the new century, public opinion about business education was becoming strongly supportive. In fact, such education programs were now widely proclaimed essential because they were deemed to contribute to the well-being of the social order. The condition of the education itself, however, was marked by out-of-control growth and utter confusion. Attempts to bring order into the new field of study were brave but not very fruitful.

THE SHIFT IN PUBLIC OPINION

By 1910 it was clear that attitudes had begun to change. For two decades and more, people such as Edmund J. James and Frank Vanderlip had been preaching the gospel of business education to unconverted audiences, no doubt wondering if their message would ever be heard. Now such proselytizing was no longer needed, as all the previous objectors—business people, educators, and the public—came to accept higher education for business as a perfectly reasonable, normal, and valuable thing. To be sure, the controversies that had raged before kept on raging, but now the majority opinion always seemed to fall on the business education side.

Controversy One: Is College Education Good Training for a Business Career?

For a couple of decades it had been universally accepted, in the press and in the popular mind, that a college education of the traditional kind not only did not help but actually hurt a young person's chances in business. Now, almost suddenly, that view was just as widely derided. One *New York Times* editorial dismissed the old belief as nothing more than a myth, while another similarly defended colleges with words that closely resembled Sir Francis Bacon's observations from three centuries earlier. The *Times* asserted that

We are confident that the young man with a college education is better fitted for advancement in modern business than the one who begins at the foot of the ladder with small learning.[1]

Such observations now had become the norm. Only a few years earlier Andrew Carnegie had attracted worldwide attention and approval with his boisterous denunciation of college men; now any such statement would be apt to trigger an irate response. One such occurred in a 1916 letter to *The New York Times* that berated the business community for its treatment of college graduates. First, the author said, business publicly scoffed at college graduates who, if given a chance, could have become superior employees; and second, business then exploited them by taking advantage of their consequent employment difficulties and underpaying them.[2]

Support for this pro-college sentiment came from several sources—business itself, educators, and the press. Businesses such as American International, Inc., the plumbing fixture manufacturer, increasingly began hiring college people and publicly announcing the policy. University of Chicago president Harry Pratt Judson wrote a widely noted book, *The Higher Education As a Training for Business* (1911), in which he reported that college imparts industriousness, intelligence, acuteness, and reliability, the four traits businesses most need in their employees. Moreover, he argued, college not only makes a better business man but a "larger man": uneducated business people make fortunes and do not know what to do with them, whereas an educated business person will know not just how to earn the fortune but how to spend it wisely. Finally, a much-reported (although undocumented) study from somewhere in the midwest showed that college graduates did well in business after all. Although some were impatient with drudgery and wanted to move on faster than circumstances warranted, they nonetheless caught on faster, analyzed facts better, and on the whole proved themselves more capable, intelligent, and efficient than non-college-educated people.[3]

Controversy Two: Is It Appropriate for Colleges to Teach Business?

Even when it came to the question of whether colleges should attempt at all to train people for a life in business—certainly a far more revolutionary idea since it attacked at the very heart of the definition of an educated man— a new attitude was evident. In 1911 Princeton University dean Andrew West wrote an eloquent and prescient article warning about the dangers of "practical" education. Universities rose and flourished, he argued, not because they helped people in their struggle for life but because they helped people rise above this struggle. But his article, which thirty years earlier would have stood unchallenged, this time provoked an equally eloquent response arguing that education, by ignoring the struggle for life, had produced the very disorders of society that Dean West condemned.[4]

On a more popular level, when the University of Texas opened its business school in 1912 the *Dallas News* did not merely approve but specifically pointed out that this development was part of a national trend:

> That studies relating to business and commerce have an educational value equal to those of the arts and sciences is being recognized by the leading institutions in this country. . . . We congratulate the University of Texas.[5]

It was true in other countries as well. In Germany the battle between the traditional humanistic curriculum and commercial studies was finally being won by the commercial studies after a struggle that grew far more acrimonious than anything the United States had seen. In Great Britain ten universities—Birmingham, Durham, Leeds, Liverpool, Manchester, Nottingham, Reading, Southampton, the Birkbeck Institute, and the London School of Economics—had already begun offering full programs in business studies (including some master's degrees) by 1916, and in 1918 no less a figure than Foreign Secretary Arthur Balfour spoke eloquently on behalf of introducing such studies at the University of London. Far ahead of any other country in the world, finally, was Japan, which after centuries of scorning commercial activity had established a system of college-level business education a full decade before the United States did.[6]

Controversy Three: Is It Even Possible to Teach Business?

The third controversy—whether business can in fact be taught at all, rather than being learned through experience—also continued to be heard after 1910, and the majority, as with the other controversies, had shifted to the yes side. The business community in Wisconsin, for example, asked the Board of Regents of the university to offer courses in business, for the purpose of remedying some specific defects they saw in their own knowledge as well as in the knowledge of the young university graduates who were applying for jobs.[7] A Kansas City school superintendent, in a prominent address at a national conference, added that business not only can be, but in fact must be taught, to correct the commercial chaos that surrounds us. He pointed out that whereas it takes four years to make a doctor, three to make a teacher, and six to make a college president, "a lazy lad dropped from grammar grades is supposed to succeed in business." It is no wonder, he continued, that ninety percent fail. He concluded, "All successful men in the future must be educated men. The business man cannot remain the sole exception."[8]

The most ringing endorsement came from a somewhat surprising source, Harvard's former president Charles W. Eliot, who, as is noted in Chapter 1, just a few year earlier had called the teaching of business subjects "monstrous" and had insisted that a traditional liberal arts education was entirely sufficient for a person of business. His change of mind reflects the change of the whole nation, which by the time of World War I had come to like the idea of business education in college with as much enthusiasm as it had derided it just a few years earlier. Eliot wrote,

> I believe commerce and industry in their higher ranges to be eminently intellectual pursuits, and I know of no other intellectual calling for which a professional school is not now provided. It used to be the fashion to study medicine by cleaning the doctor's horse and buggy, grinding his drugs, and driving around with him to make his calls, and to study law by copying deeds and briefs in a lawyer's office and reading books taken from the lawyer's library in the intervals of clerical labor; but the world has now learned that there is a professional school, where progressive systematic instruction rapidly developed is to be had. To deny that young men may be systematically trained for industry and commerce is to assert that industry and commerce are merely imitative arts to be acquired only by seeing other people do the tricks and then practicing them. In industry and commerce all things are become new, and new methods of preparing young men for these occupations must be invented with discriminating foresight, established with prudence, and maintained with liberality.[9]

BUSINESS EDUCATION AS A SERVICE TO SOCIETY

The new wrinkle in most of the pro-business-education statements was the emphasis on public service. Probably because the idea of educating people just so that they could grow rich was offensive, the stress came to be placed more and more on the contribution that sound business education could make to a well-ordered society.

Better-Run Businesses

On the most basic level, business education was to produce decency, stability, and strength in America's commercial activity. For example, when the University of Nebraska began a program in principles of selling, it did not state that the object was to help salespeople earn big commissions but that "the university authorities hope to eliminate many of the objectionable features of salesmanship." Similarly, Harvard Business School's announcement of a large study of the grocery business did not say that the purpose was to make grocers rich but instead stressed that the aim was to bring stability into the area, which exhibited more failures than any other line of business in America. In the same spirit New York University proudly announced a project in which its business students would volunteer their services to help keep the books for charitable organizations in the city. The object was to create in New York the "most scientifically managed charities in the United States."[10]

International Competitiveness

Global-minded observers added that improvement of business at home would improve the country's competitiveness in the world. Educational consultant Frank L. Glynn traveled through Europe for the U.S. Bureau of Education in 1912 and reported that "the entire scheme of European trade education partakes of an internationally competitive nature, and the training for job efficiency is primarily for the welfare of the state rather than the individual." The New York Chamber of Commerce president likewise reported his observations that the United States was far behind Great Britain and Germany in commercial education, and a Cleveland businessman speaking in New York cited figures to support his contention that business failures due to poor education were causing the United States to fall behind Europe.[11]

Improved Government Operations

Attempts to make government itself more efficient also fell into the business schools' purview, partly no doubt as a result of the emphasis on service to the public. The University of Nevada had a course in municipal accounting as early as 1912, and courses in city government were found at several institutions, including New York University, by 1914. When Cornell University repeatedly was unable to get a school of business approved, it proposed in 1914–1916 a "college of business and public affairs" that would train students for "positions in business and public service." That attempt was turned down too, but the fact that it was tried at all shows the prevailing public sentiment it had been intended to latch onto.

A Better-Ordered Society

Somewhat more arcane was an often stated conviction that betterment of the business community would contribute to the stability of the social order. "One of the greatest needs of this country," said the New York University dean as he handed out diplomas, "is for wise business men to solve fundamental economic and social questions." The University of Chicago was even more emphatic on the subject: the entire curricular philosophy of the school was grounded in the concept of service to society. One of its basic purposes, according to Dean Leon C. Marshall, was to make available the vast amount of information accumulated in the social sciences both to aid in commercial and individual development and to assist in solving social and political problems. It thus combined, Marshall went on to point out, three groups that were separate at other universities: the college of commerce, the school of social work, and the bureau of municipal research. The result, he said, was less a typical "business school" than a "social science institute," because the ultimate justification of any college must be a social justification:

> However important it may be to turn out business men who can make money, social workers who can command good salaries, civic workers who can rise to positions of influence and affluence, the most important task of all is to aid in promoting the progress and welfare of society. Our medical schools are demanded not primarily that physicians may command good fees but that society may be served. Our law schools may aid in making lawyers who will be wealthy, but the mere fact that we impose a bar examination shows that the interest of society, not that of the individual, is dominant.[12]

Foreign Secretary Balfour of Great Britain said essentially the same thing: even a man who does not need to earn a living could well devote himself to the study of commercial subjects, both because they are complex and fascinating in themselves and because commerce is the backbone of the sciences of social organization, diplomacy, and international relations. "How can such a study have a narrowing effect?" he asked rhetorically. "The University will do a great work if it will carry out such a scheme."[13]

Money earning, in short, was seldom mentioned during these years as a reason for studying business, almost as if it was too embarrassing a subject. A couple of times New York University's School of Commerce, Accounts, and Finance issued public relations releases that named salary figures— once boasting that its graduates earned more than did those of Harvard or Princeton (neither of which had an undergraduate business program) and once stating that its graduates were commanding salaries of from ten to fifty dollars a week. But except for these breaches of unwritten etiquette, one would have thought that business education, the fastest growing phenomenon in American colleges, was strictly a civic-minded undertaking.

One other motive, besides the general fear of being tainted by association with the grubby world of moneymaking, may have prompted university officials to insist on such higher civic motives: a desire to distance the new collegiate schools of business from the private "business colleges" that had acquired so poor a reputation. At Marquette University, when the regents first proposed a school of business in 1909, they were careful to make clear that they meant something different from "a glorified school of typing and secretarial science." Some of the regents, according to the university historian, "had heard of an entirely new curriculum which employed lectures by experienced merchants and trained economists," and because of this new curriculum they were persuaded to permit business studies for the first time. A speaker at the 1914 National Education Association conference went still further. After arguing fervently on behalf of business education, he then expressed absolute contempt for the typical proprietary business college, "which exists only to make money, which spends on advertising what it should spend on equipment, which enrolls anybody who pays, which has no staff, and which falsely claims to guarantee a job."[14]

Just about everyone thus seemed agreed. The high level study of business in college was now a legitimate and permanent feature of the landscape, bringing promises of increased productivity, international competitiveness, efficient government, and an orderly society. "There are few today," a New York University official could say in 1918, "who will deny the possibility of the science of business."[15]

THE STATE OF COLLEGIATE BUSINESS EDUCATION

Phenomenal Growth of Business Schools

Although the question of whether commentators approved or disapproved of collegiate business education may have had some intellectual interest, practically speaking it was irrelevant. While the commentators debated, enrollment in college business programs soared beyond anything imaginable just five or ten years earlier. Whereas only 3 such programs had existed at the turn of the century, and only 10 by 1907, there were 20 by 1911, 40 by 1915, and no fewer than 65 by 1918, with an estimated course enrollment of over 20,000. Moreover, these were only the full-fledged "business major" programs. If one counted institutions that simply offered individual courses in commercial subjects, the number was vastly greater—224 such institutions by 1913, according to one survey. Every kind of institution joined the movement, including state universities (Arizona, Tennessee, Delaware), private universities (Tulane, Columbia, Washington of St. Louis), state colleges (Oklahoma A&M, Mississippi A&M), and private colleges (Gettysburg, Whitman, Allegheny, Defiance, Davidson). All parts of the country were represented, from Lehigh in the east to DePaul in the eastern midwest, to Wyoming in the western midwest, Whitman in the west, Albion, Olivet, and New Rochelle in the north, and Stetson and Vanderbilt in the south. There was no kind or place where the rush to business education was not being felt.[16]

The Uncertainties about Business Education

Judging just from the numbers alone, it obviously was indeed true, as the New York University official said, that "There are few today who will deny the possibility of a science of business." Yet it was equally true that there were few people who would have agreed with one another about exactly what this rapidly growing science actually consisted of. Should it be divided up according to character traits that people needed to be successful in business? Or by the functions that business people are required to perform? Or by traditional academic subjects, such as history, mathematics, psychology, and English? In the absence of any previous experience to guide them, institutions devised their own curricula and formats, and as a result the field of "business" took radically differing shapes in different colleges and universities.

Names. Even what to call it was unclear. In the first few years of its existence, the new field went by at least thirty different names (Ill. 2–1)), most of them combining in some way the words "business," "commerce," "economics," and "administration," with an occasional "finance" and "accounts" or "accounting." It seems clear that the overriding objective was to find a name that unmistakably distinguished the study of the "the science of business" in colleges from the mere learning of typing and stenography in the widely discredited private business colleges.

Formats. Instructional formats likewise varied from one campus to another, falling mainly into four types. Harvard (and later Stanford) decided from the beginning that business was strictly a postgraduate subject, to be studied only after regular college studies had been completed. Such an arrangement Columbia University regarded as "unthinkable," opting instead for the "2 + 2-or-3" model, in which students would take two years of basic college work and then either two (for the bachelor's degree) or three (for the master's) more years of business studies.[17]

The Amos Tuck School (Dartmouth College) model was similar, a "3 + 1-or-2" plan in which the basic college studies lasted three years instead of just two. The University of Michigan also adopted this plan. A large number of institutions offered only undergraduate degrees and restricted the students' business studies to their final two years—thus a "2 + 2" plan. Finally, another substantial group offered undergraduate business courses over the entire four years of college, interspersing them all along with traditional college courses. The University of Pennsylvania's Wharton School fell into this category for most of its first forty years, not offering a master's degree until 1921. In Europe, still another format—the "1 + 3" plan—was commonplace, but no American college or university adopted it.[18]

Curricula. The best evidence of uncertainty and confusion, however, is found not in the names and formats of these early programs but in their chaotic content. Was the study primarily mathematical, historical, or psychological? Was it practical or theoretical, specialized or general? Was it purely for describing contemporary business practice, or did it aim instead at teaching the way business ought to be conducting itself? The answer to each question depended entirely on which college or university one had in mind.

For example, Northwestern University and the University of Chicago founded their business schools the same year and only a few miles apart, and both offered courses in railway management. But only Northwestern offered courses in public relations, real estate, investments, insurance, and

Illustration 2-1:

NAMES OF COLLEGE BUSINESS PROGRAMS
IN THE FIRST FEW YEARS

Administration and Finance

Applied Economics

Business

Business Administration

Business Administration and Commerce

Business Administration and Finance

Business and Public Administration

Business Management

Business Science

Commerce

Commerce and Administration

Commerce and Banking

Commerce and Business Administration

Commerce and Economics

Commerce and Finance

Commerce and Marketing

Commerce, Accounts, and Finance

Commerce, Finance, and Accounts

Commerce, Finance, and Journalism

Commercial Education

Commercial Science

Economics

Economics and Accounting

Economics and Business

Economics and Business Administration

Economics and Commerce

Engineering and Commerce

Finance and Commerce

Industrial Management and Business

Administration

Secretarial Studies

the psychology of business, and only Chicago offered public service corporations, industrial combinations, economic geography, the history of commerce, and, remarkably, waterways. Ohio State and Illinois, alone in all the country, taught courses in labor. And while Consular service, foreign exchange, and foreign trade were mainstays at Dartmouth's Amos Tuck School, the Harvard Business School offered no international courses at all. Business organization and business policy, two staples in curricula today, in 1910 made their only appearance at the University of Iowa. Especially strange sounding courses included "The Materials of Commerce" (California), "National Efficiency" (Wharton), "Industrial Values" (New York University), and "Drawings and Projections" (Michigan).

The courses being taught were so disparate, in fact, that even when grouped in large classifications they still form an unwieldy subject for discussion. Even with a considerable amount of forcing and trimming, they seem to require no fewer than thirty categories. Each of these categories deserves comment.

1. *Accounting* courses were taught at every school of business, from the very beginning. Many of these courses had predated the founding of a formal business program and had been attached to economic departments.

2. *Banking,* often called "Banking Practice" or "Money and Banking," was also found in nearly every business program. Even where no courses by those names existed (Michigan, Northwestern), the subject was no doubt covered under other headings, such as "Finance." At Michigan, for example, one of the six major programs in the business school was in banking, even though not a single course in the subject appears in the catalog. Both the University of Illinois and the Amos Tuck School at Dartmouth offered a course called "Practical Banking," while New York University offered a much less practical-sounding "Banking Theory and History" as well as "Banking in Europe."

3. *Communications,* meaning training in writing and speaking skills, appeared in only four business programs in 1910, under the names "Business English," "Business Writing," "Business Correspondence," and "Commercial Correspondence." Since such courses were a basic part of the work at the proprietary business colleges, most universities may have deliberately chosen to avoid them as a way of maintaining their distinctiveness. Also, since all college business programs required a heavy dose of traditional college courses, many colleges no doubt decided to leave writing instruction to their English departments. The heavy emphasis that business placed on writing skills during this time is very evident. A report from the New York Chamber of Commerce in 1917 complained that "a large proportion of [high school graduates] are deficient in practical working knowledge of fundamental subjects such as reading, writing, spelling, and grammatical construction of the English language."[19] Further evidence is found in publishers' lists between 1900 and 1920, which were full of self-help books, such as *How to Be a Private Secretary, Good English Form Book in Business Letter Writing,* and *How to Do Business by Letter.*

4. *Consular Science,* although never associated with business schools today,

was quite commonly included in the early business curricula. Besides the Amos Tuck School and the Wharton School, the Universities of California, Colorado, Illinois, Ohio State, and Wisconsin all offered at least one such course. The connection is explained by the fact that, to a large extent, the primary task of an American consul abroad was to further the commercial interests of the United States.

5. *Corporation Finance* was a standard course at nearly every business school. In many instances it had been offered earlier in economics departments and was then simply transferred to a new jurisdiction.

6. *Foreign Exchange* was taught as a separate subject at the Amos Tuck School and the Wharton School but nowhere else.

7. *Foreign Trade* courses were offered in more than half the business programs, most notably at institutions located near one of the oceans (New York University, the University of California, and the Amos Tuck and Wharton Schools). Midwestern universities (Chicago, Colorado, Michigan, Wisconsin) generally did not get as involved in international business (although Iowa, Illinois, Northwestern, and Ohio State did, and Harvard did not). Calls for improvements in America's exports were quite common. An official from the U. S. Bureau of Education went so far as to declare that "an international point of view" must permeate not just a few but all business subjects if the country was to experience success in the foreign distribution of its manufactured products.[20]

8. *Geography* or "Resources" courses were included in practically every business program. Mostly transplants from economics departments, these consisted of descriptions of principal raw materials and products from various areas of various countries.

9. *Government* courses, which as already noted lent an air of dignity and legitimacy to what might otherwise have seemed to be commercially tainted studies, were found in 1910 only at Harvard and Illinois. Both offered municipal government courses, and Illinois had a second course concerned with state government.

10. *History of Business,* the kind of nonapplicable academic subject that many business education advocates were trying to avoid, was offered in about half the business programs. But as with communication skills, even where the subject was not specifically listed in the business curriculum it may have been available in another department, either history or economics.

11. *Insurance,* taught in virtually every program, was regarded as a basic and necessary subject. When Columbia University founded its business school in 1916, for example, it specifically avoided calling it a "school of commerce" because the United States Supreme Court had declared that insurance is not commerce (*New York Life Insurance Co. v. Deer Lodge,* 1913), and Columbia considered insurance an obviously necessary element in a business program. Most schools offered multiple courses, with titles like "Actuarial Science," "Economics of Insurance," and "Insurance Practice and Law."

12. *Investment* courses, often called something like "Stocks and exchanges," were almost as common as insurance courses. Perhaps only the fear of appearing mercenary kept such institutions as Chicago, Colorado, Ohio State, and the Amos Tuck School from including them from the first. No doubt even in those programs the subject of investments was prominently discussed in finance and other courses.

13. *Journalism,* which today is never associated with business education, was a prominent part of the curriculum in four universities by 1910 and many more later. The Amos Tuck School, New York University, and the Universities of Illinois and Colorado all had journalism "tracks" for students who planned to pursue related careers, and the connection was considered so obvious and natural that it required no explanation.

14. *Labor,* as noted above, attracted almost no attention at all. Except for "Labor Problems" at the University of Illinois, and "Labor Legislation" and "Organization and Remuneration of Labor" at Ohio State University, it was not part of any college's business program—a reflection of the fact that the concept of labor as a valuable asset was slow to take hold in the United States.

15. *Languages* were of course taught at every university in the nation, but only four—Harvard, Wisconsin, Northwestern, and the Amos Tuck School—listed them as part of their business programs. In each of these, they were listed as special business-oriented courses—"Commercial Spanish" or "German Business Correspondence"—but it is not clear how much they actually differed from regular language courses.

16. *Law* courses were included in practically every business program, under a large number of titles. Harvard taught the law of contracts, business associations, and banking operations, while New York University taught bankruptcy law, real estate law, and insurance law. Several others called their course or courses simply "Commercial Law," "Business Law," or "Introduction to the Study of Law."

17. *Marketing,* including advertising, was part of the 1910 curricula at the Wharton School, Northwestern University, and New York University—all three of which were to be outdone three years later by the University of Wisconsin. Wharton had a one-term course called simply "Advertising." Northwestern's course took a more specific approach, as reflected in its title, "The Psychology of Business, Advertising, and Sales." New York University's emphasis appears to be have been in still another category: the course, called "Advertising and Selling Practice," was cross-listed as "English 2-A" and taught by members of the English Department. What the University of Wisconsin did in 1913 was to declare its faith in the marketing side of business by requiring both a one-term course in "Marketing Methods," which mostly concerned distribution, and a full-year course in "Practical Advertising," which involved cooperation with University publications and also had a strong psychology component. The absence of any kind of advertising, marketing, or salesmanship courses at the other institutions reflects the undeveloped state of the whole marketing concept at the time.

18. *Mathematics and Statistics* courses, like the communications and language courses mentioned above, were obviously taught somewhere in every university, so their absence from a list of business courses doesn't signify very much. Sometimes a course was clearly designed just for business, as with the University of Michigan's "Introduction to the Mathematical Theory of Interest, Insurance, and Statistics," but even without such specificity it is safe to assume that mathematics played some part in every collegiate business program.

19. *Office Skills,* although an embarrassment to many schools, nonetheless turned up in three of the major early programs. Both Dartmouth's Amos Tuck School and Pennsylvania's Wharton School had minor offerings in "Secretarial Work," and it was the most prominent part of the business program at the Univer-

sity of Vermont. Besides accounting, the only other courses offered at Vermont were "Office Technique" and "Stenography."

20. *Organization* courses, such as "Types of Business Organization," which are now among the most basic offered in most business programs, were still undiscovered in 1910, except for one course at the University of Iowa, where the course was oddly titled "Advanced Accounting and Business Organization."

21. *Policy,* or Business Policy, as it is now usually known, made only one appearance in 1910, again at the University of Iowa. Yet the course, called "Commercial Policies," seems to have been concerned mostly with tariff rates and other such topics more specific than what "policy" is generally understood to mean today.

22. *Production and Manufacturing* courses were few. Despite the precipitous rise of American industry, business schools did not generally know what to do with the study of production. Only four included it at all in 1910, and in those it went by four separate names, reflecting different approaches and emphases. The University of Colorado, although it offered not a single course with the words "production," "manufacturing," or "industrial" in the title, nonetheless listed "Manufactures" as one of the four tracks that business students could choose. The University of Michigan, on the other hand, offered courses entitled "Industrial Technique" and "Problems of Production" but did not include manufacturing among the six tracks its students could choose from. The Wharton School, which offered fifty courses touching on practically every field of business, included just one in this area; called "Manufacturing Industries" it appears to have been more a descriptive survey rather than a practical course in operations. Finally the University of California offered a clearly operational course called "Modern Industrial Processes." Several more years would pass before courses in manufacturing became a standard part of the business curriculum.

23. *Psychology* was virtually unknown as a business subject in 1910. Its only appearance was, as already noted, in the Northwestern University course called "The Psychology of Business, Advertising, and Sales," where the emphasis apparently was on motivating consumers. By 1913 Northwestern had decided to expand its offering to two terms, the first called simply "Psychology" and the second "Business Psychology."[21] The whole field of employee motivation, as distinct from consumer motivation, still was undeveloped.

24. *Public Finance, or Taxation,* was found in about half the business programs in 1910. It is clear that the subject was conceived of as a subdivision of "government management," since six of the seven public finance courses offered in 1910 were at state rather than private universities, and all but two paralleled a course in the same list called "Private Finance" or "Corporate Finance." "Public finance" meant simply how governments, as opposed to companies, pay their operating expenses.

25. *Public Relations* made only one appearance, in a single course at Northwestern University. Apparently the concept that a firm's image in the public eye could be important was not widely developed.

26. *Public Service, or Not-for-profit Corporations,* likewise appeared as part of only one curriculum in 1910. The University of Chicago not only offered a course called "Public Service Corporations" but even listed "Charitable and Philanthropic Services" as one of the four tracks that business students could choose.

No other school seems to have recognized any difference in management principles for these organizations, or at any rate to have recognized any substantial need for special training for them.

27. *Real Estate* was taught only at three private universities—New York, Northwestern, and Pennsylvania. At each, it was a one-semester course titled simply "Real Estate."

28. *Teaching* of business was often mentioned during this period as a field in which there was great demand, as business enrollments in public schools soared twelvefold (23,000 to 275,000) in the twenty-four years between 1894 and 1918.[22] Yet only one business school even mentioned any interest in the training of teachers, and surprisingly it was not one of the large state universities but Dartmouth's Amos Tuck School, which listed "teaching" as one of the five tracks students might choose. No doubt the flourishing schools of education at other universities included such preparation in their curriculum, but with this one exception schools of business had nothing to do with it.

29. *Transportation* studies, which can hardly be found at all today, constituted a major part of the business curriculum at almost every university in 1910, thus illustrating how different generations can divide up a single subject in different ways. To these early theorists who were trying to figure out what a business curriculum should consist of, the major functions such as financing, making, distributing, selling, and keeping accounts all seemed separable and worthy of study—distributing, or transportation, an equal alongside the others. Several schools offered courses called simply "Transportation," while others called them "Traffic Administration," "Transportation and Communications," or (at the University of Chicago) "Waterways." Most of the emphasis clearly was placed on railways: ten of these pioneer universities offered courses specifically dealing with "Railway Economics," "Railway Operations," "Railway Organization and Administration," "Railway Law," and so on. Only landlocked Ohio State offered a course in "Ocean Transportation." Clearly, distribution of manufactured goods occupied an important place in the way business was viewed.

30. *Specific Businesses,* finally, were addressed in several curricula. In addition to railroads, which as just mentioned were studied almost everywhere, Harvard taught courses relating to the printing industry, and Michigan offered courses relating to mine administration. Six years later the University of Oregon offered a course in "Lumber Accounting." Such specialization, although it sounds strange today, is probably not really much different from today's courses on the insurance, banking, or public utilities businesses.

Even as late as 1922 one major university (Mississippi) was still planning to replace its general courses in business with specific ones as soon as resources permitted: "It is not proposed at this time," its catalog stated, "to differentiate between the specific lines of business, as banking, transportation, and merchandising, but to give a general course of instruction in those subjects which are more or less important in any line of business"—but the clear implication was that this was only a temporary arrangement, and that when resources became available the university would start teaching courses in several such specific fields.

Publisher Arch Shaw sadly predicted that the same development would occur at Harvard, where he taught for a time: "I suppose, in a hundred years from now, when the work of the school is more specialized, we will have a professor of egg marketing, cabbage marketing, etc." But as it turned out he had no reason to worry: students were not signing up for such specialized courses, and universities abandoned them. When a university did teach about a specific industry, the reason was probably that external forces led it to do so. Harvard's printing courses, for example, began with a $7,000 gift from Boston's Society of Printers,[23] and Michigan's mine administration course, like Oregon's in lumber accounting, probably derived from some legislators' promptings.

The Philosophers of Business Curricula

The overall impression this curricular survey yields is inevitably one of nearly complete chaos. Except for accounting, not one subject appeared in the curricula of all the schools. Studies considered absolutely essential by one school were not even available at others. Even when several universities did offer the same subject matter, it was possibly divided up differently and probably called by different names. Now that the challenge of getting business studies into the university had been met, the big remaining problem was to figure out exactly what it was that these studies involved.

Among the people who tried to bring some sort of order into the field, three kinds of theories seem to stand out. Surveying them, one can see the floundering, as the theorists tried to confront problems of subject matter, method of approach, and format of study, with no precedents to guide them.

Group 1: The Character School

Although most people agreed by now that a "science of business" existed, some still held to the nineteenth-century view that business was simply a matter of character and therefore required only a character-building education. In 1912 the Kansas City school superintendent presented a list of fifteen qualities that business schools should develop in their students. Consisting almost entirely of ethics, personality, and good grooming, the list marks absolutely no advance whatever on the ideas that F. Hunt had written about seventy-six years earlier in the *Hunt's Merchants' Magazine* article referred to in chapter 1. Most thinkers had moved beyond such ideas by this time, but the very fact that this list—in which only one of the fifteen items relates to business—could even have been presented by a prominent educator at a national convention shows that this school of thought was not dead.

1. Thoroughness in the fundamentals of the conventional course of study in our schools.

2. Ability to work hard, to remain at a task until its completion.

3. General information of the world, its people, and their struggle for food, clothes, and shelter.

4. Familiarity with the forms and details of some kind of specialized business.

5. Skill and tact in management and direction.

6. A knowledge of local customs and special laws.

7. Power to change environment and to establish new conditions.

8. Power to decide quickly and to act promptly.

9. Willingness to co-operate.

10. Ability to appropriate, power to initiate and originate.

11. Well-developed, thoroughly trained, morally clean physical manhood.

12. Fixed habits of conduct, courtesy, and manners.

13. Personal appearance, dress, and carriage.

14. Proper attitude toward ethical concepts.

15. Good plain gumption, whatever than means, and including all that it implies.[24]

No less a figure than Norris A. Brisco, then a professor at the University of Iowa and soon to become the first dean of New York University's School of Retailing, shared this view, at least at the time. In 1917 he made a misprediction worthy of inclusion in those lists of great mistakes. "For a time," he wrote, "many favored highly specialized courses in commerce, and believed that professional schools were necessary. Today we have a changing attitude, and I believe that the professional school will soon lose favor. We need as training for business [only] a broad comprehensive education."[25] These fateful words were written just at the beginning of the greatest growth collegiate business education had ever known.

Group 2: The Classifying School

Other theorists tackled the issue by attempting instead to classify not the traits of a business personality but the actual activities involved in business. One such attempt, by the A. W. Shaw Company, resulted in the diagram shown in Ill. 2–2. Here production, distribution, and administration, the three main divisions, are each subdivided into plant and operation—each "plant" category then being subdivided into location, construction, and equipment, and each "operation" into material, labor or agencies, and organization.

The more closely the diagram is studied the more of a mess it appears. It combines, in one undifferentiated list, factors to consider before starting a business, factors to consider while building the plant, and factors to consider while the business is operating. Besides lacking any reference to financing the entire operation or using banking services to advantage, it is woefully short on the management and labor relations side, devoting as much detail to the possible kinds of product distribution ("railroad, steamship, parcel post, express") as it does to management of the employees ("hiring, paying, training, handling"). Utterly absent is any thought of considerations larger than the mechanical ones. Law (except for zoning law), the interests of stockholders, the interests of society, the motivation of employees, and the like—things that consume enormous portions of a manager's attention—are never mentioned at all.

Only slightly more sophisticated was the attempt by the Alexander Hamilton Institute, a prominent private business college in New York, to diagram "business science" as a circle (Ill. 2–3). Despite the claim of "completeness and logical arrangement"—"Nothing essential is omitted; nothing foreign is included"—the diagram leads pretty much nowhere. Economics is depicted as "the hub of all business activity," and commercial law as the perimeter that presumably sets a boundary on how far the spokes can radiate. The fields of activity consist of the three in the Shaw diagram—here called production, marketing, and accounting—with the significant addition of a fourth, finance. This addition permits insurance, investment, banking, and the raising of capital to be included, but still the diagram is hopelessly incomplete and fuzzy. Efficiency of operation and motivation of employees, for example, disappear under the vague headings of "organization" and "management," and the relation of economics to real estate is surely not the same as its relation to correspondence or auditing. In fact the central position accorded to economics caused one observer at the time to throw up his hands in despair. Economics, he wrote, "is far from the whole story. Psychology, government, sociology, the exact sciences, the biological sciences, history, all may with justice claim a part in the play."[26]

Group 3: The Inward-Outward School

Instead of viewing different classifications of activity as equal, a few people suggested a scheme in which business might be depicted as simultaneously looking inward at its operations and outward at its surroundings. The simplest of these representations (Ill. 2–4) shows production and distribution as the two ultimate functions of a business, and administration as being concerned with both of them. Although not worked out in enough detail to be of any practical value, this representation at least does recognize that administration, including accounting and finance, is a function in support of, rather than parallel with, other functions.

The same kind of reasoning led two prominent thinkers to draw other diagrams. The University of Chicago's Leon Marshall argued eloquently that knowledge of a business, even of its markets, was not enough. "Baffling

Illustration 2-2: A CLASSIFICATION OF BUSINESS ACTIVITIES

(An Abbreviation of a Chart Issued by the A. W. Shaw Company)

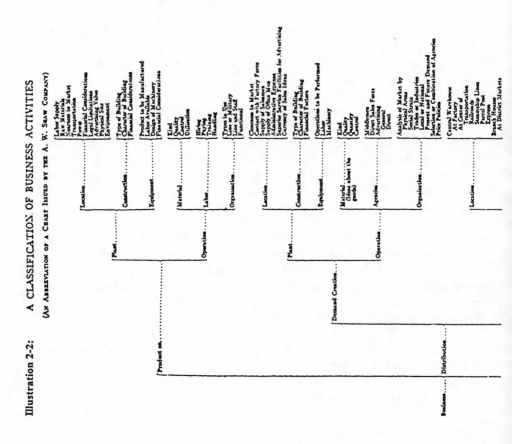

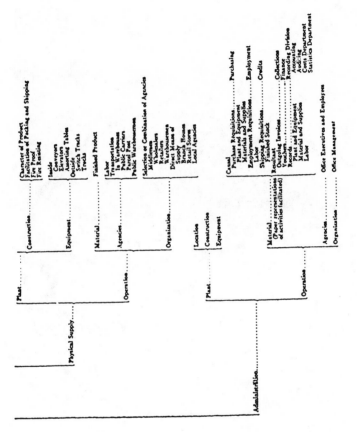

Source: Journal of Political Economy, 25 (Jan. 1917), 86-87.

Illustration 2-3:

THE ALEXANDER HAMILTON INSTITUTE'S
DIAGRAM OF BUSINESS SCIENCE (1913)

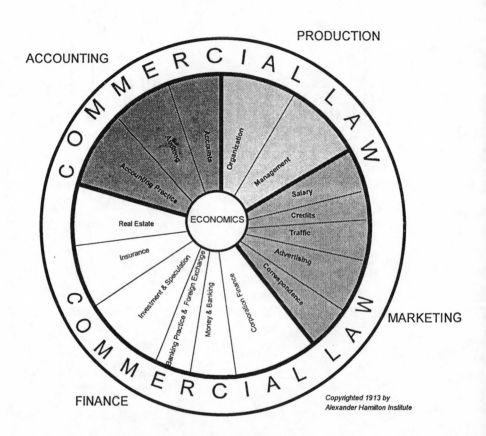

A SURVEY OF MODERN BUSINESS SCIENCE
*The four great business activities are PRODUCTION,
MARKETING, FINANCING and ACCOUNTING. ~
For purposes of systematic study each of these grand
divisions may be subdivided as shown above.*

Illustration 2-4:

A SIMPLE REPRESENTATION SHOWING BOTH INTERNAL AND EXTERNAL BUSINESS ACTIVITY

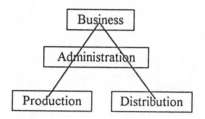

Source: <u>Journal of Political Economy</u>, 25 (Jan. 1917), 86.

as are the technical aspects of the business man's problems," he wrote, "they are after all but the beginning of his difficulties." The nearly intractable variables of value and price, he went on to say, complicate every technical decision a manager must make, but still worse are the all-permeating factors of the social environment a business operates in and the "continuous change, the influence of progress" that crisscrosses every other consideration. "Woe to the business manager," he concludes, "whose training gives him a static conception of business problems!"[27]

To include these environmental considerations Marshall suggested a diagram (Ill. 2–5) that expanded on the earlier one by showing the business manager's concerns as being both external (the environment) and internal (the business operation itself, including marketing). The arrows may be vague in their significance—with respect to the environment the manager's job is surely more to interpret than to control, and the opposite with respect to the business operations—but the implication is that far more weight must be given to environmental matters—social, legal, economic, physical, aesthetic, humane—than in any of the other schematic diagrams presented. Indeed with the A. W. Shaw diagram these things are virtually omitted, and

Illustration 2-5:

LEON C. MARSHALL'S DIAGRAM SHOWING THE MANAGER'S CONCERN WITH INTERNAL AND EXTERNAL BUSINESS ACTIVITIES

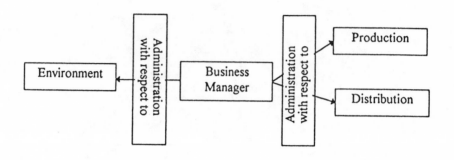

Source: <u>Journal of Political Economy</u>, 25 (Jan. 1917), 88.

with the Alexander Hamilton Institute diagram they receive only the most superficial treatment—economic forces pushing the business and legal restrictions holding it back.

To accomplish the kind of training needed to produce this kind of inward-and-outward looking manager, Marshall conceived of the University of Chicago's School of Business as a social science institute and suggested a three-level curriculum that strongly reflects this conception (Ill. 2–6). Following two introductory courses—one on environment and one on business—students would take intermediate courses in labor, finance, accounting, insurance, transportation, marketing, and social relations, before moving on to advanced courses in specific business functions.[28]

A slightly different conception was that of the Amos Tuck School's Harlow Person, who viewed education for business as a pyramid growing ever more specialized as it approached the top (Ill. 2–7). Whereas one is born with a personality, it is the earlier education (levels 1, 2, and 3) that form one's mental characteristics and the education in a graduate business school (levels 4, 5, and 6) that provides the information and experience necessary to produce the effective manager. General college education in history, soci-

Illustration 2-6:

LEON C. MARSHALL'S THREE-LEVEL CURRICULUM

Elementary Courses	Intermediate Courses	Advanced Courses
	Labor Conditions and Problems	
	The Manager's Administration of Labor	
	The Financial Structure and Financial Institutions	
	The Manager's Administration of Finance	
The Structure of Industrial Society	The Computing Aids of Adminis-tration, i.e., Accounting and Statistics	According to Resources and Local Needs
General Survey of Business Admin-istration	Risk and Risk Bearing	
	The Transport Function	
	Market Structure and Adminis-tration of Marketing	
	Social Control of Competitive Machine Industry	
	The Development of Industrial Society	

Source: Journal of Political Economy, 25 (Jan. 1917), 101.

Illustration 2-7:

HARLOW PERSON'S PYRAMID CURRICULUM (1916)

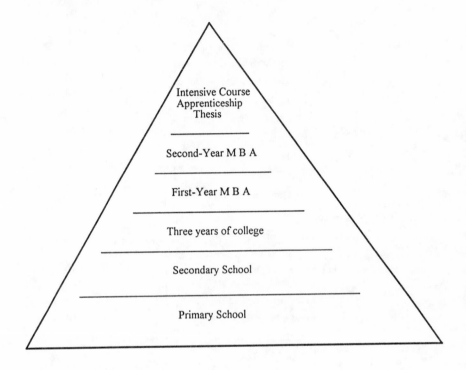

Intensive Course
Apprenticeship
Thesis

Second-Year M B A

First-Year M B A

Three years of college

Secondary School

Primary School

Source: <u>Annals of the American Academy of Political and Social Science</u>, 65 (May 1916), 117-127.

ology, political science, economics, psychology, and philosophy (level 3) is necessary before one can satisfactorily undertake and understand general business education (level 4). Only then can special business education involving specific department operations (level 5), be undertaken. And all this leads finally to the top of the pyramid, involving intensive studies, apprenticeship, and a thesis.[29]

Person's conception is admirable in its neatness and logic, even though it leaves almost every specific question unanswered. For example what aspects of history and philosophy should a future business manager study in college? What studies should a "general business education" encompass? Is "special business education in department operations" mainly descriptive (what is done) or analytical (what should be done)? In general, although both Marshall and Person stressed the importance of education outside of business subjects, Person relied much more on the traditional liberal arts offerings, while Marshall believed in special courses presenting liberal arts with specific relevance to business.

What these proposals show most clearly is that the theoreticians of business curricula were starting at the opposite end of the spectrum from the people who were actually making the curricula. While the makers were adding on courses more or less randomly whenever anyone suggested them, the theoreticians were oblivious to any empirical evidence. Instead of searching to find out what business wanted, or better still to find out what it needed, they constructed theories of business education in the abstract and assumed, or hoped, that the outcome would match what was required. Nowhere in their thinking does one find any developed ideas about surveying businesses to see what skills are required, or any thought of improving on the status quo by turning out graduates who could perform business functions better than they were being performed at the time. Curriculum making in 1910–1918 bore all the marks of the traditional academic world and almost no marks of business.

The state of practically everyone's thinking was summed up by Edward Jones, a professor at the University of Michigan, in three principles and seven propositions. As obvious and uninnovative as they seem now, they deserve attention because they show both the advances and limitations of business education thinking at the time.

The first principle states that it is important to define the type of person business schools intend to be training. This all-important point continues to be debated even to the present day, as schools wrestle with such questions as whether to provide elementary or only advanced training in business, whether to admit students who have studied only business or only nonbusiness courses, whether to train students for top-level or for middle-level management, and whether business school, in general, is for helping people get started in business or for sharpening the skills of those already there. In addition, at the time Jones was writing it was still considered important to stress that mere secretarial work was not one of the things being trained for, and in fact that consideration may been uppermost in his mind when he stated this principle.

The second principle states that patience is required in laying the foundation of instruction by systematic investigation into the ways of business. He specifically cites the wastefulness caused by the slapdash and shortsighted methods found in much of American industry and urges that educators not make the same mistakes. The implication is that education, if gone about in a systematic way, can bring about improvements in the way business is conducted. But even though this project—the construction of a workable curriculum—is obviously central to any discussion of business education, Jones has no more to say about it than that it must be done in a systematic and orderly way. Like everyone else, he recognized the importance but had few specific ideas about how to proceed.

The third principle concerns the importance of liberal studies. The subject of business education, unlike that of medicine or engineering, is human nature, Jones said, and therefore one needs broad acquaintance with all the subjects that schools had traditionally taught. This point of view was quite widely held by pioneers of business education—partly, no doubt, because they sincerely believed it but partly also because they wanted to remain part of the mainstream of university education and therefore thought it would be wise to head off critics who scoffed at business education as mere bookkeeping, typing, and stenography.

Jones's seven propositions in some degree attempt to answer the questions his principles raise, but to a large extent they merely duplicate the questions. The first four deal with the purpose, content, and method of the curriculum:

1. The purpose is to train people in managerial functions—accounting, finance, distribution, and policy—and to develop those sciences.
2. The subjects therefore should be administration, corporate finance (including accounting), and the theory of distribution.
3. New sciences are required; economics underlies them only in part.
4. Since training in investigation is basic, all these new sciences should be grounded in the scientific method.

The emphasis on accounting, finance, and distribution, to the exclusion of both the "softest" and "hardest" subjects—personnel and organization management, and production management—is typical of all thinkers at this time. The conception of business was still pretty much mechanical.

Jones's final three propositions concerned the nonbusiness parts of the curriculum and the locus and status of the education:

5. Business studies should be accompanied by the concurrent study of "liberal culture."
6. Business should normally be studied on the undergraduate level, "with the exception of a few necessary graduate schools" (presumably for training teachers).
7. Everyone should regard business as a high calling.

Like the vagueness and lack of specificity already noted, the careful attempt to show business and business education as broadly based and worthy is very typical of the sentiments of writers before 1918—and it will become even more so later.[30]

* * *

All these calls for action—for breadth, for research, and for dignity—remained nothing more than mere calls in the period before 1918. With remarkable suddenness, however, action began to occur that year, and developments in the next four years changed the face of business education forever.

3

1919–1922:
Explosive Growth, Descriptive Era

What happened between 1918 and 1922 was less qualitative than quantitative: the study of business in college did not change much, but the number of institutions offering the opportunity for such study, and the number of people taking advantage of it, simply exploded. And along with the growth in numbers came a corresponding increase in the importance the public attached to the whole world of business. Still, however, "business" remained so undefined and mysterious a subject that people could not agree even about what it included, and approaches to teaching it varied widely from one university to another.

Growth in Business Studies

It took twenty-five years from the founding of the first business program in the United States (at the University of Pennsylvania in 1881) to the founding of the tenth (at Washington and Lee in 1906). The next ten programs took only five more years, and the third ten just three more years. Thereafter they came still faster: the fortieth by 1915, the fiftieth by 1917, and the sixty-fifth by the end of 1918. Yet even that growth rate soon paled: in the four years under consideration here—1919 to 1922—the number of new business programs more than doubled, increasing by no fewer than eighty-two and bringing the total to 147 (Ill. 3–1)—up 668 percent in one decade![1]

Yet as impressive as such figures are, they tell only part of the story. For one thing they count simply the number of programs and do not reflect the phenomenal growth that was occurring within each. Exact numbers are hard to find, but where they do exist they suggest explosive enrollment. The University of Wisconsin correspondence division, for example, reported that its business enrollment grew 60 percent—from 4,296 to 6,896—in the single year from 1919 to 1920. The Harvard Business School, which had been started as a five-year experiment to see if it could survive, quickly became so popular that it could not cope with the demand. Having started in 1908

Illustration 3-1:

NUMBER OF BUSINESS SCHOOLS TO 1922

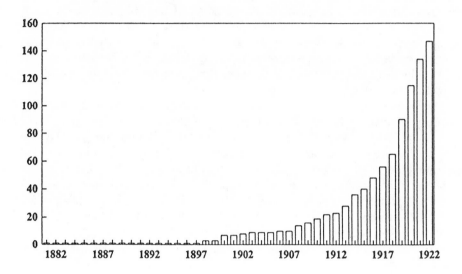

Source: Marshall, The Collegiate School of Business (University of Chicago Press, 1928), Chapter One.

with fifty-nine students, just thirteen years later it was compelled to limit enrollment at three hundred new students each year.[2]

A second complicating factor, moreover, is that these "new programs" were often nothing more than new names given to courses that until then had been parts of existing programs. The University of North Dakota did not formally announce a "school of business" until 1924, and thus it is not even counted among the 147 institutions mentioned above. Yet it had been offering business courses in its Department of Economics since 1899. From three courses that year—"Applications of Political Economy," "Public Finance," and "Banking"—it had grown to six in 1902, to sixteen in 1910, and to nine whole "groups" of courses in 1919: Economics, Banking, Commerce, Business, Insurance, Accounting, Commercial Secretaryship, Secretarial Work, and Teaching of Commercial Subjects. Undoubtedly other institutions were experiencing similar expansion not reflected in the statistics. Business education fever had gripped American colleges to an extent not even imaginable just ten or twelve years earlier.

The Growth in Reputation

Equally astonishing is the change in public opinion regarding business. Hardly a decade after antibusiness muckraking hysteria had swept the nation, and less than two decades since college presidents were expressing horror at the prospect of tainting traditional academic studies with the commonness of commerce, roars of approval were now being heard from all quarters—not just for business itself, but for the newly thriving business education industry and, consequently, for colleges and universities in general, which now were far more relevant than ever before to the life of the ordinary American.

Business. "Business" and "profession" had been considered opposites before 1900; by 1920 few people made any distinction between them. MIT president Henry Smith Pritchett foresaw in 1901 that "the time is near when those who are to direct great organizations, who are to control and develop manufactures, who are to trade between nations—in a word, the Captains of Commerce—must look upon their calling as a profession, not as a business."[3] Later, President Lowell of Harvard made some people snicker when he called business "the oldest of the arts and the newest of the professions," but he was reflecting a widespread perception that the work of a modern businessperson was as professional as that of an engineer, doctor, lawyer, or minister.

Such debates based on definitions seem more sterile now than they must have seemed in the period between 1900 and 1920, when a great deal of attention was paid to this question of whether business could qualify as a profession. The OED definition sheds some light on the central issue: a profession is "a vocation in which a professed knowledge of some department of learning or science is used in its application to the affairs of others or in the practice of an art founded upon it." Specific examples cited were divinity, law, medicine, and the military. The chief reason business could not have qualified before the late nineteenth century thus was the absence of any organized body of knowledge that constituted a "department of learning or science." But by 1918 that had all changed. As noted in the previous chapter, that year the dean of New York University could say, "There are few today who will deny the possibility of the science of business." Two years later another writer said the same thing—that the difference between a "trade" and a "profession" is the "scientific basis," the existence of an organized body of knowledge large enough to justify a person's spending time on it before starting to work. By this time, he went on, such a body of knowledge had definitely been accumulated, and thus business clearly qualified by now as a profession.[4]

Two other requirements were also often mentioned as prerequisites for professional status—a code of ethics and the existence of some professional societies. Ethics had always been discussed whenever business education was, and ethics courses were attempted, however briefly, at Harvard in 1916 and New York University in 1919. Moreover some prominent articles advocating ethics in the business curriculum appeared during this time.[5] The issues involved continue to this day to prove nearly intractable, but the fact that the discussion had become prominent is another reason that business could by 1920 be considered indistinguishable from the traditional "professions."

Professional societies, the other prerequisite, also developed profusely during this period, including the Society for the Advancement of Management (1912), the American Marketing Association (1915), the American Accounting Association (1916), the Administrative Management Society (1919), and the incredibly influential American Management Association (1923). In addition, dozens of more narrowly focused organizations were forming, such as the Mortgage Bankers Association (1914), the Menswear Retailers of America (1916), the Timber Products Manufacturers (1916), the American Association of Advertising Agencies (1917), and the National Association of Bank Women (1921). All these groups would have been entirely inconceivable a century or even a half-century earlier, and their development here, all at roughly the same time, is clear evidence that business had changed from a sweaty trade to a real profession.

But what contributed most to the elevation of business to its new status— more important than the existence of a body of knowledge, a code of ethics, and professional societies—was simply success. Maybe clergymen, attorneys, and physicians had a certain august dignity, but the newly emerged classes of white collar workers, unknown fifty years earlier, were rapidly becoming the typically successful Americans. They were clean, well educated, prosperous, and happy, and it was suddenly hard to demean them as mere merchants. They exhibited all the signs of social status that other professions had exhibited earlier, and the opportunities in such a lifestyle were expanding at an apparently unlimited rate. Just twenty years after MIT's president could ask, in an *Engineering News* article title, "Is There a Place for a Profession in Commerce?," a writer in the *Journal of Political Economy* could say plainly that, as far a business was concerned, "vocational" and "professional" now meant exactly the same thing.[6]

Thus business, just a few years after it had reached one of its periodic lows in public esteem, had soared to new heights. Once scorned as a sordid occupation, it was now fully accepted as a profession. Not one negative comment was heard when, in 1922, New York University proudly set up a special ceremony at the Morgan Library to award an honorary doctorate to J. P. Morgan Jr., hailing him as a "Prince of Financiers" who has been "called as consultant to the side of world industries and commerce."[7]

Business Education. Accordingly, educating college people in the ways of business—a prospect that just two or three decades earlier had caused Woodrow Wilson to gasp in astonishment—now seemed not just a normal but a laudable thing to do. Several commentators wrote glowing tributes to the new field of collegiate business education in the years after 1918, when (as already noted) Dean Taylor of New York University and Foreign Secretary Balfour of Great Britain had made speeches extolling it—the former saying it was now an accepted science, and the latter calling it "a great work" that would have a broadening, not a narrowing, influence on its students, a subject so "profoundly complicated" and so interesting that "even a man not needing to earn a living could devote himself to it from a purely scientific viewpoint."[8] Glen L. Swiggett of the U.S. Bureau of Education called on America's colleges to further the international interests of their country by educating their students in the ways of commerce, so that business could develop "by natural laws, with scientific methods, on economic principles, and with business practices that shall be in accord with Christian practices."[9] Harvey Alden Wooster of the University of Missouri called for the newly important schools to take the lead in developing a business code of ethics, and an official of the Business Training Corporation of New York urged that instruction in business be separated from economics departments so that its value could be fully recognized.[10] Forrest A. Kingsbury, a psychology professor at the University of Chicago, argued that education in business teaches a student to think just as much as any other kind of education does, and Edward Mott Woolley, a prominent and prolific writer on business subjects, wrote an enthusiastic article in *Collier's* magazine surveying the whole exciting new field.[11]

Almost the only negative voices heard were from an earlier generation. The brash young Sinclair Lewis did have some fun mocking Babbitt's business education, but the only real criticism came from the vitriolic pen of Thorstein Veblen in his 1918 book, *The Higher Learning in America* (which had actually been written before 1910). Calling the study of business administration "the supersession of learning by worldly wisdom," he went on to say that the work of a college of commerce "is a peculiarly futile line of endeavour for any public institution, in that it serves neither the intellectual advancement nor the material welfare of the community." Its purpose is to pursue "individual gain regardless of, or at the cost of, the community at large—and it is, therefore, peculiarly incompatible with the collective cultural purpose of the university." As entertaining as his observations are, they all were based on the false assumption that one person's economic gain is another's loss, and on the belief that unless a person actually makes a product, as opposed to financing, distributing, or selling it, that person has no right to a profit. In a time of unprecedented economic expansion in the world of commerce, it is no wonder that Veblen's ideas caused no interruption in the growing chorus of praise. To just about everyone, business education in America's universities seemed by now a perfectly normal and natural phenomenon.[12]

Colleges. The end of the prejudice against business education in college should be seen as part of the end of the long-standing prejudice against colleges in general. Formerly condemned as elitist, irrelevant playgrounds of idleness, they now became almost suddenly respectable. The fact that colleges were now willing to teach subjects of more perceivable relevance, like business, may have had much to do with the improvement in their public image. It is equally possibly that the astonishing growth in enrollment during this period deserves credit for the change: as more people were exposed to college, it became more familiar and acceptable to the public and less a strange and foreign experience. Whichever was the cause and whichever the effect, the portion of the population involved with college more than doubled, from 2.3 percent of the nation's young people to 4.7 percent, between 1900 and 1920—and this at a time when the total population was itself increasing nearly 40 percent. Not surprisingly, then, after two decades of decline, no fewer than ninety new colleges opened in the United States between 1910 and 1920. In everyone's opinion, the stature of a college education was growing fast.

In the fall of 1919, for example, America's premier retailer, Percy Straus of Macy's, wrote an article in *American Magazine* extolling college graduates and welcoming the end of the prejudice against them in business. Whereas employers used to maintain that colleges spoiled their students and made them decidedly inferior to young people whose training was entirely practical, everyone, Straus said, now knew better. Education was now as essential to success in business as in the traditional professions.[13]

The J. C. Penney Company likewise approved of college-educated employees. The director of its educational department, in a speech in New York, said college people have a bright future in retailing, both because business had become so complex it required trained minds and because business must be constantly on guard against excessive narrowness. Colleges, he maintained, equipped their graduates both to excel in analyzing conditions within business and in seeing the larger issues outside. Even J. C. Penney himself, the epitome of the self-made man, had declared that he saw nothing wrong with a college graduate who could prove his worth. "If he can and will," Penney said, "we will be glad to welcome him."[14]

These were not isolated or eccentric views. The National Association of Manufacturers issued a report in 1920, the main purpose of which was to decry the condition of American education, especially the nearly worthless vocational schools. Yet the most startling thing in the report is not its thesis but an incidental allusion to colleges: "A college education," it said, "is at least a thing admitted to be well worthwhile by the industrial leaders." That such a point could be casually acknowledged in this way shows how far opinion in the business community had shifted in just twenty years.[15]

Finally, a survey by the National Catholic Welfare Council affirmed the value of college so resoundingly it was reported as front page news by *The New York Times*. Seeking to find out who achieves "leadership in various walks of life," the survey determined that whereas only 1 person out every 41,250 elementary school graduates, and only 1 of every 1,608 high school graduates, achieves such a position, 1 of every 173 college graduates does. Faced with such overwhelming (even though rather suspiciously subjective) figures, it's no wonder that the American public vastly increased its estimate of the value of a college education.[16]

One interesting and important development was that business increased its estimate not just of the college graduates but of colleges themselves. Just a few years earlier businesses could have seen nothing of value going on in colleges, but now they actually began turning to colleges for assistance. One of the most amazing examples occurred in the spring of 1920 when the Technology Club, a group of business and academic leaders meeting at Drexel Institute in Philadelphia, established a large cooperative program designed to solve all the nation's industrial and economic problems. Under the agreement reached at the conference, companies were to furnish specifications of the kinds of training they needed for their executive and managerial ranks, and colleges would then set up programs to provide the training. The president of Drexel praised the proposed program, citing America's great shortages of truly trained executives. Unlike fraudulent shortcut courses in "business efficiency," he said, what was being proposed here was "management education of the proper kind."

In less than six weeks nearly three hundred firms had subscribed to the plan, each pledging the very substantial amount of five thousand dollars a year for three years, and even the American Council on Education had become involved. Such participation certainly indicates the confidence that business had come to have in colleges, but even more indicative were the sentiments the participants expressed. The country, they said, is facing an "appalling shortage of trained men," and problems like wages and the cost of living could be solved immediately if only companies had expert managers such as this program would soon produce.

Nothing in the news reports about this plan by the Technology Club shows any evidence of the mutual suspicion, hostility, and distrust that universities and businesses had almost proudly evinced just a few years earlier. No one on the university side demanded to know what right corporations had to be dictating a curriculum, and no one on the business side wondered what practical wisdom could ever come from head-in-the-clouds professors who taught obsolete subjects. Colleges had come to assume without question that business knew what it wanted, and businesses were willing to pledge over four million dollars to show their faith that colleges could provide what was needed.[17] (The project, incidentally, vanished entirely from view. Nothing more was heard of it after 1920, and attempts to research it have produced no results at all.)

This confidence in colleges, and especially in the business education they provided, also extended to government and society. On a festive occasion in early 1922 Dean Johnson of New York University proclaimed that the purpose of his school of business was nothing less than "to put all business on a scientific basis, lessen poverty and unemployment, destroy the germs of panic and depression, and promote the happiness and welfare of all the people." A. W. Taylor, also from New York University, went still further in a fateful speech later that year, expressing great confidence in this "first generation of university-trained business men in the world of commerce, industry, and finance." Because they have studied economic causes and effects "as a business problem rather than as part of theoretical economics," he said, panics would henceforth be things of the past, replaced forever by sound business judgment. Meanwhile, in Massachusetts, Boston University's business students were serving in internships using their newly acquired management skills for community service work, and in Belgium a new college of business stated, as one of the reasons for its founding, that scientifically run businesses were needed for the welfare of the nation. Everywhere it was agreed that colleges deserved accolades for the fine work they were doing in bringing high-level education in business to the service not just of industry but of society and government as well.[18]

The Nature of the Study of Business

Considering the chorus of praise for collegiate business education, one would have expected a little more agreement about what it consisted of. But the situation actually remained as chaotic as before. The study of business in American colleges and universities, wrote the dean at Northwestern,

> is a very ill-defined institution. It may begin with the Freshman year; it may start only after graduation from college; or it may start anywhere in between. It may represent courses in economics regrouped and possibly relabeled, or it may omit all so-called economics courses and center exclusively on practical courses in administration.[19]

Confusion of Classification. He was right, and the confusion extended all the way into the course offerings themselves. The varieties of classification attest to the schools' struggle to come to terms with the new field of study. The University of California organized its offerings into five categories, Harvard into eight, Wisconsin into nine, Chicago and Ohio State into ten, and Northwestern into eleven. While Harvard was dropping insurance from its curriculum Chicago was adding it, and Northwestern added journalism courses at the same time that Illinois dropped them. Although courses in finance, insurance, marketing, accounting, labor relations, production, and transportation were all offered by at least three of the schools just mentioned, only one school had offerings in all seven areas.

The University of Chicago's ten-part classification scheme warrants special attention because of its elaborateness. From four groups in 1910—Trade and Industry, Public Service, Charitable and Philanthropic Service, and Journalism—the school by 1921 had shed the last three groups and had expanded "Trade and Industry" into ten divisions containing eighty-one courses, as shown in Ill. 3–2. Apart from the obvious struggle with classification and terminology ("Administration of Market Problems"), the list shows strong signs of degeneration as it approaches its end and the classifications become less certain. "Psychology of Business Procedure" is unclear at best, but its fit into the laboriously constructed category of "Facilitating, Measuring, and Communicating Aids of Administration" has to be still more dubious. The inclusion of "Railroad Problems" under "Social Control of Business" suggests further impreciseness of terms. As heroic an attempt as this was to bring order into the curriculum, it did not attract any following, and it last appeared in Chicago's catalog just a few years later.

The number of courses at the University of Chicago had expanded from sixteen in 1910 to eighty-one in 1921, an explosive growth shared by all other institutions. Harvard University, even with the dropping of courses in insurance and public business, expanded from thirty-one courses to forty-seven, Michigan from twenty-three to thirty-six, Colorado from eleven to seventeen, and New York University from about forty to over sixty. What was happening mainly was a filling in of gaps. Universities that had had, for example, no courses in production or manufacturing in 1910 (Chicago, Harvard) had instituted several such courses by 1920–22. Commercial Teaching, offered in 1910 only at Dartmouth, now appeared quite widely, for example at Chicago, City College of New York, Illinois, Iowa, Nebraska, and Wisconsin. No one wanted to be guilty of omitting anything somebody else had, so everybody was adding everything.

Confusion of Course Offerings. The uncertainties about what a curriculum should consist of are plainly evident in some of the course offerings. The question of specific industries versus general business remained unsettled, as Harvard dropped its instruction in printing only to establish a department of lumbering, with courses in lumbering and forestry, general lumbering, and lumber products. Courses in the railway business became even more common by 1920 than they had been in 1910, but the University of Michigan discontinued its offerings in mine administration. The University of Iowa began subdividing its accounting courses and in 1921 offered Pharmaceutical Accounting and Accounting for Engineers. Further evidence of uncertainty is found in the curriculum of Ohio State University's "College of Commerce and Journalism," which in 1920 somehow included a "Social Service" department offering courses in family and child welfare, penology, recreation, and, incredibly, Americanization.

Confusion of Definitions. The variety and inconsistency in course offerings reflect the widespread lack of agreement about what exactly "business" meant. A report issued by Harvard after commencement in 1923 stated that

Illustration 3-2:

UNIVERSITY OF CHICAGO BUSINESS CURRICULUM, 1921

1. The Manager's Administration of Finance
   Financial Organization of Society
   The Manager's Administration of Finance
   Corporation Finance and Investments
   Advanced Banking
   Money, Prices, and the Cost of Living
   Problems in Business Finance
   Research Course in Finance
   Bills and Notes

2. The Manager's Administration of Labor
   The Worker in Modern Economic Society
   The Manager's Administration of Labor
   Education and Training of the Worker
   Types of Economic Organization
   Trade Unionism
   Collective Bargaining and Industrial Arbitration
   The State in Relation to labor
   Immigration
   Research in Labor programs

3. The Manager's Administration of Risk and Risk-Bearing
   Risk and Risk-Bearing in Modern Society
   Insurance

4. The Manager's Administration of Market Problems
   Market Administration
   Advertising and Selling Problems
   Advertising
   Purchasing
   Transportation and Traffic
   Transportation
   Industrial Traffic Management
   Commercial Cost Accounting
   Foreign Trade
   Ocean Trade and Transportation
   Marketing Seminar

5. The Manager's Administration of Production
   The Manager's Administration of Production
   Industrial Cost Accounting
   Practical Manufacturing (2)
   Field Work in Industrial Management

6. Facilitating, Measuring, and Communicating Aids of Administration
   Business Administration
   Administrative Standards, Reports, and Records (3)
   Organization for Executive Control
   Accounting (3)
   Introduction to Statistics
   Statistical Theory and Methods
   Psychology of Business Procedure
   Business Communication
   Business Correspondence
   Secretarial Work (3)

7. Social Control of Business (including Business Law)
   Social Control of Business
   Government and Business
   Business Law (3)
   Industrial Combinations--Trust
   Railroad Problems
   Principles of Government Finance
   Research in Public Utility Regulation

8. Physical Environment of Business
   Economic and Commercial Geography
   Geography of North America
   Geography of Europe
   Geography of South America
   Geography of Middle America
   Geography of Africa
   Geography of Asia

9. Development of Industrial Society
   Industrial Society
   Principles of Economics
   American Social and Intellectual History 1775-1830
   Economic History of the United States
   Social and Political Philosophy

10. Business Teaching in the Secondary Schools
    (9 courses)

90 of the 369 graduates who had specific career plans were going into business, making business the largest employer, just higher than the 89 graduates who were going into law. Yet as the report went on to show all the categories, it revealed much by its classifications methods:

90	business
89	law
44	banking
38	medicine
32	teaching
13	manufacturing
13	chemistry
11	electrical engineering
10	journalism
10	engineering
8	clergy
6	music
5	diplomacy
4	real estate
3	theater
3	architecture[20]

What strikes any modern observer is the exclusion of banking, manufacturing, and real estate from the category of "business," a word that seems to have meant exclusively the buying and selling of merchandise. Obviously, if one includes those three categories with business, then the number of graduates going into business careers is considerably larger.

With such uncertainties of definition prevalent in society at large, it is no wonder that the organization of college curricula exhibited confusion also. Thus marketing and advertising courses were part of the Commerce Department at Northwestern University, part of the Business Organization and Management Department at the Universities of California and Illinois, and separate departments by themselves at Chicago and Wisconsin. In a world where marketing could be part of management or part of commerce, where commerce could include or exclude real estate, and where banking might or might not be a business, it is quite normal that confusion of definition and classification was the most common trait in academic curricula.

Three New Subjects

Yet amid the confusion caused by uncertain definitions and rapid expansion, three additions to business curricula—international trade, retailing, and labor relations—do stand out. Hardly in existence at all in 1910, they became the fastest-growing segments of business education by the early 1920s.

International Trade. Probably because the war had heightened awareness of other countries, international business courses developed very rapidly in the early 1920s. While several schools (Dartmouth, Chicago, Michigan, Nebraska, Tulane) offered only a course or two called "Foreign Trade," others had more extensive offerings—six courses at Harvard, seven at California, and eight at New York University. The prize for most courses goes to the City College of New York (CCNY) and Northwestern University, each of which offered over a dozen. A look at the titles alone shows that the courses (especially at CCNY) seem to overlap as a result of proliferation without much control:

CCNY (1920)	NORTHWESTERN (1921)
Foreign Exchange and the Financing of World Trade	World Commerce
South American Markets	International Trade Practice
Business Methods in Foreign Trade: Marketing	International Trade Theory
	Ocean Traffic Management and Rates
Business Methods in Foreign Trade: Technique	Latin American Trade
Foreign Exchange Practice	Oriental Trade
Foreign Credits and Financing Foreign Trade	European Trade
	Geography of North America
South American Sales Problems	Geography of Asia
Russian Markets	Geography of Africa
Foreign Sales Practice	Geography of South America
Export Technique	Geology and Geography
Exporters' Problems	
Practical Steamship Operation	
U. S. and Foreign Customs Administration	
Export and Import Control	

Retailing. Similarly, the entry of retailing into business curricula was marked by wide variation among colleges and by enormous proliferation and duplication of courses. The terminology, as noted, is so uncertain one can never be too sure about what was covered in a course, but a great increase did occur beyond any question. Only three schools—New York University, Northwestern University, and the University of Pennsylvania—had offered any sort of Marketing in 1910, but by 1922 one would have had to search hard to find three schools that did not. Moreover many of the added courses dealt not simply with principles of marketing strategy but more specifically with retail operations: for example "Retail Store Management" and "Sales Management" (Harvard), "Practical Advertising" and "Selling" (CCNY), and "Merchandising" and "Sales Correspondence" (Northwestern). New York University had what was probably the largest such operation in the world in its New York University School of Retailing, which it took over from a private group in 1921. Underwritten in part by such major stores as Macy's, Gimbel's, Abraham & Straus, Saks, Best, Franklin Simon, and Stern's, it provided a combination of classroom instruction and outside training to future employees and executives in the retail industry, who normally studied in the morning and worked in the stores in the afternoons. It offered evening and day courses, plus short seminars, and it awarded the degree of Master of Science in Merchandising after two years of study. For five years it operated on a subscription plan in which the cooperating stores would pay an annual amount to the university in exchange for use of the student interns. (Thereafter it changed to more predictable permanent funding, and it continued in operation as a separate part of the university until 1963, when it was merged into the School of Business.)

This period ending in the early 1920s marked a great boom in American retailing: while the nation's population was rising 50 percent between 1900 and 1924, employment in stores rose nearly 102 percent. As noted earlier in this chapter, Macy's and J. C. Penney had expressed willingness to employ university graduates; now universities were taking the next step by training students directly for such retail work.

Labor. The third major group of additions to business curricula in these year were the "human" courses, called variously "Labor," "Labor Relations," "Industrial Relations," "Business Relations," "Personnel Relations," or "Psychology." Quantitatively, they were not especially prominent—none at all, for example, at the University of California, New York University, or Ohio State—but their presence at all marks a change from 1910, when only two schools had offered such courses. It also marks the beginning of a new era in which businesses and business schools began to acknowledge the importance of the human element in the workforce. The scientific management ideas of Frederick W. Taylor had already begun to fade in popularity by this time,[21] having never really appeared much in course titles; only Harvard, Illinois, and Colorado, among the larger schools, even mentioned scientific management or Taylor in their early 1920s catalogs. What was coming on now was the earliest beginning of a movement involving understanding of workers' motives and needs, rather than a mechanical study of time and motion.

The Descriptive Approach to Business

Indeed, except for these slight beginnings, the study of business in colleges still was overwhelmingly mechanical and descriptive. Underlying it all was obviously a continued belief in the existence of some great laws of commerce, the "invisible hand" of market forces that Adam Smith had written about in the 1770s. The reasoning was, presumably, that if students of business administration could discover these laws, they could then apply them to their own businesses and become successful. Non-quantifiable concepts such as strategic planning, corporate culture, and decision-making under conditions of uncertainty were simply unknown; descriptiveness characterized both the course offerings and the research being conducted.

Descriptive Courses. Even when a word such as "policy" appeared in a course title, it meant nothing like the "Business Policy" courses of today. At the University of Arizona in 1920 the course in "trade policies" covered not formulation of strategic policy considerations in view of environmental, competitive, and market conditions but

> [t]he character of the traffic; rates, ports, papers, and contracts employed; packaging and selling methods. The organization, agents, and policies for promoting foreign and domestic trade, such as the tariff, trust policy, navigation laws, consular service, etc.

A traditional European course called *Warenkunde* or "The Materials of Commerce," which sometimes although not very often appeared in American curricula, illustrates the point even better. "Courses bearing this name," a British scholar wryly observed, "have been among the least valuable features in many a European commercial college."

> They usually consist of the recital of a string of facts concerning hundreds of materials—classified as animal, vegetable and mineral, or more minutely as "timber" and "beans and "fibres" etc.: and the lecturer, having reached coffee or rice or whatever it might be, was expected to get the particular bottle from the museum, and display it to the class. Even at a famous commercial college it was not unknown for the lecturer to hand round 20 bottles of various beans in the hour, until the students never wanted to see another bean of any kind.[22]

Courses like this, besides being (as the writer went on to say) "a mere burdening of the memory," unmistakably reflected the mechanical or descriptive attitude toward business: that in order to conduct business properly, one must know only that this kind of bean is shipped by this kind of method and sold at this price.

Descriptive Research. Nowhere was the mechanical and descriptive approach to business more evident than in the new bureaus of business research that were springing up all over the country. The idea underlying their formation was that they could serve as a "central depository for economic facts," as one proponent called them.[23] Since few professors of business had any real business experience—most of them having come from economics or other traditional academic disciplines—and since few textbooks by really experienced business people existed, the great need that everybody perceived was for some factual information to teach. "How to provide the student with the actual practice or laboratory work which will enable him to relate his instruction to actual practice and conditions in the business world," observed Northwestern University's dean, "is the great unsolved problem of business education."[24] Thus it was believed that if businesses would send their sales, operating expense, and other such data to universities, students could thereby learn how the business world really operated. Besides, the reasoning went, universities could render a valuable service to businesses across the nation by collecting, regularizing, aggregating, and disseminating the data so that companies would for the first time have some statistical norms they could compare themselves to. A large national conference sponsored by the U.S. Bureau of Education in 1923 made this information-gathering and -sharing project its main theme. Establishment of such research centers ranked as a very high priority across the country at this time, for both reasons: to help schools and to help business.[25]

The endeavor quickly proved much more difficult than anyone had expected. The inadequacy of existing business methods was the first obstacle. "The larger number of our business men," a University of Michigan professor moaned, "keep only the crudest of records."[26] Even where such records did exist, moreover, the inconsistency of classifications from one business to the next made comparability almost impossible. Some store owners counted their own salaries as operating expenses, and some charged themselves rent for buildings they owned, while others did neither of these things. Thus regularization of record keeping became one of the first objectives of these bureaus. The director of Northwestern University's bureau wrote an article attempting to set quality standards for business research. He saw the need for five kinds of standardization: in units of measurement, in how these measurements are applied, in the form in which they are tabulated, in the form of graphic presentation used, and in the way the figures are interpreted. Clearly he believed that once these five kinds of standardization were accomplished, the laws of business would begin to reveal themselves.[27]

Others obviously agreed. Following Harvard's establishment of the first research bureau in 1911, other bureaus came quickly into being, and by 1922 important ones existed at least at Northwestern, New York University, Nebraska, Illinois, Brown, the Carnegie Institute, Ohio State, Wisconsin, Stanford, and the Wharton School. Established, as one stated, "to conduct scientific investigation in business methods and make business surveys," they undertook data-gathering activities on a scale never attempted before.[28]

Harvard's bureau, in its first few years, studied the wholesale and retail shoe industry, wholesale grocers, retail general stores, retail hardware stores, retail jewelers, drugstores, automobile equipment stores, and department and specialty stores, as well as labor terminology. Northwestern's bureau studied retail clothing establishments and retail meat stores; New

York University's studied the two local stock exchanges; and others did similar survey-type research. Still others focused on policies: the University of Illinois studied local taxation, and Brown University investigated trade cycles. Finally others devoted their attention mainly to the problems of labor, including turnover, absenteeism, and (at the Carnegie Institute) worker psychology.[29]

Except perhaps for the last of these, the studies seem to have been conducted in a rigidly mechanical way. Typical of this entire view of business research was the survey conducted by a Wharton student for his thesis in 1922. Hoping to find the secret of success in the garment industry, he wrote to all the members of the International Association of Garment Manufacturers, asking questions of the most descriptive and superficial sort:

Do you sell to retailer, jobber, or direct to consumer?

Do you employ salesmen?

Do you do an exclusive mail order business?

Do you pay your salesmen on commission, straight salary, or a combination of both?

Do you sell other lines besides overalls?

Do you employ specialty salesmen for your overall lines?

Do your salesmen carry other lines besides overalls?

Do you employ side-line salesmen?

Do you have a sales manager?

Do you give selling talks to your salesmen?

Do you have sales conferences?

Is your distribution large enough to warrant the above two?

Is your distribution local or national?

Do you do any advertising?

Do you have your own trade-name for your garments?

What mediums do you use for advertising?

Do you make a union-made or non-union garment?

Do you bring out the above fact in advertising and selling?

How many different numbers of men's or boys' overalls do you make?

Does your trade demand all these numbers?

Have increased freight rates had any effect on your sales?[30]

Although the questions remain entirely descriptive, oblivious to motives and local conditions, the head of the Wharton School was so impressed with the project that he praised it and expressed hope that other students might perform similar work in the future.

Cooperative Arrangements

Given the push for information-gathering activities, it is not surprising to find a substantial number of university-business cooperative arrangements being established at this time. Besides the extensive program of cooperation at New York University's School of Retailing, already mentioned, the most prominent example was found at the University of Cincinnati, where the "cooperative system" was born. Under the direction of ardent advocate Herman Schneider, the Engineering School and later the School of Business introduced a calendar featuring four weeks of work followed by four weeks of study.

In contrast to traditional training which, as Schneider often pointed out, paradoxically required one to withdraw from active life in order to prepare for active life, the cooperative system integrated classroom studies with real life experiences to a degree never known before. The University of Cincinnati's relatively small size and large percentage of full-time students made such an arrangement possible, whereas New York University's School of Commerce, Accounts, and Finance, although it greatly admired Schneider's ideas, would not have been able to make a program like that work. Instead, one professor suggested, large universities with many part-time students might refer to themselves as "continuation schools," where people who work at regular jobs all day can continue their education at night. Everyone sensed that, whatever the best exact form might be, cooperation of some sort was not just highly desirable but inevitable. "Neither the corporation nor the business school," wrote Dean Madden of New York University, "has scratched the surface of opportunities for effecting needed cooperation or for exploiting the possibilities of coordinated effort."[31]

A somewhat different form of cooperation was seen in the proposal for an American Institution of Industry and Commerce, to have been located in Buffalo, Niagara Falls, or Pittsburgh. Sponsored by the National Association of Corporation Schools, the institution (which never materialized beyond the planning stage) was to consist of a superschool that would train employees in the latest theories and techniques of business management. Praising the project editorially, *The New York Times* called it a "national college" for a "first class business education," noting further that when workers have reached their level of competence they can be shipped off to school to learn more knowledge to apply when they return to work. In every respect the institution as proposed seems not to have been very innovative but to have resembled a typical university school, and perhaps its redundancy explains why nothing more was ever heard of it. In any case, one can see in retrospect that the entire project was foolishly built on two wholly naive assumptions: the belief that a business can recognize the point at which an employee has reached his or her maximum level of performance with existing skills, and the corresponding belief that a school knows anything whatever about raising the employee to the next level.[32]

What had developed, then, was a paradoxical, fundamentally contradictory situation, in which nobody knew what business education should consist of although everybody now agreed that science of business did exist, and in which the universities believed that business had the answers while businesses believed that universities did. Curricula continued to range over all the spectrums from theoretical to practical, general to specific, function oriented to subject oriented, and universities kept seeking more guidance from real businesses while businesses kept sending their money and their people to universities for guidance. One professor surveyed the scene and found no fewer than thirteen business degrees being offered in 1921: BA, BS, BBA, BCS, BComm, PhB, MA, MS, MCS, MComm, PhD, DCS, and DBA. He further noted that MBA programs were of various lengths—twice as long at Harvard, Boston University, and New York University as at the University of Washington—and that now over sixty differently named departments existed in business schools. "We have no theory and no policy of public commercial education," wrote another observer, "and we need both very badly."[33]

A few people looked searchingly through the confusion for some kind of order. An anonymous writer in *The Weekly Review* narrowed and refined all the course classifications and came up with a list of ten that seemed basic and standard—Commercial Geography, Economics, Money and Banking, Corporation Finance, Transportation, Accounting, Business Law, Statistics, Insurance, and—the "most practical"—Business Organization and Management. The newly founded National Institute of Credit announced plans to establish a uniform course of study in business, consisting of thirteen fields—Principles of Business, Merchandising, Accounting, Economics, Banking, Business Barometric, Business Law, Corporation Finance and Investments, Business English and Correspondence, Bankruptcy Law, Foreign Trade, Credits and Collections, and Credit Research.[34] And several meetings of the new American Association of Collegiate Schools of Business (of which much more later) were devoted to curricular questions.

But overall not much progress was really evident: collegiate business education had to wait a while longer before it began settling into recognizable patterns.

4

1923–1930:
New Prominence, New Activities

WHILE business was famously booming during the 1920s, collegiate business education was undergoing only a few intrinsic changes. Except for the beginnings of one major shift—toward a less mechanical conception of business—it mostly just grew, continuing on a constantly larger scale all the things it had been doing earlier. What did change, however, was its prominence. Whether being widely hailed or widely damned, it had become so prominent a part of the national scene that it was constantly in the news. Its influence reached into areas not previously touched, and it also began for the first time to engage in profound and detailed analysis of its own operations.

THE STILL UNSETTLED CURRICULUM

In 1920 Dartmouth's H. S. Person had written a weary account of his search for a business curriculum. "During the more than fifteen years of our efforts at the Tuck School," he said, "we have been searching for the elements of a curriculum *which are basic*" (emphasis added). Whereas businesses and others may have wanted to hire graduates trained in the marketing of concrete or the operation of a comptometer, Person recognized that these considerations were superficial and that there must, somewhere, be some basic underlying elements that should form an ideal education for business. A superficial curriculum, he concluded, "is likely to develop limitations in the graduate rather than give him professional freedom of power"—i.e., to restrict the graduate to one job forever, rather than to train for a companywide or industrywide perspective.[1]

Expansion of Course Offerings

Ten years later the search was still going on. In a half-joking address to the American Association (later Assembly) of Collegiate Schools of Business (AACSB), Prof. H. E. Hoagland of Ohio State University coined a Malthusian law of business education: "Business courses will multiply indefinitely unless checked by a scarcity of students or a dearth of appropriations." Accounting courses, he pointed out, were constantly being subdivided and re-subdivided into smaller courses; economic geography provided almost endless opportunities for breaking courses into smaller ones; and even marketing had begun splitting its offerings into wholesale and retail, domestic and foreign, hard goods and soft. Now other colleges like engineering and law, which originally looked down on business schools, were following the business precedent and beginning to divide their own curricular offerings into smaller and smaller units.[2]

The Universities of Colorado and Iowa illustrate what Hoagland was saying. Colorado went from eleven course offerings in 1910, to seventeen in 1920, to thirty in 1930—from one course in marketing to three to eleven. Iowa, which had fourteen courses in 1910 and just over twenty in 1920, expanded without restraint to seventy-seven courses by 1930, including "Air Transport" and "The Chamber of Commerce and the Trade Association." Any new subdivision anyone could think of—whether an academic approach, a division of a business function, or an employment opportunity— became a legitimate subject for inclusion in a business curriculum.

A Trend Toward Consolidation and Regularization

Yet at the same time that some schools were endlessly expanding their curricula, some others were showing signs of slowing the growth, of consolidating their courses, of eliminating the eccentric and concentrating on the concentric. The search for an ideal classification—which sounds much the same as H. S. Person's "search for the elements of a curriculum which are basic"—obviously occupied a prominent place in people's minds. The University of Georgia's experience was typical. Its 1915 offerings under the headings "Economics" and "Business Administration"—which seem not to have been especially distinguishable—appear a hastily assembled jumble. Candidates for the bachelor's degree had to take three courses from each of the following two lists:

Economics

Economic History
Economic Geography
Elementary Principles of Economics
American Government
General Economics
Money, Banking, & Credit
Corporate Finance
Transportation
Public Service Companies
Industrial Combinations

Business Administration

Accounting
Advanced Auditing & Accounting
Commercial Organization and
 Management
Industrial Organization and
 Management

Public Finance
Labor Problems
Insurance
Agricultural Economics
Commercial German

By 1919 the two lists had been combined, and the number of courses had been reduced to fifteen (mainly by returning some of the more traditional economics courses to the now entirely separate Department of Economics):

Business Administration

Geography and Industry
Elementary Economics
Money and Banking
Corporate Management and Finance
Transportation
Marketing
Personal Insurance
Property Insurance
Advertising and Salesmanship
Elementary Accounting
Advanced Accounting
Auditing
Introductory Course in Business Law
Law of Corporations, Banking, and Insurance
Foreign Trade

Four years later, the number of courses had increased, but now they were grouped more neatly into six classifications:

Accounting and Business Law (accounting, auditing, and law)
Banking and Finance (money and banking, investments, mathematics)
Economics (history, principles, problems, labor studies, and some insurance courses)
Business Administration (administration, industrial management, personnel management, marketing, salesmanship, advertising)
Transportation and Trade (geography, railroads, railroads and government, rates and traffic, foreign commerce economics, U. S. foreign trade, import and export techniques)
Secretarial (shorthand, typing, office organization, office management, business correspondence)

This classification held for several years, except that "Accounting and Business Law" was divided in two, and "Transportation and Trade" similarly became "Marketing" and "Transportation and Utilities," bringing the number of categories to eight. Then in 1930 "Secretarial" and "Transportation and Utilities" were dropped from the catalog and "Business Administration" changed its name to "Industrial Management." At that point the number of courses offered had risen to forty-three, but the number of categories had dropped back to a neat and manageable six.

These classifications, however, were by no means universally agreed on. The struggles that different schools were going through to arrive at the ideal, or "basic," are evident in some of the course titles. The University of Alabama offered a course in "Production and Personnel," two subjects kept separate everywhere else; the University of Oklahoma offered a strange combination called "Salesmanship and Business Policy." Insurance was sometimes part of Accounting, sometimes of Economics, sometimes of Finance, and sometimes separate; transportation was sometimes separate, other times combined with Communication or with Marketing. Foreign Exchange was normally a separate course but at Dartmouth was combined with Bank Management; and at the University of Illinois "Business Law" and "Business Writing" were part of the department called "Business Organization and Operation."

The University of Chicago continued refining its complex classification system referred to in chapter 3. By 1929 it took the form of three kinds of control and eight things to be controlled. Presumably the idea was that the students should master the three kinds of control and then be able to apply them to any of the eight fields. The kinds were "Communicating" (English, foreign language, and secretarial subjects); "Measuring" (mathematics and statistics); and "Standards and Practices" (psychology, and organizational policies and methods). The eight areas to be controlled were all listed as "problems":

1. Problems of Adjustment to the Physical Environment (primarily including earth sciences)
2. Problems of Technology (including physics and other sciences)
3. Problems of Finance
4. Problems Connected with the Market
5. Problems Connected with Transportation and Communication
6. Problems of Risk and Risk-Bearing
7. Problems of Personnel
8. Problems of Adjustment to the Social Environment (including law and government)

Although the configuration at first appears neat and symmetrical, closer scrutiny raises all sorts of questions and blurs the difference between Chicago and other institutions.

Amid all the struggle and confusion, however, a definite move away from "eccentric" or industry-specific courses was occurring. Harvard, having previously dropped its courses in the printing industry, now dropped its lumbering industry courses also. The catalog for 1930 states that the program "aims to give its students familiarity with general business facts and principles. . . . It avoids any pretense of covering satisfactorily the detailed technique and routine of particular industries, since this may be acquired much more effectively in each industry." The University of Michigan thought the same way. Having earlier discontinued its specialization in Mine Administration, it now dropped Railway Administration also, and Ohio State ceased listing Municipal Administration, Social Services, and Journalism as "major groups" in its business school. The University of Iowa's dean, Chester A. Phillips, noticed the trend as early as 1925 and found it augured well for the future reputation of college business programs:

> My own belief is that the present trend in education for business is moving away from narrow technical procedure toward an emphasis on fundamentals of almost universal applicability. To the extent that this trend continues, there should be less and less criticism of the courses offered by our schools of business administration. The future curriculum of the American school of business will be designed, I believe, so as to have as great disciplinary value as our so-called culture courses of today.[3]

Not all universities took part in this movement: Arizona offered "Farm Accounting," Oklahoma added a course called "The Petroleum Industry," the University of Washington offered "Wharf Management," and the University of Chicago instituted a whole department called "Science and Management of the Packing Industry," with ten courses including "Beef Operations" and "Pork Operations." Moreover, one specific industry—public utilities—which was taught at only a handful of universities in 1920, could be found in practically every university catalog by 1930. Courses called something like "Management of Public Utilities" became standard, as the half dozen gigantic holding companies that controlled most of the nation's electric power sought people to run their local operations. But in general the schools of business did move slowly away, during the 1920s, from the industry-specific studies they had offered earlier and toward a more generalized functional conception of business.

The most noteworthy single attempt to come up with a comprehensive philosophy of curriculum design was an address by Chicago's distinguished dean, Leon C. Marshall, yet it ends up illustrating how little progress had been made. Entitled "The Collegiate School of Business at Erehwon," the address begins with some funny satirical jabs—saying, for example, that Erehwon University, unlike all others, chose to decide what it wanted to do before it actually opened. It decided to place undergraduate business education in the third and fourth years of college and then to offer a master's degree in the fifth year. Increasing specificity was the overriding principle: two years of general liberal arts education were followed by two years of general business education, and then the master's program concentrated on one of three kinds of specialization: a field of work (statistician), or an executive function (marketing), or an industry. Each university should specialize in only a few industries with which it had some particular connection, such as geographical proximity. Marshall developed the entire curriculum in an orderly and logical manner, but by the end he had come up with nothing any different from what already existed in most universities, and his idea about universities specializing in specific industries—reflected in Chicago's Meat Packing Institute—never caught on widely. The business administration curriculum in the 1920s, in short, remained a mess.[4]

Growth, Cooperation, and International Emphasis Continue

Growth. Trends that had just begun to be evident in 1920 continued and grew stronger during the next decade. Most noticeable of these was simply growth. One survey showed the number of students in college business courses increasing 85 percent—from 36,456 to 67,496—between 1919 and 1927, and the number of commerce degrees granted up an amazing 934 percent, from 640 to 6,621. In fact the increase may have been even greater, judging by figures from schools in the northeast. New York University alone reported 8,615 business students in 1926, making it by far the largest business school in the nation, despite having raised standards in 1924 in an effort to contain enrollment. Enrollment at Columbia had grown 628 percent— from 61 to 444—in just fourteen years, and at the City College of New York enrollment jumped from 350 to 529 just between the fall and spring terms one year. Applications to the Harvard Business School exceeded the quota for the first time in 1929, and even MIT acceded to the demand and began offering business subjects the next year. New buildings were also popping up everywhere: Northwestern in 1923, Columbia in 1924, Harvard in 1925, New York in 1926, City College of New York in 1927, Alabama in 1928, and many, many others.[5]

Part of the amazing enrollment growth was due to the interest by women students. In the same nine-year period when total enrollment rose 85 percent, women's enrollment rose 152 percent, and degrees granted to women rose 608 percent. The University of Georgia opened its doors to women in 1919, and the business school established a program to train them for secretarial careers. The University of Cincinnati established a "Professional School for Women" in 1923, with work in the secretarial, interior decoration, dietetic, office management, and industrial-chemical research fields. By 1924 the University of Oregon was offering a program in "Business Administration and Household Accounts" specifically for young women, so that they could be prepared for careers either in business or as wives, and New York University proudly reported the inclusion of kitchenettes in the women's rest rooms of its new building. In 1930 Hunter College announced a considerably more professional and less sexist program to train women to be "leaders for the best places in business." The program, started in response to student demand, was to have high standards and to feature a liberal and cultural education. Only ten percent of the nation's business students were women in 1927, but that was up from a mere seven percent just eight years earlier, a very sharp rise in market share.[6]

Cooperative Arrangements. The need for cooperation between universities and businesses continued to be a major topic for discussion and action during the 1920s. Everyone seemed aware of the need, even though no one seemed to know any ideal way to satisfy it. The schools needed contacts with business because they needed guidance about what to teach and also more facts to use in their teaching; the businesses wanted guidance from the schools and also a supply of well-trained young graduates.

Of course the universities were also hoping that businesses would become major financial donors, and things did occasionally work out that way. By far the most noteworthy instance was George F. Baker's five million dollar gift in 1924 to build the Harvard Business School's first permanent home. A few other large gifts did come, such as the Sachs family's $200,000 donation to Harvard and Rockefeller's $10,000 contribution for research at the Wharton School, but in general the hoped-for results never happened. Typical gifts from business were either very small or very restricted. Edward Bok of the *Ladies Home Journal,* for example, gave Harvard an unspecified sum to sponsor an annual advertising award; a French steamship line gave Harvard's library a model of one of its ships; and some understandably anonymous donor gave Columbia University a "notable" twenty-volume history of the National Wholesale Druggists' Association.[7]

International. The emphasis on world trade that began after World War I continued and increased during the next decade. In 1923 the U.S. Department of Commerce issued a booklet extolling the virtues of careers in foreign trade and urging students to take advantage of the international courses offered in most colleges. A year later the president of United States Steel made a similar appeal, urging colleges of businesses to focus on the international aspects of business, including the study of foreign languages. The universities responded to such calls with more courses and with new programs and projects. New York University taught "International Banking and Finance" and "The Economics of the Congo" as part of its "Institute of International Finance," started in 1926, while Harvard University offered courses in "Latin American Trade" and "Importing." City College of New York established an "International Institute for the Advancement of Commercial Education and Business Relations," the purpose of which was "to help in the solution of educational problems arising from the internationalization of business and finance in the United States," and Columbia University inaugurated a wide-ranging research program into the economic and business affairs of the Far East. Yet even though such developments were widely reported in the press, progress toward internationalization was actually quite modest; as a percentage of the curriculum, especially outside the northeast, international studies grew only a little.[8]

SOCIAL SCIENCES AND THE DECLINE OF "APPLIED ECONOMICS"

Already slightly in evidence by 1919, the work of "human relations" people continued to make slow advances in the 1920s, as the inadequacies of the mechanical or descriptive approach to business studies grew plainer. The change was so slow as to be practically imperceptible at the time, and examples of the mechanical-descriptive attitude continued to be plentiful. In retrospect, however, the change that occurred at this time was profoundly significant, and it marks one of the major turning points in the history of the MBA degree.

The business research bureaus at Harvard and Chicago continued to turn out studies of the profits, turnovers, margins, and inventories at dry goods, chain, and department stores, and New York University produced a detailed survey of the average income of families in the borough of Queens. When this kind of survey was applied to nonquantitative areas, however, its limitations should have been embarrassingly obvious. In 1927 the Wharton School surveyed chief executive officers of corporations to find out their average age, and the next year Harvard undertook a very large survey of fifteen thousand leading business men to find the reasons for their success. Not surprisingly, no results of this last study were ever published, and the secrets of success have continued to remain elusive.[9]

The Harvard Business Reports

Most notable among the mechanical-descriptive activities of the businesses schools in the 1920s was the ill-conceived and short-lived *Harvard Business Reports,* a much-heralded series that was to bring to an end all the uncertainty of business management. Announced in early 1924 but not first published until 1926, the *Reports* were to constitute a series of management "precedents" that would parallel the collections of precedents that had worked so well in the legal system.

As the preface to volume 1 explained, the object was to bring the science of management up to the same level as the more developed fields of law, engineering, and even accounting and finance. Many centuries ago judges decided each case individually without reference to precedent except what they recollected from their own memories. Then someone began recording decisions so that they could be applied to other cases outside a single judge's jurisdiction, and thus the modern legal system was born. Similarly the art of factory design had advanced through collective experience in an industry: when a new floor layout proved advantageous, word was spread through publications and trade conferences so that other factories could copy it. Accounting practices and financial operating ratios were freely circulated so that they became accepted standards. Why, then, should management alone keep making the same mistakes over and over, with no body of common knowledge circulating beyond each separate company?

The cases presented—149 of them in the first volume—thus were indexed according to the management principles involved. A shoe manufacturer who received a sudden large increase in orders from retail stores suspected that the stores were simply trying to place their orders before anticipated inflation occurred. Since the manufacturer confidently expected recession rather than inflation, he ordered only a fourth of the needed raw materials, and his judgment was confirmed when the recession hit and retailers canceled substantial parts of their orders. This case was indexed under "Raw material purchases during period of inflation" and "Restriction of raw material purchases." A private-label tea company confronting wholesalers' demands for bigger discounts decided to sell directly to retailers; this case was indexed under "Importer's private brand," "Increased discount requested by wholesalers," "Price-cutting by wholesalers," and "Direct sales to retailers." Such index tags, it was hoped, would make each important business decision available to other companies, and as a result the entire business world's activity could be raised to a new level.

The project endured for six years and eleven volumes before it was finally abandoned as a failure. Although the Great Depression is probably what actually brought it down, the seeds of failure lay in the basic conception. The idea of business "precedents" could never have worked, because such precedents are incapable of validation, usually ungeneralizable, and never comprehensive.

The Problem of Validation. The validation difficulty points up the flawed analogy with law. Legal principles are established by decision, business principles by success or failure in the market. Whether a legal decision is just or kind or wise never affects the question of whether to adhere to it; all that matters is that it has been decided. In business, on the other hand, no decision-making arbiter exists; a decision is a good one only if the consequences that ensue from it are good ones. Thus not only does it take longer, sometimes decades in fact, for a decision to prove good or bad, but there also will always be room for disagreement since determination of rightness or wrongness will never be entirely clear or final. The tea company's decision to bypass wholesalers and sell directly to retailers could have consequences twenty or thirty years later, some of which could be good and some bad. With results so uncertain, so incapable of verification, no company would ever choose to regard the decision as a precedent to be followed.

The Problem of Generalizability. On a more specific plane, the ungeneralizability of most management decisions prevents their wide use as precedents. Occasionally a good idea does come along which certain other companies can copy—"flex time," for example, or HMOs for employee health care—but most decisions are so firmly rooted in one specific industry or one specific situation that they cannot be duplicated in another. The shoe manufacturer's decision to order enough raw materials for just a fourth of the orders that had been placed was a good decision only because his reading of the economic future was more accurate than that of his retailers; had the economy gone the other way he would have suffered a major loss. Thus the decision is valid as a precedent to be followed only if other people facing similar choices are absolutely confident that they likewise know what direction the economy will take—or, in short, almost never. The last three volumes of *Harvard Business Reports* tried to overcome the problem of industry-specificness by focusing exclusively on one industry each: "Industrial Marketing" (vol. 9), "Marketing Airplanes" (vol. 10), and "Cooperative Advertising" (vol. 11). Still, however, ungeneralizability remained a major and obvious flaw in the whole conception.

The Problem of Comprehensiveness. The third difficulty with the "precedent" approach is that precedents can never hope to cover more than a small fraction of the decisions that managers have to make. The cases reported deal with such concepts as using returnable versus nonreturnable containers, building a warehouse in Argentina, and deciding whether employees who quit and then return to work should keep their former wage levels. These cases often make interesting reading, but they no more cover the widely inclusive field of "management" than the household hints feature in a daily newspaper covers the problem of how to raise a family. The territory is vast, and the little lessons learned from individual cases could never amount to much.

Turning Away from a Mechanical View

Harvard's recognition of the inadequacies of the approach embedded in the *Harvard Business Reports* marks the beginning of an important turning point in the history of business education. Business studies had from the first often been referred to as a branch of "applied economics," and now the conception was turning out to be inadequate. Harvard Business School historian Melvin Copeland later described the curriculum of those days as based on "static assumptions which completely ignored many of the most significant elements of business strategy and behavior, as well as many of the most important issues involved in the decisions facing an active business executive."[10]

Gradually the truth began dawning that the major problem confronting business education was not the difficulty of finding answers to questions but, instead, of finding the right questions to ask, questions that involved a much more society-based conception of business. Looking back on this moment from a later time, Dean Wallace Donham noted that "The objective of our research changed from the collection of materials for the illustration of known principles into the ascertainment of new principles." And still later he explained further,

> I gradually came to question whether we could continue to think of business as applied economics. We found that even though the men we sent out to gather the facts of business problems went with the definite primary errand of recording and putting on paper economic facts, facts they brought back did not stay economic. There were all sorts of things entering into the situations that were not within the concepts and the abstractions to which the economist was . . . limiting his thinking. All kinds of noneconomic factors and many nonengineering and nonlegal factors broke these boundaries. We made the discovery that while two and two in mathematics may always be four, two and two plus the X of human relations and other "imponderables" involved in any situation is never four. . . . It gradually became obvious that a new conceptual framework was required.[11]

What that new conceptual framework would be nobody knew, but evidence of the search was visible in many other places too. Although the curricula of most universities, as already noted, showed few new courses, some subtle changes did occur: one was that the word "personnel" replaced the word "labor." Courses formerly called something like "Labor Problems" now became "Personnel Management" at the Universities of Alabama, Chicago, Nebraska, Northwestern, Ohio State, and Oklahoma, among others. The title of a course never tells much about the content, but the change here was so widespread it must have reflected at least the beginnings of an attitude shift, from the controlling of workers to an understanding of human motivation.

Several other occurrences at the time suggest the same thing. In November 1923 the distinguished American Academy of Political and Social Science devoted the entire 232-page issue of its *Annals* to "Psychology in Business." Psychologists, professors, and business executives from around the world contributed articles about psychology's place in managing workers and in understanding consumers. In the introduction to the volume, former Wharton professor C. H. Crennan, by then an economist with a Chicago bank, wrote "At the heart of every business situation is a human nature problem. . . . The psychologist is in business to stay because business involves human nature." Among other articles was one by Harvard University's Elton Mayo, who pointed out "a strange inconsistency" in the attitude of business managers:

> If some inorganic material prove obdurate to industrial process, we employ chemist and physicist to discover why. But should the human material of industry prove obdurate to factory organization, we usually lose our tempers and stamp

about breathing forth threatenings and slaughters. In the one case we endeavor, with careful patience, to discover what unknown causes defeat our purpose. In the other case we appeal all too often to primitive force, talking darkly of conspiracy the while.

"We have long since ceased to smash inanimate things when they happen to displease us," he concluded. "But we still apply the primitive method to our brother man."[12]

A New York University professor conducted a seven-year study to determine what problems business managers face. He concluded that only fifteen percent of the problems were of the theoretical and quantitative kind that people study in schools; the overwhelming lack in managers' training was in the area of "being able to deal with people." Others shared this growing perception. When Rutgers University offered an evening course in Business Psychology in the Jersey City YMCA, over two hundred students signed up and twenty-five leading industries in the area endorsed the idea. Even the American Management Association was devoting major efforts to the study of "the human factor in commerce and industry." Clearly, a shift had occurred since Taylor's theories of "scientific management" had dominated management thinking. And yet what had happened so far was barely even a beginning of the movement to come.[13]

The New Prominence of Collegiate Business Education

Even though changes in the schools themselves during this period were only gradual and slight, the prominence of collegiate business education in the public mind grew quite astonishingly. By no means was all the attention favorable: as more and more people praised it, responses from critics, some witty, some vitriolic, were provoked. Whatever the attitude, no one in America could now be oblivious to the presence of business education in colleges.

Praises for Business

One reason for the growing prominence of business education was that business itself had now grown entirely respectable. The old question about whether it constituted a profession now seemed, to most people, absolutely settled in the affirmative. The laying of the cornerstone for Columbia University's new building in 1923 was said to mark "the development of business from a calling into a profession," and the next year at Harvard ninety-year-old former president Eliot, by now a strong convert to the cause of business education, said the same thing—that a business school is a rightful part of a university because it "inculcates high ethical purposes and aims in the profession of business, a calling which until lately was not recognized as a liberal profession at all."[14]

In Britain, H. Gordon Selfridge, the American who founded London's famous department store, noted a big change in the attitude of young people toward business careers. Before the war, he said, a person who had to go into business was an object of pity or sympathy, but now even people of great social position had come to look on a life in business as a privilege and a pleasure. This change, Selfridge declared, was "one of the great rewards or victories of the Great War."[15]

Accordingly the leaders of business were elevated to new positions approaching the status of heroes. One speaker called them not merely technicians but men of broad cultivation who see their work in relation humanity. Another went considerably further:

> Theirs is a task more delicate than that of the men who carved the Milesian Venus, more majestic than that of the men who built the Coliseum, calling for ability to dream dreams and see visions and the power to crystallize those dreams and visions into great business enterprises, even as the people of a few centuries ago crystallized their dreams and aspirations in the cathedrals of Europe.[16]

Praises for College Education in General

Virtually all of the old hostility toward colleges had vanished. Doubts about the economic worth of a college education were dissipated by surveys. A Boston University dean calculated that college graduates earn about twice as much as high school graduates and more than three times as much as those with still less schooling, and a Carnegie Institute study produced similar findings. Moreover, even apart from the economic advantages, people saw great promise for the future of society in the fact that college-educated people were now beginning to be the managers of the great businesses of both American and Great Britain. "It is not too much to hope," *The New York Times* editorialized,

> that out of the multitude of educated young men going into shops and factories there will arise in the future not only captains of industry but leaders of opinion. . . . They may be able to show others how to attain similar successes, and so become the reconcilers and pathfinders needed by the new industrial day.[17]

Considering that only three decades before it had been commonplace to deride the value of college, especially for people going into business, this newfound respect for the wisdom that college inculcates must surely mark one of the fastest public opinion changes on record.

Praises for Business Education

Since both the business community and the college community were experiencing a strong rise in public esteem, it's not surprising that business education was also riding high. During the first part of the decade the praises tended to focus on the things that business education could do for business, but as 1930 arrived the focus widened to include the great benefits that all of society would realize from the work of the business schools.

During the early 1920s, business education was quite widely extolled in the popular press. In 1923, 1924, and 1925 alone, articles praising business education to various degrees appeared in the *Saturday Evening Post, Century Magazine, Literary Digest* (twice), and *Literary Review,* as well as in the *Boston Herald,* the *New York Sun,* the *Brooklyn Eagle,* and the *Providence Journal.* Author and publisher Richard J. Walsh (Pearl Buck's husband) wrote a notable three-article series for *Century Magazine* in 1924–25—"The Doom of the Self-Made Man," "Carving Out a New Profession," and "Tools for To-Morrow"—in which he traced the history of management education, urged its further development, and called especially for more research. Whereas the main function of European universities, he noted, was to turn out researchers, American universities were shortsightedly scorning research and concentrating instead on teaching. Americans professors, he reported, presented between three hundred and five hundred lectures a year, compared with only fifty to one hundred in Europe, and one American professor-author reportedly had been reprimanded by the governor of his state, who reminded him that he had been hired to teach, not to write.

Since businesses themselves, Walsh maintained, belligerently resist new knowledge, the job of research falls exclusively to the universities and research institutes, without which the requisite body of knowledge could never be developed. He singled out just seven organizations that, in his opinion, were conducting significant management research as of 1925—Johns Hopkins University, the Carnegie Foundation, the National Research Council, the Engineering Foundation, the Mellon Institute of Industrial Research, the Institute of Economics, and especially the Engineering-Economics Foundation in Boston.[18]

Eliot G. Mears, a Stanford professor, had said similar things in the *American Economic Review* a year earlier. Although he regarded the growth of business education as "the most startling development during the twentieth century in American Higher Education," he deplored its condition and declared it still in its infancy. The chief problem, he felt, was a tendency to remain theoretical. Economics no more includes business, he wrote, than mathematics includes engineering or biology includes medicine. Pointing out "an entirely different spirit behind the courses in economics and those in business subjects," he argued that business "must be approached through different types of courses and by different types of instructors." Yet he acknowledged that no one, including himself, had any clear idea of what to teach. His own list of readings—Cicero, Pericles, F. H. King's *Farmers of Forty Centuries,* Clive Day's *History of Commerce*—certainly confirms the suspicion that, although he ardently believed in the importance of a good business education and felt profound discomfort with the present state of affairs, he had few ideas about how to proceed.[19]

Development of Placement Activities. The practical effect of this new-found confidence in the value of education was that companies now began coming to campuses to recruit. Princeton University, which had no formal business department or school, reported that companies were flocking to its campus in unprecedented numbers. Up until the war, graduates had had to go out and seek jobs from company executives who generally hated universities, and then had had to work their way up from low positions. Now, Princeton's Bureau of Appointments noted, American businesses had come to recognize the value of a college education and therefore were constantly sending recruiting representatives to the campus. Another report a few years later noted that Wall Street investment houses had similarly changed their attitude and now were giving preference in hiring to college people.

The good reputation that colleges had acquired was clearly paying off. Like Princeton, universities everywhere, and especially those with schools of business, were finding it necessary to establish "employment bureaus" or "placement offices" for the first time. Although their main function was often seen as finding part-time jobs for students still in school, the idea of helping the graduates find subsequent employment was fast catching on. Columbia, Pennsylvania, Princeton, and Yale all significantly enlarged their placement offices between 1923 and 1927.[20]

Praises for Benefits to Society

Toward the end of the decade business education began to receive accolades of a different sort. Instead of being touted for its ability to collect and analyze facts or to improve the management of America's industries, it now began to be hailed almost as a savior for society. At a New York University building dedication in March 1930, the speaker exuded that "the business future of our country will be evolved not alone in the factory, upon the highway or in the market place. It will be due even more to the patient research, the systematized thought, the profound study and the wise counsels of a proper business education within these walls." The next month the president of New York Telephone Company told a conference how urgently the nation's businesses needed leaders trained broadly and inclusively for a strengthened power of analysis, adding that business is reliable and honest and that schools must teach the ideals of fair dealing, consideration, and courtesy. And hardly a week later the New York Stock Exchange's president, speaking at Columbia University, cited a new union that business education had brought about between intellectual analysis and practical experience. America now has, he said, "a power of judgment in economic questions never before at the disposal of our commonwealth."[21]

Although these may seem at first to be brave exhortations made in the face of the newly arrived depression, they actually were continuing in a vein clearly in evidence earlier. In 1927, for example, Columbia's president Nicholas Murray Butler, not originally an ardent champion of business education, had proclaimed the arrival of the day when such studies not only were intellectually respectable in themselves but offered great value to society:

> There is coming to be a philosophy of business just as there has long been a philosophy of theology, of law, of medicine and of teaching, and it is through the door of that philosophy, that understanding of fundamental principles and higher standards, that the University seeks to lead men and women to prepare themselves for the capable and competent pursuit of this form of intellectual activity and public service.

And Harvard Business School carried the idea of public service still further by disdainfully expressing indifference to money. Any possible increase in remuneration that its graduates might happen to realize as a result of their education was coincidental and irrelevant to the purposes of the school. In fact the school proudly reported that salaries of its alumni were not appreciably different from what they would have been had they never attended, and Assistant Dean D. W. Malott stated the attitude plainly: "We don't teach our men how to make money. . . . Our purpose is to make them capable of attaining positions of real responsibility ten or fifteen years after they start in business." Not all schools were so lofty, and certainly not all students (including Harvard's) were indifferent to money, but business education was quite sincere and quite successful in representing itself as a contributor to a more ordered and just society.[22]

The great change from disreputable to reputable is well illustrated by developments at the University of Kansas. In 1904, when the university first began to offer business courses, the catalog was almost apologetic. These courses, it explained, did not "in any sense form a school of commerce or business." Instead they were called "Courses in Business in Its Higher Relations," and instead of teaching students how to conduct business they aimed "to illustrate the economic forces which control the business world" and to give "cultural training which is indispensable to the thoroughly enlightened citizen." Exactly twenty years later, in 1924, the University, now under the direction of a new chancellor known for his work in business studies at the University of Oregon, proudly established its "School of Business" with no apologies. In these two short decades, collegiate business studies had become respectable.[23]

Attacks on Business and Business Schools

Being prominent in the public eye meant attracting unfriendly opinion as well, and, with tones ranging from hilarious sarcasm to dead serious outrage, critics lined up to take shots at business education. Just as with the praises, the single most important impetus for the criticism was George F. Baker's unprecedented five million dollar gift to Harvard, an event that brought widespread attention to the already established existence of business in college.

Chapman. Yet it was in May 1924, the month before Baker's gift was announced, that the most vitriolic of all the denunciations occurred. At the annual dinner of the *Harvard Business Review,* the unlikely guest speaker was the witty, acid-penned writer John Jay Chapman, who already had made himself known as a relentless critic of his alma mater's current activities. Seizing this opportunity, he let fly at the whole concept of a collegiate business school in an address that was remembered for years.

In general Chapman was appalled at the extent to which business had taken over all of American life. "We are a mill that turns everything into business," he said at the start of his address. "Love, art, leisure, science, innocent recreation, and religious contemplation are ground up into business packages and marketed as soon as nature—prodigal, unabashed, procreant nature—produces them."

More specifically, however, he was concerned that freedom of academic inquiry was being infringed upon by the quest for profit. After citing a Harvard pamphlet extolling the visions and accomplishments of William Wrigley the chewing-gum maker, he went on,

> Do you gentlemen seriously believe that you can accept Wall Street's money and be clear of Wall Street's influence? You are idealists, indeed! It used to be thought an abuse for the plutocrat to subsidize a chair in a college and put a bit in the mouth of learning. But since business is now discovered to be a profession, such practices are perfectly all right.

Following up on that observation, he attacked the pretentiousness business exhibited by claiming to be anything other than lowbrow commerce aimed at moneymaking:

> My friends, the truth is that business is not a profession; and no amount of rhetoric and no expenditure in circulars can make it into a profession. This fact stands like a sharp-pointed, deep-seated rock in mid-channel, and against this rock Harvard is steering her craft—or raft. . . . I can imagine a man practicing medicine or law or architecture or engineering out of sheer love for the thing. But I cannot imagine a man's running a business at a loss. It wouldn't be business. A School of Business means a school where you learn to make money.

"You couldn't find," he continued,

a man in the whole world more divested of the peculiar virtues that cause the regular professions to be revered than our American prominent business man. Then why should we "accord" him the dignity and respect due to these professions? Give him something else! Give him a medal with a picture of himself and of his pile; give him praise for benefactions, for benevolence, for courage, mother wit, good luck. But don't play upon the accordion of his vanity and ignorance by according him the dignity and respect due to other things.

Finally, he aimed his barbs at the whole idea that a business leader should have an education less broad, less concerned with social issues, than anyone else should have. "Your purpose," he said to the audience at Harvard Business School, "is to turn out smart business men." By contrast, he said, "if the Harvard Law School should profess to teach lawyers how to become smart money-makers, it would lose its reputation in a night." In Britain, corporations come to the universities to recruit graduates with the greatest general world wisdom, not those with the most training in merchandising or advertising. "I think," Chapman concluded,

> that the whole view of Harvard and her attitude toward Business, as shown in her recent pamphlets, is small-pattern and ephemeral. The big Britishers will have a great advantage over America in the field of world-business, if, as appears to be the case, England relies on that class of intellect which has been able to absorb the higher education while America relies on the mind of Main Street.[24]

Ayres. Less than a year later, economist C. E. Ayres, who was later professor of economics at the University of Texas for nearly forty years, wrote a two-part diatribe in *The New Republic* continuing the attack that Chapman had begun. Ayres's particular concerns were with the corruption of the university. Seeing Greek, literature, mathematics, and biology replaced with "uncouth" courses in accounting, salesmanship, and railroad administration, he felt that a debasement was occurring:

> Business is the subject of universal disapprobation among humanists. Whatsoever things are mean, whatsoever things are low, whatsoever things are incontinently selfish and piratical, for all these things business and the trading classes have stood in the European imagination since the Middle Ages. Humanism, culture, gets its definition by contrast with commerce and industry.

Accordingly, the intrusion of such subjects into the curriculum constitutes not just a displacement of proper subjects but a positive corruption, especially since "the trading classes" were now themselves often teaching the courses, as "professors of financial manipulation" and "assistant professors of tax-dodging." Even more serious was the ubiquitous influence of business's wealth in calling the shots:

> Under the auspices of the School of Mammonry the foremost buccaneers of the period pass in solemn procession through the academic groves bearing the palms

of special lecturer. By special invitation the more intricate problems of commercial chicanery are submitted to the staff of the university department to be solved with the eager assistance of the squads of novices. All this in the name of "Extension Services," "Cooperation with Related Industries," and—crowning insolence of humanitarian cant—the "Bureau of Business Research."

"The first, primary, and quintessential condition of liberal education," he continued, "is the freedom of the mind, and as we surely do not need to be told at this late date the one important obstacle to the realization of that condition is business, . . . the imponderable, seeping influence of an established order upon which every teacher and every student depends for all the goods of life." Even civilians, he pointed out, find it hard to keep an open mind under such conditions of dependency, and business professors— the "staff officers of business"—will find the task hopeless.[25]

The Lampoon. A third sarcastic attack came the same week as Ayres's articles, in the 28 January 1925 issue of *Harvard Lampoon,* which was devoted entirely to mocking the Harvard Business School. Since award of the contract for construction of the new buildings was less than two months away, the Business School was very much on people's minds, and rebellion against it was taking shape in other parts of the university. "No one can deny the existence, right or wrong," the *Lampoon* said, "of a strong reaction against the intrusion of 'this dagger, which we see before us, the handle toward our hand.' Perhaps there is a real occasion for the attitude, prevailing in the college especially, that there is a neglect of some parts of the University body for others—the head for the stomach, shall we say?"

The *Lampoon*'s own design for the new building (Ill. 4–1) leads off the issue. Instead of Homer, Plato, Aristotle, and Virgil, the building bears the names of three contemporary swindlers and Shakespeare's Shylock. Its dome consists of a ticker-tape machine, and its supporting columns appear to be not marble but piles of gold coins. Portraits of four fictitious businessmen who serve as lecturers—a bootlegger, a bogus inventor, a crooked marketer, and a plumber—then follow in the magazine, with text which carefully notes that in fact none of them ever went to college. The attack on boorish commercialism continues later with some verses:

> Fair Harvard will at great expense
> A temple build to common sense,
> 'Tis called the Business School, and hence
> Appears the latest scholar.
> No studies there can vex the heart,
> They're learning quite another art,
> To chase the festive dollar.
>
> At "clubs" the busy students meet,
> Discuss the rumors of "the street,"

Illustration 4-1:

THE <u>HARVARD LAMPOON'S</u> DESIGN
FOR THE NEW BUSINESS SCHOOL BUILDING

Source: <u>Harvard Lampoon</u>, January 28, 1925.

And other problems to complete
Commercial education;
And this is right, because you see
It makes for new prosperity
For Harvard and the nation.

Unimpressed by constant references to "service," "satisfaction for the customer," "business ethics," and "religion in business," the *Lampoon* suspects that the true message of the school is "the world judges a businessman by the money he makes."

Pervading the entire issue of the magazine is the persistent fear that business will soon come to dominate the whole university and even all of Western culture. Dean Donham is pictured as Harvard's next president, and a cartoon shows Johnny Harvard adopting a pet lion cub named "HBS," which then grows up and eats Johnny Harvard. Two time-honored stories—Walter Raleigh laying down his cloak for the queen, and William Tell shooting the apple on his son's head—are turned into advertisements for waterproof cloaks and a new model crossbow. It is not the wittiest issue *Harvard Lampoon* ever put out, but it undeniably made its point with trenchancy.

Mencken. One other comical attack on business education in college appeared in 1928 in *The American Mercury.* Signed pseudonymously "Arlington J. Stone," it bears all the marks of H. L. Mencken's authorship. Although he approved of Joseph Wharton's original purpose, to "provide training suitable for those intending to engage in business," he was aghast at the way "the science" had developed, and especially at the way it was being used to attract funds for universities.

"All of these shrines of scientific business seem to be making money," he wrote. "Indeed, next to football teams and schools of education, they are probably the biggest money-getters in the world of intellect. At some places, as at New York University, for example, it is only the takings of the School of Commerce that enable the Chancellor to pay the university's bills." Then in horrified fascination, he recited, almost without editorial comment, a list of (to him) appalling courses he had found at major institutions: "Store Management," "Practical Table Service," "Business of the Theater," "Apartment House Management," "Traffic Management," "Livestock Management," "Cafeteria Management," "Principles of Dress," "Hosiery and Underwear," "Window Display," and "Packing House Operations" in two sections—beef and pork. To a humanistically trained thinker like Mencken, no comment seemed necessary. The very existence of such subjects in once-classical universities was, just on the face of it, monstrous and absurd.[26]

Flexner. The same classicist outrage, but without Mencken's wit, pervades Abraham Flexner's 1930 book, *Universities: American, English, German.* His primary objection to business education was simply that the subject itself was illegitimate. Legitimate subjects use intellect to attack problems, but business administration teaches how to make a profit. The proper purpose of education is to learn, not to get ahead, yet Harvard Business School's brochure proclaimed that its training "permits rapid progress" and that its graduates show "satisfactory progress." "What university school of medicine," Flexner asked rhetorically, "would dare to define its ideals and results in such terms?" The distinction he made was between studying business as a phenomenon, as economists and sociologists might legitimately do, and studying how to conduct a business. The first of these was a proper function of a university; the second was not.

More specifically, he cited Harvard's award of two thousand dollars—part of the Bok advertising award money mentioned earlier—to "a young woman who organized a campaign for Pet Milk." Such an activity, to Flexner's mind, simply had no place in a university. "Is it," he asked in exasperation, "a proper concern of Harvard University . . . to market a product of this or any other kind?" By contrast, Columbia University's course in "The Psychology of Salesmanship" met with his approval because it presented its subject in a scientific manner rather than teaching merely how to achieve certain results.

The chief problem, he explained further, was the absence of any ethical or social dimension in the content of business education. Examining the fifteen volumes of case studies that Harvard had published—including "Operating Accounts for Retail Drug Stores," "Record Sheets for Retail Hardware Stores," "Merchandise Control in Women's Shoe Departments of Department Stores," and "Methods of Paying Salesmen and Operating Expenses in the Wholesale Grocery Business in 1918"—he found "not the faintest glimmer of social, ethical, philosophic, historic, or cultural interest" in any of them.

And finally Flexner cast doubt even on the necessity for schools of business. Yale and Princeton, he pointed out, will provide as many businessmen as Harvard, even though they have no business school, just as Harvard, which had no journalism school, would provide as many journalists as Columbia. To him, the central distinction was simple: medicine and law were professions, but business and journalism were not.[27]

Others. In general, criticism of collegiate business education during this time reflects a sort of ambiguity. Those who objected could often find nothing more substantial to base their criticisms on than the fact that the subject was not a traditional one in universities, and those who championed it often had nothing more to say in its defense than that it really didn't differ all that much from traditional subjects. L. J. Nations, an English professor in the School of Business at the University of Alabama, illustrated the former attitude in a 1930 *North American Review* article in which he called the modern college an "institution of higher earnings." Unlike Pericles' Greece, where tradespeople were snubbed as barbarians, today's society glorifies them and permits the obliteration of the liberal arts by business subjects. Yet at the same time that he longed for a return to the cultural courses he cherished, Nations clearly was excited by the new field that was opening before him, as shown by the fact that he devoted most of his article to detailing the plans of his university's program.[28]

Fears about the commercialization of universities actually reached as far as the Massachusetts State Legislature. In 1925 a legislator invoked multiple figures of speech to charge that Harvard University was in the meshes of financiers, that professors dared not speak up on behalf of real scholarship, that "big business is in the saddle," that business was exercising an alarming tyranny over the entire university, that freedom of speech was dead, and that big business was forcing scholars to say only things approved by J. P. Morgan. He therefore introduced a bill calling for a legislative inquiry into whether "true culture is being crushed by big business at Harvard University." The legislature sanely refused to pass his bill on the grounds that it had no jurisdiction over a private university like Harvard, and thus the inquiry was never undertaken. But the mere fact that such a bill could have been introduced at all shows the prominence that business studies had acquired.[29]

This kind of attack explains the defensiveness that permeates an article four months later by University of Pennsylvania president Josiah H. Penniman. Although a renaissance English literature professor by training, Penniman proclaimed again and again that he welcomed the arrival of business and business influence in the nation's universities. Colleges were better organized as a result, he said, as well as more objective and systematic, and university research was being greatly furthered by business sponsorship. The influence of colleges on business was likewise beneficial: economics was now applied to agriculture, and physics to industry. Dismissing widely expressed fears "that scholarship and the market place are too close together," he again proclaimed confidently his belief "that colleges and universities have broadened immeasurably their field of observation and that business and industry have become more academic."[30]

Ethics. A case that came up in 1929 illustrated that the situation might be a little more complex than Penniman's forced optimism implied, however. That year another Massachusetts legislator demanded an investigation of Harvard professor C. O. Ruggles, who had formerly been dean at Ohio State University. Ruggles, then in his first year at Harvard, had for some time been receiving $15,000 a year—more than twice what Harvard paid him— from the New England Electric Light Association for the purpose of "overhauling" textbooks on economics and public utilities. Now, as a Harvard professor teaching "Public Utility Management and Regulation," he was continuing to receive the stipend, and the legislator smelled a rat. "I want to know," he said, "and I believe the people of this State will want to know, what is the relation between the Harvard Business School and the power interests."[31]

The case was not mentioned again in the press, as Harvard quickly determined that there was nothing improper in the arrangement. Yet the whole issue deserves to be paused over, since it shows something about the increased prominence of business education. Before about 1920, when people spoke of ethics in business they meant giving a customer a fair deal and not bribing politicians. Now, by the end of the decade, new and uncharted ethical territories were opening up. With the explosive growth of business education far more could be gained by influencing the hundreds of thousands of business students than could ever have come by fleecing an occasional customer—as much, perhaps, as by buying influence in a legislature. Therefore businesses and their associations were quite naturally investing their money where they could realize the best returns. Even when the activity was entirely aboveboard, when the people involved sincerely believed in the rightness of their cause and looked on their work as educational rather than propagandistic—as C. O. Ruggles, an upright man, no doubt did—still the possibility of influence peddling existed now as never before and created circumstances for which no ethical precedents existed. No better proof of the newfound importance of business education is needed than this. It may have been aboveboard—but, just the same, businesses knew where to put their money!

New Activities

Meanwhile, as business education was enjoying unprecedented fame and growth, it was also extending its influence into all sorts of areas it had not touched before. As noted earlier, the word "business" had still been construed quite narrowly as late as 1923, so that it included wholesale and retail trade and not much else; banking, manufacturing, and real estate were specifically excluded, and insurance probably was considered separate too. Now, by 1930, "business" had come to include practically everything—and not just new lines of commerce but managerial functions, new kinds of activities, and even a great deal of self-study.

Services and Managerial Functions

Research and teaching in business schools had from the first been based on such retail and wholesale lines of commerce as shoes, dry goods, hosiery, stationery, department stores, drug stores, radio shops, and grocery stores. These activities continued, but service businesses were soon added to them: motion pictures, hotels, hospitals, utilities, banking, air transport, radio communication, and others. Gradually functions became prominent, as schools sought to learn and teach the principles of "distribution," "store management," "marketing," "retailing," "trusts," and "export and import."

Policy Issues and the Social Sciences

Toward the end of the 1920s, the schools moved still another step away from the daily management of a business as their studies began focusing more on larger policy issues than on individual actions. They held conferences and conducted research projects on subjects such as changes in business policy during the 1920s, the change from an agricultural to a manufacturing economy in China and Japan, ways of improving capital-labor relations, and the export of capital. The social sciences continued their march into the study of business, not just through courses mentioned earlier but in student assessment, too. The Wharton School announced in 1925 a "personality audit" required of each student to assist in placement work. Evaluating students on such criteria as poise, cooperativeness, and social attitude, it was supposed to enhance their chances of a successful match with potential employers.

Self-Study

One area where business education turned its newfound powers of analysis was itself. Now that business education in college had become a major activity, self-study of all kinds began to develop. Curricular studies and surveys similar to ones conducted earlier became more numerous, as Columbia University debated whether it should offer only graduate-level courses like Harvard, Harvard altered its class schedule to give students more contemplation time, New York University consolidated its course offerings after studying to see which were most effective, and the University of Washington dropped forty courses it deemed too "vocational" and concentrated instead on scientific and technical ones.[32]

Business education in the universities of other nations also attracted attention. *The Journal of Political Economy* ran a series of articles, totaling over two hundred pages, on higher education for business in Germany, Czechoslovakia, Italy, and Great Britain. They showed strong parallels with the universities of the United States, especially in classifying the curricular offerings, resolving the tension between theoretical and practical approaches, and searching for general principles of the science of business. Differences were generally in matters of format and schedule, such as when to examine students, how much specialization to permit in the first and second year of a business program, and whether to limit enrollment.[33]

Surveys of all kinds became common. In 1923 the American Management Association and the Association of Collegiate Schools of Business announced a large survey to determine the scope and success of business education in college. Very much a descriptive type of study, it planned to include questionnaires sent to business school graduates now working in companies, to determine their age, occupation, and salary, and then to see how various kinds of business education programs produced various degrees of success. As one might expect, no results were ever reported. In 1929 a Purdue University professor surveyed graduates to find out how their salaries correlated with certain variables in their background. His nationally publicized finding was that personality had much more to do with success than grades did. Surveys also existed on a smaller scale: New York University asked its students to name their favorite courses and found (six months before the stock market crash) that finance was liked most and economics and accounting least.[34]

The AACSB

By far the greatest impetus for self-study came from the Association of Collegiate Schools of Business (later American Association, and still later American Assembly). Founded in 1916—twelve schools were represented at its first meeting—the AACSB had grown to thirty-nine schools by 1919 and had become the recognized standard organization in the field. Its annual meetings constituted a forum for exchange of views among member institutions, all of which were confronting the same baffling and unprecedented problems. In 1922 the theme was the desperate scarcity of teachers for the new courses in business—should they be academically trained or recruited from business, and should they be paid higher salaries than other college teachers? In 1923 the questions ranged more widely, covering in fact almost the whole spectrum of administration of a business program:

Questions Relating to Admissions

Is the selection of students on the basis of previous college records as satisfactory as a personal interview?

What should be the prerequisites required for admission to a graduate school?

Questions Relating to Student Life

To what extent should graduate students be permitted to engage in extracurricular activities?

To what extent may responsibility for attendance, performance of current work, and selection of courses be placed upon the students?

Should the honor system be used in business schools?

Questions Relating to Curriculum and Schedule

Should the method of instruction for undergraduates and for graduates be sharply differentiated?

In view of the period of apprenticeship generally required by business houses, is it more advisable for a student to meet this requirement while he is a student or after he has finished his studies?

Can the problem method and the part-time or full-time plan of education be worked together?

What are the merits of a thesis in applied business as compared to an oral examination as a condition of graduation?

To what extent and on what basis should advanced credit be given for work in undergraduate business courses?

How much specialization is desirable in the business curriculum?

Questions Relating to Research

How much research and of what character can be accepted of students of business?

What is the educational value of research?

Questions Relating to Faculty and Administration

Can schools of business justify a higher salary scale?

Should the dean supervise, regulate, and lead in the formulation of standards of work in the several departments of the school?

What should be an effective teaching load for heads of departments and others?

How important is business experience for the staff?

To what extent may a professor properly engage in professional activities outside of teaching?

During the rest of the 1920s the main concerns at the annual meetings were standards for membership in the association and how to enforce them, relations between business schools and departments of economics, and the establishment of a "Business Research Council," which would operate as a sort of superbureau of business research, gathering and disseminating data from bureaus in member universities. Each of these meetings, of course, also included presentations on other subjects, and many of the papers presented were later published for a wider audience, especially in the *Journal of Political Economy*. A whole new field—administration of departments and schools of business administration—had thus sprung up in less than two decades.[35]

* * *

By 1930, then, business education in college had not only continued its galloping growth but had broadened its sphere of influence to include new subjects and activities. As a result it now had a degree of prominence far greater than it had ever had before: neither supporters nor opponents could ignore the existence of business studies in college. What now remained to be seen was how it, as well as its new public, would react when the world plunged suddenly into the worst economic depression of modern history.

5

1930–1940:
Philosopher of Business and Society

As Americans gradually came to realize that the economic slump that had hit late in 1929 was not going to be a short-term affair, they began seeking explanations, solutions, and scapegoats. Unpredictably, business education came out well. Instead of blaming the nation's colleges for overemphasizing moneymaking at the expense of traditional education and thereby contributing to the collapse of the economy, public opinion sided with the business schools, even to the point of holding that they alone could lead the nation out of its predicament. The schools willingly assumed the rule of guru and extended their influence, and student enrollments continued to rise.

Gradual Awareness of the Depression

From a viewpoint of more than sixty years later, it is easy now to forget that people in 1929–30 did not realize they were at the start of a Great Depression. Stock markets had fallen before, even though not quite so far, and they had always come back up, so it was widely assumed that the depression of 1929 was going to be just as temporary as those of 1923, 1893, and 1873.

In fact it wasn't until 1931 that people began to suspect something more than ordinary had happened. That was the year that business schools—Boston University's College of Business, for example—first began to feel any effects,[1] and also the year that the general tone of public pronouncements began to change.

Throughout 1930 the activities of business schools had continued pretty much as before. The business research bureaus at Harvard, Columbia, and Wharton continued to turn out descriptive studies just as they had done for a decade or more, for example on operating expenses in the dry goods business, on public utility management, and on the effect of group versus individual bonuses.[2] A City College of New York forum dealt with "the break in stock markets," depicting Great Britain's as worse than America's

115

and showing no expectation that anything other than a temporary "break" was involved. Just two months later another such forum heard an optimistic Chase Manhattan vice president paint a cheerful picture of the economic future. Most tellingly of all, in May 1930—just seven months after the stock market crash—the Massachusetts Institute of Technology decided to teach business (as well as engineering) on a large-scale basis. MIT renamed its Department of Engineering Administration the "Department of Business and Engineering Administration" in recognition of the need for technically trained leaders in what was then the still prosperous field of business management.[3]

By the next year, however, things were clearly changing, as people realized that the economic slump was going to be around longer than they had thought at first. During 1932 and early 1933, the Wharton School sponsored large meetings on the economic decline as it affected Philadelphia, the nation, and the world. Columbia University's business library began collecting popular "depression panacea" books as a resource to help future generations understand the current bleak conditions. Harvard offered a course specifically for unemployed executives at the recommendation of executives from AT&T, Macy's, and J. P. Morgan. A hundred inquiries about the course were received in the first ten days, and final enrollment was eighty-two, despite the fact that full tuition rates were charged.[4]

Research projects also reflected the new awareness of economic realities. In 1933 alone three Harvard research projects showed distinct changes. Instead of simply describing income and expenses, an analysis of the cotton industry made recommendations stressing the consumers' viewpoint and the importance of coordination among marketing, production, and financial functions. Another large study analyzed economic policies of the American, Brazilian, and Japanese governments and pointed out how all had failed despite huge efforts. A third study dealt, as many had done before, with the fuel, food, and clothing industries, but this time, instead of simply citing figures, the study had a focus: determining whether and to what degree the Depression was affecting consumption patterns.[5]

THE ENNOBLEMENT OF BUSINESS SCHOOLS

As the Depression grew worse, and awareness of it grew stronger, there seems to have been no particular reason that business schools did not come in for a significant share of the blame. They had, after all, played a major part in the glorification and professionalization of business, and many of their courses, especially those in investments and real estate, had taught students to do the very things that had brought about the problems. Indeed Barnard College's distinguished dean, Virginia Gildersleeve, did make such critical observations in an address she delivered near the end of 1931. Arguing that the world needs the liberal arts more than ever, she flatly declared that it was the emphasis on technical training that had produced the current economic mess.[6]

Calls for More Business Education

But Dean Gildersleeve was practically alone. Instead of criticism, what resounded from all sides was a cry for still more business education. The Depression was taken as proof that business studies had been neglected and that traditional education had failed. The tide of public opinion, it would appear, could just as easily have gone the other direction. But it emphatically did not. Even when business education was specifically cited as being at fault, the conclusion people drew was not that it should be abolished but that it should be improved and redoubled.

Prominent British industrialist Sir Francis Goodenough epitomized this view perfectly in an address delivered just two months before Dean Gildersleeve's. "Obviously," he said, "many of the theories in business and commerce have been all wrong or the world wouldn't find itself in the present depression." But his conclusion, instead of being that the "science" of business was a failure, was that educators have a greater responsibility than ever before to teach economics and business on a sounder basis.[7]

The need for more and better business education was a common theme. The president of the B&O Railroad declared that the twin problems of unemployment and imperfect distribution were the curse of America, that something was terribly wrong when five million able and willing men could not find work. His solution was to turn to the universities, specifically to the Wharton School, to research the causes of unemployment. "Once the problem is clearly stated," he optimistically said, "it should not be difficult to solve."[8]

Similar confidence in the power and wisdom of universities permeated a speech by IBM's famed Thomas J. Watson, who wrote in 1932 that adequately trained young people were needed more than ever by business. "If business, finance, and science had known the right thing to do three years ago, we would never have reached our present low economic estate," he said, and then added, "I believe young men should go about the study of business as never before."[9]

Many others sounded the same call. Some cited the failure of traditional education, specifically the liberal arts, as the big problem in the current depressed economy. Professor Hugh Agnew of New York University blamed the woes on the late arrival of business education in America's colleges. Exaggerating a bit, he pointed out that no business person who was then over forty years old could have gone to business school, and that the Latin and Greek they had studied instead were not appropriate training for managing a business wisely. Four years later he made the same point in another address—that business, unlike law, medicine, and engineering, is run by people who have no specific training for it, a lack that explains its sad condition.

A similar but more pugnacious assessment was made by accounting professor Joseph Myer of St. John's University in New York, who attributed the depressed economic conditions directly to the arts and science faculties in the world's universities. They had, he maintained, deliberately blocked the introduction of business studies wherever possible, thereby retarding their progress and consequently causing the failure of many professional people who had been denied the right to study worthwhile things.[10]

Some other business education champions stressed the need for business studies programs that were broader and more theoretical. According to Chase Manhattan Bank economist Dr. Benjamin Anderson, the current economic slump derived not so much from too little education as from an education that was too narrow. Stating that the present mess was caused by the neglect of business theory and history, he urged business schools to broaden their offerings and to discard instruction in narrow and practical subjects. A prominent secondary school administrator in New York made the same point in an address a few months later. Although the city's high schools had made great progress in teaching commercial subjects, he felt that the larger issues were being neglected, and he called for the adoption of a broadly cultural business education.[11]

Most of the business education advocates argued that the problem was simply that there had been too little of it. In a long newspaper article published in 1934, Harvard assistant dean John C. Baker maintained that the new complexity of business operations required more education than ever before. Marketing now involved control, distribution, and labor problems unknown just a few years earlier. Advertising now relied for the first time on psychology and new research methods. Accounting had made the transition from bookkeeping to the philosophy and interpretation of costs, and it now required new kinds of mathematics. Finance had reached such levels of complexity that no longer could just anyone become a successful banker. The biggest changes of all, he continued, were in production, which was now as never before tied in with marketing in order to focus on producing what consumers actually wanted. And of course a major need for highly educated workers was created by the complexities of complying with modern federal regulations.[12]

In an article published in *Scribner's Magazine* two years later, business writer Herbert L. Towle argued more broadly that better business education could eliminate, or at least reduce the violence of, the boom and bust cycles that had so long plagued American business activity. While we cannot eliminate greed, we can, he said, eliminate ignorance, the true cause of the Depression that was ravaging the country. Citing an "unawareness among business men of what was going on and of its inevitable result," he went on to say that the two great lacks were "adequate grasp of economic principles and adequate fact-finding. With those things provided, it would be impossible for business cycles to rip through industry like tornadoes, leaving the work of years in ruins."

Specifically, Towle advocated a combined knowledge of economic principles and business practices, such as could come about only through cooperation between theoretical professors and practical business people. Two consequences could be expected if business education did not become better and more widespread. The first was simply a lower standard of living: "unless business men themselves learn to manage the vast mechanism which they have created, it will be necessary to go back to a simpler mechanism, with less concentration, smaller production, and less of the fruits of industry to divide." The second consequence was more ominous: improvement in business management was the only alternative to political dictatorship. If business did not shape itself up, he warned, the government would have to step in and take over.[13]

Even the government joined in the cry. In an example of flagrantly naive arithmetic, the U. S. Office of Education counted 2 million business positions in the nation and divided that figure by thirty years of working life, to come up with sixty-six thousand as a desired number of business graduates colleges should be turning out each year. Since the actual number of graduates in 1933 was only seven thousand, the office issued an urgent call for more people to study business. Certainly most observers would have regarded such a campaign for a ninefold increase in business enrollment to be wildly extreme, but still it was undeniably true that public opinion during the Depression came down firmly in favor of teaching people more, not less, about business.[14]

The Role of Guru

The business schools willingly acceded to the new position they were offered. Having been told that they possessed the wisdom to bring the nation and the world out of economic distress, the schools fairly quickly set about assuming their new role of economic and business philosopher. The change was reflected in their new mission statements, in their activities, in their public statements, and in their curricula.

Socially Conscious Missions. Before the Depression began, mission statements of business schools had generally had two components: an assurance that the science of business (as opposed to mere typing and stenography) had developed to a point where it was a worthy discipline for a university to teach, and a statement that the courses taught were designed to help graduates attain positions of prominence and responsibility in a shorter time than if they had not attended college. The University of Mississippi's statement, which first appeared in 1927 and was reprinted without change for several years, was typical:

> The purpose of the school is to provide broadly trained men capable of meeting the demands of the modern business world. The old type of business college, with its narrow curriculum, failed to accomplish this purpose. The modern business school has as its aim the training of professional business men, and to that end it has laid a broad foundation of economic knowledge. While recognizing the merits of the old curriculum—bookkeeping, shorthand, and typewriting—it goes much further, and grounds the student in those fundamental economic laws on which all business rests. So rapidly are we moving from a local to a state, and on to a world economy, that the men who would succeed in business must be broadly gauged.

From 1937 on, the focus of the school's mission statement changed. The object was still to turn out successful business people, but by now it had become clear that success depended on much more than a knowledge of one's business:

> The growing complexity of economic society and the quickening pace of business competition renders it more and more difficult for any person to attain a place of responsibility without an intelligent alertness to changing modern methods and to social forces which frequently become the predominant factor in determining whether an enterprise succeeds or fails.
>
> Skill at a given task will no longer suffice. Business men must comprehend the meaning of innumerable market influences, of changes in the banking and monetary system, of public finance, of new departures in legislation and legal interpretation, of international complications, of labor problems, and of even more fundamental questions of economics and philosophy which influence the course of a dynamic age. Without such knowledge, a man may find himself submerged beneath social forces which he does not understand.

The University of Oklahoma made an even more distinct change in its mission statement. Before the Depression hit, the emphasis had been exclusively on creating prosperous business professionals:

> The School of Business was organized for the purpose of meeting the needs of prosperous business men in the same way that schools of engineering, law, medicine, and theology have been organized to meet the professional needs of prosperous engineers, lawyers, physicians, and ministers. Business knowledge and experience have become so systematized in most branches that they can be taught in classrooms; so that business in its higher terms has come to be as much a learned profession as engineering, law, medicine, or other similar professions; and demands of those who make a success in the field a thoro scientific and practical training.

After 1930 this single aim was joined by a second one stressing the social implications of business:

> to give students such training as will enable them to understand the public problems, particularly those having to do with the interrelationships between different businesses, between business and government, and between the employer and the employee.

Even when a mission stated already contained social considerations, the Depression still caused changes. The University of Michigan, before the Depression, had stated three objectives: "(1) to provide instruction of a professional grade in the basic principles of management; (2) to afford training in the use of quantitative measurements in the solution of management problems; and (3) to assure education in the relationships between business leadership and the more general interests of the community." Beginning in 1933, and continuing the rest of the decade, a new paragraph was added, adapting the three objectives to the new economic conditions:

> Another factor evidenced in recent business conditions has a bearing upon the preparation needed for business. Earlier periods were characterized by expansion: expansion of population, expansion of total purchasing power, and expansion of the markets for new products. Now, many believe, we may look forward to growth at a more conservative rate. Whether or not the country as a whole has reached such a stage of industrial maturity, it is clear that several important industries have done so. So far as this is true, new policies and methods of business will become necessary, for the business policies of expansion are quite different from those appropriate to a period of consolidation and slow development.

Emphasis on the social and economic environment, rather than on business itself, now became standard. The University of Connecticut aimed "to offer training which, while somewhat directed toward vocational objectives, recognizes the civic responsibilities of business men and regards business as a field involving public responsibilities as well as opportunities for profits." The University of Iowa stressed economic and social principles. Its program was

> designed to build up in the experience of the student a fundamental understanding of the structure, operation, and function of our social and economic organization, as expressed in the fields of commerce, economics, sociology, and social administration. The work in commerce aims to provide vocational education for students planning to engage in commercial, industrial, or financial work, based upon the assumption that a careful training in the fundamental principles underlying our economic system is essential to an adequate grasp of the purpose and procedure of business.

Even the University of Cincinnati, justly famous for its innovative "cooperative" program combining study with actual work experience, stated three objectives that related to the environment rather than to the internal operation of a business:

(1) to give the student a broad conception of business as a means of organizing production, distribution, and consumption; (2) to build up a background of basic facts and principles relating to the material and social environment in which we live and work; (3) to assure a thorough working knowledge of economics, considered as a method of analysis, and of accounting and statistics, conceived as instruments of measurement and control.

The description went on to reiterate the school's emphasis on general principles. The program, it said, "is not concerned with the details of any particular business, but with the fundamentals necessary in the interpretation of economic movements and in the solution of business problems—problems of production, marketing, finance—problems of internal organization and of external adjustment. It is designed to prepare young men and women for positions of responsibility in the fields of public and private business."

At Harvard the major development was the inclusion of "the study of government" in its purpose statement. Citing three groups of people who need such training—business owners who must deal with government, government policy makers who must deal with business, and government regulators who must enforce the policies—the School announced new emphasis on "public business administration" and other aspects of government activity. To its two previous missions, teaching and research, Dean Donham now added a third—public service.[15]

Socially-Directed Activities. The schools reflected their new roles also in the greatly expanded activities they sponsored. Conferences and special programs had existed before, but never in such numbers. Information just from Pennsylvania's Wharton School illustrates the point abundantly. It sponsored a conference on unemployment in 1931; on the Depression in general in 1932; one on the international depression and another on the NRA in 1933; on the influence of commodity prices on the economy in 1934; one on the TVA and another on the gold standard in 1935; on the federal budget in 1936; one on the monetary situation and another on government control of economic cycles in 1937; on the role of government in regulating the economy in 1938; and on the Pan American economic situation in March 1939. Then to top them all, its conference in May 1939 concerned the all-embracing topics, "the weakness and strength of the United States, the future of society, and the effect of war on the democracies."[16]

At Columbia University, the annual reports of the dean illustrate again how a business school viewed its role. One year the dean said it was Columbia's duty to attack world problems; another year he stressed the importance of cooperation to replace competition; in 1934 he envisioned changing the whole emphasis so that instead of a school of business it became a school of "business and public affairs"; and the 1935 report focused exclusively on helping to solve the problems of the nation's economy.[17] With expressions like these coming from the top administration, it's easy to understand the growth in Depression-related conferences and programs at business schools.

The theme of cooperation, mentioned in the Columbia dean's report for 1933, became quite important during these years, especially in the last half of the decade, as observers seem to have realized that the separate efforts of thousands of individual enterprises would never be able to lift the nation out of its problems. Twice representatives of the federal government's Bureau of Foreign and Domestic Commerce made appeals to business schools to establish cooperative arrangements on a national scale. In November 1936 the head of the bureau urged creation of an "industrial research division" that would gather figures and coordinate the information being gathered in the more than fifty business schools in the country.

Three years later, the bureau held a meeting, billed as the first of a series, at the University of Virginia for the purpose of exploring ways in which government and business schools could cooperate to help businesses. Again the possibility of a central clearinghouse for research was discussed. In both meetings it was noted that the exchange of information was highly desirable from an overall economic viewpoint but absolutely impossible if such matters were left entirely to highly competitive individual businesses. A similar point was made by Dean Taylor of New York University in 1937. Pointing out that neither theoretical economists nor businesses could solve social problems without the other, he called for cooperation on a scale greater than anything that had been tried before.[18]

Social Concerns in Curricula and Research. Reflecting uncertainty about how to react to the unprecedented problems of society, the business schools made no great changes in their curricula during the 1930s. A few, such as Wisconsin, Ohio State, and Harvard, added some courses in governmental relations. A few others, notably Michigan, New York University, and Northwestern, increased their offerings in personnel management. Almost all by this point were teaching courses in real estate. But none of these changes amounted to much, and certainly no national trend of any kind could be found. Most of the schools simply reorganized their offerings a few times but kept the content pretty much as it had been when times were good.

Not so, however, with research. Here not only were the subjects more community oriented than before but the research methods themselves were more sophisticated. The subjects being researched, as mentioned before, were much more likely now to have social and governmental implications rather than to be strictly confined to the internal operation of a business. At the extreme, proposals were made at different schools to undertake large studies of the human problems of society, labor in New York City, and socioeconomic problems in general.[19]

But even in the less extreme cases the concern for social implications was clear. Instead of merely reporting on unemployment, the Wharton School analyzed it by race, sex, and age and calculated its economic impact on the city of Philadelphia. Instead of simply compiling and publishing expenses and revenues, as they had done for years, research studies now began making recommendations: the shoe, hosiery, and wool industries were told that they ought to restrict production; cotton industry companies were told they should decentralize; states were urged to adopt uniform unemployment insurance laws; and the accounting profession was urged to make changes to protect investors.

Studies like these required research techniques more sophisticated than mere bookkeeping methods. At one point during the early part of the decade a Columbia University professor severely criticized a Harvard research project for having produced a flawed study by, among other things, using outdated expense accounting rather than cost accounting. Apparently the methods employed in subsequent projects were changed as a result of his criticism.[20]

High Enrollments

Just as nobody knew what effect the Depression would have on the general reputation of business schools, so nobody knew what to expect of enrollments. It was soon discovered, to the surprise of many, that business enrollments actually rise in bad economic times. At the City College of New York, the number of business students rose from 350 to 529 the very first term after the stock market crash, and the next year New York University reported the largest graduate enrollment ever. Harvard reported a 24 percent increase in applications for 1936, and New York University reported undergraduate increases of 17.5 percent and 21.7 percent for 1934–35 and 1935–36. Nonbusiness schools were finding the same trends. Princeton, Yale, Vassar, Smith, and Wellesley noted that more students were choosing courses in economics and political science, and fewer in traditional courses in languages, literature, and Bible studies.[21]

Both employed and unemployed people seem to have contributed to the enrollment surge. Employed people, *The New York Times* reported, wanted to acquire extra skills in order to be sure they kept their jobs.[22] Unemployed people, unable to find work, figured they could best use the time by preparing themselves for employment when times got better. To be sure, times were hard for the unemployed, and one business dean urged the government (unsuccessfully) to make tuition payments tax-exempt to help them out. Campus jobs became more in demand also, as enrolled students sought to meet expenses with less help from home. But however difficult the day-today economic problems were, they did not dim the public's confidence in business education: it still, everyone was convinced, offered the best guarantee of future security.[23]

A Paucity of Critics

Thus the public, the schools themselves, and the students all held collegiate business education in higher-than-ever esteem during, and as a result of, the Depression. Anyone surveying the writings at the time has to be struck by the near total absence of negative comments either about the value of business education to individuals or about its importance to society. Almost everyone seemed to believe absolutely that the cause of this worst and longest Depression in the nation's history was not too much business education but too little. Only small and very occasional cracks could be discerned in the gleaming facade of public approval.

One such crack was quietly covered over in 1933, when Harvard Business School and Yale Law School announced a joint course. Public announcements stressed the importance of understanding the strong interrelationships of law and business, and downplayed as a mere curiosity the strange fact that Yale's Law School, rather than Harvard's, was involved. In fact the real reason for the interuniversity cooperation was that the Harvard Law School dean regarded the Business School with scorn and would have nothing to do with it. Such attitudes were not common anymore, but this episode shows that they still existed.[24]

Another criticism, this one concerning the shallowness of business education, came from Benjamin Anderson, the economist quoted earlier. Formerly editor of the *Chase Economic Bulletin* he was by 1940 teaching economics at UCLA, and he expressed concern about the tendency among his students to shun any subject that lacked immediate practical value. Psychology, he said, was valued only insofar as it told of devices that could be used in advertising, and from economics his students wanted not principles and historical perspectives but only facts relating to banking and finance. No one showed any interest in history, literature, science, or the fine arts. Even from a practical perspective, Anderson warned, such an education was a poor one, since changing economic and social conditions were causing exclusively "practical" knowledge, without an understanding of underlying principles, to become obsolete quickly.[25]

Yet Anderson's criticisms, like the earlier mentioned views of Dean Gildersleeve of Barnard College, show no evidence of having influenced anyone. Collegiate business education had not just survived the Great Depression but had prospered because of it, and its own rhetoric showed how much it had come to accept the importance status that the public had accorded it.

Such attitudes gave rise to a warning from Dean Donham of Harvard. He argued, in an impassioned article in the *Harvard Business Review,* that the nation had become fragmented and individualistic when what was needed was leadership based on an understanding of interrelationships. Politicians, he said, lack broad enough training and understanding to do the job, and therefore people look to the legal profession. Lawyers, however, have become concerned almost exclusively with finding some way of satisfying individual clients, and therefore people look to business for the answer. But alas, the businesses of the nation turn out to be probably the narrowest of all in their vision:

> Their executives behave first, last, and nearly all the time as if their companies had no function except to manufacture and sell. They have a fine understanding of their own business, too little grasp of their industries as a whole, almost none of the relation between their particular interest and our general social and economic structure, and far too little grip on the social consequences of their activities.

As an example he cited the banking industry:

> We create great banks. Their leaders too often know little beyond finance. When through intrusion of new social and economic forces, thousands of banks fail, they and the community think of improving the management of banks rather than of restoring social equilibrium. Yet lost social equilibrium rather than bad management accounts for most bank failures.

The same narrowness of focus, Donham said, characterized the entire business community, as shown in its fierce opposition to agricultural reform:

> When the farm problem becomes a major catastrophe, business knowing little of the subject either ignores the plight of one-third of our nation or actively opposes plans to regain balance. It makes little effort to design better plans.

Therefore when the nation's leaders, wanting to make good laws, turn to law or business for guidance, they receive only "specialized advice relating to the narrow individual environment of the advisor."

Thus it was, Donham feared, that the nation's leaders might be just about to turn to the highly revered schools of business for guidance. The academic field of professional business administration was a noble one, he acknowledged, but academic thinking is limited too, because university professors are specialists in narrow fields just as surely as all the others. "We criticize the politician for not following our advice," Donham said, "but our advice rarely deals with the range of variables he must take into account." Warning against the sin of overweening pride that business schools seemed to be in danger of giving in to, he concluded,

> Above all men, university scholars should be humble before their inadequacies. If in this critical period of the nation's history it should turn over to a university

faculty the political and practical decisions which must be made by politicians and men of affairs, calamity would result. The nation suffers badly from overspecialization of its business leadership. Universities with less excuse have the same fault. Nowhere do we train men to study general social relationships with the broad vision and the philosophic view needed if social science is to be valid in a complex and changing world.[26]

* * *

Donham's warnings do not seem to have had much effect. The business schools did, as already noted, turn their attention to social matters during this decade, but they showed no signs of becoming humble. And when a new national emergency struck early in the next decade and the government called on them to help, they responded by getting involved in the country's affairs to an even greater degree than before and enlarging their collective ego still further.

6

1940–1945:
War

DURING World War I the business schools in America's colleges had
hardly been noticed; they were of no more importance than any other
college department. By World War II, however, everything had
changed. Business schools had grown to be among the largest divisions of most universities and, more importantly, now occupied positions of great significance and respect in the public mind. Through
their extensive activities and research, they stood right at the center
of the nation's war effort and helped to lay plans for the nation's
future. In doing so the business schools accumulated even greater
reserves of public esteem and self-esteem.

WARTIME ACTIVITIES

Faculty and Staff at War

Since almost all professors and administrators in the schools of business
at America's universities were male, were comparatively young, and had
been trained in some sort of useful activity, they were obvious candidates for
military conscription. Many schools consequently found themselves with
greatly depleted ranks of instructors. The Massachusetts Institute of Technology, because of its famed engineering prowess, was called on to make
extensive loans of its faculty members to various war training programs.
The University of Georgia reported that half its business college's staff,
including its dean, were on leave for war-related work, and Louisiana State
University's business division lost the services of fourteen faculty members,
or two-thirds of the department. Across the whole country, courses were
frequently listed as "offered when possible."

War Training Programs

Well back in 1940 and early 1941, everybody knew war was coming—
although practically everybody expected it from Europe, not Japan—and

128

business schools were already being geared up for wartime training. In April 1941 Dean Croft of the University of Iowa told the annual AACSB convention that schools of business were establishing defense programs in four specific fields: leadership, logistics, efficiency, and organization. Dean Donham of Harvard addressed the same conference on "Defense Training—Graduate School of Business Administration," stressing the large number of special activities undertaken there in close cooperation with the army.

By the time America became involved in hostilities, three main series of war training programs had been established, and almost every university housed at least one or two of them. The navy had its "V" programs—V–1, V–5, V–7, V–12—each of which trained for a specified war-related function. Of most relevance to schools of business was V–12, which provided three years of college-level training for pre–Supply Corps candidates. After successfully completing the prescribed course, students were assigned to the Navy Supply Corps School for another five months, and then were commissioned as ensigns. Nine universities made their facilities available for these, including North Carolina, Tulane, Indiana, Illinois, Minnesota, New Mexico, and Washington.

The army had its "ASTP" (Army Specialized Training Program) courses on even more campuses. These courses were of shorter duration and were aimed at very specific skills such as welding or typing. Business schools were involved where their expertise was relevant, but most ASTP courses seem to have been more closely related to engineering or science. Among the dozens of universities participating were Stanford, Wyoming, Michigan, Iowa, Kentucky, and Florida.

Most widespread of all were the U.S. Office of Education's "ESMWT" (Engineering, Science, and Management War Training) courses. These short-duration courses were offered, free of charge and often in off-campus locations, to members of the public, with the intent (as the University of Utah's catalog explained it) of qualifying people already employed in industry for more advanced positions, and of providing preemployment training for people not already engaged in a war-related industry. In some places, such as Indiana University, the program was actually administered by the school of business, obviously a major task in view of the very large enrollments. Louisiana State University offered twenty-two of these courses in one year, and cumulative enrollment in the war years was often in the thousands—2,000 at the University of New Mexico, 3,000 at the University of Maine, and over 13,500 at Indiana University itself. Subjects included accounting and auditing, budget administration, organization and procedure analysis, purchasing and procurement, and courses for specific industries such as railroads and electronics. They were supervised by each university's academic departments and taught by practicing experts from cooperating industries in the community.[1]

War Research

Since war-related research had to be secret, few details of such activities in business schools were released at the time, but it was absolutely clear even then that such research was being quite widely conducted. Half a year before Pearl Harbor, Dean Taylor of New York University called on the country's business schools to shift the direction of their research. Although he gave no details, he pointed out that national defense has different requirements and that schools should move away from their normal peacetime studies. His comments may have been aimed directly at rival Harvard, where the Bureau of Business Research was continuing at the time to turn out studies of department stores, variety stores, and distribution costs.[2]

Others were having the same thoughts, and for the next four years business research took on a new meaning. Sometimes a university would say secretively only that it was conducting "much research" (Missouri), but a few others gave more detail. The Wharton School, which had long made a specialty of research into the textile industry, now conducted a research project on "The Impact of War on the Textile Industry."

Most projects, however, concerned prosecution of the war itself. At the Massachusetts Institute of Technology, a research project on production methods led to compilation and publication of a *Handbook of War Production,* and other research there concerned improvement of efficiency on production lines. The University of Minnesota conducted extensive research on wartime distribution techniques, and New York University surveyed the effectiveness of war-bond financing. In the summer of 1945 Harvard published a book, commissioned by the navy, on the appropriate tonnage to keep after the war as merchant marine. From general comments in university catalogs the time, it is obvious that far more work was going on than we know about; these few examples give a general ideal of the kind of research projects business schools were being called on to undertake.[3]

The War Curriculum

Changes in the curriculum were being forced by staff shortages at just about every college, but far more important than these were the modifications made for the purpose of bringing business school training into line with the war effort. Changes ranged all the way from the addition of a course or two to total revamping of the curriculum. One great need perceived by the military early in the war was for vastly increased numbers of typists, stenographers, and file clerks. Accordingly Louisiana State University instituted a one-year program in office skills, "purely a service program which has been inaugurated to help solve the urgent needs of the Armed Services." Indiana University likewise expanded its office skills training, as did several others.

Some universities added special "war" courses. Louisiana State and Northwestern Universities both offered "Accounting for War Procurement Contracts," and the University of Massachusetts offered an unusually specific course called "Army Administration":

A study of the procedures that pertain to the administration of an infantry rifle company and an infantry regiment, which are, with only minor variations, applicable to similar organizations throughout the Army. The first part of the course treats with company administration and the second part regimental administration.

The University of Tennessee added "Economic Problems of War and Post-War" and also "Problems of Procurement of Supplies and Equipment," in which "special attention will be given to the effects of a war economy"; and the University of Georgia offered "The Economics of War" and a new war-related course in "Industrial Management."

The University of Mississippi's School of Business took a different approach and modified the description of all its existing courses to make them war-relevant. Thus, the following course descriptions appeared in the 1944 catalog:

Marketing: An analysis of modern methods as they are related to consumers and producers living under the conditions of war. Effects of rationing. Attention is given to both wartime and peacetime products.

Labor Problems: A consideration of the major problems confronting the wage earner in a modern economic society, with emphasis on the position of labor in a war economy.

Investments: A study of the characteristics of investment securities, personal and institutional investment problems, the methods of testing the investment worth, and public and corporate securities, with consideration given to the effects of war on investment programs.

Merchandising: . . . adjustments necessitated by governmental war measures.

Salesmanship: . . . the importance of training for the post war period will be emphasized.

Business Organization and Finance: . . . Full consideration of the effects of the war on organization and finance will be stressed.

Personnel Management: . . . Attention will be given to the relation of personnel work to the war program.

Advanced Money and Banking: . . . The problems of inflation in war periods will receive attention.

Transportation: . . . War demands on rail and air transports are stressed. Dependence on transportation in a war economy is observed.

Business Cycles: . . . the possible future effects of current war conditions.

Finally, a few universities instituted new curricula altogether. Columbia University established a "war-time program" aimed at training women, men not in the military, and prospective inductees to be qualified as accountants, personnel specialists, statisticians, geographers, and teachers. The University of Michigan did the same on a larger scale. Designed to train women and men not in the service, Michigan's "War Services Courses" included four courses in accounting, four in business administration (Management, Business Mathematics, Industrial Mobilization, and Industrial Relations), four in economics, and three in factory management. Beyond question, the University of Michigan's commitment to the defense effort was gigantic: in the *Announcements* for 1942–43 the description of the university's war activities required seventy-eight pages.

The emphasis on women's programs was not unusual, since women now were being permitted, even sought, to occupy jobs traditionally held only by men. The University of Washington thus announced a "Special Business Training Course for Women," concerned with "war and essential civilian activities." Late in 1942 both Columbia and New York Universities reported that firms were "clamoring" for women accountants, and earlier that year a University of Chicago survey had assured women that it was now acceptable to be smart and hold a job—that it did not hurt their chances of marriage.[4]

Special Schedules and Credits for Soldiers and Veterans.

Almost all universities made adjustments in their calendars and schedules during the war in order to facilitate completion of studies. For several (Tulane, Indiana, Florida, Wharton) these adjustments meant switching to the trimester system so that students could take courses for three rather than just two terms each year and could thereby complete their work in two and two-thirds years instead of four. For others (Maine, for example) a change to the quarter system accomplished the same objective. Several—the University of Maine and the Wharton School, among them—went still further and altered their prerequisite structures so that students who were in a hurry to acquire needed skills—such as business skills—could do so at an earlier point in their college careers.

The question of providing academic credit for some of the military training programs mentioned above, and also for military service itself, came up often, as would be expected. Dean Elwell of the University of Wisconsin devoted his address to the 1944 AACSB Conference to possible credit for ESMWT courses, and Indiana University had already taken the lead by giving returning soldiers college credit for their experience where possible. Courses in the navy's V–12 (Pre-Supply) program were convertible into credits in the college of economics and business at most schools (for example, the University of Washington), permitting graduation after only a little additional work.

Returning veterans, who showed a strong propensity to study business, were often given special consideration to facilitate their work. Columbia offered special refresher courses for them, and New Hampshire, Tulane, and Illinois created special schedule arrangements for them. But the University of South Dakota stood alone in generous recognition of the veterans' services: it granted free tuition to all returning South Dakotans.

Harvard

Undoubtedly the defense commitment at the Harvard Business School was the most absolute in the nation. "No other school," writes Jeffrey Cruikshank in his history of the Harvard Business School, "had so completely abandoned its civilian program or was committed contractually to the government to such an extent."[5] For the last two years of the war the school had no regular students at all. All were uniformed, taking shorter term courses dealing with material almost entirely new to the faculty, material that had had no place in the prewar curriculum and would not be needed again after the war. Among the subjects Dean David cited in his talk at the 1944 AACSB convention were "Navy Aviation Supply," "Navy Industrial Accounting," and "Classification and Control of Surplus Stocks." While other universities were sponsoring selected navy "V" programs, army ASTP courses, or Office of Education ESMWT courses, Harvard Business School participated in everything and even invented more of its own, including an "Industrial Administrator Program," a program for the Quartermaster Corps, a highly successful and influential Army Air Force Statistical School, and a program for retraining active executives for war-related work, called at various times the "War Production Training Course," the "War Production Re-Training Course," the "War Industry Training Course," or simply the "retreads" course. A full description of these programs occupies seventy mammoth and fascinating pages of Cruikshank's book.

Thus because business was profoundly relevant to the war effort, especially with respect to accounting, purchasing and procurement, personnel management, administration, efficiency analysis, and office skills, all the nation's schools of business, Harvard most of all, found themselves constantly involved in war-related activities. Moreover the tendency of returning military personnel to be interested in business studies placed still further demands on them. Even though they were often overwhelmed with day-to-day details of these almost entirely new activities, they still knew that the end of the war was coming, and with it would come changes of a magnitude they had never confronted before.

PLANNING AHEAD FOR AFTER THE WAR

Discussions of anticipated postwar changes began early, in one optimistic instance even before the attack on Pearl Harbor. In some places, such as the University of Maine, the plans were merely acknowledged but not specified: "Ground work is also being laid for effective service in the post-war period." The University of Mississippi, as noted earlier, emphasized "training for the post-war period" in its salesmanship course, and "future effects" in its course on business cycles. Still others expressed the general conviction that business education on the college level would grow more important after the war. LSU's dean predicted a doubling of enrollment, and Dean Calkins of Columbia predicted that the suddenly increased amount of knowledge about business would raise the educational requirements for business leaders and cause increasing demands on business schools.[6]

Two themes commonly stressed were the need to emphasize general rather than specific skills and the importance of keeping in mind that service to society, rather than mere profit making, was the principal objective. Dean Stevenson of the University of Minnesota agreed that training in techniques was appropriate, but he urged that they be more general ones than before. The head of the New York City Board of Higher Education addressed a Wharton School conference on 1943, decrying the tendency of colleges to teach specialized skills and methods when their purpose should be to train "fact-finders." He also said that business should learn to regard itself as a "channel for social services," not as a means toward self-aggrandizement.

A month earlier Dean Taylor of the New York University had similarly said that plans should be laid now to confront the economic and social problems that soon would replace the current military ones—that a strong business community is needed to implement the economic life of society. The president of the Massachusetts Institute of Technology noted in his 1943 report that his school was undertaking a major effort to determine "the proper reflection in our course content of the ever-broadening social responsibilities of the industrial administrator."[7]

A major statement on the same theme was found in a long *Harvard Business Review* article in 1944 by Columbia University's new dean, Robert Calkins. Entitled "A Challenge to Business Education," the article argued that business schools had been too narrowly defining their mission—that it should be to educate "not for business alone, but to direct and operate the wide variety of economic institutions of modern society." Actually, Calkins wrote, such had been the ultimate purpose of business schools all along, but the method of accomplishing the purpose has failed to keep up with changes in the social and economic structure.

Specifically, he pointed out that the economy "is not, as some appear to regard it, a fabulous oriental bazaar in which greedy people make a living by cheating each other. . . . It is a productive system on whose output we all depend. We all have a big stake in having it better run." Therefore the duty of educating men and women to "direct, manage, and conduct economic affairs through whatever sort of economic system exists for the purpose is an enduring necessity." Back when business organizations ran the economy, the schools, appropriately, taught people about business. But now that the system had proved to be more complex than business alone could manage, the schools should feel a responsibility to broaden the education they provide—still with the same purpose of directing, managing, and conducting the world's economic affairs but no longer through business alone.

The kind of education needed thus had changed, he concluded, but the underlying purpose remained. Moreover, the schools must recognize that the process of change was a continuing one, and that they could not merely substitute one kind of curriculum for another without remembering the ultimate objective. "The institutional structure may change further," he said, "but the educational need will not." Teaching the "prevailing practices and pat solutions" of an existing system would not satisfy the need. The business schools must reconceptualize their task as teaching not just business but the management of the economy.[8]

Emphasis on psychology, personnel management, and labor relations was also a very common theme among planners for the postwar period. Citing lessons learned from the ESMWT programs, Dean Stevenson (Minnesota) urged greater emphasis on industrial relations, personnel administration, and labor management. The director of public relations at Manufacturers Trust Company made the same argument, and he referred to a previous study at the Massachusetts Institute of Technology to bolster his point. The school had placed a number of selected graduates in important New England industries, and the president at the time had asked the employing corporations to watch them carefully and report on their progress. The result was that not one single example of technical deficiency was ever reported; but "wherever the men were not succeeding as well as had been expected the assigned cause was inability to work with others or some personal trait which short-circuited their natural aptitude." Awareness was now growing fast that the real problems for business educators to address were the human ones.[9]

Everyone realized that major adjustments in production objectives and techniques lay ahead. As early as August 1941 Dean Taylor (New York University) had called for a council to find a new objective to replace war materials production, and similar calls were heard later, as the war actually did begin to die down, from deans at Harvard and at MIT, among other places. New production and management techniques learned from the war experiences were also quite widely noted, and calls were made for them to take a prominent place in postwar curricula.[10]

A new awakening to the importance of international business was also widely predicted. The dean of Ohio State's business school urged bureaus of business research to turn their attention to international studies, and in Arizona planning was underway for a whole school—the Thunderbird School, or American Graduate School of International Management—which would be aimed exclusively at training Americans for overseas business.[11]

Several people noted that an emphasis on small business, rather than exclusively on corporations, could be expected after the war, and others foresaw a need for more stress on marketing, more cooperation with industry, and more adult education programs. It is easy to see how all four of these expectations arose from war-related experiences. Many returning veterans were showing interest in running their own companies; the change to peacetime production would require new and more aggressive marketing of consumer products; and wartime training programs had proved the effectiveness of industry-university cooperation and the value of educating older workers.[12]

RETIREMENTS MARK AN ERA'S END

Three influential business deans in the Northeast reached the end of their administrative careers during the war, and their departures from the business school scene seem both actually and symbolically significant.

At Columbia University, Dean Roswell McCrea retired in October 1941, devoting his final report, rather typically, to the importance of cooperation between economics and business departments. Each is necessary to save the other from itself, he concluded, since economics alone is only "closet philosophizing" and business alone would degenerate into "detailed descriptions of business organization and procedures, with no organizing principle other than the possible one of search for competitive devices, and with no clear vision of the social goal of business activity."[13]

Whether or not his point was valid, it clearly was out of touch with the times. In the 1920s people had debated economics/business relations and had searched for an "organizing principle," but raising that question at a time when the world was on the verge of disintegrating into international war indicates that McCrea was far out of date, more an inward-directed program manager than a leader tuned in to the actual and potential role of a business school in national and world affairs.

At Harvard, Dean Wallace Donham retired in May 1942 to choruses of praise from all quarters, including *Time* magazine and a *New York Times* editorial.[14] He was immeasurably more accomplished than his Columbia counterpart, and he had brought strength and stability to the business school during the worst worldwide depression on record. He had, moreover, directed the movement away from the mechanical conception of business toward a more people-oriented conception. Yet his concerns were, like McCrea's, primarily inward-directed: he was, most of all, a superb manager of the Harvard Business School. An era was about to begin in which business schools were to take their place on the public stage, and the departure of one dean and the arrival of a new one was an appropriate and significant milestone to mark the change.

The point applies also to New York University's A. Wellington Taylor, who retired as dean in September 1943. Although he did speak out frequently on economic issues, his main interests had been in developing the science of management and establishing a financially secure school with a big endowment and a booming enrollment. These obviously remain major goals of every business dean today, but with Taylor they reflected his association with business schools from their earliest and most insecure days (he first published an article on business education before World War I), and they seem out of keeping with the era that was to come.

*   *   *

The main impression that one gets from reading through the business education documents during World War II is one of expectations. The schools, already having achieved prominence as philosophers of business and society, now had proved their practical abilities as well. It would take a little longer before any actual changes were visible, but a real sense of great importance was there and was going to lead soon to startling developments.

7

1945–1950:
Regrouping, Rethinking

THE day-to-day problems of coping with an avalanche of returning veterans occupied America's business schools to such an extent starting in 1946 that not much else got done. What did occur was a lot of talking and planning, much of it visionary, and the result was a swirl of confusion and contradictions in which theory sometimes moved ahead of practice and practice sometimes ahead of theory.

SURGING ENROLLMENTS

Two factors—the sheer number of students coming to universities, and their propensity to study business—worked together to overwhelm the nation's business schools during this six-year period. A few figures will illustrate the first of these. By January 1946, not six months after the war ended, Harvard was already reporting that it had 5,500 applicants for a mere three hundred openings. Just three months later a speaker at the annual AACSB convention noted that 200,000 returning veterans were already enrolled in colleges, and that an astounding 750,000 more were expected to enroll by September. Since the total enrollment of all the nation's colleges and universities together was less than 900,000, this surge amounted to more than a doubling in less than twelve months. Over the next few years it grew still faster. Bachelor's degrees more than doubled in two years (from 157,349 in 1946 to 317,607 in 1948) and more than tripled (to 496,874) by 1950. Master's degrees followed an almost identical pattern: from 19,209 in 1945, to 42,432 in 1948, to 58,183 in 1950. The effort merely to provide enough classrooms and enough instructors absorbed all the energies of college administrators and effectively prevented any attention from being to paid to innovations.[1]

It is more difficult to document the surge of interest in business as a field of study, but the trend was unmistakably there. Dean Reid McClung of the University of Southern California noted that the returning veterans "are seeking education that is immediately useful rather than the cultural offerings of the arts colleges," and that "they want the most in the shortest span of time," observations borne out by the large number of nonuniversity veterans who enrolled in proprietary business colleges. A look at the academic fields in which degrees were awarded two to four years later confirms the sudden switch to an unprecedented interest in business. In the surge of enrollments from 1947 to 1949 all fields grew substantially—foreign languages by 20 percent, English by 37 percent, chemistry by 43 percent, history by 47 percent, mathematics by 50 percent, economics by 62 percent, and education by 70 percent—but business and management grew faster than any other, by no less than 88 percent. As the fastest growing component of a fast-growing enrollment, business schools were nearly submerged in a tidal wave of students.[2]

TALKING AND PLANNING

Preoccupation with the logistics of daily operations may have slowed down any actual changes in the business programs, but it did not prevent deans and others from talking about their work and planning for the next decade. Among the issues most often brought up were service to the nation, the importance of human relations and of a general rather than a specialized emphasis, and the emerging fields of international business and small business, as well as the role of women in business.

Service to the Nation

The sense of national and international crisis that enveloped the United States following the Second World War probably made it inevitable that business education would esteem itself according to its service to the national welfare and security. The Wharton School announced early in 1948 a plan for a two million dollar fund-raising campaign to enable it to expand its operations so that it could help the nation answer five questions: (1) What adjustments will be needed now that the United States is the world's dominant power? (2) How can the nation minimize the instabilities of economic cycles? (3) How can the nation provide military security without too much disruption of civilian production? (4) How can atomic energy be developed most effectively? and (5) How can independent individual enterprise be stimulated during a time of increased taxes, government control, and guaranteed security?

The University's president, speaking a few days later, similarly stressed that the business school's true importance lay in its value to the national welfare. Noting that the United States, with only one-sixteenth of the world's population, produced one-third of the world's goods, he concluded that political freedom and a prosperous economy were inseparably linked, and that the United States needed highly trained business leaders to maintain its position in the world, especially in view of the growing Communist threat.[3]

A strange development at Harvard illustrates again how important the business education effort was considered to be in the great struggle against Communism. In early September 1947 Harvard issued a pamphlet entitled *Education for Business Responsibility,* which for some reason struck a chord with *The New York Times.* In a major article almost as long as the pamphlet itself, entitled "Stress Social Responsibility as Factor in American Life: Business, Intellectual Leaders Start Cooperating to Spread Free-Enterprise Idea," *Times* reporter Russell Porter hailed the pamphlet as "a remarkably significant document" that demonstrates

> a growing sense of social responsibility on the part of American business leaders, many of whom cooperate closely with the school, giving it both moral and material support, and of growing intellectual backing for the idea that economic as well as political freedom is essential to a free society.

Up until now, the article continued, intellectuals around the world had championed "Marxist propaganda that private property and the profit motive are inherently evil and anti-social," while intellectual support for American free enterprise had at best been only "feeble and ineffective." Quoting almost the entire one-page preface by Harvard president Conant, the article extolled the publication of this pamphlet as marking a turning point toward intellectual recognition of the virtues of capitalism as practiced in America. "No matter how much defeatism there may be among some intellectuals about this way of life," the article concluded, "others are determined, as illustrated by Dr. Conant and Dean David, to help responsible business leaders preserve and strengthen it."[4]

The most amazing thing here is the astounding contrast between the newspaper's resounding praise and the utterly modest little pamphlet itself. Only nineteen pages long—and many of those nineteen pages filled with photographs—*Education for Business Responsibility* is nothing more than a minor recruiting publication designed to attract prospective students and donors to the Harvard Business School. It describes the case method of instruction, tells how faculty members keep current by staying in contact with business, discusses the importance of research, outlines some of the school's programs for active business executives, describes the physical facilities available at the school, and asks for financial contributions. Yet apparently—and especially because of the charged atmosphere of the Communist-capitalist conflict—the mere announcement that business studies were proceeding on a rational and intelligent plan, with clear objectives and with a clear relation to political freedom, was by itself enough to trigger this torrent of adulation.

Confirmation came in June 1949 when John D. Rockefeller Jr. gave the Harvard Business School a matching gift of five million dollars, citing his belief in individual enterprise as the reason for the donation. As strange as it sounds now, less than half a century later, one of the major assets that business schools had at this time was the public's perception of them as mighty weapons in the war against Communism.[5]

Human Relations

As previous chapters have noted, an awareness of the importance of human relations in business had been growing for several decades. It was the experiences during World War II, however, that finally provided the great impetus that had been lacking before. Speaking at the 1946 AACSB convention, Dean McClung of the University of Southern California noted that business schools had done especially valuable service in the human relations area during the war, specifically in providing panels of experts, in arbitration, in consulting, and in teaching ESMWT courses in personnel administration and labor management. "Labor unions as well as management leaders," he said, "are looking as never before to our business schools for leadership, counsel, and guidance."[6]

Harvard had by that time already made important moves in this direction. Late in 1945 and early in 1946 it appointed Dr. Benjamin M. Selekman as professor of labor relations and Dr. Fritz J. Roethlisberger as professor of human relations, thus signaling the beginning of a new emphasis on the human aspects of management. Optimistically projecting an era of good feelings following the cessation of hostilities, the school believed (according to *The New York Times*) that "it is important in the post-war era that men learn to work and live together in the business field as well as in other spheres." A former course in industrial relations was expanded into an area called "administrative practices" in the hope that not only would there be "management and labor without strife" but that work would become a more fulfilling experience for everyone.[7]

The business schools at other universities were making similar changes. From the University of Alabama to the University of Washington it was now more common than not to find several course offerings in human relations areas. Sometimes the offerings were extensive: eight courses were offered at the University of Michigan, nine at Tulane University, and ten at the University of Cincinnati. When, in June 1950, representatives of eleven universities with business schools and fourteen major businesses met in New York's Waldorf-Astoria Hotel to discuss ways of improving the liaison between education and management, they heard one speaker declare that ability to manage was the scarcest element in American industry, and another that the greatest need in business education was in teaching human relations.[8]

In the three years preceding that meeting, Americans had seen the founding of the National Labor-Management Foundation, the Industrial Relations

Research Association, and the influential Society for Human Resource Management. After a couple of decades of getting started, human relations in business and business education had finally arrived.

The Dangers of Over-Specialization

Almost from the very beginning, as previous chapters have shown, educators and business people alike had stressed the importance of training that is general rather than specific. The main characteristic that supposedly distinguished poor education—that provided by the proprietary business colleges—from good education was that the former trained people to perform a specific job while the latter trained for a whole career by developing intellectual and reasoning abilities and fostering moral integrity. Yet it was during the five years following the Second World War that these ideas received their fullest endorsement.

President Harold Stassen of the University of Pennsylvania issued a call for the Wharton School to expand its vision "beyond the technical phases of its curriculum" and to place emphasis instead on providing leaders for the nation. Columbia University made several prominent announcements about a new curriculum it was adopting that would stress "management in the broadest sense," including analysis of data, recognition of interrelationships, and formulation of policies—although it admitted it was making no actual changes in its program at the time.[9]

Speakers at AACSB conventions displayed the same concern about avoiding overspecialization, as well as the same uncertainty over how to go about doing so. While declaring that "our various curricula should not become too narrow and specialized," Dean McClung of the University of Southern California made it clear that he actually had few ideas about what a "general" business education should consist of, beyond saying that "We should develop as rapidly as possible a body of recognized standard concepts." Dean Calkins of Columbia University was even more open about his lack of ideas:

> But what are these fundamentals? What qualifications make for competence in the careers for which we train? Frankly, I do not know, and I can think of no one who does. But it is high time we found out.

This, then, was a major and paradoxical characteristic of the postwar period: much talk about the nature and importance of collegiate business education, but almost no practical changes to show as a result.[10]

Relations with the Business Community

Another paradox lay in the business schools' attitudes and responses to industry. People in all quarters expressed interest in increasing the interactions between business and education. A high-ranking official from the Department of Commerce spoke to an AACSB convention about the importance of such interaction, specifically naming internships, faculty exchanges, cooperative projects, cooperative bureaus of business research, and government-sponsored fellowships as possible activities. Columbia University appointed a high-level committee to seek stronger ties with the business community, and several business schools began making greatly increased use of active business executives as part time faculty.[11]

Yet at the same time that the schools were seeking ways of cooperating more closely with business, the educational philosophy they were espousing was exactly the opposite of what business said it wanted. Whereas universities kept insisting on the value of a generalized education and the dangers of being too practical, businesses were expressing the reverse. The prestigious Society for the Advancement of Management conducted a two-year survey of what CEOs thought about management education, and the result was an overwhelming call for more courses in practical and immediately applicable skills. Writing, speaking, and accounting led the list, and also in the top half were law, finance, cost accounting, and production methods. The bottom half of the list mainly consisted of courses in the more theoretical subjects such as personnel studies, psychology, management principles, and the history of industrial development.

A Dun and Bradstreet survey of business leaders in 1948 produced a similar result—that business wanted the schools to spend far more time on economics and business courses than they currently did, and far more of that time on business than on economics. Economics courses, they felt, were ridiculously theoretical.

Three years later, in 1951, The Controllers Institute conducted a similar survey and provided similar results: the inability to speak and write clearly was regarded as the greatest weakness of modern business graduates, and inadquate abilities in planning, control, forecasting, and accounting followed closely. Nowhere did management philosophy or personnel psychology show up on the list. Ordinarily a survey by controllers might be suspected of bias in such directions, but in view of the other two surveys just mentioned the results here seem entirely credible. While the schools were clamoring for more generalized and theoretical studies, businesses wanted learning that could be put straightaway into practice.[12]

Lesser Concerns: Women, Small Business, and Internationalization

Three other subjects that later were to become prominent in collegiate business education attracted some minor degrees of attention during the postwar period.

At this point in history, business education was still almost entirely a masculine venue. Neither the Harvard Business School nor the Wharton

School at the University of Pennsylvania had ever admitted women students, and the percentage of women business students across the nation remained quite small. When women were admitted, it was still often into special programs focusing on stenography or other skills associated with the stereotypical abilities of females rather than into the normal business course.

Yet a few changes were beginning to be evident. Although it was still the custom, both grammatically and socially, to say "men" when one meant people of both genders, a few universities now began to say they were educating "young men and women" to become the "business men and women of the future." And at the AACSB convention in 1946 Dean Weidler of Ohio State University specifically added an influx of women students to the trends that he could foresee in business education.

Small business was the subject of a whole program at that same AACSB meeting. The deputy director of the Commerce Department's Office of Small Business addressed the convention and stressed the new interest that students were showing in starting their own businesses. Two businessmen joined him in arguing that business schools could contribute substantially to the movement.

Finally, the movement toward internationalization of the business curriculum received at least some verbal attention, as several commentators mentioned the importance of a strong business community in order to assure stability of the world order.

BUSINESS EDUCATION AT MIDCENTURY

This seems a convenient time to stop and survey the state of the suddenly developed and now enormous business education industry as it existed in 1950. Utterly undreamed of a century earlier and just barely in existence at all a half century earlier, the school of business had in the subsequent fifty years grown to be the largest single part of many universities. From less than 1 percent of all baccalaureate degrees in 1900, business had grown to account for 3.2 percent by 1920, 9.1 percent in 1940, and 15.3 percent in 1950. It had changed the face of American higher education—and yet the changes still to come would dwarf these.

For one thing, business education in college in 1950 was still almost exclusively an undergraduate affair. When one spoke of studying business at a university, it was assumed that the studies were for a bachelor's degree, and discussions among business school deans focused almost entirely on their undergraduate programs. For every one master's degree awarded in business that year, there were over sixteen and a half bachelor's degrees—a ratio that would shrink to 10:1 by 1960 and 5:1 by 1970, before finally settling in at 3.5:1 by 1980.

The MBA degree where it did exist—and only 4,335 were awarded in

1950—was primarily regarded as a fifth year of business study for the purpose of permitting greater specialization. After two years of liberal arts courses, undergraduates would take general business courses for the last two years of college, and then the few who wanted to study a particular industry or a specific problem would stay for a fifth year and get a master's degree. Accordingly, MBA programs were quite commonly of two types: a one-year program for graduates of undergraduate business programs, and a two-year program for those who came from other fields of study. The Universities of Arkansas, Georgia, and Michigan, as well as Northwestern and Tulane Universities, all specifically maintained both one- and two-year programs, depending on the amount of previous business education the applicant had completed.

Outwardly these programs, both undergraduate and graduate, showed a fair amount of diversity, or even eccentricity. The University of Tennessee, for example, offered a major in building materials merchandising, and the University of Colorado offered a ten-course program in medical records. The University of Alabama offered a major in "clothing and textile merchandising," the University of Idaho in "the extractive industries," and the University of Georgia in "aeronautical administration." (Since all these majors were established at state universities, the natural inference is that such specialized programs originated from legislative pressure.)

Even where no distinctive major program was involved, outward diversity was evident. Many schools by this time had eliminated or at least reduced their earlier extensive offerings in railway management, leading a hasty observer to assume that the changes were part of a movement toward general rather than specialized studies. But in fact a substantial number of schools— including those at Tennessee, Arkansas, Cincinnati, Ohio State, Illinois, Oklahoma, Colorado, and Stanford—had by 1950 started offering courses in airline or airport administration, suggesting that the attachment to current trends—or fads—was still strong. And finally, secretarial studies, which in earlier decades had been anathema to status-conscious business schools, had made a strong comeback, no doubt as a result of their securing a foothold during the war. The roster of universities offering unabashedly secretarial subjects in 1950 included some of the most prestigious ones, such as Washington, Tulane, Oklahoma, Northwestern, Michigan, Indiana, Illinois, and Colorado.

Yet beneath the outward diversity, the curricula of business schools were really quite similar. After several decades of experimentation the schools had pretty much come to an agreement on what the major areas of instruction ought to be. Whether divided into seventeen fields (as at Mississippi and Northwestern), or thirteen (Tulane and Indiana), or eight (Nebraska, South Dakota, and Vermont), or five (Cincinnati and Illinois), the subjects taught had become increasingly standardized. Every school offered, and most required, courses in accounting, economics, banking and finance, marketing, and statistics. Most also had basic courses in types of business organization and business law. Management was offered almost everywhere, but the content of the courses seems to have varied widely: it included airport management at Oklahoma, industrial relations at Michigan, purchasing at Illinois, and break-even point calculations at Northwestern. Some schools emphasized psychology and personnel management by making them a separate area, and many, although not all, offered courses in insurance and real estate, often lumped together. A good number of universities—including Washington, California, Idaho, Michigan, Northwestern, Oklahoma, Arkansas, and Florida—also had by this time separate course offerings in international business or foreign trade. A few, but not many, taught Production.

Disappearing fast from most curricula were some subjects that had been standard thirty years earlier. Such academic-type subjects as geography or economic resources were becoming scarcer, as were courses in economic or business history. Peripheral fields such as consular service and journalism had all but vanished from business schools. And a few earlier subjects had fallen victim to reclassification. Transportation, originally one of the most prominent offerings, was now generally subsumed under marketing, and investment was usually covered in finance courses.

Northwestern University in particular deserves separate mention for having structured its programs more carefully than others had done. Besides being adjustable from one to two years to accommodate students with different amounts of preparation, the MBA program was divided into "basic," "core," and "advanced" courses—the first group containing introductory subjects, the second methods (such as "administrative accounting" and "marketing management"), and the third more specialized subjects. Northwestern seems to have been the first to adopt this kind of classification, which later became quite widely accepted.

In short, business education over the first half of the century had gone from stumbling, academic-heavy beginnings, to an undisciplined proliferation of courses, to a gradual settling-out process in which main divisions became clear. The process can be illustrated by the changes in the curriculum of a single major institution, the University of Utah. From no business courses at all before 1909, Utah adopted in 1910 a "program in commerce and industry" within the School of Arts and Sciences. Not a regular department, it amounted to an arrangement that permitted students to select, from any of several different areas, existing courses somehow related to business. Three of the seven courses listed—"Contracts," "Agency," and "Bills and Notes"—were clearly concerned with legal matters such as correct completion of official forms. Two courses were from the Department of Economics—one called simply "Economics" and the other "Investments." A sixth was "Diplomacy," reflecting the identification of foreign service work with business interests. The seventh, strangely entitled "Psychology and Ethics," must have dealt both with consumer motivation and the philosophy of the profit motive.

Just ten years later these confused and eclectic beginnings had grown unrecognizably. No longer a "Program in Commerce in Industry" in the School of Arts and Sciences, the business offerings now appeared in their own "School of Commerce and Finance" along with the courses of the Department of Economics, and the seven business courses previously listed had now grown to sixty-six (counting only business, not economics). The long, single, undifferentiated list contained courses dealing with business functions, types of business, philosophy, academic subjects, and several other categories, no doubt reflecting the fast growth of the subject and also suggesting a large degree of chaos in administering the new school. Included were, among others, courses in accounting, geography, Western natural resources, Western economic resources, business history, salesmanship, conservation, Latin American trade, American-Asiatic relations, rural credits, insurance, commercial languages, banking, law, stenography, ethics, statistics, posters (as used in advertising), and commercial dairying.

By 1930 a sense of order had been imposed, along with a new name and a new level of degree. The randomly proliferating courses were now bundled into seven groups—accounting, banking and finance, business management, marketing, statistics and research, general business, and economics. The former "School of Commerce and Finance" had now become the "School of Business," a change reflecting the increasingly broad definition of business in the 1920s: no longer just trade and money handling, business now included new elements such as management principles and marketing research. Also, by 1930 the university was offering master's degrees in business for the first time.

Ten years later, in 1940, the curriculum still looked very much as it had in 1930. The seven fields of study had been reduced to six (by simply combining "Business Management" with "General Business"), and minor advances in the direction of human relations studies were evident: one new course called "Labor Problems" and another called "Personnel Administration." Apart from these minor changes, the only other development was that the University of Utah had by now become a member of the American Association of Collegiate Schools of Business.

Changes by 1950, on the other hand, were so great they had remade every aspect of the school. The "School of Business" had now been promoted to a "College of Business"; its M.A. and M.S. degrees in business had been replaced by an MBA degree; and it now offered, for the first time, a PhD in business. While the number of academic fields in its curriculum had shrunk again, to five, the number of individual courses had exploded to over 175, including 18 in accounting, 22 in marketing, 26 in management, and 31 in banking and finance. "Management" now included several human relations courses such as Personnel Administration, Personnel Problems, and Industrial Relations. "Economics," from which the original business program had sprung just forty years earlier, was by this time a department in the College of Business. And alongside it, as a monument to the inconsistencies that have always characterized the building of a business curriculum, stood a twenty-five course program in secretarial studies.

Looking over this forty-year history of business education at one university, one can only be struck by its unprecedentedness. No parallel exists in academic history for a subject that grew in only four decades from small and random beginnings to one of the largest components of a university. It was unique, and it was by far the most significant development in American higher education in the twentieth century.

                                    *   *   *

Yet even with this astonishing history, leaders in business education at midcentury were uncertain about the future. At an AACSB convention, where much attention was being paid to handling the rush of returning veterans, several speakers remarked on their uncertainty about whether enrollments would continue high after the postwar bulge ended. As things turned out, they had no need to worry. The biggest bulge had not yet begun.

8

1950–1959:
Growth, Conformity, and Generalism—
The MBA Takes Off

AFTER years of being an unimportant sidekick to the bachelor's degree, graduate education in business came into its own around 1950 and ever since has been the main center of attention. Besides the unprecedented growth in numbers, business education during the 1950s was characterized by two developments: a strong pull away from individuality and toward conformity, and a remarkable emphasis on the general rather than the specialized.

THE GROWTH

Until midcentury, "business education" meant the undergraduate level. Master's degrees existed, of course, but they amounted to only five or six percent of the total. Looked at in isolation, the growth from 110 master's degrees in business in 1919 (only a little more than two for each state in the union) to 4,335 in 1949—a 3,840 percent increase in thirty years—is certainly impressive. But during those same years bachelor's degrees in business were growing even faster, from 1,576 to 72,137—a 4,477 percent increase. During all this period, the ratio of about fifteen bachelor's degrees for every master's degree did not substantially change. In short, graduate education in business, during the first half of the century, simply was not very important.

The other major trend to take into account in this statistical tangle is the growing importance of business studies on the whole higher education scene. In 1919–20 only 3.2 percent of all undergraduate degrees awarded (or one out of every thirty) were in business; by 1949–50, a mere thirty years later, that figure had more than quintupled to 16.6 percent, or one out of every six. Yet even this astonishing rate of increase tells only part of the story, since it fails to show the growth in sheer numbers. The total bachelor degree production of American colleges during those thirty years increased no less than ninefold, from 49,250 to 434,000—and thus the fivefold increase in business's share signifies something like a fortyfold increase in the number of business degrees. Nothing like such an increase had happened before or was ever to happen again.[1]

The New Look and New Importance of the MBA

Until 1950 the MBA had, in truth, not been a very attractive degree program. In all but a few institutions it amounted to nothing more than an extra year of college for business majors, permitting them to specialize in some subject that interested them. Although some of the wilder eccentricities, like meat packing and the printing industry, had disappeared a decade or so earlier, one still could find programs in mining, building materials, and medical records, as well as many in railroad and airline management. Whatever fundamental core of required knowledge did exist had not been very well defined or very widely accepted, and few programs showed evidence of any of the intellectual integrity that results from comprehensiveness of design. But all this changed during the next ten years. By 1960 the MBA had a new look, a new emphasis, and a new and enhanced reputation.

The New Look

One clear change in the MBA's appearance during the 1950s was an expansion of its course offerings. Schools simply found more things to teach. At the University of Wisconsin, courses in production increased from 7 to 9, in insurance from 10 to 14, and in accounting from 18 to 23. At the University of Utah, office administration grew from 25 courses to 30, management from 26 to 37, and accounting from 18 to 33.

Yet much more significant than the growth in numbers of courses offered was the movement toward—at long last—an agreed-upon core of subjects to be studied by everyone. The search for such a core, it will be remembered, had been occupying deans and directors since the very beginning. Its arrival now was due not to a sudden discovery by somebody but to a sort of weary acceptance of what had dwindled down from the experiments of the past.

Typically a school of business now offered instruction in seven, eight, or nine standard fields. Four of these—accounting, finance, management, and marketing—were found everywhere, apparently without exception. A fifth—mathematics, including statistics—was almost universal. As for the others, they were not so much separate fields as the results of different classifications.

Banking, investments, and real estate, listed separately at Penn State and Nebraska, were part of finance at most other universities. Business law, separate at Indiana and Dartmouth, was part of management elsewhere.

The areas that were least agreed on at this point were quantitative studies (sometimes relegated to the math department, sometimes taught separately at the business school, sometimes combined with statistics, and other times separate), economics (usually a separate department, but in all cases a subject of debate about its proper relation to business), and production (sometimes separate, sometimes combined with management, and other times combined with quantitative studies). The number of schools offering economic geography, transportation, and business history continued to decline, and foreign languages had by now all but disappeared from the typical business school.

In many respects the agreement on these basic fields resulted from a broadening of terms. Thus the University of Florida changed its Latin American trade course to "Inter-American Trade," and the University of Idaho renamed its program in the "extractive industries" to be "Business and Applied Science." The graduate courses at the University of Illinois had names much broader sounding than anything seen before: "Administrative Behavior," "Legal Problems of Business Management," "Controllership," and "Statistical Controls for Business."

By the end of the 1950s, new terminology, such as that at the University of Illinois, was quite widespread, and it contributed greatly to the new professional look of the MBA. Stanford University's catalog listed courses offerings in decision theory, information systems, and organizational behavior—three names entirely unknown in business schools at the start of the decade. Wisconsin added operations research, linear programming, and data processing, as well as courses in business policy and business ethics. Besides its new look, the MBA was getting a new sound.

Although it is true that this new paradigm more or less just "happened," it also did receive official recognition. In 1949 the annual AACSB meeting approved a resolution designating the main fields in a business school:

> As the foundation for training in administration, instruction shall be offered in the fields of economics, accounting, statistics, business law, finance, marketing, and production or industrial management. In general, candidates for the undergraduate degree shall receive basic instruction in each of these fields. Opportunities for advanced work shall be available in at least three of the above fields.

The statement, which appears to have resulted from some political lobbying and compromising, is less a piece of legislation than a recognition of what had already come to be accepted. But it did have the effect of making it official. Economics, law, and statistics still had some details to be worked out, but accounting, finance, marketing, and management were from this time on established as parts of the business education canon.

Emphasis on Social Relations

Yet even with these developments it may be that the truly most striking change in business education during the 1950s was neither the growth nor the new core but a new overall emphasis. Just two decades earlier, as shown in previous chapters, business education was still mostly concerned with the descriptive and mechanical aspects of business operations, and statements about social responsibility and human relations were still novelties. By the end of the 1950s, in contrast, it was unusual to find any school that did not stress such responsibilities and relations above all else.

Indiana aimed at inculcating an understanding of social responsibilities; Colorado at preparation for "satisfying living and constructive citizenship"; Alabama at developing one's "appreciation and understanding of the problems and larger relationships of our social economic organization as a whole"; Nevada at teaching about "the human relations involved in business activities, especially the important social and civic responsibilities of persons in business"; Idaho similarly at giving its students "an appreciation of the social importance and responsibilities of business men"; Dartmouth at recognizing "the need for an integrated economic and social philosophy" and an "acceptance of ethical considerations as an integral factor in business decisions"; Georgia at providing "a foundation of general culture" and at broadening the viewpoint and developing social thinking; and Northwestern, comprehensively, at fostering "greater understanding of the world and its peoples." Even the business-minded *Business Week* joined the chorus. When Harvard selected a new dean in 1955, the magazine expressed the hope that he would spend less time on hype and fundraising and more on developing the school's sense of social responsibility.[2]

Independent studies of business operations were confirming the importance of this new emphasis on people rather than on machines and money. A survey of dismissed employees in the Chicago area revealed that 91 percent of them had failed at their jobs because of deficiencies in personal behavior—eleven times the number that had failed because of the lack of technical skills. Top management in corporations, one observer said, was now concerned not so much with manufacturing as with creating the most favorable conditions under which manufacturing could occur.[3]

New Importance

Accordingly, it is not surprising that the MBA began to enjoy a much-enhanced reputation, as people began to think of it as a servant of society rather than just a short cut to making lots of money. Harvard's Dean David noted the new attitude in his address at a University of North Carolina dedication in 1953. Business schools, he said, had increased their usefulness and expanded their purpose and thus had gained wider acceptance. Their mission, he concluded, was no longer simply to teach people how to run a business but "to provide creative leadership for business, labor, and government." His view was confirmed in practice when other schools recognized the virtues of the education business schools were providing and began to emulate it. Some engineering schools, for example, such as the one at UCLA, added business courses in the mid-1950s for the purpose of training engineers to become executives.[4]

International confirmation came, too, sometimes from unexpected places. In 1952 none other than the august Oxford University established its "Summer Business School," a nondegree program for young executives, where industrialists could (and still can today) learn more about economics, and economists more about industry. And in Brazil, the Escola de Administracao de Empresa de Sao Paulo (EAESP) was founded on an experimental basis and in the face of great opposition. Since the universities scorned business as disreputable and regarded it as nothing more than a sideline of economics, EAESP was set up as a separate institute. But even so it had an uncertain start, since business people expressed contempt for the idea that management could be taught in school. In less than a decade and a half, however, the school grew from this shaky start to have over two thousand students, and demand for its graduates became so great it decided its placement office was unnecessary and closed it.[5]

Further evidence of the new prestige came from both students and employers. In an article called "Popularity Swamps the B-Schools," *Business Week* reported a sudden rush of business students in America's colleges. The immediate consequence, the magazine said, was a severe teacher shortage, but in the long run the consequences would be positive—greater selectivity leading to higher standards, eventually raising business to the level of a revered profession like medicine, with equally demanding training. Graduation rates confirm the magazine's observation: between 1953 and the end of the decade, undergraduate business degrees rose 44 percent and master's degrees an astounding 80 percent. Another *Business Week* article published less than two years later reported that even during an economic slump the demand for newly trained MBAs was keeping up with the greatly enlarged supply. Companies were reported to be enthusiastic about the abilities of these new graduates and willing to pay a premium to get their services.[6]

Most resoundingly, the new look and new importance of the MBA were celebrated at the start of the 1950s in a *Fortune* magazine article by Peter Drucker, who at the age of forty-three had already established himself as the nation's leading business philosopher with *The Future of Industrial Man, The Concept of the Corporation,* and *The New Society: The Anatomy of the Industrial Order.* Pointing out the eightfold increase in MBA degrees awarded since 1941, Drucker surveyed the nation's graduate business schools and astutely observed that three emphases had come to be agreed upon. The first—"operating a profitable business"—was of course the one that had existed from the beginning. The other two, however, "managing a human enterprise" and "relations with economics and society," had been derived since 1930. Most of the credit for their introduction, in Drucker's view, belonged to Harvard's longtime dean, Wallace Donham, who had perceived the limitations of "applied economics" and had steered the business school toward a much wider view of its functions. Beyond any question, "managing a human enterprise" and "relations with economics and society" would have been inconceivable, in 1925, as major emphases of business schools.

Drucker also cited three big problems that all business education, especially that on the graduate level, had to face—problems that continue to dog business schools to the present. The first is that much of what a business person needs to know is learned through experience, and experience cannot be taught in a classroom. The proper relation between theory and practice has been a subject of debate and experimentation since Joseph Wharton's time. The second problem is that business requires an entrepreneurial spirit, but schools and entrepreneurship are intrinsically opposite—one encouraging conformity while the other demands daring and independence. And finally, Drucker noted the tendency of young MBA holders to be too ambitious, to want to move upward more quickly than the corporation would permit—or the "crown prince" syndrome.

Drucker's survey of the MBA radiates with optimism. Citing two recent gifts to graduate business schools—Mellon's six million dollars to the Carnegie Institute, and Rockefeller's five million dollars to Harvard—he points out that master's-level education in business, formerly only "a tiny appendix to the undergraduate business school," had now become both large and important in its own right, and that businesses everywhere had come to accept and even covet its graduates.[7]

The General versus Specialized Debate

One cry that arose with great persistence during this period of new growth and respectability was the championing of a generalized education for business and a warning about the dangers of overspecialization. Such a point of view was not new, but it had never before received such urgency and frequency of expression. During this decade of conformity to a standardized curriculum no articles about innovations in business education were published. However, nearly three dozen articles extolling the virtues of a general rather than a specialized education for business did appear.

Some of these advocates simply wanted education to concern itself with general principles of business rather than company-specific methods of performing day-to-day operations. When a prominent business executive told a large conference of other executives that business people need a "broader, more liberal educational background" and that "how-to-do-it" is best taught in the company itself, not one dissent was heard. This same philosophy formed the entire basis for the founding of MIT's Sloan School of Management in 1952. There were to be no specialists on the faculty, and the curriculum was to be not fragmented into departmental courses but fully integrated. Organization theory—the forms of organization, how they fit into society, and how people work together—was the focus of instruction. Whatever practical learning took place was to come from visits by active business executives, with whom the school kept closely in touch.[8]

Other general education advocates, however, spoke not so much about the nonspecialized view of business instruction as about the inclusion of humanities courses in the business curriculum. To many of them, the humanities were to be valued merely because of their practical applications, especially in developing good writing and speaking skills. In 1951 the National Education Committee of the Controllers Institute cited "inability to speak and write clearly" as the biggest single failing of modern business graduates. The schools agreed and by 1956, according to *Business Week,* were placing strong emphasis on English, both spoken and written, as a vital common tool—more so, in fact, than on mathematics. In 1958 a dean from one of the California state colleges wrote about a nationwide movement back toward "cultural" subjects—by which he meant instruction aimed at resolving the problems of graduates who could not write or speak at acceptable levels.[9]

Another practical use of the humanities, to some minds, lay in their supposed contribution to the maturity and sophistication with which people conducted themselves in their daily lives. One observer undertook a study of the reasons for job dissatisfaction and found that poor adjustment to new people and new surroundings was the main cause. As a result he urged schools to devote more time to training their students in subjects that could facilitate personal adjustment. A similar conclusion emerged from a survey of the 1955 graduating class of MIT's Master of Science in Industrial Management program. These were all experienced executives who had taken a year off from their companies to study full time for the degree, and their opinions therefore carry more weight than would a survey of typical graduates. They felt that they had been away from their jobs too long, that the required master's thesis was a waste of time, and that the examinations they had to take were infantile. But what they did find valuable was their newly discovered ability to persuade people to do things, an ability that gave them personal confidence.[10]

One further practical application of the humanities—a strange-sounding one indeed to today's ears—was expressed by Inland Steel chairman Clarence Randall in 1956. Just as earlier observers had found business courses to be a weapon against Communism, he advocated the teaching of liberal arts subjects for the same purpose. Basing his case on the idea that a liberally trained mind is better at synthesis and correlation of results, he said that such minds were needed to counteract the tendency toward specialization and the corresponding blindness that accompanies it. Anyone trained in the liberal arts, he maintained, would be able to conduct a critical examination of all the world's economic systems, like analyzing one's competitors in business, and thereby to see the virtues of the capitalistic system.[11]

Yet still others felt that the real value of the humanities could be found not in their practical applications but in their contribution to the development of the mind. This point of view was, of course, the one that had prevailed for centuries—the whole purpose of studying Greek and philosophy and ancient history had always been, ultimately, to develop the mind and character of the individual. But now, in the face of the newly arisen movement toward practicality in education, it seemed to many people that this purpose needed urgent restatement. A *Fortune* editorial in 1953, arguing that technical training must be supplemented by a general liberal arts education, quoted two important industrialists to support the position. Retired U. S. Steel chairman Irving Olds said,

> The most difficult problems American enterprise faces today are neither scientific nor technical, but lie chiefly in the realm of what is embraced in a liberal arts education.

And, according to Standard Oil of New Jersey chairman Frank Abrams,

> The need for technically trained people was probably never greater than it is now. At the same time, we were never more aware that technical training is not enough by itself.

Robert E. Wilson, chairman at Standard Oil of Indiana, made similar grandiose claims for the value of nontechnical training. From them, he wrote, the students acquire "a sure grasp of their cultural heritage" and become "mentally and morally disciplined and trained to evaluate data and arrive at sound decisions in all aspects of life."[12]

Dean Courtney Brown of Columbia University, himself recently come from Standard Oil of New Jersey, was more specific. He (with the concurrence of several other business leaders) listed four contributions that the liberal arts make to a business education:

1. they nourish the qualities of a free society that permit business to flourish;
2. they counteract narrow specialization;
3. they lead to an understanding of how to manage people; and
4. they develop the capacity for self-expression.[13]

Such arguments were forceful enough to persuade the business community to experiment with special liberal arts courses for its executives. The stimulus came, apparently, from top executives who perceived the need for broadening among their middle management ranks and saw the liberal arts as a possible answer. The Aspen Institute for Humanistic Studies was founded by Container Corporation of America chairman Walter P. Paepcke for this purpose. Several colleges and universities—including Clark, Wabash, Southwestern, Pennsylvania, Swarthmore, Dartmouth, Williams, Northwestern, and Pomona—also established intensive short-term programs, usually in the summer. Some companies, such as Bell Telephone of Pennsylvania, started in-house programs for their management. In 1957 it was estimated that three hundred thousand executives were back in school studying the humanities.[14]

The success of such efforts is by nature almost impossible to measure, a fact that explains why the literature on this back-to-the-humanities movement contains many arguments about why the instruction should be beneficial but no assessment whatever about whether it actually was. One might well ask, as indeed some did, why the world had not improved more than it did during those centuries when its leaders had been educated in the liberal arts. In any case, whether because the liberal arts did not work as a means of expanding people's minds, or whether it was simply that they could not prove that they did work, the movement gradually lost steam and quietly disappeared from the scene.

In fact many observers had all along questioned whether the business community really had any sincere commitment to a liberal arts education. At a much-publicized "Industry-College Conference" in White Sulphur Springs, West Virginia, in 1953, academics hooted at the business executives' call for more general liberal arts education. They pointed out that, at the same time that top executives were calling for people to be trained in the liberal arts, their representatives were on campuses recruiting technically trained people and paying them more. William H. Whyte succinctly made the same observation in *The Organization Man* (1956): "Between 1953 and 1956, the number of business speeches bewailing over-specialization increased. So did the demand for specialists."

Also widely noted was the fact that, when it came time to make charitable donations, corporations inevitably gave their money to the technical schools, not to the liberal arts divisions. The corporations' rather lame excuse—that they had to satisfy their stockholders—simply served to confirm the academic opinion that the advocacy of liberal arts was nothing more than lip service.[15]

A front-page article in the *Wall Street Journal* in 1958 debated the issue at length. Both corporations and universities, it reported, were divided in their opinions about a business education. Some people condemned the undergraduate business program, advocating instead a liberal arts education followed by a graduate business degree. Others, however, condemned the whole system. Companies professed to love the liberal arts but emphasized business in both their recruiting and their in-house training programs. The dean at the Wharton School threw a new—and profound—consideration into the debate by claiming that businesses wanted liberally educated people, but that "liberally educated" did not necessarily mean the same thing as the liberal arts.[16]

* * *

Yet all this arguing was meaningless: the market once again was overruling all objections. By the end of the 1950s, the MBA had reached an unprecedented 5,601 degrees, and had risen from 5 percent to 15 percent of all master's degrees. While the theorists were arguing about what a business education was, what it should be, and even whether it was any good, the students were racing to get one in increasing numbers, and the corporations were hiring them as never before.

9

1959–1967:
Midcourse Deflection—The Foundation
Reports

In the fall of 1959, both the Ford Foundation and the Carnegie Corporation issued reports on the condition of higher education for business in the United States. Although the reports themselves were not actually sensational, both of them were very negative and critical, and they attracted a fair amount of sensational attention in the nation's newspapers and magazines. Widespread public opinion at the time held that the two foundations had really sent the business education community reeling and that the colleges had to scramble to get their affairs in order and rescue themselves from disgrace. Even today, nearly forty years later, it is common to hear 1959 referred to as the watershed year in business education history, the year in which business schools reformed themselves in order to avoid further public humiliation.

Closer scrutiny, however, casts real doubt on this whole theory. The foundations were no doubt entirely well intentioned in undertaking their studies, but the reports that resulted were unoriginal and highly predictable, and they furthermore created a fair amount of unnecessary ill will. Long-term effects, moreover, were few—and almost without exception those few were extremely unfortunate.[1]

The Reports and Their Criticisms

The two reports, totaling over 1,200 pages, ran through similar litanies of complaints. Primary among them was the poor quality of the students. "Business administration," the Ford report declared, "gets a much larger fraction of poor students and a much smaller percentage of the best students than do the traditional professional fields." This criticism was especially directed against undergraduate programs, which, the Carnegie report noted, "concentrate their efforts almost exclusively on average or even mediocre

159

students." The Carnegie report further presented pages of statistics to show that, "Judged on intelligence test scores, undergraduate business students do not compare favorably with other important student groups," and that "hardly any undergraduate business schools . . . follow selective admission policies."[2]

A second, and similar, criticism was aimed at the curriculum. Although the school of business at almost every university purported to teach broadly conceived fundamental principles of business, it was still common to find ludicrously over specialized courses such as "Freight Claim Procedure" and "Principles of Baking: Bread and Rolls." The number of courses also came in for criticism, since they seemed to the report writers to be proliferating without restraint. "Other things being equal," the Ford report declared, "the quality of a business school tends to vary in *inverse* proportion to the number of business courses it offers."[3]

Third, both reports cited problems arising from inadequately trained faculty, specifically the use of teachers trained in other fields and the low percentage of doctorates. Professors of mathematics, statistics, psychology, and sociology were found to form a large portion of business school faculties, even though many had neither experience nor interest in business. The same was true of an even larger group, professors of economics, who often viewed their subject only in a theoretical way and had little use for practical business applications. The lack of doctoral degrees among business professors, both reports noted, was about to become much worse, as student enrollments were poised to double and triple while production of Ph.D.s remained stable. The proportion of Ph.D.-holders among business faculties was placed at 40 percent, with the expectation that it might drop to 21 percent in the next ten years.[4]

Fourth, the dearth of quality research coming from business schools sounded alarms in both reports. The Carnegie report summed up the deficiencies this way:

> Much of the research at these institutions is heavily weighted on the side of description; much of it centers on particular companies or local trade groups; much of it is undertaken because of its practical usefulness; very rarely is emphasis placed on developing analytical findings which can be fitted into a general system of principles and tested in a scientific manner. This misplaced emphasis is almost as serious as the dearth of research itself.

The Ford report added that "more significant research of ultimate value to business has come out of nonbusiness departments of the university"—psychology, mathematics, statistics, economics, sociology—"than out of the business schools." Both reports also noted that the business community seemed virtually unaware of any research activities going on at business schools. Thus in all respects—"meager amount," "low level," and the "quite striking" failure to communicate the results to businesses—academic research in business was found severely wanting. Everyone interviewed for the Carnegie report agreed that "business schools have seriously underrated the importance of research."[5]

Finally, one other problem was cited in both reports: the uncertain relation between undergraduate and graduate work. Should the MBA degree be only for people who have already studied business on the undergraduate level? Or should it be restricted (as at Harvard, Stanford, and a few others) to people who have studied widely in the humanities or sciences? All other graduate programs—in mathematics, for example—quite naturally require their applicants to have had substantial advanced training in the specific field before beginning graduate work. Yet in business schools, there were strong pressures to avoid narrowness and overspecialization, and these were leading some MBA programs, including the most prestigious ones, to admit and even recruit people whose previous training had been entirely in other fields. Although the MBA was the fastest-growing degree in America, no one seemed quite sure just what it was or who it was for.[6]

The reports contained other criticisms as well—scarce resources, for example, and overworked and underpaid teachers—but the five just mentioned are the main ones. And since issues like inferior quality attract media attention, while scarce resources and overworked teachers do not, these five were the ones that the reports became known for.

Short-term Public and School Reactions to the Reports

Concurrences in the Popular Press

Reactions were immediate and strong. *Business Week* predicted that the reports would have tremendous impact. More specifically, they would "knock the stuffing out of business schools." *The New York Times,* in an article headlined "Two Studies Assail Business Classes—College Courses Are Found Inferior—More Emphasis on Humanities Urged," the newspaper's education editor reported the allegations that business schools "offer inferior education to a carelessly selected mass of students" who "fall near the very bottom of the ranking list." Especially noted was the reports' emphasis on the humanities, basic mathematics, and the sciences, "work that will develop general capacity and understanding." This view of the impact of the two reports continued to prevail long after the publication year. Five years later *Business Week* reported that business schools were "still smarting from the criticism," and *Business Topics* remarked that "the Ford and Carnegie attacks have hurt."[7]

Early Dissenters

Other observers, however, began to express reservations about the value
and even about the significance of the entire effort. In a *Harvard Business
Review* article Prof. John Fielden called attention to the strong liberal arts
bias evident in both reports and noted that business education—a compromise between the theoretical demands of classical economics and the practical demands of corporations—is certain to offend anyone with such a bias.
For that reason he suspected that standards may have been made to appear
a great deal lower than they actually were. Moreover, since it has long been
known that achievement levels in college do not correlate very strongly
with achievements levels in life (and in business in particular), he wondered
what difference the loudly proclaimed low standards really made. What the
reports did do, he astutely observed, was to provide ammunition to the
academic-minded deans who were seeking ways to upgrade their schools
along traditional lines.[8]

Prof. John Hutchins of Cornell University took a different approach, criti-
cizing the reports for what they failed to say. He pointed out that the reports
never addressed the differences and similarities between "business administration" on the one hand and "entrepreneurship" on the other, to suggest
whether perhaps one emphasis or the other would be more apt to produce
business leaders. He also noted that the reports failed to consider anything
about how the business schools ought to relate to the nation's economic
system: is the training for CEOs, for millionaires, for middle managers, or
for consultants?[9]

Economist Leonard Silk, at the time a senior editor at *Business Week*,
made similar critical observations in an abbreviated version of the reports
the Ford Foundation and the Committee for Economic Development hired
him to write. Going beyond mere condensation, he noted that both reports
were the work of people trained in classical economics, and both prescribed
traditional remedies for what they saw as deviations from academic respectability—but that neither report contained any research whatever to indicate
what kind of education would actually most benefit the business world.[10]

Two other commentators made what may have been the most devastating
observation about the reports: that they were boring and, once the sensa-
tionalism had passed, did not really say very much. A committee appointed
by the American Accounting Association to study the reports noted sardoni-
cally that every critical observation made was inevitably going to be true
of at least one of the 560 institutions studied and added that the reports "say
almost everything that could have been said and also succeed in hedging
just about every statement to which anyone could take exception." And by
1963 the dean of Michigan State University could observe in passing that
the reports, which had cost so much and been launched with such fanfare,
already seemed outdated.[11]

The Lack of Originality

He was absolutely right, just as all these last five observers were. For one thing, as previous chapters of this book have shown, the charges leveled against business schools, although proclaimed as if they were recent discoveries, actually date back as far as collegiate business education itself. The low academic quality of business studies, for example, had been the subject of the University of Pennsylvania student magazine attack on the new Wharton school in the 1880s, and the problem of poorly or inappropriately trained faculty had dogged every school, from Dartmouth to New Mexico, since the beginning. Many of the criticisms in the reports were simply rehashes— although with tables of statistics to back them up—of the charges that traditional academic disciplines had leveled against business studies all along.

But another, and more serious, problem was that the reports were not original in another, more immediate sense. Because they were based largely on interviews with deans of existing business schools, who used the opportunity to express their frustrations with the present and their wishes for the future, the reports simply brought into public view the problems that people in the business of business education already knew about and were working on.

In fact, almost everything in the two 1959 reports had been said six years earlier in an AACSB-commissioned self-study by Dean Richard L. Kozelka of the University of Minnesota. Entitled *Professional Education for Business,* this remarkable report addressed the problems of inappropriately trained faculty, low quality students, unfocused curricula, uncertain missions, and inadequate facilities—in fact much more directly, simply, and readably than the later reports did. Partly because of the Kozelka report, these issues were all clearly in the minds of business education leaders as they were being interviewed by the Carnegie and Ford report authors, and thus these two later reports—although presented as based on original research—actually contained only the thinking of the people already in the profession.[12]

As a result, publication of the Carnegie and Ford reports caused a certain amount of ill will among business schools, which correctly felt that their efforts at self-analysis and self-improvement had been turned into instruments for public humiliation. Consequently, when schools announced reforms over the next few years, many felt obliged to specify clearly that initiative for the reforms had already been well underway before the foundation reports had appeared. The Wharton School, for example, announced in early 1961 that it was increasing the nonbusiness, or "general education," portion of its undergraduate program from one-third to one-half of the curriculum, a change that accorded with the recommendation of both reports. In reporting the change, however, the dean was careful to note that the change was not just a case of "panicking in the face of criticism of business education." The plans, he said, were in the works fully five years before the foundation reports appeared.[13]

LONGER-TERM EFFECTS OF THE REPORTS

The biggest failing of the reports, however, lay not in any temporary effects they produced but in three long-term, possibly permanent, effects that are still being felt today. Although the report writers had no such intentions, their work weakened the control that some universities had over their undergraduate programs, and it created two new industries that often are viewed as out-of-control monstrosities—the Ph.D. in business industry and the business research industry.

Loss of Control over Undergraduate Programs

The reports produced one undesirable effect by attempting to go counter to the direction of the market. Neither report actually advocated closing down undergraduate business schools, but both laid such stress on the importance of a general or liberal education and on the evils of overspecialization in the undergraduate program that they cast a shadow over all undergraduate business studies. As a result several universities took the step of idealistically declaring the discontinuation of their undergraduate business programs so that business could thenceforth be exclusively a graduate-level study—as it already was at the prestigious business schools of Harvard, Dartmouth, Columbia, Chicago, and Stanford.

Unfortunately, these declarations occurred just at the start of the fastest decade of growth undergraduate business education had ever known—from 58,000 to 116,000 degrees awarded—and virtually no university could afford to take an action so flagrantly contrary to the prevailing market winds (Ill. 9–1). What happened at one large state university may be typical:

1. Alarmed by the fact that an unprecedented 33 percent of its undergraduates were registering as business majors, the university decided to abolish the undergraduate business program altogether, in order to raise intellectual standards.
2. Two years later, university officials decided it would, after all, be all right to offer undergraduate business courses in the evening division, because evening students had different needs and because the controls on the evening division's degree requirements were less strict.
3. Almost immediately, vast numbers of day students signed up for evening courses so that they could study business.
4. Within a few years, the evening division became as large as the day division, and it no longer seemed to make sense to keep them separate. Therefore "in the

Illustration 9-1:

UNDERGRADUATE BUSINESS DEGREES
DOUBLED DURING THE 1960s

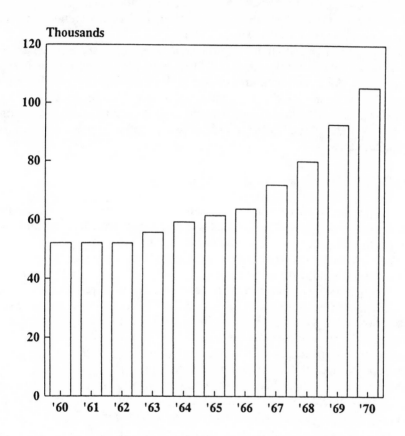

Source: USOE/NCES Earned Degrees Awarded Series

interests of efficiency" and "to eliminate duplication," the university decided to merge the two divisions.

5. At present, about 60 percent of the undergraduates at this university (compared with 33 percent at the beginning of this saga) now major in business.

In short, whatever effect the reports produced in this respect was not only short-lived but may even have weakened the humanistic content of the program by causing the university to lose control of its curricular design. "We thought we were strengthening our curriculum," one administrator said, "but all we did was to give away the charter."

Similar, although not identical, experiences appear to have taken place at universities such as Emory, Rutgers, Marquette, UCLA, and the University of Michigan. All abandoned undergraduate business studies in 1959 or early in the 1960s (some of them actually before the foundation reports were published), and all later reinstated them. Only a very few colleges continue today to resist the market pressure to offer business study to undergraduates.

The Ph.D. in Business

Both reports cited the low percentage of Ph.D.s among business faculties and the low quality and quantity of research. Actions were already underway to remedy these perceived problems before the reports appeared, but the impetus the reports gave caused startling and rapid changes that have affected business education ever since.

Nothing shows the academic bias of the reports more clearly than this attack on business schools for having too few Ph.D.s. For all of the history of business education, the field had been criticized for being too theoretical and bookish, as opposed to being practical and experimental. Yet since experience is hard to quantify, while a low percentage of doctorates is easy, both reports cited the latter and not the former.

As a result, a new industry—the production of Ph.D.s in business studies—sprang quickly into existence. According to one survey, no fewer than fifty new doctoral programs in business were founded in the next ten years—or one every seventy-three days—programs which have absolutely redefined the nature of the field. The number of doctorates awarded grew from 124 the year before the reports to 1,097 fifteen years later (Ill. 9-2), and it soon became the norm, almost a requirement, for faculty hired in business schools to have their degrees specifically in this particular field.

The effect, however, has been not to make these faculty members more capable but merely to assure that their knowledge of business is almost entirely academic rather than being grounded in experience. Since experienced businesspeople seldom had any reason to earn a Ph.D., and Ph.D. candidates seldom had any time or inclination to work in business, the

Illustration 9-2:

PhDs IN BUSINESS, 1958-1975 —
Up 884% IN 17 YEARS

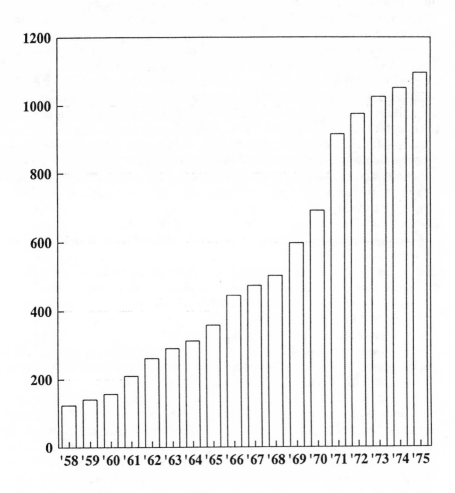

Source: USOE/NCES Earned Degrees Awarded Series

sudden rise of this new requirement has served mainly to drive an even bigger wedge than before between the theoretical and practical approaches.

Just a cursory look at titles of doctoral dissertations in business administration is enough to confirm this observation. Even when conducted with the highest standards of scholarship, most of the studies remain firmly in the theoretical camp. The largest group is model building—studies in which the student identifies a problem and then constructs and tests a theoretical way of handling it.

Such an approach is very common in marketing, where many elaborate models were proposed to determine how consumers make purchase decisions—for example, "An Empirical Investigation of the Performance of a Situational Multi-Attribute Attitude Model in Predicting Consumer Purchase Behavior and in Monitoring Change." Models are also often found in the quantitative fields like investment, debt management, and compensation analysis—for example, "The Prediction of Management Compensation Preferences: Some Multivariate and Multivariable Models."

Model building in the "softer" fields such as leadership, decision making, human relations, and corporate culture also has become very common—for example, "Development of a Theory of Committee Formation" and "Quantification of Decision-Making in the Field of Advertising Management."

A second large group of dissertations consisted (and still does consist) primarily of descriptive studies in which surveys are used to compile and analyze large amounts of empirically collected data—for example "An Exploratory Study of Communication Regarding Data Processing in Thirty-One Midwestern Banks" and "A Study of the Relation Between the Economic Period and the Education and Experience of Personnel Elected to Top Management Positions in United States Industry."

Rather often these studies were turned inward and directed toward either the field itself or the schools and their policies. As the body of theory in business administration grew, it became possible to conduct studies of the study of business administration, such as "A Comparison of Behavioral Assumptions of Management Accounting and Some Behavioral Concepts of Organization Theory." As operation of the schools themselves became more complex, studies appeared such as "An Inquiry into the Curriculum Change Process in Graduate Schools of Business with Particular Emphasis on Management as a Generic Concept." Finally, wandering even further from anything related to the actual practice of business, young scholars researched such topics as "The Influence of Selected Factors on the Choice of Fields of Study by Nigerian Students in the United States"—and as a result received Ph.D.s licensing them to become professors of business administration.

The result of all this activity, one observer has said, was that "in less than two decades, the dominant members on business school faculties were young people, most of whom had never succeeded in business but who could tinker both mathematically and behaviorally with significant problems and who often deluded themselves and others into believing that they had actually found solutions."[14]

Even if one doesn't fully accept that dim view, it should be obvious that the authors of those studies just cited would have far less appeal to the business world as employees than to the academic world as professors. Whether the expertise is in the theory of committee formation, the education and experience of top executives at different points in American history, or the course choices by Nigerian students, business itself would have a hard time finding an appropriate use for it, and thus the call for an increased number of Ph.D.s has had the effect of even more sharply dividing the theorists from the practitioners.

The Birth of the Research Industry

The call for more and better research, which must have seemed beyond dispute to the authors of the foundation reports, can likewise be viewed in retrospect as one of their most grievous failings. From the standpoint of academicians—a category that includes the authors of both reports—the desire for academic respectability ranked high on the list of motives, and, in the academic world, research activity is and has always been the surest way of achieving respectability. Little or no thought, however, appears to have been given to the specific requirements of research in business as opposed to research in history or any other academic subject.

As a result a huge amount of research activity began to take place, the great bulk of which, one suspects, has had very limited significance for actual practitioners in business. Although the last half of that statement is hard to prove, the first is easy. The number of periodicals publishing business research tripled from about 1,600 in 1959 to nearly 5,000 just twenty-five years later, and the number of business books published annually in the United States quadrupled from about 290 in 1959 to over 1,200 (Ill. 9–3 and 9–4). An enormous "research industry" has sprung up, which has had an incomparably greater importance for the academic than for the business world. Professors sit in their offices writing articles to one another, with almost no impact on the actual conduct of business. Instead of answering questions that business is asking, they invent their own questions and answer those instead. The actual number of significant contributions that academic research has actually made to business, it has often been observed, can be counted on the fingers of one hand.

A true anecdote will illustrate the point further. In the business school of a major university, a distinguished professor of quantitative studies had just finished explaining to the class a highly complex mathematical theorem. One student raised her hand and, quite sensibly, asked, "But where is this

Illustration 9-3:

NUMBER OF BUSINESS AND ECONOMICS
PERIODICALS IN EXISTENCE, 1900 TO 1984

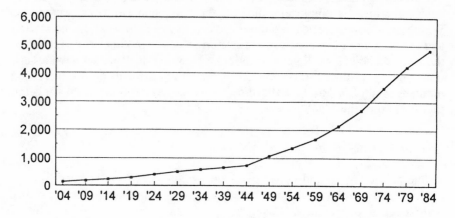

Source: Ulrich's

Illustration 9-4:

NUMBER OF BUSINESS BOOKS PUBLISHED
IN THE UNITED STATES, 1910 TO 1980

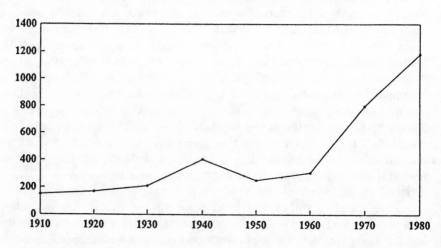

Source: Bowker Annual

used?" The professor thought for a moment and said, "Right now, it's used at UCLA and Carnegie Mellon"!

Thus, with respect to research, as with the increased number of Ph.D.s, the reports seem to have had the effect of widening the chasm between theory and practice. From the very beginning, business schools could and probably should have been built on the model of medical schools and law schools, where research and teaching have a close relationship with actual practice. Quite possibly even as late as 1959 it would have been possible to make this kind of change of direction. But the directions set in motion by the two foundation reports that year seem to have permanently eliminated any such possibility and to have cast business education forever in the academic mold.

PARALLEL DEVELOPMENTS IN GREAT BRITAIN

The problems the foundation reports dealt with—and created—were not unique to the United States. In Britain in 1959 the Ministry of Education appointed an Advisory Committee for Further Education in Commerce to suggest ways of improving commercial education. Its recommendations reflect a profound lack of knowledge about the subject, as well as the most naive assumptions about university professors' ability to teach principles of business.

Fifty years after apprenticeship had ceased to be a viable way of learning, it recommended apprenticeship schemes. Another recommendation was group release from work, so that the workers could study together at school—but with no suggestions about what they were to study or how the school would know about it. Other recommendations were for new (but unspecified) kinds of courses, refresher courses, and, incredibly, courses in salesmanship and in modern foreign languages and customs—subjects that American schools had all but completely dropped by this time.[15]

Four years later, when nothing had happened as a result of this report, several industry and government organizations hired Lord Franks, provost of Worcester College, Oxford, to devise a plan for enhancing management education in the country. His report—which attracted less attention than it might otherwise have because it was issued just a few hours before the world learned of President Kennedy's assassination—showed many of the same weaknesses found in the previous report and in the American reports. Although it did acknowledge that business differed from other fields by being "an intelligent form of human activity, not intellectual nor academic, but practical in nature," the report went on to recommend very traditional academic approaches.

Business knowledge was divided into two types, "framework" and "skills or techniques"; methods for integrating the theoretical and practical were left unspecified; and most of the instructors were to be drawn from the university's full-time faculty. Unquestioned throughout was the assumption that management education is a fairly simple and straightforward process— that is, that the knowledge needed to run a business is available and that university professors have it and can teach it. In fact, a smaller portion of the report is devoted to those profoundly basic issues than to trivial questions like whether Great Britain's business schools should be located in the country or in the city.[16]

REAL REFORMS IN BUSINESS EDUCATION

In some ways the biggest disservice the foundation reports did to business education was to distract public attention from the real reforms and innovations that were already underway at the time. For most of the period from the end of World War II to the mid-1950s, discussed in the two previous chapters, not many substantive changes had taken place in the nation's MBA programs. Enrollments had soared and the prestige attached to graduate business education had greatly magnified, but the education itself remained pretty much as it had been for the previous decade. Starting in the second half of the 1950s, however, changes began taking place in several respects.

First, much more thought than ever before was being given to the purposes and methods of business schools; assumptions that had until then always been accepted were now being brought under scrutiny. In addition, public attention was being paid to the output of the schools—the graduates and their careers—for the first time. Finally, schools and businesses were testing new relationships. All these developments could have made collegiate business education more prestigious and influential than it had ever been, and to some extent they did. But business education also had to contend with the evil odor that the foundation reports had cast upon it, and thus it did not achieve the prestige it might have had.

Increase in Self-Study Activities

Purposes. The new interest in self-study took many forms. In a couple of informal articles Dean Courtney Brown of Columbia discussed the whole purpose of business education in ways not generally heard before. Business students, he noted, needed to acquire knowledge, attain abilities, and develop appropriate attitudes; and it was the last of these—the development of appropriate attitudes—that was the highest obligation and challenge of a business school.

Somewhat alarmed by the recently developed emphasis on "managerial problem-solving," Brown asked whether it was "an appropriate concept around which to construct a complete program of collegiate study." More specifically, he pointed out that the making of wise decisions requires not so much knowledge of specific tools or situations but an ability to bring a huge breadth of knowledge to bear on specific problems—and the precise nature of this knowledge was still proving elusive. He then went on to ask a question that had in fact been heard before: whether university professors, most of whom have had no business experience at all, are in fact the best people to develop in students an understanding of business.

This kind of questioning was reflected in the new curriculum Columbia instituted under Brown's direction in early 1959. It placed as much emphasis on the environment in which business operates as on the internal administration of the business, and it required all students to take a course in the philosophical foundations of business.[17]

Pedagogical Methods. Meanwhile—for the first time in about twenty years—colleges were now devoting attention to curriculum design. Several commentators advocated new approaches to bridging the perpetually troublesome chasm between theoretical and practical education in business. A professor in one of the California state colleges commented on a trend he perceived, the tendency to move away from "hands-on" instruction and toward "applied theory." Noting that traditional predictors of success— mainly academic grades—showed practically no correlation at all with later success, while personality traits of various kinds did show some correlation, he concluded that books are far less important than experience and that people, not machines or math, are always the biggest problems. Consequently he advocated further development of applicable theories from the social sciences, especially psychology, sociology, and anthropology, all of which he considered more important even than economics.[18]

Similarly, two MIT professors called for something like the "laboratory training" used by the sciences. Business education, they said, suffers even more than medicine and law from the theory-practice dichotomy for three reasons: education is not a proven necessity for success in business, colleges have no clear way of simulating the reality of business, and no clear agreement exists about the exact content of a good business education. The solution they recommended, therefore, was greater involvement and participation in business by university students, using business as a laboratory for learning about the underlying processes.[19]

This quest to avoid purely descriptive or mechanical instruction at one extreme and overly theoretical instruction at the other occupied the attention of most schools, as it had in the past, but now with renewed vigor. The University of Southern California eliminated everything that could be considered descriptive and added experts in sociology, philosophy, physics, and political science to its faculty. At MIT, some professors had for years been developing the "incident process" method of teaching, in which a bare incident is noted and then more details are gradually added as needed. This method, they and others believed, far excelled the widely used case method by being much more realistic and much less purely descriptive.

Standard Oil president M. J. Rathbone made a speech in which he too stressed the importance of developing the reasoning ability rather than merely learning the mechanics of business. As for whether business education should be general or specific—"the old question," he accurately called it—he said it obviously should be both, but the main objectives should be to produce students who reason clearly and logically, who do not get upset by complexity and uncertainty, who communicate well (including listening), and who possess skills of persuasion, leadership, and command.[20]

Humanities and the Liberal Arts. Yet the call for a broader education was somewhat different this time from the vague calls for "education in the humanities" that had been heard a decade earlier. Starting in the late 1950s commentators began delving deeper than the traditional general love-for-the-liberal-arts and analyzing the subject more carefully. When the University of Pennsylvania's Institute for Humanistic Studies was founded in 1953, it included from the first a program for evaluating outcomes, testing whether the participating executives experienced changes in their knowledge, attitudes, motivations, and values as a result of exposure to humanities courses. The closely scrutinized results showed a definite increase in knowledge and some increased propensity toward independent thinking, but no changes in interests, attitudes, or values—thus casting some doubt on whether such traditional training had any value in the improvement of human relations.[21]

Meanwhile other scholars were experimenting with different kinds of training in the humanities in order to see if they could find the perfect mix. At the Carnegie Institute, the Program for Executives included a humanities component so thought provoking the editors of the *Harvard Business Review* spent two pages exuding over it. Participants read and discussed writings ranging from Sophocles to Luther to Freud to Thornton Wilder and covering the nature of human beings, humans as social animals, our knowledge (physical and spiritual) of the cosmos, the workings of our minds, and our efforts at self-government. At the University of Virginia the highly challenging humanities course in the engineering school was proposed as a model also for business, since literature—including plays such as *Macbeth, King Lear, Faust,* and *Oedipus Rex,* the works of Plato, and novels such as *Lord Jim*—provides great examples of leaders grappling with problems.[22]

Other observers were directing their thoughts toward the difficult question of when and how this kind of humanistic exposure should ideally take place. A significant part of the problem, one widely read book pointed out, was that the breadth of learning associated with liberal education in the humanities is more highly valued as one rises to the top levels of management, and correspondingly it is the more technical and specialized courses that help most at the beginning and middle stages of a career. The traditional method of education—general courses followed by specialized ones—which had been praised and considered almost inviolable for a century, was thus called into question. This kind of thinking no doubt was what prompted some participating deans at the 1964 AACSB meeting to note that although education for business should definitely be broad and professional the typical undergraduate liberal arts program was not doing the job.[23]

Innovations in the Business Schools

Computers and Business Games. Not all the changes taking place were philosophical. Almost every business school in the nation now began, for the first time in several years, to experiment with new subjects in the curriculum. One large category of changes dealt with computers, which started making their way into business education in the second half of the 1950s.

In January 1959 UCLA opened the country's first university computer laboratory dedicated exclusively to solving complicated business management problems, and a year later it was reported that twenty-one computer simulation games were in use in America's business schools, in addition to a large number also in use in industry. By 1962 Harvard Business School was using an elaborate game that featured a competitive model of several firms, each making three products. The results, according to a Harvard professor, showed that students learned more from the game method than from the case method for three reasons: the game was better at showing interrelationships of various courses of action, it gave the students active roles in ongoing decision processes, and, most importantly, it provided an arena where the students could test what they had learned in class.[24]

The most elaborate of the business games appears to have been the University of Chicago's INTOP (International Operations), which was so large it required a division of labor among its participants. Although focused on international business INTOP involved many business decisions applicable to domestic firms as well, and it featured almost limitless entrepreneurial opportunities rather than the limited routines found in some of the earlier games. Designed to be endlessly expandable, it was still being worked on several years after its initial introduction.[25]

International Business Studies. International programs were developing faster now than at any time in the past. Early in 1959 New York University established an Institute of International Finance, one of the first in the nation, and three years later American University followed with the marketing-oriented Center for International Business. Stanford University's International Center for the Advancement of Management Education, founded with Ford Foundation assistance, differed from the others in being a training center for professors and managers from other countries. Participants came from all over the world for one-year programs that rotated annually among four topics: finance, marketing, personnel, and production.

By 1963 many schools had international programs of one kind or another, including the Center for Multi-National Business at Harvard. Thus when Indiana University held a conference on international business education at the end of that year it was heavily attended and widely reported. Calls for international emphasis had been heard as far back as World War I, but nothing like this amount of interest had ever been shown before.[26]

Entrepreneurial Studies. Another newly awakening emphasis was small business, or entrepreneurship as it now was being called. Traditionally, small businesses had felt a strong bias against MBA schools, calling them "prep schools for the industrial giants" and scorning the graduates they turned out. The schools, correspondingly, had traditionally exhibited a major blind spot when it came to small business. "Instead of teaching small business," one dean reportedly remarked, "we should teach small business to think like big business."

But by the early 1960s this mutual standoff had begun giving way. Many small businesses were hiring at least one MBA on their staffs to analyze complex problems, and a number of schools were showing increased awareness of small businesses' needs. At Harvard the students set up their own "Student Small Business Placement Program" to compensate for what they perceived as indifference in the official placement office. One sixth of the 1963 graduating students were interviewed for jobs at the smaller companies, reflecting the students' belief that giant corporations were inelastic, depersonalizing, and myopic in their failure to make use of individual talent. The university fostered this interest with two courses—"The Management of New Enterprises" and "Small Manufacturing Enterprises"—and many other schools did likewise. The movement, and the need for it, had become prominent enough by 1964 that the dean of one major university listed "developing managers with an entrepreneurial and innovative attitude" as one of the four main challenges facing business education.[27]

New Emphasis on Tools of Analysis. One final change that was underway during this time was the growth of interest in analytical tools. These had been evident since the end of World War II, but they began receiving unprecedented emphasis in the late 1950s and early 1960s. Mathematics, statistics, and "controls" experienced almost a new birth, and terms such as "quantitative analysis," "operations research," "linear programming," "systems analysis," "Gaussian curves," "PERT," "probability," and "Bayesian decision theory" appeared almost everywhere. Harvard even established a chaired professorship of management controls in 1963. These techniques—which led some observers to comment that business education was now beginning to draw more from the sciences than from the liberal arts—appeared to offer the ideal compromise between theory and practice that had been sought for so long. Neither pure theory nor mere practice, they seemed to parallel engineering in their applicability, and they promised a scientific basis on which management decisions could be made. At the AACSB's annual meeting in 1965 the major question addressed was how to preserve the idea of a general education when faced with the increasing number and increasing importance of these specialists' tools.[28]

School-Business Relations. Another area of experimentation at this time was in the business schools' relations with business. The call for close relations had been heard since the beginning of the century, but these relations had usually taken the form of lectures by visiting executives or student tours of a factory. Things were changing now.

In 1964 the top executives of the Boise Cascade Company spent three full days at the Stanford Business School and, with vows of confidentiality, let the students in on all company secrets in a free exchange of views. Later the same year a Stanford conference brought together marketing professors and practitioners for a free-swinging exploration of the abyss between theory and practice in marketing analysis and marketing techniques. At the University of Florida a chaired professorship of real estate was established, paid for entirely by privately raised money from real estate boards, appraisal institutions, and mortgage, finance, and insurance companies—the first privately supported professorship in the United States. And business executives, such as the president of Remington Rand, were speaking up much more often about their views on education and urging their fellow executives to do likewise.

All this activity marked a notable change from just a decade earlier, when *Fortune* editor William H. Whyte had observed that businesses and universities usually spoke to each other only at industry-college conferences where nothing got done because of the emphasis on agreement and cooperation. At last businesses and universities were now starting to speak openly to each other.[29]

Output Studies. Both businesses and universities now began paying attention for the first time to the output of educational institutions. For nearly three-quarters of a century people had argued a priori about what would be an ideal education for business, but nobody had made any systematic effort at evaluating the results. What happened beginning in the late 1950s still did not qualify as very systematic, but it did constitute more of an effort than anything that had happened before. As AT&T chairman Frederick Kappel sensibly pointed out, what degree one has is not a criterion for success; the only criterion is ability to perform. Yet for seventy-five years no one had paid much attention to such output considerations.[30]

Most of the studies were very upbeat and served to give business education a strong boost. A 1959 survey of middle-sized manufacturing firms showed that whereas the number of executives had increased 64 percent in the previous decade, the portion of those holding business degrees had increased 118 percent, or almost twice as fast. Many companies had by this time adopted tuition-reimbursement policies for employees who wanted to study business, and another study showed such plans to be popular among the employee-students and beneficial for the companies.

Surveys of the hiring practices of major corporations now began appearing regularly every year. In 1962 companies were reported to be hiring graduates in accounting and mathematics, and in 1963 job offers and salary levels reached new records: a University of Chicago MBA graduate had to choose among seven offers ranging as high as $8,700. Existing employees in companies were reported to be resentful of the high salaries being offered to the educated newcomers. But two years later the policy was continuing and even reinforced. Many employers now reported doing their recruiting only at business schools, and 74 percent said they found that business school graduates made the most satisfactory employees.[31]

INCREASE IN PUBLICITY AND PRESTIGE

The Press

Not surprisingly, business schools were coming in for an increased share of public attention during this time, and except for continued fallout from the foundation reports and the loudly expressed opinion of one cranky executive, most of the attention was very favorable. *Forbes* magazine ran several highly complimentary articles noting that the tide had turned in favor of business schools and that such distinguished alumni as Secretary of Defense Robert McNamara had high praises for the training they had received. Sixteen specific schools were singled out for special praise—Harvard, Pennsylvania, Dartmouth, MIT, Carnegie Tech, Columbia, New York University, Chicago, Stanford, The University of California at Berkeley, Michigan, Pittsburgh, Northwestern, Purdue, and the soon-to-be-founded Virginia—but no ranking or systematic evaluation was involved.

In 1964 one observer confidently predicted that within ten years business schools would no longer be looked down on, and by 1966 the president of the American Management Association could say that he saw fantastic challenges and growth ahead for business schools. He predicted that within fifteen years the MBA would become required for top executives, and that a Ph.D. in business would be an advantage. When the chairman of the Chock Full o' Nuts Company made a couple of public pronouncements deriding the value of business education, his comments were widely reported, but they were drowned out by the rising accolades.[32]

Government Interest

One testimonial to the rising prestige was the interest that government began showing in business schools. In 1964 all the officers of the Department of Commerce met with deans of thirty-three business and engineering schools to ask for advice on what the department could do to improve its operations. Two years later a Harvard Business School conference was used for a call to businesses to participate in the "war on poverty." Such conferences were becoming increasingly common, and they often touched on prominent national issues, such as when U. S. Steel chairman Roger Blough spoke in November 1966 at Northwestern about the money supply and inflation. An economics professor pointed out, about this time, that universities themselves might well take advantage of the management and budgeting expertise that business schools could provide—evidence that the long-standing enmity between economics and business had dwindled away in view of the business schools' rising prestige.[33]

Foreign Schools on American Models

The most impressive testimony to the rising reputation of business schools came in the form of foreign imitators. Between 1959 and 1966 major business schools were established in (among others) Britain, France, Italy, Switzerland, Spain, Turkey, Nigeria, India, Pakistan, Japan, Brazil, and Peru, many of them with direct assistance from universities in America. After decades of inaction due to either indifference or outright skepticism, other countries were now moving fast to try to catch up with what was perceived as America's lead. Although one could occasionally hear somebody say that European managers were better than American ones, the consensus clearly went the other way, and America was beginning to be widely imitated.[34]

FUNDING PROBLEMS

One thing that did not improve as the reputation improved was the financing. Business schools are always reputed to be rich, and nonbusiness students on many campuses have sarcastically named the business school building Fort Knox or Fort Mammon. When Vanderbilt University was considering establishing a business school in 1964, one objection raised was the fear that it would be a financial liability—that money formerly given as a general donation to the university would now be earmarked for the business school.

The reality of business school financing, however, is and always has been quite different from the reputation. In 1961 Harvard University received $18 million in gifts, but only $25,000 of that, or about one-seventh of one percent, was designated for the business school. The Committee for Economic Development reported in 1964 that only 1.7 percent of money donated to colleges and universities was specifically for business schools, and in 1965 the figure was reported to be still less than 2 percent. Business schools were gaining

in prestige, but they had to wait another decade and more before their material stature grew as well.[35]

*   *   *

The era beginning with the foundation reports, then, can best be viewed
as a temporary interruption in the quest for the golden mean, the proper
balance between academic theory and commercial practice. The reports
served to pull business education toward the academic side, but for the most
part the deflection was not permanent, and the publicity surrounding the
reports was certainly far more than their actual content merited. The MBA
in particular grew in both scope and numbers during this period, and chances
are that it would have grown still further had it not been for the bad aura
cast by the reports. But a second assault was about to take place, one that
would throw not just business education but the entire business community
on the defensive.

10

1967–1971:
War and Protest—MBA on the Defensive

AFTER decades of earnestly trying to get closer and closer to business, the nation's business schools awoke during the Vietnam War to find themselves being denounced for having gotten too close. In response to the criticisms, the schools took several steps, including moving strongly toward ethical and social concerns, reexamining the proper relationship between businesses and schools, and paying more attention to the graduates and their careers. Meanwhile, enrollments continued to grow, and the amazing MBA emerged from the fracas stronger than it had been before.

VIETNAM AND THE ATTACK ON THE UNIVERSITIES

Universities had been trying for years to establish connections with America's large and hugely prosperous business community, but the extent to which they had succeeded by the mid-1960s must have come as a surprise to almost everybody. Two books published in 1968—*The American University* by Jacques Barzun and *The Closed Corporation* by James Ridgeway—bared the secrets and made sure no one would be surprised again. Since protests against the Vietnam War, which had begun to be heard two and three years earlier, were reaching their resounding peak by this time, the impact of the books was considerable.

Barzun's was by far the milder of the two. Its point was simply to show how far the modern university had shifted from its original teacher-and-student model to become a player on the scientific, cultural, political, and social scenes. Recently, he noted, they had "become the arena of political battles and the target of demonstrators who proclaim that by accepting government subsidies the university is abetting crimes against conscience and humanity." His observation applied to universities' involvement not just with government but at least as much to their involvement with business.[1]

Ridgeway's work was more specific. In relentless detail he chronicled the

181

links that connected almost every major university with President Johnson's merciless and unpopular destruction of Vietnam:

> MIT and Johns Hopkins run centers which design missiles; half of MIT's budget and three quarters of Johns Hopkins' budget come from running defense labs. Cornell designs more effective bombs for Vietnam; Princeton breaks codes and runs conventions for the CIA. Michigan is first in photo reconnaissance and helps out with counterinsurgency. Pennsylvania and fifty other universities have recently been involved in chemical, germ, and biological warfare research. . . . Princeton and the Davis campus of the University of California are working on new ways to get leaves to fall off trees, thus helping us to defoliate more of Vietnam. The University of Pittsburgh's Washington office is noted for its new tank gun sights and clever methods of sowing river and beach mines. The state college system of California runs a leadership project to teach young Vietnamese to think like Americans. And the University of Rochester in upstate New York manages the secret Center for Naval Analysis in Alexandria, Virginia.[2]

Since business was perceived to be deeply involved in the war—manufacturing planes, bombs, guns, ammunition, poisons, defoliants, and so on, at a well-publicized cost of a billion dollars every two and a half days—it became as much an object of hatred as the government was, and university-business connections, from specific contracts to mere ownership of stock, attracted a large portion of the protests.

Even the best-intentioned and seemingly most harmless acknowledgments of the business community attracted an avalanche of abuse. At the University of Michigan, business history professor David Lewis proposed a "Business Leaders Hall of Fame, . . . a national memorial to America's greatest businessmen." Before any plans were made or funding obtained, however, antibusiness sentiment burst through and thwarted the project. Denouncing the whole idea as "obscene," an English professor (one of many people who participated in the attack) wrote to the university newspaper,

> As there is no evidence in the proposition of any redeeming social value, but rather candid pandering to the basest of unnatural desires, the plans for this gilt brothel or mercantile mecca should be confiscated and destroyed, and its shameless advocates incarcerated.[3]

A grant-funded study to determine why the nation's best students were not going into business elicited similar sentiments. Top undergraduates from several universities and colleges were given brief training and then sent for summer-long internships with major companies. Most of them returned with negative feelings about business, saying that they would prefer to spend their lives making social contributions rather than just earning money to guarantee personal security for themselves. "If you want to fulfill yourself," one said, "go into a profession. If you're a hungry money-grubber, go into business." Others expressed the wish that corporations would use their wealth and ingenuity to solve the nation's growing social problems. The people who undertook the study seem to have thought that the fast pace of business life was what was deterring students; the results must have rudely awakened them to a different and deeper problem.

Even at Harvard the same sentiments were present. The Business School, according to the *Wall Street Journal,* was widely disparaged within the university as a mere trade school. The socially conscious student newspaper dismissed the entire field of business study as "uninteresting," and Prof. John Kenneth Galbraith said the school prepared its students not for meaningful lives but for "dull and tedious administrative jobs."[4]

THE UNIVERSITIES RESPOND

Business schools correctly felt that they could not ignore the criticisms or pretend that no reply was called for. Their reactions ranged from direct rebuttal and denial that any problem existed to major changes in the direction of increasing the ethical and social content of the curriculum.

Rebuttal or Denial

Indiana University had the misfortune to dedicate its new building for the school of business in the fall of 1966, just as student protests were beginning to reach their shrillest. Although Dean W. George Pinnell could be content to allude briefly to society's criticisms of business and then point proudly to the "more than 16,000 alumni of the School [who] now make their contribution to the conduct of business affairs," guest speaker Oscar L. Dunn, a General Electric vice president, felt the need to confront the raging criticisms directly. One by one he cited and refuted the nine allegations against business most often heard by GE's recruiters:

—that profit is the only concern, even if it means compromising quality and utility

—that the insistence on routine performance of duty dehumanizes the employees

—that business life is exciting only at the top echelons; others simply follow orders

—that conformity reigns, and individuality is crushed

—that further training programs are redundant and amount to corporate brainwashing

—that business employees, unlike Peace Corps workers, never get to see the people they help

—that most of the work is simply paper-shuffling

—that one never encounters new ideas in business life, but instead keeps treading the same ground

—that the only reason for choosing such a life is to make money, not to achieve self-fulfillment.[5]

In the summer of 1967, *Nation's Business* confronted the poor image that business had among young people and concluded that the real problem was not hostility but ignorance. It was, the magazine editor said, the business community's job to teach youth that business has meaning and purpose and can make a significant contribution to the world. Among other things, he suggested that business could help its image by making summer jobs available.[6]

But, as the war continued and protests mounted, business schools noted with relief that the ultimate measure of their public image—demand for admission—was not being affected. In early 1968 *U. S. News and World Report* published a probusiness article showing that graduate business en- rollments had actually grown faster than other graduate enrollments—101 percent to 71 percent—over the previous five years. Placement directors were quoted as saying that the widespread perception of antibusiness senti- ment among students was exaggerated. An article in *Nation's Business* the following year said essentially the same thing: that in this era of campus disruptions and violence, the business schools were remaining largely un- touched. Interviews with a number of deans revealed widespread optimism. They saw no effect on the quality or quantity of students, and they expected the favorable conditions to continue.[7]

Ethical Emphases

Several business schools responded to the criticism by enhancing the ethical content of their curricula. The dean at American University surveyed a number of schools and found a trend toward preparing managers who would be professional in every sense, including ethics. Most universities, he reported, were treating business ethics as a separate field from other branches of ethics, stressing that profitability must be achieved with integ- rity, equity, and morality, and that temporary penalties must often be en- dured for the sake of ultimate good. At roughly the same time, the University of Virginia's Darden School established its Center for the Study of Applied Ethics, and the Harvard Business School, in a move that probably had ethical overtones, established a joint degree program with the Harvard Law School, thirty-six years after the idea had first been proposed.[8]

Emphasis on Social Concerns

The main response business schools showed to social unrest came in the form of specific moves designed to increase their involvement in society's problems. Concern about America's role in Vietnam, one must remember, was almost dwarfed in the public mind by urban racial unrest here at home. The main changes at the business schools, accordingly, were in the attitudes expressed by administrators and students, in efforts to increase minority enrollments, in alterations to the curricula, in special efforts at educating business executives in social concerns, and, in some cases, in actual involvement in remedying social problems.

Changes in Attitudes. As previous chapters have noted, the place of business in society had occupied an increasingly prominent position in the mission statements of business schools, starting even before World War II. Now, however, expressions of social concern were much less likely to take the form of "training our graduates to occupy positions of civic responsibility in their careers" and more likely to take aim at specific problems. When Arjay Miller, former vice chairman at Ford Motors, took over as dean at Stanford early in 1969, he did not stop at mentioning "corporate social responsibility" but declared that graduates of business schools from now on would be the ones to lead the nation in the fight against poverty, ghettoes, poor housing, pollution, and unemployment. Similarly, when Lawrence E. Fouraker became dean at Harvard Business School the next year, *Business Week* called it the start of a new era and specifically noted how terms like "social relevance" and "urban" had started appearing in the school's catalog, and how students were increasingly choosing to work for companies which they thought would give them more opportunity to concentrate on social problems. A study reported in the *Wall Street Journal* later that year showed that MBA students were strongly in favor of companies assuming greater responsibility in dealing with social concerns.[9]

Increased Minority Enrollments. One thrust of this new emphasis was an effort to get more minority, specifically black, students into MBA schools. The thinking behind such efforts clearly was to bring minorities more into the mainstream of economic life, and such thinking may have been part of the U.S. Office of Education's motive, in early 1967, for establishing a twenty-million-dollar loan fund for business students from lower income families. By the end of the same year—after the worst summer of rioting in memory—schools were mounting earnest campaigns to attract not merely lower income but specifically black students. According to the *Wall Street Journal,* Wharton, Harvard, Chicago, Northwestern, and Stanford all had established fellowships, instituted special recruiting efforts, and adopted special standards in an attempt to attract and retain black students. Such efforts were even more widespread by the fall of the next year, when Harvard—which had had only twenty-four black students altogether since the end of World War II—included twenty-eight in its new entering class. A number of universities, led by the University of Rochester, established a consortium to encourage minorities to enter graduate business programs, and the University of Massachusetts by itself announced a program, consisting of one summer of preparation followed by a year of graduate-level work, to train minority workers to fill management positions.[10]

Such efforts met with such success that early in 1970 the Sloan Foundation awarded a million dollar grant to nine major MBA schools—Columbia, California, Carnegie-Mellon, Cornell, Tuck, Harvard, MIT, Wharton, and Stanford—to establish a "Council for Opportunity in Graduate Management Education," a five-year program to attract and educate minority students. In July of that year the Black MBA Students Association was formed, and an observer at Harvard in the fall of that year commented on the greatly increased number of black students in evidence.[11]

Curricular Changes. Enrollment changes proceeded faster than changes in the curriculum. Although the *Wall Street Journal* reported in mid-1968 that business schools were stressing social issues as never before, the catalogs themselves show hardly any evidence of significant changes in the traditional curriculum. The article, which dealt primarily with Harvard, Wharton, and New York University, reported that the new initiatives were taking two forms—educating whites about their responsibility to society and educating blacks about business—but that four problems were holding back the efforts: (1) lack of freedom among the younger professors who might be most interested in such work, (2) lack of experience among business professors, leading to easy discouragement; (3) fear of offending the traditional business community; and (4) the superficiality which characterized most of the efforts.[12]

Cornell's experience may be typical. As a response to the nation's urban crisis, it not only offered but required of all students a course in urban problems. Yet further examination reveals that the course consisted entirely of a computer game on land use that primarily showed how changes in single-parcel land use shape the development of a city. Clearly, the *Wall Street Journal*'s fears about the superficiality of efforts were well founded.[13]

Yet exactly what a more socially conscious curriculum would have consisted of, had it existed, has never been even remotely clear. Any socially oriented course that fell within the normal scope of a business school would have been susceptible to the charges of superficiality and hypocrisy, and courses outside the normal scope of the business school would have been deemed to belong somewhere else. Two professors wrote an article in which they proposed a grid for a curriculum that would relate business to its social environment (Ill. 10–1). Based on the premise that higher level management education should focus not on getting a high rate of return but on what the firm and the environment do to each other, it argued that the manager of each of ten business functions (listed vertically) should be educated to see the interrelationships of every decision on each of four environmental areas (listed horizontally). Ideas about practical implementation of such a grid remained hopelessly vague, however, and nothing more was heard of the idea.[14]

Many schools' curricula were no doubt affected to some degree by the movement toward social concern, but the fact that specific changes are hard to find suggests that the changes weren't very extensive. The Wharton School in 1970, for example, proudly stated that it trained its students not just for business management but for management of all sorts of other enterprises such as cultural and social organizations. Yet the curriculum listed in the catalog for that year resembles that of all the other schools, without any specific features that relate to such an emphasis.[15]

Executive Education. At least two major universities used special programs for executives as a way of responding to the social crises. The University of California at Berkeley used its Advanced Management Training Program to provide executives from big companies with four weeks of courses on poverty, health costs, and crime—on the principle that these people needed no further training in practical matters or in traditional business subjects but instead needed to develop an understanding of social change. Less elaborate and more practical was a seminar on the urban crisis offered to executives by the University of Michigan. Its purpose was to assist them as they prepared to embark on large-scale hiring of the hard-core employed.[16]

Actual Involvement. In a couple of instances universities became involved in hands-on efforts to assist minorities. Although the projects were not long-lived or very significant, they still deserve to be mentioned as illustrations of the responses by business schools to social unrest.

In a program that continued for several years, the Woodrow Wilson Fellowship Foundation provided funds to send business school graduates to assist the administration of several southern black institutions such as Tougaloo College in Mississippi. From the viewpoint of a quarter of a century later, such a program sounds patronizing and insulting to colleges that had been running their administrations without assistance for many years, and it also appears to have been of dubious value, since recent business school graduates would have had little to offer. But the *Wall Street Journal*'s report on the activity, which was then in its third year, was entirely laudatory, so the colleges apparently were able to find some kind of work for these young graduates to do.[17]

A 1968–69 program at Stanford Business School, in which advanced students were sent to assist black businessmen and women, seems open to the same suspicions and doubts. Although the program directors openly acknowledged and dealt with the problems of race and of young inexperienced students advising older business operators, the aura of patronizing still remains, as well as a self-consciousness that reveals much about the

Illustration 10-1:

A DIAGRAM OF ENVIRONMENTAL-BUSINESS RELATIONSHIPS FOR USE IN CURRICULUM DESIGN

Business Elements	Environmental Factors			
	Educational	Behavioral	Legalpolitical	Economic
Planning				
Control				
Organization				
Staffing				
Direction				
Marketing				
Production				
Research & Development				
Finance				
Public Relations				

Environmental-Business Interrelationships

All business functions (listed vertically) directly interrelated
with environmental constraints (listed horizontally).

Source: __Management International Review__, 7 (1967), 143-154.

business education community's defensiveness in the face of widespread criticism.[18]

International Emphasis. As in every period, emphasis on international business continued to grow in the late 1960s, but this time the developments had a slightly different twist. Partly, no doubt, because of America's increasing unpopularity abroad, the traditional means of emphasis—adding courses in exporting or international investing—no longer seemed enough. Thus in late 1967, Education and World Affairs, a nonprofit organization established by the Ford and Carnegie Foundations, sponsored a report and subsequently a conference in which fifty business school deans met to discuss the issues of international business education. The purpose was to stimulate international thinking in America's business schools, over 75 percent of which, according to the report, offered no international courses at all.

Activities were taking place on a smaller scale too. Rollins College, for example, undertook an international venture of its own, sending twenty-five of its graduate business students to Europe to meet with overseas business managers. The purpose—to teach the students about international business—could well have been influenced by a desire to rehabilitate the image of business and of America.[19]

ATTEMPTS TO FURTHER THE PHILOSOPHY OF BUSINESS EDUCATION

Perhaps because it is hard to think while demonstrators are chanting protests in the halls outside an administrator's office, few advances occurred during this time in philosophical speculation about the right and proper nature of an MBA program. Some observers concentrated on specific problems, and others correctly noted with alarm that the gap between practical businesses and theoretical schools was widening. But no one made any intellectual breakthroughs in analyzing the field, either in this country or elsewhere, and the problems that were plaguing Great Britain's newly developing schools sounded just like the ones that continued to plague America's older ones.

Focus on Specific Problems

The difficulty observers had in formulating a comprehensive overview of management education's problems is well attested to by the few instances in which they tried. For example, at the dedication of Indiana University's new building for its school of business in November 1966, the dean listed the three biggest problems that he saw confronting management education. The items in the list, instead of being concerned with philosophical foundations as one might expect, all seem peripheral, short-term, and limited:

society's poor opinion of business, the need to accommodate great increases in enrollment, and the need to provide lifelong learning opportunities.

Likewise, the papers presented at the annual AACSB conferences from 1966 through 1970 dealt almost exclusively with near-at-hand concerns like audio-visual technology or with vague older topics like "the liberal arts and the business school." Even a collection of studies assembled in 1969 under the title *The Dynamic World of Education for Business: Issues, Trends, Forecasts* contained nothing more important than articles on such topics as "The Relationship of Graduate to Undergraduate Education in Business Administration." The late 1960s were simply not a time of breaking down old paradigms or creating new ones.[20]

More specific problems were, however, discussed rather widely. One scholar undertook a survey to determine which areas of employment were most satisfied with MBA graduates. The results showed that, whereas nearly 70 percent of all MBAs were found to perform at a "very satisfactory" level, only 29 percent of the ones in personnel work were rated that highly. His conclusion was not only that the MBA schools should place more emphasis on personnel work, but that personnel departments themselves were partly to blame because they had little idea what they wanted. Another study produced similar findings with regard to management education, which, the author said, had degenerated into simplistic models resulting from flawed experiments. Noting that "most management education has little management in it," he called for research to bridge the gap between theory and practice.[21]

The Theory-Practice Gap

Other observers were likewise alarmed by what they perceived as a widening gap between the theoretical instruction being handed out by universities and the practical requirements of business. Instead of finding ways to bring the two sides together, forces seemed to be driving them further apart. Nobody seems to have had concrete suggestions about what to do, but the awareness of the gap was widespread.

In a much-noticed *Fortune* article published in 1968, "The MBA: The Man, the Myth, and the Method," reporter Sheldon Zalaznick pointed out that the degree had grown far more respectable over the previous fifteen years. Not only had academic standards increased, but business schools by this time were hiring top intellectual leaders from other disciplines (sociology, psychology, mathematics), and research of all kinds was being conducted everywhere. Although such developments would be considered good in most other fields, in business education they could be viewed as sources of concern. The problem was that the newly won respectability was all of the academic kind, and that it had been acquired at the cost of relevance to business itself. Zalaznick quoted Peter Drucker as expressing concern because the new breed of academic-minded young professors had no real acquaintance with actual business. Instead of doing work which could have relevance in society, they devoted themselves entirely to abstract concepts and theoretical models. Thus, Drucker concluded, the new developments that had brought high standards, interdisciplinary studies, and greater respectability were actually to be deplored:

> The business schools no longer see themselves as social instruments. They want to be "respectable" as, say, mathematics departments are respectable. But this is wrong. Professional schools are not intellectual institutions but social institutions. Old-timers at the business schools had one great strength; they knew what they were talking about.[22]

A year later, two prominent business school deans separately expressed the same reservations about the new direction that business studies were taking. University of Pittsburgh dean Gerald Zoffer saw the gap between schools and businesses constantly widening, to the point where business education now meant only that professors with no real-life experience were training students to be technically proficient in computer simulations. As a result, he said, both the employers and the new graduates were growing dissatisfied. The companies were appalled at the aggressiveness that young graduates exhibited, as well as at their reliance on unproven tools and techniques and at their lack of respect for experience, tradition, nonquantifiable variables, and loyalty. The graduates, on the other hand, found the business world boring, slow, and unreceptive to new ideas.

Dean James S. Hekimian of Northeastern University focused his criticisms on what he perceived as alarming developments in research that, instead of being viewed as something that could contribute to business practice, had now begun to take on a life of its own. It had grown less and less connected with business until it had now become, in the eyes of the business school professors, more important than contact with the business community it was intended to serve. Three results of what he called these "increasingly sophisticated analyses of an increasingly unreal world" were (1) business faculty members who had no business connections, (2) unreal expectations on the parts of both the employers and the graduates, and (3) very weak financial support of business schools by the business community.

And yet, for solutions to these problems, the two deans could only come up with two standard recommendations that had been heard for decades: more communication between schools and businesses and more emphasis on such programs as internships.[23]

Developments in Britain

The very same problems that American business educators were worrying about (except, of course, for the ones related to the war in Vietnam) could be found in Great Britain. Like all the European countries, Britain had been slow to take to management education in college, and in fact it was not until the 1963 Franks report, mentioned in chapter 9, that formal programs even existed within British universities.

As of 1967 one of the two new business schools—that at the University of London—had turned out a mere one hundred graduates, and the one at Manchester had turned out just eighty. By 1970 it had become obvious that this pace was far too slow, since the rate of production would have to quadruple in order for the number of master's degrees merely to equal the number in Canada, which had less than half Britain's population. Two public reports issued in 1969–70 called attention to Great Britain's dearth of business schools and attributed America's great lead in business not to technology but to the superiority of management education. One of the reports advocated vast and immediate expansion of Britain's business schools, but even such expansion, the *Economist* lamented, would merely bring Britain in 1975 up to where the United States had been in 1960.[24]

By late 1970, however, people were beginning to have second thoughts. Instead of lamenting that there was not enough management education, doubts began to surface about whether that kind of education did any good anyway. From the very beginning the Manchester Business School had often been considered too "behaviorist" and had been criticized for neglecting business and instead teaching social science. Now, however, the criticism spread to London also, and the *Economist* cited a wide gulf between what the schools were doing and what industry thought they should do.

When the queen opened a new business education building in Regents Park in what was supposed to be a happy and upbeat ceremony, the main speaker used the occasion to lambast Britain's business schools for their irrelevance and low quality. Citing the fact that the teachers were recruited from traditional colleges without any special training and therefore were inexperienced and not even acquainted with business, he found it inevitable that school-industry relations should be as bad as they were. The schools, he said, knew and cared little about business, instead offering irrelevant course to students who themselves had never worked. But his solution, unfortunately, was even less imaginative than the "more communication" urged in America: he attributed the problems to the fact that the schools were in private rather than public hands, and he called for the government to take them over.[25]

EMPHASIS ON THE OUTPUT OF SCHOOLS

One interesting development in the late 1960s was that observers began to pay unprecedented attention to the output of graduate business schools—to the young MBAs entering the work force. As noted in the previous chapter, output had begun to attract attention in the early 1960s, but that was insignificant compared to what happened next. The most likely explanation lies in the defensive position that business and business education had been forced to assume. Since critics had attacked MBA students as selfish and materialistic, the next logical step was for someone to study them a few years after graduation and see if the charges were accurate.

Many of the comments dealt directly with the question of supply and demand. In fact, starting about 1968, reports on the job market for MBA graduates became regular annual events in the press, although sometimes contradictory ones. In June 1968 *Forbes* reported an acute shortage of MBAs, but three and a half months later the *Wall Street Journal* reported that hiring during the year had eased off, with fewer companies making offers, and at lower salaries. Exactly six months afterward, the *Wall Street Journal* noted that each Harvard MBA graduate commonly received a dozen job offers, and that salaries were correspondingly much higher than the year before. When the 1970 economic recession arrived, the paper included reports on five separate occasions about how MBA graduates were continuing to find jobs, although with fewer offers to choose among. Within less than a decade, the subject of employment availability for new MBAs had become major news.[26]

Other reports coming out at this time analyzed the job preferences shown by new MBA graduates. Two professors conducted a study in 1969 that found manufacturing industries, especially automotive, to be the graduates' first choice, while the insurance industry ranked last. (Banking and finance were not included in the study.) Another survey found a strong trend toward working for smaller companies: 42 percent of graduates chose firms with fewer than a thousand employees, and 25 percent chose ones with fewer than a hundred. A similar trend was reported at Harvard. From these studies it is unmistakably clear that new MBAs were now finding themselves in great enough demand that they could largely control the market.[27]

In confirmation of that last point, a new organization, the Business Graduates Association, came into existence in Britain about this time and began exerting influence to improve the life of its members. Displaying an attitude that in any earlier age would have been called unmitigated arrogance, three of its leaders wrote an article telling major corporations how they should treat the new recruits. The mere publication of such sentiments illustrates the growing power and prestige that graduate business education was beginning to command:

First and foremost, the business graduate has an immediate need for an opportunity to perform—to put his professional training to use and, in particular, his abilities to analyse problems concerned with broad aspects of the business. A further formal training period is unnecessary and usually the last thing he wants is to be put on an introductory graduate training programme.

He wants to feel that he is entering a company that is receptive to new ideas and business methods and that his views will be considered on merit rather than dismissed as coming from someone with little experience. He wants to work for a man whose ability and knowledge he respects—someone from whom he can learn and who understands the graduate's capabilities—this is often the deciding factor for the business graduate when he takes a job. He expects to be rewarded and promoted on his ability and performance alone, rather than his age. The first job is insufficient in itself; he needs to have an idea of his career path and what he can achieve in the next five years and beyond.[28]

One negative trait long associated with MBA graduates was their inclination to move freely from one job to another rather than remain loyal to one employer. The *Economist* reported that graduates of European business schools were very mobile, and *Business Week* said the most-asked question at Harvard was not "What will I do" but "What will I do first?" But late in 1970 the *Wall Street Journal* reported that (perhaps because of the recession) job hopping was becoming less prevalent: the portion who had changed jobs in the first two and a half years had recently declined from 40% to 28%. The group that conducted the survey, MBA Enterprises, announced that it would continue to monitor the situation and report the results monthly— again demonstrating how important a news item the output of graduate business schools had become.[29]

THE GOOD REPUTATION OF THE MBA DEGREE

Whatever opinions individuals expressed, the economic facts show unmistakably that corporations continued to have a good opinion of MBA programs and their products. In a survey, 88 percent of the CEOs of *Fortune* 500 companies agreed that the MBA degree gives young executives an advantage, and another executive said that he found young MBAs above average in intelligence, perseverance, and dedication. Other reports told of companies spending millions of dollars to send their senior staff back to take special seminars at business schools. "Colleges are producing a generation of high-powered minds—super intellects," one executive said. "You've got to keep up."

Among the universities sponsoring such seminars in 1967—many of which were filled to capacity—were Harvard, Carnegie-Mellon, UCLA, Pittsburgh, Hawaii, Stanford, MIT, Columbia, and Michigan. The next year thirty-nine institutions were offering summer institutes in liberal arts studies specifically for business executives. A few less enthusiastic comments about smart-alecky young know-it-alls could always be heard, but the evidence clearly shows that corporations held advanced business studies in high regard, almost approaching awe.[30]

Demand for the young MBAs continued to be strong. At Columbia, the graduates received an average of 4.7 job offers each, and administrators worried that enrollments were not keeping up with industry's demand for "highly trained executive manpower." RCA executive David Sarnoff saw a growing shortage of international managers and predicted that the need would double (to eighty thousand) in the next six years.[31]

Accordingly, salaries started going sharply up, and any reluctance to discuss them vanished completely. In previous decades, as already noted, some schools had thought it undignified to discuss money openly; now almost every report on a business school mentioned salaries from the first. Two business professors—one of them later to become a prominent dean—published a major article advocating the use of salary figures as the best means of evaluating graduate schools of business. A *New York Times Magazine* profile of the Harvard Business School in 1968 reported that starting salaries for its graduates had risen a thousand dollars each year for the past four years, and *Business Week* went still further in breaking down salaries by field of work: consulting, investment banking, and brokerage paid $16,000, while insurance paid $14,500 and communications $12,000. University catalogs and recruiting materials now also regularly mentioned salaries. Even though the emphasis on social contributions was greater than ever before, the schools clearly knew that it was mainly money, not social contributions, that attracted students and built reputations.[32]

And, of course, graduate enrollments—the ultimate indicator of success—continued to rise at a faster and faster rate. While undergraduate business enrollments rose a remarkable 43 percent over the four year period ending in 1971, MBA enrollments rose an astounding 201 percent and business Ph.D. enrollments 81 percent. The rise, far higher than anyone had expected, continued to catch even the experts by surprise. The director of the University of California's Center for Research in Management Science made a prediction about MBA enrollments just three years in advance—and his prediction turned out to be more than 40 percent too low.[33]

* * *

As the 1970 recession began, some observers began to predict dire things for the MBA. Two prominent business magazines strongly criticized the same executive seminars that had been so highly praised just three years earlier, and a front page article in the *Wall Street Journal* proclaimed the end of good times. "The halo over the MBA is fast becoming tarnished," a prominent university placement director said, and other people noted the "growing disenchantment with MBAs." The number of job offers made at eighty well-known schools was said to have declined from 6,554 to 3,706 in just two years, leading the *Journal* to declare a gloomy future for the MBA.

Such predictions were not just wrong but were horrendously wrong. What happened in the next decade would have stunned even the most optimistic of optimists.[34]

11
1971–1979:
The Golden Age of Innovation

FOLLOWING the brief but troubled war interlude, the MBA defied all predictions and began the fastest growth in its history. Besides growth in numbers, the 1970s saw the introduction of an astounding number of innovations, a greatly increased emphasis on research, and an unprecedented increase in the public attention attracted by graduate business education and the students it turned out. Along with the positive side, this success produced two negative results: universities began recognizing the MBA as a source of money, and doomsayers again began predicting the demise of the degree.

THE GROWTH OF THE MBA

Just months after the *Wall Street Journal* said that demand for the MBA was past its peak and beginning to decline, graduate education in business began a period of growth that can only be described as explosive. During the 1970s more MBA degrees were awarded—over 387,000—than in all the previous seven decades combined. By the end of the decade far more than half of the MBA holders in American industry had received their degrees during the 1970s. Degrees granted in the 1970s were almost four times as many as those granted in the 1960s—which had been more than two and a half times as many as those granted in the 1950s—which had been twice as many as those granted in the 1940s (Ill. 11–1).

Equally astounding is the growth in the number of universities that offered the MBA degree. Between 1950 and 1975, according to one report, five hundred institutions (or twenty a year) began offering the degree. By 1975 the growth rate was between twenty and thirty a year, and by 1978 it was thirty-five a year, or a new MBA degree program every ten days. Most of the growth in MBA production came from established programs, which often were experiencing 35 percent, 50 percent, or 60 percent growth in any two-year period in the 1970s, but these rapidly multiplying new schools certainly contributed to the total.[1]

196

Illustration 11-1:

MBA PRODUCTION BY DECADE
1920s THROUGH 1970s, IN THOUSANDS

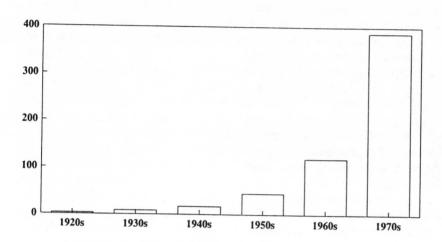

Source: USOE/NCES Earned Degrees Awarded Series

One explanation for the precipitous rise is that America had grown tired of antiwar just as quickly and as surely as it had grown tired of war. The excesses and violence of the protesters. produced a negative reaction in a sizable portion of the student-age population, to the extent that the number taking the Admission Test for Graduate Study in Business nationwide surpassed 95,000 in 1970, as compared with just 40,596 in 1965. In 1971 the United States Chamber of Commerce magazine, *Nation's Business,* noted proudly—albeit with a touch of sarcasm—that the number of people studying graduate business was six times as great as those studying social work and twenty times the number studying public administration.[2]

A second reason was the overcrowding being experienced in other professions. Around 1970 it became obvious that college teachers were in oversupply, and consequently people who previously would have studied for Ph.D.s in philosophy, history, and English now enrolled instead in business school. About the same time the legal profession was experiencing a glut, and business schools attracted many students who would otherwise have studied law.[3]

A third explanation may account for as many of the new applicants as the other two combined. For all its history, the MBA had been a man's degree. Many universities had always admitted women to their business programs, but enrollment of women in business schools had never been great, and during the 1950s it had actually declined. It was not until 1961 that Harvard Business School admitted women, and not until 1968 that Dartmouth's Amos Tuck School did.

Now, during the 1970s, women's enrollment suddenly began growing far faster than men's. Typical was the experience at the Wharton School, where the proportion of women students rose from 4 percent to 25 percent during that one decade. Only about 8 percent of those taking the national admission test in 1971 were women, but by 1975 the figure had risen to 22 percent.

Nationally, women averaged about 10 percent of enrollments by 1975, but some universities were already far ahead of that figure—for example at Columbia, where women accounted for 27 percent of the enrollment that year. The University of Western Ontario went from graduating one woman MBA in 1971 to graduating thirty-three in 1978. During the first half of the decade both Simmons College and C. W. Post University established special MBA programs to encourage women, and by 1974 *Nation's Business* was reporting that women with MBAs were in great demand. Almost as if a door to success had opened for the first time, women rushed to MBA programs and greatly swelled the enrollments in the country's business schools.[4]

Minorities and international students also enrolled in larger numbers than before and contributed to the overall increase. *Nation's Business* said that minorities were in great demand in business, and *MBA* magazine reported that minority enrollment in graduate business programs had soared from fewer than fifty in 1966 to between two thousand and three thousand in 1977. Florida A&M University began a drive to become the country's leading center for black students' business education and achieved national attention for its efforts.

Growth in international enrollments, although less spectacular, was still substantial. Between 1970 and 1973 Harvard's foreign student enrollment, for example, rose 57 percent from 75 to 118. One reason was that economic conditions abroad improved while the dollar fell in value, and another was simply that American multinational corporations were growing, and many foreigners wanted to work for them. More than a fourth of the students, however, ended up remaining in the United States.[5]

But what, more than all else, moved young Americans to go to graduate business school was the promise of success and security—in short, money. Throughout the 1970s, loud and clear messages came forth indicating that the MBA was a sure ticket to prosperity.

In 1972 a *Harvard Business Review* article pointed out that a Harvard MBA graduate from 1947, just twenty-five years earlier, had a one in three chance of having already become a CEO, and that 20 percent of the nation's CEOs in 1972 had MBA degrees. In 1974, a recession year, several news reports came out championing the value of the MBA. While other people were vainly looking for work, new MBA graduates were finding that corporate demand for their services was up 10 percent and salaries were up 5 percent. Harvard MBA graduates, the *Wall Street Journal* reported, were being offered salaries from $1,000 to $1,500 higher than had been offered in the previous year when the economy was actually better. In 1975 *Business Week* reported that Harvard MBA salaries were up 8 percent, and by 1976 the proportion of CEOs with MBA degrees was said to have risen to between 25 percent and 30 percent. By 1978 Northeastern University was advertising its MBA program as "a go-go ticket to success."

When asked whether the MBA degree helped young employees get ahead, 45 percent of companies (as opposed to just 32 percent ten years earlier) said yes. MBA salaries that year were reported to be $3,000 to $4,000 higher than for people with bachelor's degrees. With such reports coming from individuals, colleges, and companies, the signals were clear, and a rush to enroll in graduate business school was inevitable.[6]

Two side effects of this rush were a splintering into specializations and a shortage of teachers. The desire to create specializations was probably inevitable as the field of graduate business studies grew larger in both enrollments and subjects covered. Typical of new degree programs devised were a Master of Science in Taxation (Bryant College) and a Master of Science in Labor and Industrial Relations (Baruch College). The teacher shortage meanwhile had become very serious, as Ph.D. production in business studies, which rose for a few years in the mid-1970s, fell again after 1976, so that the number of doctorates granted in 1979 was the same as in 1971— although MBA enrollments had risen during that period by more than twenty-three thousand students.[7]

CONTINUED SOCIAL CONCERNS

Although the antiwar protests and concern about social unrest had died down, they still had left their mark on graduate business education. One cannot label the 1970s as a decade of really strong social consciousness, but evidence shows that most business schools did remain aware of a larger duty. Courses in some aspect of urban affairs, for example, could be found at Stanford, the Wharton School, MIT, New York University, Columbia, and the University of California at Berkeley, although they were conspicuously absent at other schools, such as the University of Chicago.

Stanford was especially committed to urban concerns. Its catalog for 1973–74 lists courses in urban political process, structuring decisions for the urban manager, urban workshop, comparative economics of poverty, urban finance, urban economics, decision making in the public sector, minority employees in white organizations, black economic development, small business management, and new enterprise management—as well as a course in the American woman at work. Harvard and Wharton had courses in management of not-for-profit organizations, and arts management courses could be found at Wharton, SUNY Binghamton, and a few other schools.

Several universities, including Southern California, Indiana, Wisconsin, Rochester, North Carolina, and Washington University of St. Louis, received large grants from the Ford Foundation to increase their minority enrollments, and these enrollments often led to other kinds of involvement in minority business concerns. The Association for the Integration of Management (AIM) came into existence during this decade, joining the increasingly active National Black MBA Association.

Other student groups also were formed for the purpose of exerting social pressure on corporations. The National Association of Concerned Business Students was matched on the local level by the Effective Communication through Interpersonal Seminars (ECIS) at MIT and chapters of the Committee for Corporate Responsibility (CCR) at Stanford and Harvard. Even ethics made a faint appearance, when the University of Michigan was awarded $10,000 by the Exxon Corporation for integrating ethics into its business curriculum.[8]

MBA INNOVATIONS

The main characteristic of the 1970s, however, was not social concern but curricular innovations—or, to those less sympathetic, gimmicks and fads. Unlike previous periods, where the curriculum always resembled and often duplicated that of the preceding decade, the 1970s saw the introduction of new concepts at a dizzying pace. In an effort to establish for itself a niche distinct from all the other schools' niches, almost every institution introduced innovations on some level, ranging from the entire aim and purpose of the school, to the auspices under which the instruction was offered, to changes in individual departments and courses.

Innovative Aims and Purposes

Yale. For most of its seven decades, the MBA curriculum had been witnessing a movement away from mechanical and formalized measurements and toward a deeper understanding of human motivation. Yet nothing in all that time had come close to approaching the single-minded commitment of the founders of the new Yale program in the mid-1970s. The school was named not "business administration" but "The Yale School of Organization and Management." Its purpose was to be the nation's leading management school, just as Harvard was the nation's leading business school. It aimed at teaching not profit-making skills but the kind of management and negotiation skills required by a government agency seeking congressional approval. It trained for leadership in either the private or the public sector, since basic to its conception was the idea that government and business must interact and that the artificial walls which separate them must be broken down. While other schools were training people for positions in corporations, Yale's "O&M" school aimed at producing leaders for government, the military, private, foundations, or in fact any kind of organization at all.

Press coverage of the new school was quite extensive, and its appeal to students was unquestionable: 2,000 application forms were requested in the first month after its announcement, and applications were received at the rate of 150 a week. Demand for places at all graduate business schools was rising, but the demand for Yale's program was much stronger than most.[9]

Vanderbilt. Several years before Yale announced its nearly total commitment to organizational studies, Vanderbilt University had done almost the same thing. Its original plan in 1965 had called for "a new kind of school of management that can and will set educational patterns of national significance in the years to come," and the new emphasis it chose to follow was largely behavioral and organizational. Of the twenty curricular modules it adopted, seventeen were entirely behavioral. The new dean who came in 1970 announced that the school would differ from all others by focusing on one thing. Just as Wharton was distinctive because of its emphasis on finance, Harvard because of its case method, and Carnegie-Mellon because it stressed theory and numbers games, Vanderbilt would emphasize "the management of change" as its distinctive focus.[10]

Wharton. In contrast to Yale and Vanderbilt, the Wharton School, already widely known for its emphasis on finance, decided to anchor its activities more securely in the world of real business, rather than move in the direction of theoretical studies. It established the Busch Center for Research, which would undertake specific research under contract with businesses. Such an arrangement was seen to have both academic and practical advantages. It was intended at least partly to be a response to the criticism of traditional academic research in which students and professors devised elaborate theoretical answers for artificial problems. By having its students participate in research on real problems, Wharton would take a large step toward bridging the much-discussed chasm between theory and practice.

From a practical viewpoint the use of contract research was seen as a source of revenue, and especially as a financial safeguard in case student enrollment should start to decline. In addition to a small full-time research staff and the graduate students who worked on the problems, the Institute was to use also the services of faculty members, "buying" their time from the school. Such a move toward conducting research at the behest of the business community raised a number of philosophical questions about the relation between universities and businesses and thus marked a potentially major development in the aims and purposes of graduate business education.[11]

New Auspices for Business Education

Some of the innovations during this period consisted of new places, new times, and new ways for reaching students. Few people were as ambitious as Carnegie Mellon's dean, who announced in 1970 that his school (which he already regarded as the best in the nation) would embark on a massive effort to disseminate its instruction through new technology. Besides using videotapes to supplement regular classroom work, he wanted to run television and computer lines into major corporations and thereby offer the MBA degree to on-the-job engineers and administrators. His confidence in the viability of the project was unbounded. Before his Graduate School of Industrial Administration came along, he said, "there were two things you could say about business education: it was dominated by the Harvard case study approach, and it was all bad."[12]

A couple of years later a kind of MBA-by-TV did come into existence. Through the facilities of South Carolina Educational Television Network, the University of South Carolina piped graduate instruction in business administration to special "TV classrooms" in seventeen cities and towns around the state. The three-year course of study proved very popular: 100 people had graduated by 1975, and 140 new students enrolled that year. Since students still had to assemble at specific locations, rather than hear the lectures in their own homes or places of work, the project was less grandiose than what Carnegie-Mellon's dean had envisioned, but it still amounted to a notable enlargement of the traditional classroom.[13]

Other schools were conducting similar experiments in bringing education to people rather than having the people come to them. St. John's University in New York City offered an MBA degree for employees of Chase Manhattan Bank entirely on site within the bank, and Adelphi University on Long Island began its "MBA on Wheels," offering classes on railway cars to commuters traveling to and from New York City.[14]

The leader in all this movement toward innovative auspices was surely Pace University, which undertook new activity on every front and capitalized on the growth wave of the MBA. Besides an Executive MBA Program (of which more later), it instituted a Ph.D. program for executives who wanted still more training, an in-house MBA program at AT&T headquarters in New York for one hundred of the firm's top managers, and other non-degree courses at various AT&T plant sites. In addition it extended the hours of instruction in its regular MBA program both earlier and later, so that classes were meeting from 7:00 A.M. to 11:00 P.M., and also on weekends, and it opened branch campuses in two suburban locations. Finally, it established an advisory council of over 130 prominent New York business-people, representing such firms as AT&T, Chase Manhattan, Morgan Guaranty Bank, First National City Bank, Manufacturers Hanover, Irving Trust, Bankers Trust, Chemical Bank, and Pepsico. At one point, 112 corporations were providing grants of five thousand dollars annually to the university. What had been a small and extremely localized college suddenly became a major presence in business education in New York.[15]

Curricular Innovations

By far the greatest innovations of the 1970s in both numbers and significance were those that affected the curriculum itself. On all levels, from the grand curricular design to the smallest detail of teaching method, innovations were being introduced, especially in the middle years of the decade, at an absolutely astonishing rate.

At Southern Methodist University, for example, the school set up a real company for its marketing students to run. With a two-hundred-thousand-dollar grant to get them started, the students examined a number of potential products until they found a promising one, and then undertook to market it to the public, using skills they had learned in their courses.

Nearly every major business school had developed some kind of real-world experience component for its students by 1975. The most popular form was the consulting team, in which students set out to solve real problems or find real answers for real business clients. The businesses liked the service because it was inexpensive; the students liked it because of its relevance to the actual business world; and the placement offices liked it because it was proving to be valuable in helping students get jobs after graduation. Rutgers, UCLA, Emory, Dallas, Purdue, and dozens of other universities were finding such programs to be strong attractions in their efforts to recruit outstanding students.[16]

A school in South Africa went still further by not just requiring real-world experience but placing it at the very beginning of the program. The University of Stellenbosch's Graduate School of Business had all its students take a four-week minicourse, without textbooks, in seeking financing for a new business. Under supervision, students conferred with leading businesspeople, went to banks for loans, and drew up business plans for new ventures—all before even starting their formal studies. The director, a Dutchman, instituted the idea in reaction against traditional theory-first methods, which he regarded as worthless.[17]

Another rebellion against tradition led to adoption of an innovative modular curriculum at the University of North Carolina. Weary of a calendar that made all courses equal in length regardless of their content, the School of Business adopted a complex schedule that permitted students to study some

Illustration 11-2:

THE UNIVERSITY OF NORTH CAROLINA'S
MODULAR CURRICULUM, 1973-74

Financial Accounting	Financial Management	Management Accounting	Financial Management
	Production Management		
	Marketing Management	Oral Communication	Production Management
Human Behavior in Management		Stabilization and Economic Growth	Marketing Management
Managerial Economics			
Quantitative Methods I		Quantitative Methods II	
		Laboratory in Integrative Management	

Source: MBA, 8 (May 1974), 33-34.

subjects more intensively than others and some for longer periods of time (Ill. 11–2). The amount of vertical space on the chart indicates the number of class days per week, and the horizontal axis represents number of weeks per year, beginning with the fall term at the left. Thus Financial Accounting was to meet five days a week for eight weeks, while Managerial Economics met three days a week for sixteen weeks, and the Laboratory in Integrative Management once a week for the first half of the year and twice a week for the second half. The arrangement was adopted in an effort to improve interrelationships among various disciplines.[18]

Several business schools created new departments to meet the changing curricular needs. In 1975 alone, for example, the Wharton School created a Department of Decision Sciences, the Sloan School a program in healthcare management, and the University of Virginia's Darden School the Center for the Study of Public Policy, reflecting, respectively, new classifications, new subjects, and new missions.[19]

Sometimes even when the name of the department remained the same, the emphasis changed so much that it became unrecognizably different. In the early 1970s the University of Chicago adopted a new set of mathematically oriented courses and placed them in the Department of Management, with the result that its management curriculum resembled that of no other university anywhere. In most schools, "management" courses still included all the "soft" topics, like organization, motivation, and negotiation. The much more traditional management curriculum at the University of Cincinnati, less than three hundred miles from Chicago, illustrates the contrast:

Courses in the Management Department

University of Cincinnati 1972–73	University of Chicago 1972–73
Management	Mathematical Analysis for Business Decisions
Administration	
Management Decision Problems	Linear Algebra for Business Applications
Personnel Administration	
Administrative Practices	Digital Computers and Applications
Problems in General Administration	Mathematical Analysis for Business & Economics
Administrative Organization	
International Management	Control Theory
Administrative Planning and Control	Extensions of Linear Programming
Interpersonal Relations	Non-Linear Programming
Administrative Theory	Mathematical Inventory Theory
Industrial Management	Selected Topics in Management Science
Production Administration	
Materials Management	Introduction to Queueing Theory
Industrial Planning and Control	Graph Theory and Network Models
	Information, Decision, & Control

Also, of course, innovations appeared in endless numbers simply on the course level, where departments and instructors were constantly chasing after new ideas to improve education and bring attention to their schools. Behavioral science courses, being less bound by tradition to start with, were especially likely to feature innovations. At several schools, Purdue and Rutgers among them, special laboratories with one-way glass were constructed so that students in an observation room could unobtrusively take notes on the behavior of people in meetings and other business activities. At Cornell University a professor of organizational theory made news by introducing a course in the use of Machiavellian tactics in business. The object was to show students not just how to recognize such tactics but how to practice them in order to further their careers. Some professors expressed doubts that Machiavellian tactics were productive in the long run while others feared the damage that such a course would do to the already precarious reputation of business and business schools. Such experimentation in course in the social sciences was quite widespread.[20]

The humanities also came in for a major share of innovating. Dissatisfied with the traditional instruction in liberal arts subjects, yet still sure that the liberal arts possessed value for developing and broadening the minds of business students, several colleges undertook innovations to make the humanities more practical. At the University of Chicago, a course ambitiously called "Politics, Rhetoric, Economics, and Law: The Liberal Arts of the Practical" was introduced in 1973 "to apply knowledge to seeking practical solutions to public policy questions."

Two years later the U.S. Department of Education's Fund for the Improvement of Post-Secondary Education funded "competency-based curricula" at a number of colleges around the country, such as Alverno College in Milwaukee. Although these last efforts were not specifically related to business education, they obviously drew heavily on existing business curricula in their effort to make the liberal arts more marketable. Eighty competencies were identified, grouped into eight main categories, which in many ways bore a striking similarity to the departmental arrangement of business schools:

   communication
   analytical capabilities
   problem-solving skills
   independent value judgments
   social interaction
   individual/environmental relations
   awareness of the world in which the individual lives
   responsiveness to the arts and humanities

One further piece of evidence that business-type innovations were being introduced across the entire curriculum came in 1973, when a letter writer to *The New York Times* complained about the new jargon found in colleges and especially in business schools, which he called "the worst jargoneers of them all." Among the phrases he cited were "partially disclosed principal," "corridors of indifference," "selective aperception," "cranial data systems," and "bilateral frontal structure." The wave of innovation was in full motion, and no area of a college curriculum escaped it.[21]

Other Innovations

Some other significant changes were occurring, too. International programs made some gains, and emphasis on small business development also grew somewhat. The concept of the executive MBA reached full development, and, for a short period, accounting departments looked as if they were about to secede from business schools and form their own separate entities.

International Emphasis. Like every previous era, the 1970s were full of advocates for internationalizing the business curriculum. In April 1974 AACSB added the phrase "an international perspective" to its description of the required common body of knowledge. In the two years following, Golden Gate University and the Wharton School, among others, announced an international emphasis in their curricula, and the Thunderbird School in Arizona, which had made a specialty of international education ever since its founding, deepened its commitment by adding Chinese, Japanese, and Arabic language studies to its curriculum. Even before the AACSB requirement, New York University had established a graduate student exchange program with universities in Britain and France. Initially financed by grants from the Ford and Exxon Foundations, this program was seen as the start of a nationwide trend. The dean overoptimistically announced that within a year all students would be offered full scholarships, to be paid for by United States corporations.[22]

In general the international sensitivity in business programs during the 1970s does seem to have been higher than before. A survey of *Fortune* 500 companies found that executives considered MBAs from the period after 1971 to be significantly better in international business than their predecessors. These companies specifically wanted young MBAs who had been trained in international financial matters—monetary systems, capital markets, exchange rates, international financial reporting, and the economic effects of various trade restrictions—and accordingly they advocated more courses in international financial management. In contrast, production and advertising ranked at the bottom of the desired course list, the companies apparently preferring to leave management of those fields up to the local staffs in each country. Yet despite the expressed interest in enlarging the international component of MBA education, few companies were placing their young MBAs in international work. No one was opposed to an international emphasis, and many people were earnestly in favor of it, but it still could not yet be called a major thrust in graduate business education.[23]

Entrepreneurship and Small Business. Like international business, small business came in for an increasing, through still not major, share of attention in the 1970s. Harvard set the pace in 1972 with a three-week institute for owners of small businesses. One reason given for establishing the institute was that recent MBA classes had been clamoring for the school to place some emphasis on entrepreneurship, alongside the traditional emphasis on the workings of corporations. Although the Advanced Management Program was already in existence to serve the needs of practicing businesspeople, few small business owners had attended because they could not afford to be away from their businesses for the required twelve or thirteen weeks.[24]

By the middle of the decade, Harvard students had formed a "Small Business Club" whose main purpose was to supplement the work of the placement office by locating jobs with small businesses that normally did not engage in recruiting. Only 8 percent of the previous year's graduates had gone to work for small businesses, and the Small Business Club apparently aimed at increasing this number. Other schools reported similar expressions of interest by students. Indiana University experienced a tripling of enrollment in its small business course between 1975 and 1978, as students were attracted by the freedom they felt such work offered. Yet most students nationwide continued to take positions with large firms after graduation, probably just because the pay was better. Both Indiana and Carnegie-Mellon reported few of their graduates going to work for small firms, and by 1978 the portion of Harvard graduates taking that route still remained at 8 percent.[25]

Executive Education Programs. After flagging briefly at the beginning of the 1970s, special graduate business programs for mid-to high-level executives came back strongly later in the decade. Testimony about what caused the decline in 1970 is confused. It was a recession year and some observers felt that companies could not justify the considerable expense of sending senior people back to school. But others complained that the programs themselves were deficient. Articles in both *Dun's* and *Business Week* recited a litany of complaints by participating executives.

Primary was the claim that the programs were taught not by experienced businesspeople but by inexperienced educators, with the result that the practitioners consistently knew more than the professors. The textbooks likewise came in for criticism for being either too theoretical or absolutely irrelevant. The programs often were found to be standardized rather than tailored to a company's specific needs, and the universities were further criticized for admitting an unusually large number of foreign students—50 percent rather than the normal 20 percent—to fill up the classes when American companies stopped sending large numbers of their executives.

Two other criticisms also were noted. The lesser one was that the participants regarded the programs not as a learning opportunity but as a license to revert to their adolescent behaviors; drinking and fornicating were commonplace in the dorms. This report lends credence to the charge that the content of the programs was poor, since the executives found little to take seriously.

The other complaint dealt with the "sensitivity training" component in the programs, and here the reactions were strongly negative. Such training often involved deep probing into personal motivations and antagonisms, and the charge of "practicing psychiatry without a license" was more than once leveled at the program designers. Some of the exercises were ludicrous beyond belief. An executive from an electronics firm gave this report:

First we took off our shoes, then we paired off and faced our partners from opposite sides of the room. Next we were told to run at each other as fast as we could! After the collisions, we were supposed to talk about what we felt. Looking back on it now, I'm struck by three things. One, no one was hurt. Two, we actually did what we were told. And three, the company spent a fortune on that sort of bullshit![26]

Either the universities heeded the criticism and improved the programs, or the corporations ignored the criticism and kept participating, because, when the economy improved the next year, executive education soared to new heights of popularity. By the middle of the decade the *Wall Street Journal* reported that "executive MBA programs" were growing everywhere. Typically these programs were open only to people who had had about eight or ten years of managerial experience. Classes met on weekends in order to accommodate executive schedules, and instruction was on a higher level than in ordinary courses, in recognition of the different backgrounds of the participants. Chicago, Pittsburgh, Columbia, Rochester, Pennsylvania, Stanford, Southern Methodist, Illinois, and Wisconsin had especially prominent programs.[27]

Variations on the standard pattern were quite widely found. Pepperdine University's program was open exclusively to presidents, chief executive officers, and occasionally, senior division managers; New York University established a certificate program in finance for advertising executives; a European university gave a sixteen-week course, in eight two-week segments, to approximately ninety executives from a single company, focusing on the functioning of the organization rather than the individual; Hofstra and Cornell Universities joined to offer programs in "Management by Objectives" and "Human Relations and Management Psychology" to executives; and in 1974 more than forty universities were offering advanced management courses specifically for managers of arts organizations. Whatever slump had existed in the popularity of executive business programs had entirely vanished before the middle of the decade.[28]

Separate Accounting Schools. One innovation that never quite happened on a large scale was the secession of schools of professional accounting from business schools. The movement gained enormous support in the 1970s and for a while appeared to be inevitable. According to one count, the bibliography of writings on the subject surpassed 160 items by 1978. The American Institute of Certified Public Accountants in 1973 endorsed free-standing accounting schools as "one way, and perhaps the preferable way" of teaching the subject. Three years later the National Association of State Boards of Accountancy passed a resolution recommending the establishment of such schools, and the National Association of Accountants went on record as believing that "professional, accredited schools would contribute more effectively to the preparation of individuals planning accounting careers." The Arthur Andersen firm pledged a million dollars to support universities with separate schools, and as many as six universities did make the move.[29]

Among reasons cited in support of the separation were those relating to identity, autonomy, and support. Many accountants felt that their profession would acquire much more prestige if universities granted it a status equal to that of the management schools. Embedded in this argument was the conviction that accounting qualified as a profession much more clearly than other fields of business did. Second, since the career needs of accounting students were perceived as distinct from those of other business students, accountants felt that administrative autonomy would give them the required freedom to design their own curricula and the flexibility to make more rapid changes. They believed quite strongly that MBA programs as they existed included many things that accountants did not need and omitted many things they did need. Finally, many people predicted that practicing accountants would be much more likely to give financial support to separate schools, since they would know that their gifts were going to support accounting rather than some other field like behavioral science. In addition, several observers predicted that separate schools would lead to higher standards, but no specific evidence was ever adduced to support that claim.[30]

At least part of the reason for the movement, however, probably lay in the fact that the field of business administration had developed enormously over the preceding four decades, to the point where accounting, once the most prominent subject in the curriculum, was in danger of being ignored as merely a minor part of business education. Whereas accounting courses might have constituted a third to a half of the early curricula, even into the 1930s and 1940s, by 1975 they amounted to perhaps only a tenth in a typical university. Studies in human relations and organizational management, unheard of in 1925, had developed tremendously and now occupied the major part of most schools' curricula, and quantitative studies had likewise expanded beyond recognition. To people who believed that accounting formed the basis of a business education, the newly emerged MBA curriculum seemed not just far off the mark but an actual insult to accountants.

Research also figured strongly in the motivation for the separation movement. As noted in previous chapters, ever since the end of World War II and especially since the 1959 foundation reports, American schools of business had gradually been moving toward emphasis on research rather than on teaching as their primary mission. Professors were evaluated now more on the books they had written than on the quality of their teaching, and many were able to use their extensive publication records as bargaining tools for higher salaries and reduced teaching loads. But research of the kind being rewarded—empirical or model-based—did not easily match the needs of accounting, as it did in marketing or organizational behavior. As a result, accounting departments found themselves either squeezed out of the reward structure or forced into kinds of research not appropriate to their discipline. A separately administered school of accounting, they believed with good reason, would offer them a better chance to be rewarded for doing what they should be doing.

GROWTH IN PUBLIC ESTEEM FOR THE MBA

All through the 1970s, the MBA degree was becoming more prestigious. Once scorned or barely tolerated, it was now acquiring a glowing reputation in both private industry and public service. Criticisms continued to be heard, of course, but they were less frequent and less convincing.

Good Reputation in Industry

The traditional reluctance of executives in industry to acknowledge anything good about the MBA degree was slowly giving way. As late as 1968, only 32 percent of those surveyed said that they thought the degree gave young people an advantage, but by 1973 the figure had risen to 45 percent. The wonder is that the figure wasn't still higher, in view of statistics published in 1974 showing the growing prominence of the degree among chief executive officers (Ill. 11–3). Just in the last eight years being studied, from 1964 to 1972, the percentage of CEOs holding MBAs had more than tripled, while the percentage of those holding law or other degrees, or no degrees, had declined. Every major industry had by now adopted the methods that business schools had long been advocating. The home building industry was one of the last to give up its resistance, but by 1972 even it had done so and was for the first time being run by business people rather than carpenters, according to the *Wall Street Journal*. The president of the American Management Association championed the new MBA graduates as the best ever because, instead of being overspecialized as in the past, they possessed broad management skills. And in Great Britain, a recent participant in a three-month seminar at the London Business School raved about the high quality of his education, saying that it was, in fact, so advanced he had been unable to persuade his company's tradition-bound directors to adopt the new ideas.[31]

The corporations were matching their words with deeds. Even during the oil crisis recession years in the middle of the 1970s, hiring of new MBA graduates was at an all-time high. One reason suggested for the increase was that placement directors had become more aggressive in seeking out firms to recruit students. Another was that the students themselves were more appealing to employers because they were more mature and purposeful than ever: these students, unlike the previous generation, were studying business because they wanted to, rather than merely to avoid being drafted into the Vietnam War.

Illustration 11-3:

DEGREES HELD BY TOP EXECUTIVES
Percent--Selected Years

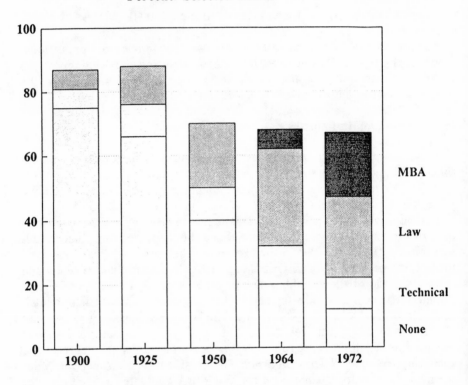

Source: Harvard Business Review, 52 (Jan. 1974), 101

But a third suggested reason is probably the most convincing: that the MBA degree had come of age and was by now increasingly valued, especially in economically troubled times. Banks and accounting firms were by far the biggest recruiters, with consulting firms second and oil, real estate, chemicals and pharmaceuticals, health care, and food and beverage companies coming on strong. Beginning salaries were 3 percent to 10 percent higher each year, usually in the $16,000 to $20,000 range, and, astoundingly, women and minority graduates were in such demand that they were receiving the highest offers. Every school, according to one survey, reported an upturn in MBA recruiting activity at a time when the energy crisis was causing thousands of layoffs on other levels.[32]

The public sector was equally enthusiastic. With encouragement from all levels of government, the business schools started emphasizing management of social and political institutions as never before. The Wharton School, MIT, New York University, Harvard, and California at Berkeley all offered such courses, and Columbia established a joint program between the Business School and the School of Architecture leading to both the MBA and a Master of Urban Planning.

But no other school matched Stanford's commitment. Whereas business education formerly, it said, meant making a product and selling it at a profit, business managers of the future had to learn how to deal with political processes, urban and racial problems, and federal, state, and local financing. While many business schools were ignoring the political leadership side of a business education, and many schools of "government" were ignoring the business side of a political and leadership education, Stanford was focusing on both and even requiring a summer internship in urban government. The emphasis everywhere, and especially at Stanford, was on planning well, so that the future would not repeat the urban problems of the present.[33]

One source of public sector praise for the MBA (as it turned out, an ironic one) was the administration of President Carter. Determined, as one observer said at the time, to make the White House "a model of management efficiency and organizational reform to be emulated by the other federal agencies," he brought a group of highly professional young managers with him to help manage the affairs of his office. "The President," this observer went on, "is seeking a place not only in the history books but in the management texts as well." Such confidence in the contribution that young MBAs could make to a government would have been entirely unimaginable twenty or even ten years earlier.[34]

Growth in Media Attention

Not surprisingly, the media began to report more news about MBA programs as their reputations grew. It now was commonplace to find national news reports about business schools competing with one another for a bil-

lionaire's fortune, about a tuition rise at Harvard, about the need for corporations to assist schools, or about increases in minority enrollments—
subjects that would never have received more than local coverage just a few
years earlier.[35]

Individual Institutions. In addition, individual schools now became objects of major attention. *The New York Times* ran lengthy articles profiling
the business schools at Stanford University, the University of London, the
University of Pennsylvania, and Harvard University, and the *Wall Street
Journal* did the same about Chicago. *MBA* magazine featured a student's
view of daily life at the Wharton School, and the Conference Board's prestigious journal *Across the Board* similarly focused on a student's experiences
at Harvard. Even *Canadian Business* published a long and highly favorable
article about the Harvard Business School. Not even medical or law schools
were attracting so much attention as business schools now were.[36]

National Surveys. Some observers focused not on individual institutions
but on nationwide trends. A University of Oklahoma professor surveyed
two dozen business schools and found recent trends emphasizing research
and methodology, real-world problems, service industries, applied fields
(real estate, career planning, investment by portfolio analysis, entrepreneurship, city planning), business games, and environmental and social concerns.
A *New York Times* article surveyed an entirely new phenomenon, the business school magazines that were suddenly appearing across the country.
Besides the long-standing *Harvard Business Review,* other major ones now
noted were *Tuck Today,* the *Wharton Magazine,* and *The Executive* from
Cornell.[37]

Students. The students passing through these business schools also became subjects of interest to the media, and to a rather surprising extent.
Three times in less than three months during 1978 *The New York Times*
featured major articles about the experience of business students and the
kinds of careers that awaited them. The first reported on the Wharton
School, where a third of the graduates were now going into banking and
finance, and where beginning salaries had risen nearly 14 percent in just one
year. The second article, a more general one, was headed "Students Are
Bullish About the MBA." It noted the more than ninefold increase in MBA
degrees in the sixteen years from 1960 to 1976, the great growth especially
in the number of part-time students, and the 20 percent to 25 percent pay
differential between master's and bachelor's degree holders in business. Finally, an article headed "Harvard MBA: A Golden Passport" was mainly
devoted to interviews with students who were looking forward to lucrative
careers. Salaries offered Harvard graduates had risen an incredible 60 percent in just six years, and alumni from ten years earlier were now averaging
an impressive fifty six thousand dollars a year. Figures like these are enough
by themselves to explain the attention being accorded to graduate business students.[38]

Rankings. Since business schools were so much in the news, it was probably inevitable that someone should try to find out which schools were the best. The movement started slowly, early in the 1970s, but by the end of the decade it had become something like a national pastime.

In 1973 two Columbia University researchers undertook a survey to find out which professional schools, in the opinion of deans, led all the others in their fields. They asked deans to list the best schools and then counted to see which were named most often. "We assumed that the deans, as the leading officers of each school, have the knowledge and experience for these evaluations," they wrote—an assumption that later was strongly called into question. Harvard, Stanford, Chicago, Wharton, and Carnegie Mellon led the list.[39]

At almost exactly the same time two Georgia State University professors came up with a rating system based on the number of articles published in major journals by faculty members from different universities. They counted articles in the leading journals in accounting, finance, marketing, "management sciences," and "administrative science" and thereby derived a list of the "Twenty Leading American Schools of Business and Commerce." Since the survey did not take into account the widely diverging sizes of business schools, those with very large faculties had an obvious advantage. Thus, two campuses of the University of California—Berkeley and Los Angeles— came out on top, while Harvard ranked fourteenth and Carnegie Mellon seventeenth. *The New York Times* noted the unfairness of the survey and suggested conducting it instead on a per capita basis. No one suggested, however, that other criteria such as quality of education or number of distinguished alumni would make more satisfactory ways of rating business schools.[40]

Six months later, two Columbia University students published a ranking of business schools by a criterion considerably closer to their own interests—the employability of graduates. They simply asked corporate recruiters to name the schools they considered best, and the ones most mentioned made up the "top 12" list. Harvard ranked first and Stanford second, and Chicago, Columbia, the Amos Tuck School, the Wharton School, and MIT tied for third. (Others on the list were California at Berkeley, Carnegie-Mellon, Michigan, and Virginia in fourth place, and New York University in fifth.)[41]

At the end of 1974, *MBA* magazine published a survey—the first of what became an annual feature—in which business schools were ranked not solely by academic or employment criteria but by a combination. Surveying both deans and current and recently graduated MBA students, the magazine asked them to rate schools by academic quality and, separately, by employment value. In the resulting "combined academic-employment ranking" for all respondents, Harvard, Stanford, Chicago, Wharton, and MIT's Sloan School led the list. In one (and only one) category, academic quality, Stanford was listed above Harvard. This poll attracted only a small amount of attention, and no one seems to have asked the obvious question about how students, or even deans, at one school would know anything about either the academic quality or the employment value of another school.[42]

The second annual survey, however, attracted more attention and did elicit criticism. The poll showed Stanford, Chicago, and the Sloan School as the top three, and Harvard fourth, leading *The New York Times* to headline that Harvard was "slipping." But many of the deans who responded to the survey criticized the entire concept as well as the method. Several people questioned the need for ranking at all, and both the lack of specific criteria and the omission of many smaller, regional schools were singled out for criticism.[43]

But the ranking craze was not to be stopped by criticism. Three separate surveys, each with its own special method, appeared during 1976. Professors from Oregon State and Wisconsin conducted a survey in which professors in each field—accounting, finance, marketing, management science/operations research, and organizational theory and behavior—identifed what they considered to be the outstanding schools in the field. The resulting lists, although more complicated, contained few surprises. Stanford, Harvard, and Chicago led, in one or another order, in nearly all categories. By asking professors rather than employers or recent graduates, this survey clearly allied itself with evaluation of the academic quality.[44]

Later in the year a prominent banker declared that a strong microeconomics program was the key to a good MBA, and he went on to rank business schools according to his perception of their quality in microeconomics. The resulting highly eccentric list—Chicago and the Sloan School first, Rochester fourth, London ninth, and Stanford not ranked—surprisingly provoked no responses, probably because its focus was too obviously narrow for it to be taken seriously.[45]

This year, when *MBA* magazine came out with its annual December survey, the method had been changed. Readers as well as deans were now asked to rank schools, and the two criteria were "quality" and "reputation." The results, as the magazine noted, were very likely to be skewed in favor of larger and older schools which had the most graduates, but again the list contained few surprises, as Stanford, Harvard, and Chicago led the rankings.[46]

The ratings game expanded during 1977 and attracted some critics. Two surveys early in the year ranked Canadian universities and also, strangely, the MBA programs at schools that grant doctorates in business. Later, a Wharton student wrote an article about how Wharton students all suffered from a "Harvard complex" because Harvard always outranked Wharton in the surveys. The annual end-of-the-year ranking in *MBA* magazine again placed Stanford first and Harvard second, and the results were widely noted in the media. *The New York Times* took the ratings very seriously and even suggested that Harvard was instituting changes in order to climb back into first place.

But two prominent academic people voiced sharp criticism. Harvard professor Theodore Levitt pointed out that Harvard's reliance on the case method places great demands on the professors and causes them to spend less of their efforts on writing scholarly articles—thus making them less visible to their counterparts at other universities. Adherence to the case method, he argued, was the main reason for the Harvard Business School's greatness, but the survey method of *MBA* magazine projected the opposite conclusion. A month later the dean at the University of Chicago severely denounced the magazine's methods also, pointing out that the market, not the opinion of professors, should be the sole determinant of quality.[47]

The mania for ranking thus had grown from its small beginnings in 1973 to a major event by 1978, despite shortcomings that should have been obvious to everyone. But two major conclusions do emerge from the experience. One is the revelation that no one—neither the students, nor the schools, nor the public—had yet decided just what the purpose of a business school was. Was it to rank highly in academic circles because of its scholarly production, or was it instead to get good jobs for its graduates? And the second conclusion is that graduate business education, an insignificant side activity just twenty years earlier, had become so important that a large segment of the American public now paid attention to it. It would have been inconceivable that major magazines and newspapers would devote articles to a ranking of schools of anthropology or social work, but schools of business had now come strongly into their own as subjects considered newsworthy by all.

International Attention

The boom being experienced by American business schools attracted attention overseas as well, and their influence was clearly evident in many countries. Toward the middle of the decade, however, reaction set in as the schools in other countries grew stronger and felt less need to imitate American models.

U.S. Influence. For a long time European business schools had not been noted for much of anything. With the exception of INSEAD in France, CEI and IMEDE in Switzerland, Cranfield and Henley in Britain, and IESE in Spain, they had mostly been low-profile, low quality, non-degree-granting institutions that offered only short-term courses on specific aspects of business.

Beginning sometime in the late 1960s, however, this situation changed, partly due to grants by the Ford Foundation for the purpose of strengthening European business schools. By 1971 *Business Week* could report a sudden boom, as older schools revitalized and new ones were founded, many times under the direction of prominent Americans. Business professors from

Wharton, Harvard, Stanford, and Carnegie-Mellon, for example, took temporary or permanent positions at INSEAD, IMEDE, CEI, the West Berlin Institute of International Management, and the European Institute for Advanced Studies in Management in Brussels. The high reputation of American schools was bolstered by comments such as the one from an engineer who said that two years at Harvard Business School had given him the equivalent of ten years of experience in French industry. Even the great enemy, Russia, recognized that it could learn from America. Early in 1971 it held a conference of Russian and American managers in Kiev to learn about human relations in management. Up to that point, "management" in Russia had meant simply properly organized production; awareness of concern for a worker's motivation and welfare was only slowly dawning.[48]

Reaction Against U.S. Influence. Although American influence continued to be strongly evident all the way through the 1970s (in Israel for example), a strong sense of independence from America became the dominant theme by about 1973. One notable attack on servile imitation of American models came from an American, the Wharton School's D. F. Berry, who was serving as director of INSEAD, near Paris. Arguing that only experience can teach business and that business schools therefore must teach only the language and style of business, he urged European schools to take their lessons from European society, not from remote and inapplicable elite American models. His voice was one among an increasing number of Europeans who argued that in fact their brand of management education was already better than that practiced in the United States.[49]

At almost exactly the same time, the London School of Business was making a similar break from traditional models. Under the direction of an American-educated Briton, it began introducing more flexibility and more innovation into its programs and establishing more connections with business on the European continent. Long known as an imitator, it was now becoming an innovator as it tried to escape from the ivory tower model and close the "notorious gap" between education and industry.[50]

Other overseas business schools were likewise innovating toward the middle of the decade. INSEAD established a program in which ninety or more executives from a single company were brought to the campus eight times over a two-year period for two-week seminars focusing on the organization rather than on individual needs. In India the Jamnalal Bajaj Institute of Management Studies (with help from a Ford Foundation grant) abandoned traditional models—"colonialism in disguise"—and stressed practicality through fieldwork.

In South Africa, as noted earlier, the University of Stellenbosch not only required a fieldwork component but placed it chronologically first in the curriculum. And in Great Britain, the University of Manchester took on the role of international education center, bringing to its campus students from all over the world—including Venezuela, Nigeria, Turkey, and Hong Kong—for "a progressively international programme of business education."[51]

These examples serve to illustrate the increasing independence of worldwide business education programs from the American models that had dominated them earlier. By the middle of 1976 the independence was evident in another way also. The *Wall Street Journal* reported a distinct decline in the prestige associated with American MBA degrees among French companies. Although it had for a while been very fashionable for young Frenchmen to come to the United States for their graduate business education, employers in France now clearly preferred graduates of their own universities. Harvard and other universities accordingly were reporting a decline in applications from France. Ironically, the success of American business schools had had the effect of inspiring foreign schools to improve—to the extent that American schools were now less in demand.[52]

GROWTH IN SELF-STUDY

At the same time the nation and the world were paying more attention to business schools, the business schools were paying more attention to themselves. More studies than ever before now began to appear concerning the mission and the management of the schools, as well as the students who attended them.

The Continuing Practical-Theoretical Debate

The question of whether business schools exist to teach students the underlying philosophy of business or to teach them how to do their jobs probably will never be settled to anyone's satisfaction. Certainly it had not been by the 1970s. Early in 1973 UCLA's new dean, the former CEO of the Norton Simon conglomerate, granted a long interview to *The New York Times* in which he argued fervently for increased emphasis on the practical side of instruction. He specifically blamed the 1959 foundation reports for causing business schools to stress theory above all as a way of gaining academic respectability. Now, he said, schools must move back toward practicality, since it does no good to analyze situations or even to identify problems without also knowing how to implement solutions.[53]

Shortly afterward, two other prominent voices from the business world echoed these sentiments exactly. Malcolm Baldrige said "Too many people from B-schools are over-educated and under-experienced," and Ross Perot lamented that MBAs view themselves as "planners, thinkers, consultants, and advisers." They are taught, Perot said, that once they've defined a problem their job is done. "That's the fun part," he concluded, "but solving the problem is more important. Making it happen is the tough nitty-gritty of business."[54]

Three professors undertook a survey of companies in the *Fortune* 500 list and found these pro-practical sentiments to be widespread. Many employers agreed that the post-1959 shift toward the general and theoretical had gone too far, and they now saw the need for less theory and more functional application. They agreed that "broad administrative skills" were desirable, but they also wanted the new graduates to demonstrate considerable knowledge of "functional specialization" in finance, marketing, management, or accounting. Two other professors found similar results when they surveyed employers with reference to the computer skills of new MBAs. Employers found that many of the young graduates were trained in programming but few had sufficient skills in actual business applications.[55]

As the University of Virginia's Darden School celebrated its twentieth year in 1975, its historian confronted this issue in a slightly more analytical way. Whereas other observers had more or less equated the "practical vs. theoretical" dichotomy with the "specialist vs. generalist" one, he separated them. In accord with the other sentiments noted so far, he predicted that the Darden School in the future would become more practical as opposed to theoretical, but at the same time it would, he said, become more generalist as opposed to specialist. Attempts to define these approaches in the abstract are apt to produce only sterile debating exercises, as one struggles to identify exactly what a practical generalist would be. But at least the implication is clear that to some minds practicality did not mean excessive specialization.[56]

In 1977 the practical-theoretical issue was the subject of a debate between two leaders in business education, former SMU dean C. Jackson Grayson and University of Washington dean Kermit O. Hanson. Grayson claimed that executives find that young MBAs are characterized by—among other faults—too much talk and not enough action, too much theory and not enough practice, inability to carry through, and inability to design plans and achieve goals. Pointing out that grades in MBA school show no correlation with later success, he argued that business schools are focusing on the wrong rewards and incentives. Whereas managers want employees who can do something, schools are turning out graduates who can only think. The schools should instead become more responsive to their students' needs rather than the faculty's needs, by such actions as emphasizing relevant rather than theoretical research and rewarding practice-oriented behavior as much as scholarly academic behavior. Faculty members, Grayson said, usually operate from hypothetical solutions rather than from actual problems. They say, "Here is a concept or technique that I find exciting. I hope you find it useful." Instead, they should be saying "What are your problems? Maybe I can be of some help." He went on to accuse universities and the AACSB itself of standing in the way of innovation out of fear that they would be reducing business education to a trade-school level. Yet such practically is approved of and expected in other fields, he argued. It would be inconceivable to have a medical school in which professors have never practiced medicine and students have no hands-on training.[57]

Hanson's reply relied mainly on two points: that the tension or dialogue between the practicality that business wants and the theory that universities can provide is very valuable and productive, and that, because of this dual emphasis, business schools had become much more respectable in recent years to both the business and the academic community. While acknowledging that a proper balance between theory and practice is difficult to define or attain, he felt that business schools were doing well at it in their present state. And he also dismissed as a myth the accusation that AACSB inhibited universities.[58]

Public sentiment seems to have been more on Grayson's side. In the same year that this debate appeared in the *Wharton Magazine,* the Wharton School was founding the Busch Center for Research, as described earlier, and the next year the University of Chicago announced a totally practical marketing course in which students were to design and market a new product for the Kraft Foods Co. About that same time, two businessmen conducted a survey of alumni of the operations research department at Case Western University in order to find out what they thought of their education. Overwhelmingly the alumni felt that the curriculum contained too much theory and too little practice—that they had learned the tools but not how to make them work. A good addition to their education, they said, would have been regular lectures by on-the-job practicing managers.[59]

Increased Attention to the Management of Business Schools

Although the evidence is somewhat sketchy, the 1970s seem to have marked a distinct advance in the art of managing schools of management. Before the decade began, few observers had paid much attention to the specific problems of managing a business school. Now that business schools had become a big business in themselves, such studies began appearing frequently.

The fact that business schools had been long operating blindly and in a vacuum, with no clear idea of what they should be doing or how to do it, was clearly illustrated as late as 1971, when the Confederation of British Industry announced, together with the British Institute of Management, another massive survey of businesses to find out exactly what it was that they wanted from business schools. The specific event that gave rise to this effort was the previously mentioned embarrassing episode at which a speaker used the royal dedication of a new business school building as an occasion to lambast business schools in general for their irrelevance and incompetence.

The mere fact that such a survey was the establishment's response to the incident is the most revealing part of the whole affair. Ever since the very earliest years, before 1920, business schools had been surveying businesses, asking them to send in question and problems, and inviting executives to come in and describe their needs. More than fifty years of such activities had produced nothing but platitudes and unexceptionable truisms, yet schools, having developed little philosophy of mission on their own, still at this date knew nowhere else to turn for guidance than to industry itself.[60]

This situation soon began changing. Early in 1975 a Pennsylvania State University professor published results of a different kind of survey. In it alumni who had become executives were asked to rank thirteen stated goals in importance, and their ranking was compared with that of professors. The comparison (Ill. 11–4) showed surprisingly strong general agreement, but nonetheless it did document for the first time the intuitive expectation that on-the-job executives would tend to rank practical matters higher and theoretical matters lower than faculty members would. "Developing an understanding of the political, social, and economic environment of business" ranked fifth-highest with the professors but only eleventh with the executives, while "providing realistic knowledge about the business world," which the executives ranked fifth, scored eleventh with the professors. "Getting things done" and handling oneself under fire similarly ranked much higher with the executives than with the professors.[61]

A few months later Dean Paul Gordon of the Indiana University Graduate School of Business wrote an article in which he listed ten ongoing problems that face management education. Written in response to a superficial diatribe denouncing American business education as vastly inferior to European, the article is important because of its focus on the enormous gaps that existed (and still exist) in the whole philosophy of educating people for business.

With reference to the subject of business education, for example, Gordon pointed out that although people had long recognized that the categories of "unique" and "universal" do not include all management thought, little progress has been made on identifying the intermediate areas. In the early days of business schools, educators had operated on the assumption that business knowledge was of only two kinds—subjects uniquely applicable only to a particular job, and those universally applicable to all business management. Now that theorists and practitioners had finally recognized that not everything which is not unique is therefore universal—that there is, in short, no set of "management principles" that can be taught to people to qualify them equally well for positions in every field of business—a great deal of work had to be undertaken on determining the nature and boundaries of the third category, whatever it might be. This acknowledgement—that "management science" either does not exist or at least is not very comprehensive—marked

GOALS OF MBA SCHOOLS, RANKED IN ORDER OF IMPORTANCE BY EXECUTIVES AND EDUCATORS

GOAL	RANK BY EXECUTIVES	RANK BY EDUCATORS
Developing skill in problem identification	1	1
Developing skill in arriving at creative solutions to problems	2-3-4	2-3
Developing skill in written and oral communications	2-3-4	2-3
Developing skills in implementing decisions, getting things done	2-3-4	8-9
Providing realistic knowledge about the business world	5-6	8-9
Developing analytical abilities	5-6	4-5-6
Developing skill in how to handle oneself "under fire"	7	11
Education for eventual upper-middle or top management	8	4-5-6
Developing leadership skills	9-10	10
Providing concepts and tools for self-education throughout the career	9-10	7
Developing an understanding of political, social, and economic environment of business	11	4-5-6
Education for starting level positions	12	12-13
Building enthusiasm, a spirit, for a career in management	13	12-13

Source: MSU Business Topics, 23 (Spring 1975), 41-47.

a notable departure from what people had been saying just a few years earlier.

With respect to the business community itself, Gordon made similarly incisive and startling observations. For one thing, he pointed out what should have been obvious years earlier—that no evidence existed to indicate that business had any idea what kind of education it needed. Moreover agreement was absolutely lacking on the three most basic questions of all: how to change individuals, how to change organizations, and—most tellingly—what kinds of change may be desirable. Finally, very basic questions relating to the place of business in society—social responsibility, political action, executive and personal ethics both in and out of organizational life, and the legitimacy of corporate power—were, Gordon noted, still utterly unanswered.

Reaching some kind of resolution regarding all these problems and questions was clearly, as Gordon pointed out, prerequisite to evaluating the quality of management education in America or anywhere else. Such a point of view, although it was beginning to seem reasonable 1976 and today seems entirely obvious, would have been unimaginable in the 1950s or 1960s, when business education was enjoying a golden age, unbeset by any doubts or critical self-analysis.[62]

By 1978 rumblings of discontent could be heard concerning the practical side of business school operations as well. As employers fell in line to pay more for MBA holders, schools offering quick and cheap MBAs began popping up everywhere. As noted earlier, one report stated that thirty-five new MBA programs were being started every year, or one every ten days. In the Washington, D.C., area, mostly because the government and the military gave automatic raises and promotions to employees who earned MBAs, no fewer than fifty such programs were operating. The University of Beverly Hills was offering an MBA for $1,800, and for an extra $500 it would waive the bachelor's degree requirement. Within the schools, resources were not keeping up with increased enrollments, and student/faculty ratios were rising by more than 30 percent. The turnover rate among business school deans reached 20 percent a year, the highest among all deans and twice the 1968 rate. Such developments had begun to happen more or less while no one was noticing, and it was only now, with the increased self-study that was occurring, that any alarms began to sound.[63]

Increased Attention to Students and Graduates

Newspapers and magazines also turned their spotlights on MBA students, this new breed of energetic young businessmen and businesswomen who seemed to offer both themselves and their country the brightest of futures. An altogether unprecedented amount of coverage suddenly began to be devoted to the questions of who these students were, what they were study-ing, and where they chose to work—along with how much they made.

Who They Were. Until the second half of the 1970s no one much noticed the characteristics of the young people who were filling the business schools in unheard-of numbers. These numbers, however, along with the apparently unlimited prosperity they encountered after graduation, made more notice inevitable. A *Business Horizons* article in 1976 pointed out the interesting fact that the average age of MBA students, unlike that of other graduate students, was not declining—meaning that more businesspeople in their 30s and 40s were recognizing the value the degree offered them. Confirmation came in a 1978 *Wall Street Journal* article showing that twice as many stu-dents now had work experience as in the late 1960s. An economic explana-tion of this change was reported in a study that compared the financial benefits of full-time and part-time MBA study and concluded that part-time actually paid off better in the long run.[64]

Much more comprehensively, a major *Fortune* article in 1977 analyzed the current MBA students and found them the best ever—partly because the schools, with the increasing demand, were able to be more selective, but also because the students themselves were more realistic in their expec-tations, showing less impatience and egocentricity than in the past. Empha-sizing the newly coined phrase "fast track," the article noted how students were seeking high visibility above almost all other considerations. Having chosen investment banking for that reason in the 1960s, they more recently had been choosing consulting; now, however, the investment business was making a comeback. Whatever they studied and wherever they chose to work, it was becoming increasingly plain that the MBA degree was "the ticket required for the executive suite."[65]

Other studies had a more specific focus. One tried to see if any personality and motivational differences could be found between male and female MBA students—and concluded that not many differences existed but those that did were in women's favor. Another created a complex model for predicting new students' choices of business schools. Besides the expected determi-nants like cost and location, the authors found that published rankings of schools and the reported starting salaries of graduates did have an impact on students' decisions.[66]

Course Choices. Some attention also was paid to shifts in students' cur-ricular tastes. At Harvard, Investment Management, the *Wall Street Journal* reported, declined in enrollment from 445 students in 1972 to a mere 100 by 1975, while Corporate Financial Management rose from 400 to 600 and courses in corporation financial report analysis and capital markets were increasing even more sharply. As noted earlier, Harvard students also showed a strongly increased interest in small business and even started a Small Business Club on their own initiative.[67]

Jobs and Salaries. More than in the coursework, the nation was interested in what happened to the students after they graduated. In the face of this great amount of interest, any reticence about mentioning successful careers and high salaries entirely vanished. The *Wall Street Journal* reported that all the members of Harvard's class of 1976 had jobs at or soon after graduation and that their average salary was $20,000, compared with $18,000 the previous year. Consulting jobs, averaging $24,000, were the most popular, with commercial banking ($19,000) and investment banking ($20,000) following. *Forbes* reported that, nationwide, the average salary was $26,620 and further noted that the average undergraduate business student earned only $10,644—a differential that had doubled in a decade. *The New York Times* called Harvard's MBA degree a "golden passport" and cited figures to prove it: in the six years from 1972 to 1978 starting salaries had risen over 37 percent, and alumni out of school for ten years were earning, on average, $56,000. Women MBAs came in for a share of the attention also: *Fortune* reported that after only five years on the job, Harvard's first women graduates were earning $32,250.[68]

A University of Chicago professor took the study further by analyzing in great statistical depth the factors that affect starting salary offers. He found that salaries were positively associated with work experience and grade point average, and therefore that black students, who tended to have more experience, received higher offers, while women, who tended to have less, received lower ones. Other factors, such as field of study (accounting lower, consulting higher) and region of the country (New York City higher, overseas lower) did matter also.[69]

THE GREAT SUCCESS OF MBA HOLDERS

Indeed, the one major driving force behind the media's sudden attention to business schools was, as one would expect, the amazing success of their graduates. Critics might doubt, from a theoretical viewpoint, whether business skill could be or should be taught, but the high salaries that young MBAs were earning were indisputably there for all to see.

Figures have to be used with caution, since different observers rarely presented exactly the same ones. The same year when *MBA* magazine declared it "the best year in a decade" and *Nation's Business* noted an "upswing in the MBA market," *Business Week* was calling it "a cold market for new MBAs," the bleakest in four years. But in general everyone saw the news for the second half of the 1970s as unprecedentedly good.[70]

In 1974 Harvard's new MBA salaries were averaging around $20,000, up 5 percent or more from the previous year. In 1975 *Dun's* called the recruiters' efforts to hire MBAs a "scramble," and *Business Week* noted the 8 percent rise in salaries and said that MBAs could continue to get jobs when nobody else could. The following year, with the recession ending, salaries rose between 6 percent and 10 percent, and some schools reported that each graduate was receiving three job offers. By 1977 the news was uniformly good and widely noticed. *The New York Times* called it the best year ever, and salaries were reported to have risen 10 percent or 11 percent. Harvard salaries reached a $25,931 average by 1978, the year *The New York Times* called the degree a "golden passport." The same year, the Wharton School's salaries passed the $20,000 mark by a wide margin, showing an increase of more than 10 percent in two years. *Forbes* worriedly reported that the consulting business was paying salaries ranging from $25,000 to $40,000 to newly graduated MBAs who had no experience at all.[71]

As noted, all reticence about mentioning salaries was long gone by now. Placement offices regularly released such information to the press, and catalogs and other recruiting materials listed salaries prominently. Between 1972 and 1978, *Business Week, Forbes, Dun's, Institutional Investor*, the *Journal of Business, International Management, MBA, The New York Times*, and the *Wall Street Journal* published more than twenty-five articles stating salary figures from various schools of business. When one school's figures were featured in an article, a subsequent issue frequently would report another school's figures, which obviously had been supplied by the second school in an effort to keep up with the competition. Little was heard now about contributing to the welfare of society or to the strength of the nation. The selling point in the 1970s was money.

As a result of these figures and the publicity accorded them, graduate business schools experienced a great increase in applications. *Business Week* justly called it a "stampede." Eleven major schools surveyed reported that applications rose from fewer than 15,000 in 1972 to over 25,000 just three years later. The University of Chicago experienced a 35 percent increase in applications in 1975, the Amos Tuck School a 50 percent increase, and the University of California at Berkeley 60 percent; nationwide, takers of the Admission Test for Graduate Study in Business increased 45 percent in three years. On the undergraduate level, business majors, already the largest group, were reported to have increased between 20 percent and 30 percent in just two years. No one could ever doubt again that business education prospers during recessionary times. *The New York Times* and the *Wall Street Journal*, as well as *MBA Magazine*, all acknowledged that people were going to school because of the recession: since jobs were going only to the most qualified applicants, young people might as well use this period of joblessness to get the qualifications.[72]

Two other factors, both impossible to measure, may have contributed to the precipitous rise in the popularity of the graduate business schools. One was an improved attitude toward business among young people, as Vietnam began fading in their memories and the desire for normality reasserted itself. Antibusiness protests, still plentiful and loud in 1972, were far less common by 1975. The other factor, probably much more important, was the tuition-

payment policies adopted by corporations around the early part of the decade. As the MBA had grown in esteem, businesses decided that it was in
their interest to encourage their employees to return to school part-time and
earn the degree, and so they agreed to subsidize part or all of the cost of
the education. This is a subject worthy of a full study by itself, but whatever
the specific details it is inevitable that the policy of granting such subsidies
must have had a substantial effect on enrollments.[73]

THE OMINOUS RISE OF CRITICISM

The 1970s were indeed a golden age for the MBA, but not absolutely
everything had been positive. Critical voices, although not loud ones, had
been heard all along, expressing doubts about the value of the degree from
the individual's and the employer's points of view, and about the appropriate-
ness from the university's.

Poor Preparation for a Career

Early in the decade the *Harvard Business Review* rather surprisingly published an article critical of business schools. The surprise lay in the fact
that the criticisms were aimed at debunking claims most business schools
had never made. As earlier chapters of this book have demonstrated, it had
long been acknowledged that good grades in business school showed no
correlation with business success later, but the article trumpeted such observations as if they were new discoveries:

> How effectively a manager will perform on the job cannot be predicted by the
> number of degrees he holds, the grades he receives in school, or the formal
> management education programs he attends. Academic achievement is not a valid
> yardstick to use in measuring management potential.

Yet instead of concluding that management skills, not being a cognitive
matter, are incapable of measurement by grades, the article went on, with
dubious logic, to lay the blame squarely on the schools:

> Managers are not taught in formal education programs what they most need to
> know to build successful careers in management.

The clear implication was that MBA school did not make any contribution
to the career prospects of an aspiring young business executive. These observations received wide exposure through Great Britain's *Economist,*
which reported them to a worldwide audience the following week.[74]

The British, in fact, seem either to have been disposed to criticism of business education or else to have had such poor luck with it they had more to criticize. Ten years after the Franks Report (mentioned in chapter 9), several observers took a moment to observe the state of business education in Britain, and they did not like what they saw. The *Sunday Telegraph* accused the schools of perpetrating "something very close to a confidence trick," and no one came forward to advance any significant evidence to rebut the charge. Sir Arnold Weinstock, managing director of the GEC, declared that schools were useless since "management skill" consists mainly of judgment and therefore can't be taught. A survey of CEOs, conducted by *The Director* magazine in 1974, showed tacit agreement: in listing requirements for new executives over the next twenty-five years, not one of them even mentioned business schools. Whatever claims were being made elsewhere about the boost that an aspiring young executive could get from earning a business degree, it's clear that this opinion was not universally shared.[75]

Irrelevant to Employers

Further evidence of problems in Britain came when the two main business schools, Manchester and London, undertook to raise seven and a half million pounds from British industry. The effort led to such grumbling that the British Institute of Management set up a commission to find out the sources of dissatisfaction. The panel's report, "Business School Programmes" (June 1971), made the usual criticisms about the students, the curriculum, the instructors, and the graduates. The students were of low caliber and had no business experience. The courses offered had little orientation toward actual tasks or real life conditions; instead of production, marketing, and industrial relations they concentrated heavily on finance. The instructors, like the students, were perceived as not especially bright, and they often had almost no real business experience. Yet the graduates emerging from this unhealthy situation were cocky and pushy, as if they had actually learned something that put them ahead of the people who had been working hard in industry for years.[76]

In the United States, relations between schools and businesses were far better, but even here some occasional discontent surfaced. One of Chicago's largest financial institutions, the Harris Bank, announced in April 1977 that it would no longer hire MBAs. Its reasons were that its in-house training programs produced all the people it needed, and further that new MBA holders were simply too expensive: whereas new bachelor's degree holders could be hired at $9,000 to $12,000, new MBAs were commanding $16,000.[77]

University Critics

Finally, relations between the brashly successful business schools and their tradition-bound mother institutions continued to show occasional signs of strain. In Britain, one commentator stated flatly, "No university likes a business school." Although such a statement might have been too strong for America, plenty of caustic American observers were in evidence. Yale University's outspoken chaplain, William Sloan Coffin, denounced the founding of a business school there, saying that the university should be feeding the hungry rather than creating a school dedicated to increasing business profits. At almost the same time, the *Harvard Educational Review* published an article denouncing career education as contrary to the mission of a university, and Cornell University's business dean stated outright that universities still regarded business schools as disreputable.

In a *New York Times* opinion article, Amherst College English professor Benjamin DeMott elaborated on the conflict between academic purists and utilitarians by pointing out three problems that the utilitarian view caused: (1) students and schools were showing blind faith in "hot" subjects which would inevitably cool later; (2) meanwhile weaker-appeal subjects were being banished, in effect permanently, from the curriculum; and (3) college administrations tended to believe in parity or equality of one subject with another—three credits of marketing were, to them, the same as three credits of philosophy, history, Shakespeare, or any other traditional subject. Such sentiments, no matter how well reasoned and expressed, thus were never quite absent from the scene. But they were drowned out by the overwhelming voice of the majority.[78]

Business Schools as a Cash Cow

Universities began to notice, sometime during the 1970s, that business schools offered a source of revenue unlike anything else available. As far back as 1928 (as noted in chapter 4), H. L. Mencken had mentioned the fact that business schools were profitable:

All of these shrines of scientific business seem to be making money. Indeed, next to football teams and schools of education, they are probably the biggest money getters in the world of intellect. At some places, as at New York University for example, it's only the takings of the School of Commerce that enable the Chancellor to pay the university's bills.[79]

By the 1970s business schools had become so successful that universities were turning to them for support in an altogether unprecedented extent. This new policy created a major source of unhappiness for business schools, since it virtually destroyed any incentive they had for raising money. The problem loomed so large, in fact, that it was addressed at the AACSB meeting in 1975. Columbia University had required its business school to turn over $750,000 of tuition to the central administration in 1973, $1,200,000 in

1974, and an astonishing $1,700,000 in 1975, a 227 percent increase in two years. As a result, the business school's dean resigned after only two years, and the issue came to national attention in the ensuing publicity. By early 1978, *Business Week* reported, it had become standard for business schools to be allocated only 30 percent of the money they generated, and the percentage would probably have been still lower if deans had not stood firm at that figure.[80]

PROPHECIES OF DOOM

Predictions that the MBA was soon destined to collapse were more common at this time than ever before. One reason may have been the criticisms mentioned earlier; another may have been the inequitable financing arrangements just described, which seemed to suggest that the business program existed less for business than for the purpose of supporting the rest of the university. But beyond any doubt, the biggest reason for the dire predictions was simply the phenomenal growth the degree had experienced. No educational segment had ever grown like that, and many people quite understandably doubted that it could continue.

In the early part of the decade the warnings mainly concerned the economics: too big a supply would depress the salary level. *Nation's Business,* the national Chamber of Commerce magazine, suggested (perhaps hopefully) that the growing supply of MBAs might keep salaries low, and a *Harvard Business Review* article in 1974 noted with alarm the increase in starting MBA salaries and worried that MBA holders would soon price themselves out of the market.[81]

The later part of the decade featured more general statements of doom. Dean Fouraker of Harvard was among the first, in 1977, with a dire prediction that, because tuition was rising faster than salaries, "there will be a collapse in the 1980s." Even *MBA* magazine suffered from the same fears. As concern mounted that the National Defense Student Loan program was about to be eliminated, the magazine asked "Will the MBA Balloon Burst If the Feds Cut Student Loans?"—and the comparison with a balloon suggests little confidence in the degree's durability.[82]

During 1978 alone five separate major predictions of an MBA glut made the news. The College Placement Council, *Business Week,* and a major executive recruitment firm all warned of a coming surplus. A mathematics professor at Carnegie-Mellon constructed a model that showed a forthcoming decline in enrollments, and *The New York Times* noted that schools everywhere were studying their curricula to find new ways of attracting students.[83]

One other observer, however—a business and economics professor at Indiana University—dismissed all such predictions. Declaring that the future would be determined not by statistics but by the policies of the schools, he pointed out several trends that would, in his estimation, keep the MBA degree alive and healthy. Most important was the fact that the degree had become the "ticket of admission" to business. Since the previous generation of MBAs had by now been promoted to the senior manager level, they were hiring more people with the same credentials, and thus the degree was becoming self-perpetuating. In addition, he noted growth in three sectors— international students, part-time students, and students interested in the public and not-for-profit sectors. Together, he said, these developments indicated a growth far greater than anyone would predict from simple extrapolation of statistics.[84]

* * *

He was correct. For one more whole decade the MBA was to continue its phenomenal growth, so that half the MBA degrees ever awarded were to be granted in the next twelve years. A storm of criticism was brewing, but, for a while at least, it was not going to stop the MBA express.

12

1979–1984:
The Critics Turn It On

AFTER a mostly sunny decade, MBA schools suddenly became the objects of a storm of criticism in the early 1980s, with complainers ranging from the new president of Harvard to nearly every business magazine and every major newspaper in the country. Although some of the criticisms had substance to them, most seem to have arisen in reaction to the phenomenal success the schools had enjoyed for so long. Much of the criticism, in fact, was already obsolete by the time it was made, since business schools had been continuously working on self-improvement.

THE CRITICAL ONSLAUGHT AND ITS CAUSES

Criticism of business schools was certainly nothing new, but this time the number of critics and the virulence of their comments caught everyone by surprise. Most of it began in April 1979, when Harvard's President, Derek Bok, wrote a report calling for changes, mainly in the direction of social awareness, in the work of the Harvard Business School. Other sources, some even before Bok's report made the news, were expressing negative opinions about MBA schools, ranging from predictions of a declining market for degree holders to philosophical criticisms about the ethics of the profit motive. During 1979 alone, *Business Week, Management Review,* and *The Wall Street Journal* each featured two major articles critical of business schools, and *The New York Times* published six.

In 1980 those four publications continued to print more unfavorable articles, and they were joined by the *Atlantic, Dun's* (twice), *Management Today, Human Resources Management, Money, Advertising Age,* and especially the *Harvard Business Review.* Beyond any question, the dominant tone of press coverage had changed by the end of that year, from the adulation of the 1970s to a cynical and downbeat attitude.

The next year, 1981, marked the low point, with negative articles about MBA graduates in *Industry Week, Business Week, Management Review,*

Interfaces, Fortune, and *Canadian Business;* attacks on the curriculum in *International Management* and the *Academy of Management Review;* and expressions of disillusion and philosophical disapproval in *The New York Times* and *The New York Times Magazine, Management Today, Interfaces,* and *Canadian Business.*

The barrage continued in 1982 and 1983, with three major critical articles each in *Business Week* and *Interfaces;* two in Britain's *Management Today;* others in *Industry Week, International Management, Institutional Investor, Academy of Management Review, Fortune, Canadian Business, Financial Management, Sloan Management Review,* and *Business and Society Review;* and no fewer than eleven *New York Times* articles denigrating the MBA. By this time it was not unusual to find an article entitled, "Do Business Schools Teach Absolute Rot?"

In 1983 and 1984 the rate of attack began to subside somewhat, although more publications joined in. *Forbes, Business Horizons, Personnel Management,* the *Economist,* and even *Esquire* included jabs at what was perceived to be going on in business schools, along with continued attacks in the other journals.

The reasons for this sudden turnaround in journalistic attitudes—from admiration in the 1970s to contempt in the early 1980s—are interesting to speculate on. Certainly the criticism reported in chapter 11, which expressed dissatisfaction with the MBA from the point or view of employees, employers, and universities, played a part. Another major reason, undoubtedly, was the mere fact of the MBA's stunning, relentless growth. No one believed it could continue to be so successful, and thus everyone was looking for signs of cracks in its structure. Even more important than these, however, was the almost sudden realization that America's competitiveness in world markets had slipped, and the feeling that something specific, such as business schools, must be to blame.

Another reason may have derived from the failure of so many of the innovations of the 1970s to yield anything like the results they had promised. A few of them did survive to become permanent parts of the MBA scene— South Carolina's MBA-by-TV, for example—but most faltered within a decade.

Wharton's triumphantly announced Busch Center (for conducting practical research under contract with industry) limped along for a few years doing research mainly for the Busch firm that underwrote it, and then it quietly folded. Carnegie Mellon never built the television lines that were to carry business instruction into major corporations, and Adelphi University discontinued its commuter train MBA in the early 1980s. MIT's health-care program silently slipped from the catalog; Wharton's Department of Decision Sciences merged with another department; and the many college courses designed to make the humanities more practical almost completely vanished.

The vaunted behavioral science observation rooms, equipped with one-way glass so that students could observe behavior in business meetings, were soon sitting vacant or used as storerooms. People had watched the innovations of the 1970s with great hope; when nothing happened, disillusionment was bound to set in.

THE CRITICISMS

The complaints of critics ranged over the entire spectrum of possibilities, including dissatisfaction with the curriculum, with the schools' whole way of viewing business, and with the attitudes displayed by graduating students. Many critics also pointed to evidence that industry was losing interest in the MBA, and they therefore accused the programs of perpetrating a hoax on students by building up false hopes. And finally, nearly everyone predicted that doomsday was near for the MBA.

An Unresponsive Curriculum

Although a few academic traditionalists might still have been found who sneered at business studies for being mere vocationalism, the overwhelming chorus of critics condemned the studies for the opposite reason—for not being practical enough, for being too theoretical, abstract, and removed from anything that could be put into practical use on the job.

Even a national magazine for consultants, which might have been expected to be more sympathetic with the theoretical approach to business education, editorialized that business schools were too scholarly and sarcastically noted that studies in behavioral science were now widely used as a replacement for line experience. Two prominent journal articles in 1981 and 1982, both by business professors, criticized the schools for elevating theory and ignoring practice, and *The New York Times* noted in mid-1982 that "business school professors don't have much idea what goes on in companies."

A *Fortune* article about the pressures of working in California's Silicon Valley companies observed that new employees with MBAs usually lasted only about seventeen months because, although well educated in the theory, when it came to the daily grind "they can't cope." *Business Week* reported a widespread feeling everywhere that the schools had swung much too far toward the theoretical side.[1]

A more specific variant of this criticism was the growing belief that perhaps no science of "management" actually existed at all. Many people expressed the opinion that one can learn how to manage a specific company or industry but not how to "manage" in the abstract. One feisty commentator, Admiral Hyman Rickover of the U.S. Navy, made that his main point in an address to Columbia University's School of Engineering and Applied Science. "Many who teach 'management' in our universities," he said, "do their students and society a disservice." He went on,

> By focusing on the techniques of "modern management," they promote the idea that by mastering a few simple principles of how to handle people and situations one can become a universal manager, capable of running any job without having to know much about the work to be managed.

A good manager, he continued, has to know specific details of the work being done, in order to be able to maintain control and take responsibility for completion of a job. The notion that one can separate the management of work from the work itself was, in his view, responsible for the widely discussed decline in U. S. productivity.

> In searching for its causes, we should not overlook the impact of the many professional administrators who run large corporations. Though trained in management at our leading universities, they are often unskilled in the technical aspects of the company.[2]

Prof. H. Edward Wrapp of the University of Chicago said similar things in an interview with *Dun's Review*. He expressed contempt for "professional managers," saying, like Rickover, that managers must know the industry in order to be effective. When asked if business schools were to blame, he replied, "Certainly. We have created a monster. . . . The business schools have done more to insure the success of the Japanese and West German invasion of America than any one thing I can think of." The blame, he concluded, should be placed not on capital underinvestment, government interference, or poor attitudes by workers, but directly on the fraudulent science of "management."[3]

When investment banker and novelist Michael M. Thomas was asked by a *New York Times* reporter, "How would you educate people for business careers?," he replied, "I'd close every one of the graduate schools of business and every one of the management consultant firms." He went on to explain, although still answering the question only in a negative way, that

> [p]eople go to the schools for a job, a meal ticket, and management consulting firms consist of people who came right out of those schools. So you have this unedifying spectacle of companies that have gotten into difficulty being presented to by young men and women six months out of business school.[4]

Canadian business writer Andrew Weiner found many similar opinions in his conversations with Canadian industrialists. Whereas companies had dreamed of hiring ready-made managers from the business schools, he wrote, they quickly found that the absence of on-the-job know-how was more serious than the presence of any abstract management theories. Professional managers had good conceptual skills but a shortage of training in nuts and bolts; lots of solutions but no knowledge of how to implement them; too much finance and too little manufacturing and production. Professional management, he concluded, is a myth.[5]

Overemphasis on Finance

Many commentators similarly noticed industry's emphasis on finance rather than manufacturing and placed the blame squarely on the business schools. The most prominent of such attacks was an influential 1980 article in the *Harvard Business Review,* "Managing Our Way to Economic Decline," in which two Harvard professors argued that business schools had taught the principle of maximizing short-term financial returns at the expense of long-term competitiveness. They cited statistics to show that while technical and marketing people were becoming less likely to be chosen as company presidents, finance and legal people were moving up at a far faster rate than ever before. These people's bias toward making money rather than making products, a bias inculcated in business school, was the principal cause of America's economic decline.[6]

These views found a large and sympathetic audience. Nearly two years later, *The New York Times* published a detailed feature about the *Harvard Business Review* article and its authors. In mid-1982 a published satire defined "MBA" as meaning "Make a Buck Anywhere," and by 1984 such criticisms were so widely accepted they even made their way into an article defending the nation's public elementary and high schools. Although many people believed that poor public schooling was the reason for America's decline, the author rejected that view. "The disastrous American emphasis on short-term, bottom-line management," he wrote, "owes less to science classes at Central High than to MBA classes at Harvard."[7]

Two articles in the British journal *Management Today* showed that similar criticisms existed abroad. One expressed puzzlement about why companies kept hiring people trained only in "management by calculator," "management by numbers," or "management by remote control." The other pointed out a vast imbalance in emphasis: at the London Business School, thirty-three people taught finance, as compared to only one in production management and one in industrial relations. Awareness was growing that, wherever business schools grew, productivity began to take second place to profit making.[8]

Underemphasis on Human Relations

Not many American schools had, as London did, only one person teaching industrial relations, but nonetheless the feeling was widespread that Americans too were drastically underemphasizing the human side of busi-

ness. *International Management* magazine reported in 1981 that MBA programs were commonly criticized for doing little to teach interpersonal skills
even though people generally agree that such skills are the basic and essential ingredient of management. *Business Week* echoed the criticism in an
article unfavorably comparing American business with Japan's: whereas
American managers base their decisions on statistics, Japanese managers
base theirs on human considerations and personal relationships.[9]

Such criticisms became more frequent over the next few years. The president of Johns Hopkins called college graduates "highly skilled barbarians,"
and a prominent insurance company executive lambasted the business
schools for teaching "subjects" rather than "people." Another American
professor criticized the schools for emphasizing numbers and computers
rather than people and relationships, and a British professor similarly but
more comprehensively attacked the whole philosophy that schools had been
operating under since the beginning. Instead of teaching such mechanistic
matters as output per man-hour—concepts which, he wrote, had done so
much damage to industrial relations and caused alienation from the work-
place—the schools should be teaching business how to create a climate
for knowledge workers and should be concerned with appropriate career
structures. Management, he concluded, had less to do with academic learning than with vision, leadership, creativity, and attitude.[10]

Indifference to Society

Awareness of the role of business as an instrument of social change was
growing, and business schools were often criticized for not responding to
the challenge. As previously noted, President Bok's 1979 report at Harvard
was aimed mainly at getting the Harvard Business School to think more
deeply about its social responsibility. He called specifically for four important changes: (1) a reconsideration of objectives, especially those not
linked with profit; (2) a study of ethical conflicts that people are likely to
encounter in business; (3) a study of the proper roles of government and
business with respect to each other, especially with regard to matters of
regulation; and (4) a deeper consideration of consumer involvement in corporate affairs. These suggestions, understandably, were widely interpreted
to be hostile to business education, and also to be aimed especially against
Harvard's famed case method. Eight months later the Harvard Associates—
a group of distinguished alumni and corporate supporters—published a reply to Bok in which they defended the school and the case method. Their
defense was so fatuous, however, that it merely served as a hilarious validation of all Bok's criticisms. Other critics likewise said negative things about
the case method, most notably that it emphasized quantitative-based decision making with little regard for social and industrial relations
implications.[11]

Lack of International Scope

Another common criticism held that business schools were too provincial, that they continued teaching business the same way they always had even though business itself had now gone global on an unprecedented scale. *Business Week* noted in 1980 that businesses had grown disillusioned with MBA programs and that a major reason was the weakness of instruction in international matters. Two years later *Interfaces* magazine similarly observed that the failure of schools to prepare students for competition in the international marketplace was one of the biggest causes of the recent outburst of criticism. An alumnus from the Harvard Business School specifically cited the lack of international studies as one of business education's big failings, and *The New York Times* reported in 1982 that the international component in business schools was only then getting started—five years after a report from the American Council on Education that 75 percent of doctoral students in business had had no international coursework at all.[12]

Ambitiousness and Materialism of Graduates

Tensions between older experienced workers and bright young upstarts from schools had always existed, but charges that new MBA graduates had unduly high expectations began to be heard much more often now. One particular complaint was about job-hopping. A prominent executive recruiter in San Francisco observed that MBA graduates had developed a strong network which enabled them to learn how much their classmates were earning and to demand equality or to quit for higher pay elsewhere. Hiring young MBAs was a good investment, he said, but only if the company could hold on to them, and such an outcome was becoming less likely. A widely reported study at the time confirmed his views: MBAs were found to have unrealistically high expectations and self-assessments and were characterized by elitism and chairman-of-the-board complexes. They quit if not quickly promoted, with the result that turnover rates for MBAs were demonstrably higher than for other groups.[13]

A Wharton School professor mollified the criticism somewhat by arguing that job satisfaction and personal fulfillment, rather than mere money, caused most of the job-hopping; in fact, he said, such job-hopping had always existed, but it was not until salaries rose to high levels that companies began to complain about "disloyalty." Whatever the cause, excessive ambition was cited also by executives-in-residence at several graduate business programs: the young graduates, these seasoned businessmen said, had too high expectations about their careers.[14]

General Disillusionment among Employers

Doubts about the value of young MBA holders to their corporate employers became fairly widespread in the early 1980s. Using such terms as "disillu-

sionment," "disenchantment," "disappointment," and—more elegantly—
"demystification," the press reported a wave of negative sentiment that it
found among corporations.

Within a few months of one another toward the end of 1980, the *Wall
Street Journal, Business Week,* and *The New York Times* all reported a
widespread feeling among the business community that the high salaries,
fast pace, and generally poor fit of young MBA employees were creating a
backlash. Undergraduate business students, executives said, were cheaper,
more realistic, and more adaptable. A few months later the senior vice president of American Can Company attacked even more strongly. Saying that
the young MBAs were all identical, all concerned only with quantified risks,
fast paybacks, and short-term results, he accused them of being too well
trained and too well paid to take time out to get experience. Most tellingly,
he pointed out that a recent survey had found that one-sixth of the nation's
1,300 largest companies were run by MBAs, and yet nobody had any evidence that these companies were better managed than the other five-sixths.[15]

By 1983–84, *Fortune, Industry Week,* the *Economist,* and the *Harvard
Business Review* had all run further articles reporting and commenting on
industry's perceived disenchantment with MBA education. Among the spe-
cifics cited were that the young people's pursuit of power irritated senior
employees, that corporations were increasingly beginning to doubt that management ability was teachable, and that the schools were more useful as
screening agencies than as educators. No longer the "wondrous white
knights" of industry, young MBAs were now scorned as "instant wonders"
and "business magicians."[16]

The same problems existed in Great Britain, where the MBA degree was
reported to attract little public notice, and most of that was negative. As in
the United States, graduates were said to know statistics and graphs but not
how to motivate people, and their career expectations were regarded as
unrealistically high. An article in *Management Today* wondered aloud about
why corporations kept hiring the unproven products of business schools.
Noting a widening gap between what businesses wanted and what the
schools actually provided, it forthrightly suggested that companies should
start examining more closely exactly what it was that they were paying for.[17]

A Fraud against Students

Since critics perceived that employers were growing disillusioned with
the graduates of MBA programs, the obvious next steps were to accuse the
schools of perpetrating a fraud on students and to warn the students about
the realities that awaited them.

Writing in *Forbes* magazine, a reporter—who later would join *Business
Week* and become a champion of MBA education—launched an assault on
the programs at all but the prestige schools, and on some of those, too.

Citing advertisements from various schools that called their programs "the right step for your career," "the difference between a job and a career," and "preparation for leadership in tomorrow's business world," he concluded that the MBA was "the most oversold degree in the history of education." He called the MBA a "cruel hoax on 140,000 students" and blamed both colleges and employers for the problem: colleges because they found business programs to be a lifesaving source of revenue, and employers apparently because they could use universities as screening agencies to eliminate the less-serious job applicants and as a replacement for expensive in-house training. To support his contentions, he quoted an executive at General Electric as saying, "It's criminal what has been foisted on young people today," and, even more directly, "There's no value to the MBA degree."[18]

Another reporter in *Forbes* had argued the previous year that the cost of an MBA program to a student was greater than the rewards the student would later realize, mostly because of lost opportunity costs. Yet despite the statistics cited, the author had to acknowledge that the advantages of the degree were rising as the recession came to an end, and as a result her argument was not strongly convincing. Nonetheless it stands as an example of the press's hostility toward business schools.[19]

Finally, the MBA was seen in another report as a fraud from a different perspective—that of the foreign student in the United States. Although the report dealt exclusively with Arab students, its conclusions applied to others also. Following a period in which outstanding students around the world were routinely sent to America for what was regarded as the finest business education available anywhere, a backlash began to set in as the students' home countries observed some unwanted results. With respect to the coursework itself, many observers noted that the concepts being taught were very specific to the American scene and not easily transferrable to other cultures.

With respect to the students, three other problems had surfaced. A substantial number of students were choosing to remain in the West, where lifestyles were more appealing and career opportunities more abundant, and their home countries began to be alarmed at the prospect of a brain drain. Second, those students who did return to their own countries often had problems readjusting, since their training in the United States had raised their professional expectations far beyond what could be attained at home. And finally, many Arab observers were shocked at the erosion, or at best the Westernization, of the returning graduates' moral values. To be sure, some countries did continue to send students to the United States for business training, but the earlier enthusiasm had definitely subsided.[20]

Too Many MBAs

Doomsayers prophesying the end of the MBA's popularity became more common and more vociferous than ever during this period, as would have been expected in view of the avalanche of criticism. During 1979 alone, *Business Week, The New York Times,* and the *Wall Street Journal* all published articles predicting that the market for MBAs would soon be saturated. MBAs were starting to take jobs that formerly required only a bachelor's degree, and the director of one university's placement office predicted that the market for MBAs would be entirely flooded in just four more years. *The New York Times* article—headlined "MBA Rush: That Glitter Isn't All Gold"—warned that the oncoming recession would cause employers to stop paying tuition for their employees and that potential students would no longer see the MBA degree as a guarantee of success. The *Wall Street Journal* even more directly headlined its article "MBA Glut? MBA Recipients, Once Eagerly Sought, Now Eagerly Seek Jobs in Tighter Market." It cited several stories about difficulty finding employment, predicted that many MBA schools would drive themselves out of business by producing a surplus of MBAs, and quoted a Ford Motor Company spokesman as saying "You may find MBAs driving taxicabs."[21]

The following year *Dun's Review, Money* magazine, and *Management Review* all joined in the doomsday prediction, again citing the large number of graduates and the growing disillusionment among corporations. One of the articles concluded that "MBAs have become a luxury many companies have decided they can do without," and two prominent deans agreed, saying they foresaw no market for their MBA graduates. The other two articles based their pessimism on the proliferation of nonaccredited MBA schools, blaming them for having inflated the number of new graduates beyond the absorption capacity of the market.[22]

By 1982 it was beginning to be evident that no glut was going to occur, yet in the first half of that year direful predictions were still abundant. Proclaiming that "The MBA Glut Is Now Hitting the Top 10," *Business Week* cited decreases in internships, recruitment interviews, and salary offers at Harvard, Cornell, Stanford, Chicago, MIT, Virginia, and Wharton. *Fortune* added that "a few discouraging cautionary flags have begun to wave," specifically the lack of significant salary increases for young MBAs in their second, third, and fourth years on the job. Astonishingly, the salaries of Harvard Business School graduates, according to the report, had not increased at all between 1970 and 1980, when adjusted for inflation. *The New York Times* similarly pointed to the alarmingly large number of MBA graduates (up from 5,000 in 1952 to 50,000 in 1982) and to the proliferation of third- and fourth-rate schools, and it added still another observation to support the woeful prediction: that the knowledge taught in MBA schools was now said to be obsolete within five years.[23]

REFORMS ALREADY UNDERWAY

As forceful as some of these criticisms may have sounded at the time, and still sound today, they were in fact obsolete before they were ever made.

The schools themselves had already recognized all the problems that the critics later pointed out, and reforms had been underway for several years.

Real-World Business Involvement

On all levels, from the broadest philosophy of the whole subject to the smallest detail of the curriculum, business schools in the early 1980s underwent what *Business Week* called a "swing to practicality." The involvement with real businesses this time was different from what had caused concern during the Vietnam war period, but it nonetheless was unmistakably growing and becoming a major movement in the schools.

A New Attitude toward Business. Simply on an abstract level some evidence shows that business schools were growing uneasy with the theoretical approach to business that had dominated their work for so long. Admissions decisions, for example, which had long been based principally on undergraduate grades, now began to rely more heavily on work experience, a sign that schools were finally acknowledging the well-known fact that grades are a poor predictor of success. In Great Britain, the example of Henley College of Management, which admitted only full-time managers, was attracting more and more attention. Its approach to education was to take real problems these managers had encountered at their work and to bring theory to bear on them. Such thinking, one Henley professor forcefully argued, should underlie all management education everywhere. Instead of consisting of theory with practice added, it should consist basically of practical work with theory added where needed.[24]

The American Management Association had been thinking along similar lines, and in 1980 it undertook a new kind of MBA program, the first truly innovative one to appear in half a century. Instead of teaching business as a cognitive subject consisting of information to be learned, it viewed its job as developing certain skills, or "competencies," that managers need in business. After considerable research, the program's founders identified four categories of competency—goal and action management, directing subordinates, human resource management, and leadership—and they designed tests and instructional modules to evaluate and develop the nineteen competencies that fell into these categories (Ill. 12–1). The advocates of the program—which turned out its first graduate in 1982—constantly stressed that the program was output oriented, unlike every other program in existence, and that it emphasized skills, not knowledge. They confidently predicted that the concept would surely be adopted by management educators everywhere.[25]

More Practical Curriculum. Curricular changes reflected the new concern for practicality. Some of the changes, however, were very reminiscent of the early decades of business study: courses in retailing, for example, which had been out of fashion since the 1940s, began to grow again, although

Illustration 12-1:

THE 19 COMPETENCIES IN THE AMA's COMPETENCY-BASED MBA PROGRAM

Accurate Self-Assessment

Conceptualization

Concern with close relationships

Concern with impact

Developing others

Diagnostic use of concepts

Efficiency orientation

Logical thought

Managing group process

Perceptual objectivity

Positive regard

Proactivity

Self-confidence

Self-control

Spontaneity

Stamina and adaptability

Use of oral presentations

Use of socialized power

Use of unilateral power

Source: Richard Boyatzis, <u>The Competent Manager</u> (New York: Wiley, 1982), p. 269.

not necessarily to any great prominence. Likewise at the University of Maryland a new program in "practical humanities"—featuring courses such as Law and Ethics of Business, Analysis and Problem Solving for Business, and the History of Business and Financial Institutions—actually differed little from curricula of an earlier era.[26]

Much more significant change toward practicality came in the form of new emphasis on manufacturing and production courses. After years of taking second place to finance, production experienced a surge of interest in the early 1980s, rising from attracting a mere 5.1 percent of the students at Harvard Business School in 1982 to an astonishing 28 percent the very next year. Although the pay was generally lower in production jobs, new technology was making the work more interesting and challenging, and professors—especially those who had ties to real-life manufacturing businesses—were encouraging students in that direction. In addition, industry itself was now more likely than before to promote people from production and manufacturing areas into its executive ranks.[27]

Student Participation in Business. Nearly every major university had by this time established some sort of arrangement through which students could actively participate in a business while still enrolled in school. Most such arrangements took the form of student consulting teams, in which advanced MBA students were sent to study and resolve a real problem in a real company. Rutgers University, Brigham Young University, and the University of Southern California had established programs of this kind early on, and other schools had followed until "field-work" existed quite widely. Columbia revived the old "alternating work and study" idea that the University of Cincinnati had pioneered back in the 1910–1920 period and made it an option for MBA students, although it was apparently not widely used. Interestingly, European schools were making even more use of student consulting programs than American schools were, since apparently the Europeans felt no ethical concern about using university resources in support of private business.[28]

Colleges Reach into the Business Community. Even where the arrangements were less formal than an actual consulting team, business students were widely involved in some degree of participation in real business. Students at the University of California at Berkeley, for example, received credit from the university for attending executive meetings at Kaiser Aluminum, and students in Prof. Farok Contractor's international business class at Rutgers University worked with small domestic firms to show them how to become exporters. Entire MBA programs on site in a corporation, an idea that had been tried since 1970s, continued to exist in some places: Maryville College of Missouri, for example, offered such a program in McDonnell Douglas's headquarters in St. Louis. General Motors meanwhile was sending as many as one thousand managers to Northwestern University's Kellogg School for training in how to manage change.[29]

Sometimes such close ties between colleges and businesses raised questions about propriety, especially in the United States. A number of American college professors held positions on corporate boards of directors, and some people thought that such service presented a conflict of interest and a threat to academic integrity. So strong were these criticisms that the dean of Dartmouth's Tuck School felt obliged to answer them in a newspaper opinion article, arguing that professors had no more conflict of interest than anyone else did, and, more importantly, that they could make valuable contributions to the work of corporations.

In Britain, as at the continental European schools, such industry-university ties were not viewed as unethical, and consequently virtually every business school program there included work tied closely to industry. All British business schools, even the tradition-bound University of London, now stressed practicality, and in most of them the students were involved in practical projects specifically designed to help businesses.[30]

The Business Community Reaches into Colleges. Simultaneously, practicing business executives were taking a larger and larger part in the work of business schools. Three major schools—Stanford, New York University, and the Wharton School—all chose senior executives to be their new deans, and schools everywhere were inviting older business people to join them as "executives in residence." This position was not always well defined, and schools sometimes had difficulty figuring out what to do with the executives once they took up their residence, but the concept was very popular and quite widely adopted. Carnegie Mellon University went even further by hiring a whole board of business executives to evaluate plans devised by student teams as part of a major computerized business simulation game.[31]

Other Connections. Besides the major trends, many smaller arrangements were established during this period to help close the theory-practice gap. Business schools were establishing more joint programs with law and engineering schools and were holding special programs for executives. Columbia University, and probably others too, established advisory committees consisting of executives from businesses, to advise the school on its activities in marketing, accounting, production, and other fields. At the University of Pittsburgh, professors met every six weeks for discussions with active executives. The University of Chicago created a "laboratory" course in which students worked on developing new products for real companies, and other schools increased their work with computers, government relations, and the social context in which businesses operate.

It is no surprise, then, that the MBA degree was acquiring a new look. In 1979 Stanford's retiring dean declared that corporations could find no better investment than the hiring of a new MBA. Unlike education in economics, which he regarded as nonanalytical and narrow, education in business had developed, he said, to the point where it trained people to understand government, society, the market, and other forces that affect the operation of a business.[32]

In short, in his opinion as well as that of others, business schools had at last begun to find the long-sought proper balance between theory and practice. Although keeping their distance from the "mere vocationalism" that they always abhorred, they had moved distinctly toward restoring practicality to a business education.

More Substantive Curriculum

Reforms went further than just increasing the contacts with the business world. Curricular changes, especially in manufacturing and entrepreneurship, flatly contradicted the charge that business schools taught only finance. Students choosing to study finance still constituted a majority, but the changes underway at the time make it clear that the schools were earnestly trying to broaden rather than narrow the students' conception of business.

The Return of Manufacturing. As mentioned briefly above, production courses experienced a resurgence in the early 1980s. Early on, the *Wall Street Journal* reported a widespread realization that American companies were not making things very well and that the lack of production-trained managers was a major reason. Neither engineers (who did not know business) nor finance specialists (who did not know engineering) could handle the problems. This realization, the *Journal* went on, had given rise to a resurgence of manufacturing courses in the business schools, and, correspondingly, to a shortage of faculty qualified to teach the courses. *Business Week* added that enrollment in production courses at Columbia had doubled in one year, that the courses at the Wharton School were oversubscribed, and that Cornell, Carnegie Mellon, and UCLA were experiencing similar growth. It had been thirty years, another report said, since manufacturing had been in the limelight at business schools. After years of emphasis on finance, "operations" was now the new buzzword.[33]

Stanford University's Business School drew special attention for its production courses. Its new dean, Robert Jaedicke, listed management of technology and innovation as one of the four major challenges he saw facing business schools, and the results of this emphasis were soon clear. A wave of new courses in production subjects appeared in the school's catalog, and all students were required to take courses in both production and R&D. Students toured plants, studied robot assembly lines, and prepared cases dealing with production schedules and labor contracts. Within a two-year period, the number of Stanford students choosing careers in the manufacturing side of business rose more than 28 percent.[34]

Other schools were doing similar things. Carnegie Mellon established a number of joint production and operations management courses with its engineering school, and Columbia likewise set up new courses which were soon oversubscribed. Duke University's Fuqua School entered into a three-year project with IBM to "bring the factory to the classroom." It divided the manufacturing operation of a business into twelve phases and devised highly developed computer simulation modules to teach students how to control each phase. All the evidence in the early 1980s points to a growing awareness of the importance of manufacturing, on the part of both the students and the schools. In fact by 1984 a Harvard professor was complaining that the new emphasis was causing the school to neglect the service sector, which was growing to be even more important than manufacturing.[35]

The Rise of Entrepreneurial Studies. Almost as important a trend in business school curricula was the new emphasis on entrepreneurship that developed toward the middle of the decade. An enthusiastic *Nation's Business* article in 1982 reported that entrepreneurship courses were growing fast, but it actually named only three universities, three community colleges, and one Ohio technical school that offered them. Later that year the same message, but equally undocumented, came from eighty-six-year-old retired industrialist Royal Little, who addressed Columbia University's MBA students and stressed that entrepreneurship was the fastest growing area of interest in the business world.[36]

By middecade, however, documentation was plentiful. In 1984 the *Wall Street Journal* reported that entrepreneurship courses had risen a remarkable 61 percent in just four years, and *Business Week* said that the number of universities offering such courses had exploded from just 6 in 1967 to 150 seven years later. Among the major schools now teaching entrepreneurship were Harvard, Stanford, Northwestern, and the University of Washington, and the deans at Arizona State, Wharton, Carnegie Mellon, Tuck, Miami, and Chicago all listed entrepreneurship as one of the major challenges facing their schools. Although most of the emphasis appears, as would be expected, to have been on teaching young MBAs to start their own companies, another major focus was on entrepreneurial activities occurring within large corporations. IBM's recent success with its special start-up team that designed and marketed its first personal computer served as the model.[37]

Stanford, New York University, and Columbia all came in for special notice for their entrepreneurial work, but a nagging doubt remained about the value of such studies so long as no measures of effectiveness were available. Many people doubted that schools could teach the kind of aggressive, risk taking, visionary skills needed to start a business, and others expressed fears that training in entrepreneurship would actually cause adjustment problems if the graduates went to work for corporations. To test the value of these courses, three midwestern professors undertook an extensive survey of students who took them. The results were positive: the courses, they found, attracted entrepreneurial-minded students, affected their thinking, and led to new businesses being created.[38]

International Emphasis. Although some critics derided MBA schools for not being sufficiently global minded, the schools were in fact more so now than they had ever been, and they were moving faster and faster in that direction. In 1979 AACSB found that schools everywhere were emphasizing international studies by instituting new courses, redesigning existing courses, and undertaking exchange programs. Four years later a survey by the dean at Cornell found international emphasis in all major MBA programs without exception, as evidenced by an increased number of faculty and by notable changes in the curricula. He especially noted the programs at Harvard, Northwestern, Stanford, Virginia, Wharton, Arizona, New York University, and Cornell. By the end of 1984 the *Wall Street Journal* could state that international business education, along with computer studies, was the new rage at business schools.[39]

Early in 1982 AACSB adopted a requirement that every MBA student be exposed to international business studies of some sort, and the deans seem to have taken the requirement seriously. The deans at Arizona State, Carnegie Mellon, Chicago, Miami, Stanford, Tuck, and Wharton all named international work as one of their major challenges, and several of these schools, as well as notably global-minded New York University, established exchange programs in which MBA students went overseas for all or part of their studies. International business was very popular at Columbia, where the separate International Division was eliminated in order to make global business an integral part of every course across the curriculum. Harvard professor Michael Porter predicted that Harvard would soon have courses in developing and managing global strategies. Country-centered courses, he declared, were simply obsolete.[40]

Meanwhile Japanese students were studying in Stanford's MBA program, and several American universities, with the guidance of the U.S. Department of Commerce, were helping to set up an MBA program in China. The Chinese programs were especially interesting because of the direct involvement of American schools: in Beijing, Dalian, and Liaining, professors and administrators from New York University, the University of North Carolina, the State University of New York at Binghamton, and Georgia Tech, as well as from the Department of Commerce, were teaching in and directing the programs. Not one dissenting voice was heard about any of these programs. Regardless of what the critics claimed, business schools were unanimously behind the international movement.[41]

Concern with Social Problems and the Arts. Although the schools were sometimes accused of producing soulless, number-crunching automatons, the evidence shows clearly that social and artistic concerns were strong and always near the forefront. A reporter with a long history of antibusiness bias attended a national conference of MBA students at Duke University and was surprised to find strong expressions of concern about social problems. A professor who made a career of advocating the solving of social problems through experiential learning surveyed all the AACSB-accredited business schools and found that a large number of them had such programs, especially on the West Coast, in New England and Pennsylvania, and to a lesser degree in the midwest. At Harvard, where new courses in inter-personal behavior and self-assessment were proving very popular, one of the professors commented, quite accurately, that the public generally did not recognize how socially sensitive the curriculum had become—and his observation was equally applicable at other schools.[42]

When deans were asked to name the biggest challenges they faced, social concerns occupied a large portion of the list. Human relations, government relations, corporate responsibility, and the special problems of women and minorities constituted from twenty-five percent to forty percent of the prob-lems they identified. One of them scoffed at the idea that America's moral value problems were attributable to business schools, and another agreed, calling the charges silly. Still another declared that MBA programs, because they confronted these new challenges directly, had now become more valu-able than ever.[43]

Executives and professors agreed. Three prominent accountants said they found no more arrogance in MBAs than in anyone else, and they further denied that MBA programs were too much oriented toward quantitative studies. One professor said he found business curricula very responsive to society's needs, and another, when asked about the charges that the schools were mathematical and cold hearted, asked a telling question: such accusa-tions may sound valid in the abstract, but are there really any schools like that?[44]

Likewise in the arts, things were happening that belied the general image. Yale's new school won prizes and praises for its architecture; Cornell estab-lished an art gallery in its business school; Dartmouth operated a fully subscribed summer program in the humanities for executives; and Rutgers established an innovative program, "Business and the Arts," which took students into arts organizations and activities to see how they functioned and why they were worthy of support. The critics' charges of indifference to social and aesthetic matters were, simply, wrong.[45]

Ethical Concerns. The charge that business schools were indifferent to ethical questions was on somewhat solider ground, but the reason was less that the schools were callous than that they simply did not know what to do about the problem. Starting in 1979 AACSB accrediting requirements included a provision that students must be exposed to some sort of ethical instruction, but one observer found not a single program that he considered thorough and conscientious. Most, he said, were only superficial responses to the requirement, sometimes taking the form of nothing more than a sen-tence in a school's mission statement.[46]

Ethics studies, which could be separate courses, integrated into other subjects, or a combination of both, were tried at a number of schools. One executive in residence at a major university argued that only the case method, as opposed to a structured theoretical approach, could effectively teach the subject. But a Harvard student writing in the *Wall Street Journal* denounced all such courses as useless, regardless of method. Students, he wrote, are no more or less ethical than anyone else, and no more or less ethical after taking the courses than before. Likewise, business is neither more nor less ethical than it has been in the past. The only way to increase the number of ethical graduates going into business, he concluded, is to admit into the business program people who are already ethical to begin with.[47]

No one was even remotely inclined to dismiss the subject entirely, but even the advocates lacked any clear ideas about what to do. Two schools— Emory University and the University of Pittsburgh—offered joint master's programs in their business and theology schools, apparently hoping that the interaction of the two fields would produce benefits to both. Others, however, simply stayed with traditional approaches, trusting that an examination of theories and examples would produce higher ethical behavior. Whenever *The New York Times* wanted insights on the ethics of corporate takeovers, it went to a business school to interview a professor, because the idea persisted that business professors had special knowledge on ethical subjects.

That idea may have been valid, but still, so far as teaching this special knowledge was concerned, the professors were baffled about how to communicate it. One avid advocate of ethics instruction argued fervently for inclusion of ethics in the curriculum—but then concluded by acknowledging that he could provide no details because he had not worked out exactly how it should be done.[48]

Improving the Personal Attributes of MBAs. As noted earlier, from at least the sixteenth century and probably before, businessmen had been regarded as deficient in culture and grace—in short as crude and boorish. Quite naturally the same criticisms were often directed—for example by Sinclair Lewis and James Thurber—against young people (especially men) studying to enter business. They were regularly accused of being stupid and inarticulate, of lacking social graces, and of having no interests other than money.

But by the time this most recent barrage of attacks occurred, in the late 1970s and early 1980s, these criticism were already obsolete. With reference to the fixation on money, for example, several studies had appeared demonstrating that in fact other things were more important. The majority of Stanford graduates in 1984, the *Wall Street Journal* reported, did not take the highest paying employment offer they received. A Wharton professor surveyed graduates four or five years out of school and found the same thing: most were satisfied with their salaries and were seeking not more money but more challenging work.[49]

The idea that psychological fulfillment, rather than simply higher salaries, was what motivated students received support from other studies. The dean at Europe's most distinguished business school, INSEAD, commented that the reason young MBAs were regarded as arrogant and ambitious was simply that business, with its rigid structure, did not know how to make proper use of them. The head of a prominent recruiting firm made the same observation after interviewing hundreds of discontented young workers: they did indeed job-hop, he reported, but the reason was far more likely to be discontent and disillusionment than a quest for higher pay. The B. F. Goodrich Company prided itself on avoiding these problems through a special career-planning program for MBAs. The senior vice president, in an article describing the program, specifically credited the loyalty and hard work of these carefully mentored MBAs with having saved the company from financial disaster, thus echoing the other observers who blamed business, not the young graduates, for the widely reported poor fit.[50]

Communication skills of MBA students had been coming in for more and more attention over the previous two decades, at least partly because the 1959 foundation reports had singled out poor writing and speaking ability as one of their targets. Programs in communication had sprung into existence in virtually all major business schools by this time. Membership in the Association for Business Communication grew 255 percent in just seventeen years, from 649 in 1968 to 1,654 by 1985, and a new and more advanced organization, the Management Communication Association, was formed by a select group of major universities in 1979. Maryland, Rutgers, Illinois, Virginia, Tulane, Utah, Duke, and literally dozens of other schools—besides Harvard, Yale, MIT, Michigan, Chicago, and Stanford—had business communication as part of the curriculum well before 1980.[51]

Social graces made a strong appearance also. John T. Malloy's *Dress for Success,* first published in 1975, was widely read among business students, and his seminar presentations on the subject proved immensely popular at Wharton and other major business schools. Interviewing skills were quite widely taught—for example at Columbia—sometimes separately and other times in connection with the business communication program. Few schools, however, went as far as the University of Chicago did, where students were offered two forums on wine selection to aid them in impressing future clients. The fact that the schools were offering all these courses serves as confirmation of the need: the critics must have been right or the schools would never have responded. But here as in the other instances cited, the critics were late. By the early 1980s these problems were all already being addressed.[52]

Business-Oriented Reforms in the Schools. Even before the critics started complaining that the business schools knew nothing about business or about how to prepare people for it, the schools themselves were undertaking many reforms and self-study activities to improve their responsiveness to the needs of business. Their whole approach to the teaching of business was

Illustration 12-2:

FACTORS BRITISH BUSINESS EXECUTIVES CONSIDER
WHEN RANKING A BUSINESS SCHOOL (1982)
(in descending order)

1. Teaching reputation

2. Past experience of use

3. Opinions of other users

4. Curriculum design

5. Intellectual reputation

6. Well-known faculty

7. Teaching facilities

8. Research reputation

9. Consultancy

10. University status

11. National register of opinion

12. Accommodation

Source: Industrial Marketing Management, 11 (Oct. 1982), 303-310.

undergoing close scrutiny, and the results were felt in all parts of the curriculum.

On the general question of what opinion business held about business schools, a British professor of management conducted an interesting and revealing study he called "Marketing a Business School to Industry." He surveyed 142 major businesses to find out what criteria they used in choosing general management programs for their employees, and in doing so he uncovered major discrepancies between industrial and academic values (Ill. 12–2). Whereas universities had long been basing their rewards to professors primarily on the amount of research they conducted, businesses ranked research far down on the importance list. Teaching and curriculum design were much more important to them. In fact almost the only other things that mattered were the "status" or "reputation" of the particular university.[53]

American studies conducted at this time were likewise identifying discrepancies between what business wanted and what the schools were doing, and as a result the schools were beginning to institute major changes. An AACSB survey (Ill. 12–3) pointed up astonishing differences in the importance that the business world and the academic world attached to each curricular subject. The more theoretical subjects of economics and mathematics—ranked first and fourth by the professors—were given much lower rankings (third and tenth) by the executives, while the less traditional business policy and human relations courses, ranked fourth and seventh by the executives, scored just sixth and ninth with the professors. Another study revealed a further discrepancy with respect to teaching method. The case method, which Harvard pioneered and championed and which many other schools attempted to emulate, was, according to this report, scorned by industry as a "prime source of irritation" because it stressed the CEO's viewpoint and the making of rapid decisions, while ignoring social and industrial repercussions of problems under consideration.[54]

Such studies had the effect of bringing about reforms in the business schools in the direction of practicality. AACSB began work on an outcomes-based accreditation system that would evaluate how skilled the graduates were in various areas, rather than rely on measures like the number of Ph.D.s and the size of the library. Such an approach, had it ever materialized, would have marked the single most radical change in business education in its entire history. From the start, emphasis had always been placed on input measures, with the unstated and untested assumption that these would somehow correlate with output measures later. Another example of the new stress on practicality came in September 1980 when the Canadian Federation of Deans of Management and Administrative studies adopted a ten-point agenda for developing the teaching of business (Ill. 12–4). The overwhelming emphasis in these ten points is again on the practical: words like "skills," "capabilities," "results-oriented," and "entrepreneurship" stand out, and traditional phrases like "grounding in the basic intellectual disciplines" are noticeably absent.[55]

Changes quickly showed up on the curriculum level. Harvard undertook a thorough reexamination of its curriculum in 1984, with the aim of making it more practical and less theoretically analytical. Neither Harvard nor any other university, however, was willing to go as far as the "creative MBA" proposed by one professor, in which the entire second half of the curriculum would have consisted of courses in international studies, languages, and

Illustration 12-3:

DISCREPANCIES BETWEEN BUSINESS AND ACADEMIC RATINGS OF THE IMPORTANCE OF SELECTED SUBJECTS (1979)

Rating by Business Executives	SUBJECT	Rating by Professors
1	Accounting	2
2	Finance	3
3	Economics	1
4	Policy	6
5	Marketing	5
7	Human Relations	9
10	Quantitative Studies	4
13	International Studies	13

Source: Business Week, Nov. 19, 1979, p. 171.

travel—subjects that this professor believed would be useful on the day-to-day level.[56]

Curricular changes, both actual and proposed, reflected the same trend. In accounting, a proposal to require a fifth undergraduate year for the specific purpose of preparing for the CPA examination generated some controversy. In computer science a movement away from programming and toward applications was strongly underway. In marketing, sampling and survey techniques became more important, even to the point of having a special master's degree devoted to them in at least one school. And in personnel management, where a traditional course, "Introduction to Personnel Management," had ruled for years, new surveys of corporations were conducted

Illustration 12-4:

RESEARCH AGENDA ADOPTED BY THE CANADIAN FEDERATION OF DEANS OF MANAGEMENT AND ADMINISTRATIVE STUDIES
September 1980

1. Research to broaden the management education curriculum.

2. Research to streamline the management education curriculum.

3. Research to implement lifelong continuing professional education for managers.

4. Research on training for "results-oriented" management education.

5. Research on producing the distinctive skills and knowledge required by managers of different kinds of organizations.

6. Research on instilling the international understanding and capabilities needed by prospective managers.

7. Research on recruiting and training managers from non-traditional segments of the population.

8. Research on educating for entrepreneurship.

9. Research on preparing managers to cope with the emerging relationships of Canadian organizations with new external constituencies.

10. Research on educating managers to understand changing values, philosophies, and lifestyles.

Source: Sloan Management Review, 53 (Winter 1982), 68-69.

to determine exactly what skills a student should master in order to perform well on the job.[57]

The MBA Keeps Prospering

The biggest error the critics of MBA programs in the early 1980s made was in saying that the degree was past its prime, both in numbers and in importance. Demand for MBAs kept increasing, leading to constantly growing enrollments, and the prestige of the degree increased steadily the whole time. Thus whatever criticisms the commentators were making were ultimately rendered meaningless by reality.

Heavy Demand for MBAs. Salaries, always a good measure of demand, had been rising five to ten per cent a year for several years, and by 1979 most graduates were receiving initial offers of more than $20,000. Starting in 1979 the demand began to pick up sharply. At Harvard, salaries in that one year rose nearly 17 percent, to an average of $28,000, with the average offer from consulting firms reported at $33,863. Yet as strong a demand as these figures suggest, evidence shows that the demand in Canada was even stronger—in fact several Canadian observers declared that an actual shortage of MBAs existed and was responsible for the slow growth of Canadian industry.[58]

The same trends continued the next year, but more intensely. The *Wall Street Journal* reported in February 1980 that recruiting activity was higher than ever, especially among consulting firms, and that salary offers were reaching $40,000 to $50,000, with bonuses as high as an additional $20,000. Two months later the *Journal* reported that salary offers everywhere were up by 7.6 percent, and that some people were actually predicting a shortage of MBAs by 1990. A third report, in September, confirmed the earlier ones by noting that recruiters at Harvard were engaging in all sorts of competitive activities in their efforts to snare the best students.

The New York Times similarly found demand strong and salaries high at Harvard, Columbia, and Stanford, and it reported that Harvard was finding it necessary to impose restraints on recruiters to try to reduce the intensity of the competition. Companies had been using such high-pressure tactics as the "exploding bonus"—$2,000 if you sign up today, $1,800 tomorrow, $1,600 the next day, and so on—and the university ordered a stop to the practice. Other reports presented evidence that consulting showed no signs of faltering and that even lowly marketing, traditionally a weak field for salaries, was showing strong demand.[59]

In 1981 Harvard again imposed restraints on the recruiting process, as zealous employers continued using high-pressure techniques. This time the university tried to head off early offers by forbidding any acceptance until early April, an easy-to-evade edict that apparently had little effect. Corporate enthusiasm abounded everywhere. According to one report, the Exxon Corporation attempted to hire the entire 1981 graduating class at the University of Chicago, and other reports told of salary offers that confirmed the picture: nationwide, salaries exceeded the previous year's by 6 percent to 12 percent, and at the Wharton School the average salary for all fields surpassed $30,000 for the first time.[60]

The two following years saw much quieter activity, but by 1984 the news was good again. Salaries rose 5 percent to 10 percent at Harvard, Tuck, UCLA, and Columbia, and over 15 percent at Northwestern. By this point, salary offers in financial services and consulting commonly reached $40,000 to $60,000, not counting bonuses. *Business Week* reported instances of salaries as high as $150,000 for new MBAs with computer and information technology expertise. As in previous cycles, just when it had begun to appear that the doomsayers were right, demand for MBA graduates bounced back more strongly than ever.[61]

Rising Enrollments. Because demand for graduates was strong, demand for admission to MBA schools continued to be strong as well. Between 1974 and 1978 applications at Columbia University had increased 10 percent a year; in 1979 alone they grew 22 percent. Nationwide the number of degrees awarded, which had grown only 4 percent and 3.5 percent in 1977–78 and 1978–79, grew an average of 6.3 percent for each of the next four years. Specific groups were growing also. The percentage of black students among the MBA recipients rose from 3.5 percent to 3.7 percent in the late 1970s. The number of practicing executives coming through special weekend programs increased vastly during this time; from ten programs in existence in 1974, the number grew to almost a hundred by 1984. About ten thousand executives were said to be participating in all such programs, degree and nondegree, by 1984. In Great Britain short courses for practicing managers proved so popular that the schools could barely keep up with demand. Growth there was put at 20 percent a year, a phenomenal rate in view of Britain's long history of indifference to management education.[62]

Shortage of Faculty. A consequence of this growth was that too few instructors could be found to teach the burgeoning numbers of students. In 1981 articles in both *The New York Times* and the *Wall Street Journal* pointed out a growing discrepancy between doctoral and master's graduation rates: whereas master's degrees were growing at 5 percent and more a year, the number of new PhDs available to teach them had been falling since 1975 and by this time had already dropped more than 27 percent. Of particular concern were courses in manufacturing, since instructors with hands-on experience were required, and few of the people getting Ph.D.s had such experience.[63]

In 1982 the AACSB attracted wide publicity by releasing a committee report on the shortage of faculty. According to the report, 20 percent of college teaching positions in business were going unfilled, and finances played a large part in creating the shortage. New Ph.D.s reportedly earned $4,000 less than the starting salaries of the MBAs they trained, and, moreover, the process of earning the Ph.D. degree involved the loss of $100,000 in tuition and opportunity costs. Such solutions as flexible accreditation, the use of Ph.D.s from related disciplines, the use of experienced businesspeople, and a special nonresearch doctorate were proposed. The problem would have been considerably worse, it was noted, had it not been for the foreign students who were coming to the United States in increasing numbers to get their business Ph.D.s.[64]

High Prestige. Finally, signs indicate that despite the criticisms, the MBA degree grew to be more highly esteemed than ever during this time, in both the industrial and academic worlds. In industry 60 percent of all employers agreed that MBAs performed better than non-MBAs and that the MBA degree was an important addition to a bachelor's degree. A prominent executive search firm reported that MBAs progressed faster in corporations and earned higher salaries, and a British study reported that, after some early reservations, major corporations there were now quite happy with the graduates they were hiring. In Canada, a similar report found widespread agreement in industry that the degree was a worthwhile investment.[65]

More specific votes of confidence came from the advertising, food, and electrical industries. Advertising executives generally expressed approval of the degree, saying that MBAs seemed smarter and made better presentations because of practice in schools. A food industry expert noted that, after years of avoiding MBAs, food stores were beginning to come around: one company had now begun hiring them, and others would soon follow, as the need for more intensive analysis of business operations became clear. No less an industry giant than General Electric, which had a long history of outstanding in-house training programs, established a joint MBA program with Purdue University, in which much of the instruction and homework was transmitted by computers and the rest was handled in intensive weeks of study on campus.[66]

Among academicians also, a new note of admiration for business studies was evident. In addition to the by now commonplace claims that MBA programs were socially responsive, were not narrowing, and were more important than ever now that business growing more complex, several professors and deans commented on the suddenly evident improvement in quality as compared to the liberal arts programs. Good students, several of them commented, used to go into the social sciences and humanities, while the poor students turned to business studies, but that was true no longer. A combination of limited opportunities in the other fields and new and challenging developments in business studies was now attracting good students to schools of business. The result, one management expert observed, was that the MBA had become the new mark of a well educated person, replacing the liberal arts.

This development had come about rather quietly and without much public notice, but it was unquestionably true. The 1959 foundation reports had mocked business departments and schools for accepting the worst students, but now, less than twenty-five years later, the situation had to a large extent reversed itself, and business was an entirely respectable subject for study. Even the august London School of Economics now proudly acknowledged its work in practical subjects like accounting, which had begun there back in 1902 but only recently grown to be considered "a distinguished tradition."[67]

GENERAL CONFORMITY AND INCREASED EMPHASIS ON RESEARCH

Two characteristics of MBA programs during this period—a tendency for schools to become more alike, and an all-consuming focus on theoretical research by faculty members—were probably undesirable and should have attracted criticism. Surprisingly, neither did. While the critics were leveling obsolete attacks against the MBA, both these negative developments escaped their wrath.

Conformity Reigns

MBA schools seem to have become more alike during this period. The reason may have been that, in the face of sudden criticism, they instinctively retreated to safe common ground, like an individual seeking protection in a crowd. Whatever the reasons, the strength of the pressure to conform was evidenced by the smaller number of innovations and the poor reception accorded them, the gradual disappearance of differences among institutions, and the apparent influence toward conformity exerted by the AACSB.

Innovations. Through most of the 1970s, published articles about MBA programs had been filled with descriptions of innovations, but a decided drop-off in their numbers was evident by the end of the decade. In 1982 it was reported that women's networks were springing up in business schools, almost the first new idea to be heard in three years. The following year likewise saw only one new suggestion, a strange proposal to replace grades with number of hours worked.[68]

When a viable new idea did come up, it seemed to have difficulty thriving. At the beginning of this chapter the American Management Association's competency-based MBA was described, in which students would have to demonstrate their mastery of certain skills in order to receive their degrees. The idea obviously had a great deal to recommend it, since it was based on output rather than input—producing graduates who could actually do something rather than graduates who had simply sat through certain numbers of hours of classes. Although the program did get established and still continues to the present day, predictions that the concept would quickly be adopted everywhere by management educators turned out to be dead wrong. The force of conformity proved so strong that no other MBA program has ever followed in that path.[69]

Erasing Differences. A perusal of school catalogs for the period yields the clear impression that fewer major differences were evident from one university to another. In general such an impression is hard to document, but in the case of two institutions the conforming trend seems plain. The Thunderbird American Graduate School of International Management, which had been founded in 1945 as a distinctly different kind of business school, became more and more like the other schools. *The New York Times* profiled it in mid-1980 and left an unmistakable impression that, although the school still retained its original emphasis, it was growing to be more like other schools and in fact had established joint programs with several others. Yale's School of Organization and Management likewise seemed to start losing some of its individuality. Founded, as noted in chapter 10, as a school unlike any other, it soon became very much like all the others. After its original dean resigned in 1979, an economist was chosen to replace him, a clear indication that the exclusive emphasis on behavioral studies would soon come to an end, as it indeed did.[70]

AACSB Pressures. Several observers expressed the view that the national organization was causing much of the conformity pressure. A British reporter plainly said as much in 1981, citing AACSB-inspired conformity as one of the big weaknesses in America's MBA programs. A professor at a nonaccredited school, Houston Baptist University, echoed the sentiment two years later, pointing out that nonaccredited institutions had a distinct advantage, since the quest for AACSB accreditation was preventing other schools from seeking innovative solutions to their problems. For example, one of the state schools in Wisconsin briefly adopted a policy at this time of using sales people as part-time instructors in order to ease the faculty shortage problem—but it was clear that if they expected to use such a policy extensively they would do so instead of getting accredited, since AACSB severely limited the role that part-time teachers could play in a business school.[71]

The Apotheosis of Research

Meanwhile, the research craze in business schools, which had started in the 1950s and had received a great impetus from the 1959 foundation reports, continued its growth until it reached new heights. In the late 1970s *The New York Times* devoted a whole feature article to the price war among universities bidding for the services of highly productive scholars. The article focused on one professor who had written twelve books and twenty-nine journal articles in nine years and had used that record to command higher and higher salaries. In 1973 a salary of $25,000 was high; by 1977 a $32,000 salary still was newsworthy. But by the mid-1980s a few universities were paying over $100,000 to professors hired for the specific purpose of turning out large numbers of publications.[72]

The ranking of business schools by the amount of published material their professors produced—a strange phenomenon that had begun in the 1960s and 1970s—continued in this period. Following the pattern of an earlier study published in the *Journal of Business,* a 1980 article in the prestigious *Quarterly Review of Economics and Business* detailed the publishing records of the finance, marketing, organizational behavior, and general business departments at various universities, counting not just the number of articles produced but even the number of pages. The results showed a strong research surge at several institutions not previously much in the news for their business programs—for instance, Florida, Pennsylvania State, Indiana, and Georgia—indicating that research was now the main thrust at a wide assortment of institutions rather than only at the traditionally most prestigious ones. Although the study included several disclaimers, and although it made no attempt to adjust its figures to account for the different sizes of different schools, the implication that high publication rates signify a better school was inescapable.[73]

Since quantitative measurements—number and length—were attracting attention, it is not surprising that professors directed their efforts toward frequency of publishing rather than toward contributing ideas of importance. One financial executive said that the research contributions in the 1950s and 1960s were significant, but that a slacking in significance was evident by 1970, and by 1980 the published research had become simply "nit-picking," containing only answers to questions no one was asking. A Wharton professor conducted a purportedly serious study in which he found that lower readability and less valid logic were more likely to lead to getting published and that the most prestigious journals were the least readable of all. Yet such negative observations as these were seldom heard at this time; the research express was going full speed, and everyone wanted to be on board.[74]

*   *   *

Criticism of MBA schools in the early 1980s was mostly just a fad, caused primarily by the phenomenal success they had been, and still were, experiencing. The problems people criticized had generally been solved several years earlier, and the attacks left few or no lasting effects. Over the next few years management education would come back stronger than ever, and not until after the 1980s had ended would the long-predicted decline in demand begin to become evident.

13

Since 1984:
The Active MBA

CONTEMPORARY history never falls into neat compartments the way the past does, but still a few clear outlines have emerged over the past dozen years that indicate what may lie ahead for the MBA. The most significant and undeniable development is that business schools everywhere have been frantically trying to change in order to get away from the model that dominated for most of the previous seventy-five years. The reasons for these efforts lie mainly in profound and unprecedented changes occurring in the business world. The resulting alterations in the schools have been of every imaginable kind, but most seem aimed at making business education more practical, more participatory, and more active. As a result, at a time when it might have been expected to decline, the MBA degree has actually increased in public esteem.

CHANGES IN THE BUSINESS ENVIRONMENT

A Reduced Demand for MBAs

Central to all the recent changes in the business environment is the new concept of a job. Whereas companies used to hire people to fill a certain position, they now increasingly think of hiring people to do certain work. Rather than having six assistant vice presidents whose job descriptions include a large range of activities, they have become more inclined to start from the activities themselves and plan their staffing around those. Instead of being asked "What kinds of things do you think an assistant vice president ought to do?," a candidate for employment will be asked "Can you plan a marketing campaign designed to sell 75,000 units of our product the first year?"

This change, which has been occurring very gradually since the mid-1980s and has grown in momentum in the 1990s, has had, as intended, the entirely predictable effect of thinning the ranks of managerial employees. Calculating staff requirements from a "work produced" point of view, rather than from a structured or "job title" point of view, produces a smaller number of people required. The belief is growing that Americans for the past many generations have been the most oversupervised workers in the world, with far more managers per worker than in other countries. Consequently the dramatic downsizing that has been occurring has hit the management ranks very hard. Many of those eliminated fall into the category of "general management": so long as the work gets done, according to modern reasoning, no one cares whether it's been "generally managed" or not. And since supervisory positions are where most MBA holders have traditionally ended up, the reduction has (or should have) produced a glut of employees with general management MBAs. So long as employment was expanding, there was room for the ninety thousand new MBAs the schools produced each year. Now, in a time of apparently permanent contraction, such is no longer the case.

Declining Enrollments

The message—that MBAs aren't getting jobs as they used to—has slowly worked its way back to young men and women considering going to business school, and as a result the number of applicants for MBA programs stopped growing for a while and in some cases even went down. The trend began showing up in the early 1980s, although no one paid attention to it at first. From 1980–81 through 1983–84 the number of people taking the Graduate Management Admissions Test (GMAT), which had risen steadily ever since the test began, declined by nearly 15 percent. *Business Week* pointed out the decline early in 1985 and attributed it both to a surplus of MBAs in the business world and to a decline in the size of the youthful population. Shortly afterward, the *Wall Street Journal* picked up the theme and estimated that 25 percent of the nation's business schools might have to close. Both articles pointed out a dramatic increase in executive education programs and speculated that these might be the principal form of graduate business education in the future, and the *Journal* further suggested that business schools would have to start differentiating themselves by finding special niches, as Duke University's Fuqua School had recently done with its computer-simulated technology program.[1]

By 1986 GMAT takers and enrollments had turned up again, leading some observers to think that the decline had ended and that the widely heralded obituary for the traditional MBA had been premature. Although the deans at both Columbia and Fordham predicted the continuation of hard times, the figures kept rising for two or three years, and most pessimists quieted down. In mid-1988 *The New York Times* reported that most people now thought the decline had been only temporary. The University of Iowa, among others, was experiencing an altogether unmanageable surge in its undergraduate business enrollment, with 3,500 students competing for 1,300 places in the upper-division program. At the University of Illinois the dean noted that "It is easier to get into some of the Ivy League business programs than it is here, and that isn't sitting too well around the state." A teacher shortage existed across the nation, according to the *Wall Street Journal,* forcing the business schools to offer unprecedentedly high salaries to attract faculty.[2]

But within another three or four years it was again being speculated that the interruption had been only temporary, and that a major and apparently permanent decline had truly begun. The number of people taking the GMAT started dropping again after 1991, until it was actually lower in 1992–93 than it had been in 1980–81. Applications were declining almost everywhere; at the Wharton School, for example, they fell more than 20 percent from 1990 to 1993. *Forbes,* under the title "Another Boom Ends," reported in early 1992 that large portions of graduate business schools' graduating classes had no jobs by commencement time—15 percent at UCLA, 20 percent at Texas, 25 percent at Tuck, and 33 percent at Yale. A survey of 250 companies, conducted by Northwestern University, revealed a more than 8 percent drop in demand for MBA graduates in 1991 alone, on top of another decline the previous year. Graduates of British MBA schools were having similar experiences.[3]

On the undergraduate level, the AACSB reported, signs of the decline were even more serious: in just five years, undergraduate interest in business careers had plunged an incredible 40 percent. By 1994 the *Wall Street Journal* could declare that the nation's business schools were clearly operating far below their capacity. Corporate downsizing and belt tightening were affecting not just jobs available for graduates but corporate tuition support for employees who wanted to return to school while working. Nationwide, such support was reported to have fallen 18 percent between 1985 and 1992; one university reported that only half its working students received such support in 1994, as opposed to three fourths in 1984.[4]

Britain was likewise experiencing financial support problems, but of a different sort. Instead of relying on corporate support, British management schools had depended since their beginning on a government subsidy, and in 1987 a movement to eliminate such subsidies gained strength. The idea, first proposed in 1985 and then later endorsed by the government, was intended to force the schools to operate like businesses and therefore to avoid the complacency that guaranteed subsidies can bring. After all, it was pointed out, French and American business schools had always operated without subsidies, and they were far healthier than the rather anemic British ones had ever been. Ironically, the head of the London Business School, who had assumed his position in 1984 with a promise "to push the place further into the real business world," now had to argue that schools were different from businesses and therefore needed government backing to operate successfully.[5]

Another source of concern for business schools was competition from industry itself, which now began increasing its in-house training programs and even establishing highly professional business schools with full accreditation. Most companies had extensive education programs for their management at all ranks—70 percent for top executives and over 75 percent for middle managers, according to one report, at a cost of over $40 billion in 1986. MBA degrees were offered by several companies, including Wang and Northrop in America and Arthur Young in Great Britain, and the Rand Corporation even offered a Ph.D. With the schools' overcapacity problems they would gladly have taken on these training challenges, but the fact that such in-house programs were growing at this time suggests that corporations felt more confident about their own programs than about the ones the schools offered.[6]

Finally, competition came also from the sudden development of new MBA schools in parts of the world that had not had them before. A few were established through cooperative arrangements with American universities, but most were independent and indigenous. The Amos Tuck School set up a program in Japan, SUNY Buffalo in China, Indiana University in Budapest, and the University of Rochester in Sydney, among others, normally under short-term contracts designed to help the new schools get started. Other countries, such as Ecuador and Russia, sent observers to the United States to study American business schools so that they could emulate them. But the most striking development was the founding of vast numbers of new schools independently of any existing ones. By 1986 the *Economist* was warning about proliferation of dubious quality MBA schools in Europe, but the extent of the boom would become evident only later. According to one estimate, up to 400 European business schools opened just in the last half of the 1980s, 225 of them in Spain alone. In Great Britain a large number of new programs were set up after two government reports called for greater emphasis on management, specifically for a quintupling of MBA graduates in the next thirteen years. Even Oxford and Cambridge, after years of disdainfully refusing to get involved, announced the founding of MBA programs in 1989. The effect of these developments on enrollments in American schools cannot be measured with any precision, but it had to be significant.[7]

One other factor—the loss of female and minority enrollments—may have played a part in the general decline that business schools found themselves facing at the start of the 1990s. After rising inexorably for at least two decades, they now stopped growing as fast, or even stopped growing altogether, thereby contributing to the end of total enrollment growth. In fact women's enrollment, as noted in an earlier chapter, explains much of the enormous growth of MBA enrollments in the 1970s and 1980s. With the end of this growth, leveling off was inevitable. Minority enrollments actually declined, starting around 1987, and, since minorities are expected to constitute a larger and larger segment of the population in the next few decades, this decline foretold bad news for future enrollments.[8]

The decline in women's enrollment figures was at least as alarming as that for minorities: from 31 percent of MBA graduates of the class of 1988, they declined to 27 percent in 1990. At the University of Pittsburgh women had constituted 48 percent of the class of 1985; by 1989 the figure had fallen to 33 percent; at Chicago it fell from 30 percent to 27 percent in one year. Explanations offered were that women were choosing new careers, were staying home, or were entering business careers without an MBA. Several studies showed that despite their equality at the time of graduation, women's prospects for advancement in business were less than men's, and the message may well have caused women to turn their attention to other fields.[9]

Although by 1990 enrollments were surging upward again, the unsteadiness of the previous five years' figures had left a mark. Business schools observed the tremors much as an investor observes those in the stock market. They had a profound effect on every school.

THE SCHOOLS RESPOND

Faced with the alarming—and, for them, absolutely unprecedented—prospect of actually losing enrollment, the graduate schools of business began scrambling to implement changes. Up till this point they had always been able to ignore criticism and cite the relentlessly rising market as proof that they were doing things right. Now, they had to take the criticisms seriously.

Changes were fast and frequent, in the curriculum, in the methods of teaching, and in the underlying philosophy.

A New Curriculum

The curriculum of 1985 differed very little from that of 1965. Courses matching the usual divisions of a corporation—accounting, production, marketing, personnel, finance—made up the bulk of the offerings, with additions from a few support areas like mathematics and statistics, economics, computers, the international and social environment of business, and business policy. By 1995, however, major changes had occurred, throwing unprecedented emphasis on global business, entrepreneurship, ethics, leadership, nonfinancial aspects of business, and a few other areas not previously represented.

Global. Every decade since World War I had seen emphasis on international business, and in the 1970s and 1980s the emphasis, as has been noted many times, had become very strong. But what happened starting around

1985, reflecting changes in the business world's operations, was truly without precedent.

The period starting around 1980 has been said to mark "the end of geography." No longer did it make sense to think of a business as originating from or operating in a country. International firms, which had had headquarters in one nation and manufacturing or marketing operations in another, gave way to multinational firms with ownership and operating functions scattered among many nations, to the point where companies now are often larger and more important than some countries. No longer is it possible for a company to have a separate department of "overseas" or "foreign" business: all aspects of business—ownership, management, and workforce—now transcend national boundaries.

At the end of 1985 the *Wall Street Journal* commented on the newly observed wave of international courses at business schools. New York University, Columbia, and Harvard had all taken big steps toward globalizing their curricula, and Wharton achieved national recognition for its global work, through both the University of Pennsylvania's Lauder Institute and its own programs such as the U.S.-Japan Management Studies Center. Administrators at the Massachusetts Institute of Technology complained that the growth of interest in the subject had now created a serious shortage of qualified international business professors.[10]

Other schools, including smaller ones, were moving quickly in the same direction. Point Park College in Pittsburgh instituted a "Masters in International Business Management," and the University of Maryland established an International Business and Management Institute. In Canada, many institutions, including St. Mary's University in the east and Simon Fraser University in the west, built up programs stressing training for work in international business.[11]

As the decade came to an end, the emphasis grew steadily greater. The *Wall Street Journal* announced that international subjects had replaced computers as the hottest items in graduate business schools, and within three years Chicago, Virginia, Harvard, George Washington, SUNY/Buffalo, and dozens of other universities were regularly featured in news articles because of their international work. British and continental European schools made similar moves, at least as emphatically and maybe even more so, and by 1991 one could find whole articles and books devoted to giving advice on how to convert a nation-centered program to an international one.[12]

Individual examples indicate more fully the extent of this movement. The University of Pittsburgh states that its curriculum "provides a global management perspective in every phase of the program"; the University of North Carolina says that it "puts great emphasis on incorporating the international realities of business into every aspect of the program to assure that students are poised to compete in a global environment"; the University of Rochester more simply declared its program "a model for global management." The University of Chicago became, apparently, the first of the large universities to offer an entirely separate degree, the International Master of Business Administration, starting in 1995. Specific courses around the country ranged from the functional ones (International Accounting, International Finance, International Law, International Marketing, and so on, as taught at the University of Alabama) to more comprehensive ones such as "Global Strategic Management" (Utah), "Management and the International Economy" (Vanderbilt), and "International Business Analysis" (North Carolina). Stanford's curriculum in 1995 contained seventeen separate courses in international business, making it probably the most comprehensive and thoroughly committed to global studies; yet even among the smallest schools and those furthest from the oceans, every single curriculum by now reflects the new emphasis on business beyond national boundaries.

Entrepreneurship. To a person of the 1990s the relationship of entrepreneurship to education in business seems so obvious it needs no explanation. But, as previous chapters have shown, the idea did not make its first real appearance until the 1960s, and its growth in the next two decades was steady but not really fast. Starting with the mid-1980s, all that changed. More and more, people came to see all business as a kind of entrepreneurship, whether within corporations or independently, and business schools responded by elevating the subject to the first rank of importance.

Awareness that entrepreneurship had arrived as a business school subject came rather abruptly in 1985. The extent to which it had already grown by then is startling. The *Wall Street Journal* reported in April of that year that the number of schools teaching entrepreneurship had grown from just 6 in 1967 to 240 in 1985, and in August *The New York Times* reported a different set of figures, even more startling, for the same period—an increase from 10 to 340. Regardless of whether the actual increase was thirty-four-fold or forty-fold, it clearly constituted one of the most striking developments in business education during the 1970s and early 1980s. By the summer of 1985 the *American Journal of Small Business* saw the movement as significant enough to warrant devoting an entire issue to the subject, with an invited keynote article entitled "The Educated Entrepreneurs: A New Era of Entrepreneurial Education Is Beginning."[13]

As with all such major developments, the movement did meet with some resistance. Traditional academics, who had always regarded business as administrating rather than risk taking, viewed it as a temporary fad. Some predicted it would last only about three years, and a Harvard professor dismissed it as merely a gimmick for getting money from rich alumni. One strong advocate of entrepreneurship education viewed this reluctant attitude as grounded in nothing more than self-interest:

> Researching larger organizations led to consulting contracts, board positions, funded chairs, and other perks that corporate America was ready to fund. Over

the years, the result was the evolution of a system of management education with an implicit value system that clearly favored the large organization over the small, the ongoing business versus the emerging, the follower versus the leader, the steward versus the creator and risk taker. Those who bucked this system found the road a rough one.[14]

But this time the entrepreneurship movement was unstoppable. Major schools had become deeply involved and were experiencing great success. New York University encouraged its entrepreneurial students by offering to invest $5,000 in any project they came up with that got approval from a venture capitalist. The Wharton School moved so strongly into entrepreneurship it attracted *The New York Times Magazine*'s attention, and even the University of Chicago started offering it in 1986. Babson College in Massachusetts, one of the early leaders and ardent champions of entrepreneurial education, sponsored a conference devoted to the subject in early 1987. By the end of the 1980s, the movement was so strong that virtually no school was without some sort of entrepreneurship program, and yet complaints were being made to the effect that the schools had not gone far enough in providing this valuable kind of instruction.[15]

The demand for an opportunity to study forming one's own business was huge by 1990. By 1993 *Business Week* reported that the already large number of entrepreneurial-minded MBA students was still increasing, and that schools were adding more courses, providing students with links to venture capitalists, and encouraging students to enter entrepreneurial competitions. The magnitude of the movement can be gauged from the fact that more than one-fifth of UCLA's MBA graduates in 1993 had gone into start-ups, buy-outs, or businesses with fewer than two hundred employees, as compared with virtually none just a decade earlier. The movement existed also, although perhaps less strongly, in Great Britain, where the International Management Centre sponsored master's theses on entrepreneurship as well as on "intrapreneurship"—a 1980s-coined term denoting entrepreneurial activities within a large firm. The emphasis was on implementation: one of the studies undertook to determine what conditions needed to exist in order for the intrapreneurial ideas proposed in a theoretical thesis to be put into practice in a corporation.[16]

Most of the schools simply called their courses "Entrepreneurship" and taught them as surveys of the field. Stanford offered six such courses, with names such as "Entrepreneurial Investment and Venture Capital." At other schools they went under related titles, such as "Small Business Counseling" (Utah) and "New Ventures" (North Carolina), and in many instances, such as at Rutgers, these courses were tied in closely with student fieldwork, under names like "Entrepreneurship Development and Consultation."

Quality. The movement toward teaching Total Quality Management (TQM) was slower getting started but ultimately more important. Although

Japan sponsored an institute on the subject in Europe in 1986, it was not until 1988 that TQM began appearing prominently in the United States. In July of that year, Fordham University in New York established a Center for Advanced Management Studies, basing its work on the principles laid down by the venerable W. Edwards Deming.[17]

Yet despite some national attention attracted by the center, other schools still were slow in following Fordham's lead. In 1991 *Incentive* magazine could report that major corporations, such as Motorola and Xerox, were angry over business schools' failure to teach quality. A lively book, *Quality or Else,* published that same year, quoted several vociferous critics who berated the schools for not teaching about quality. Columnist Robert J. Samuelson tellingly pointed to the statistics:

> Between 1962 and 1987 the annual number of MBA graduates (in the U.S.) rose from 5,787 to 67,496. There are now more than a million MBAs. If they were improving the quality of U.S. management, the results ought to be obvious by now.

TQM expert Armand Feigenbaum added that the schools had not yet recognized "that quality is fundamentally a body of knowledge, an important body of knowledge, a teachable body of knowledge." The secretary general of the European Foundation for Quality Management decried the fact that, as of the time he made his statement, not one single school, either in Europe or in the United States, was teaching TQM as it should be taught—not as one more discipline, alongside finance and marketing, but as "a stream across the existing disciplines." W. Edwards Deming himself took the most pessimistic view of all: Teaching of quality in a business school is "absolutely impossible because there is nobody in the faculty that knows anything about it. . . . What they do is teach students how business is carried on. That's how to perpetuate it, exactly what we do not need. Nothing could be worse."[18]

But resistance was beginning to dissolve. In 1989 Procter and Gamble, Xerox, Motorola, American Express, General Motors, IBM, 3M, and other major corporations established annual events, called "TQ Forums," to encourage the development of TQM components in business and engineering schools. In 1992, at the fifth forum, a $9 million grant program for universities was announced. Later that same year *Management Review* magazine reported that of all the new areas of curricular experimentation in business schools, TQM headed the list. One school in particular, the University of Tennessee, began to attract attention at this time as perhaps the first to adopt TQM as the organizing philosophy for its entire MBA program.[19]

Within a year, TQM had spread across the nation so fast that there was no keeping track of it. An *Industry Week* cover story cited it as the single subject of greatest importance and the subject most added to curricula in the past two years and described in detail the programs at Rochester, Penn

State, Michigan, Dayton, and Wharton, in addition to the impressive one at Tennessee.[20]

Thus some thirty years after the quality revolution in Japan and ten years after American firms had begun to take notice, schools of business had finally and irrevocably recognized TQM as a basic, and sometimes as the basic, subject to be studied. At present hardly a school exists that does not have a course called "TQM" or "Quality Management," or at least include substantial amounts of TQM instruction in the course descriptions.

Ethics. Unlike TQM, which was unheard of in business schools before the 1980s, business ethics courses have a long history. The 1846 article on "The Education of a Man of Business" (referred to in chapter 1) mentioned moral principles as one of the most basic requirements, and several early MBA programs, such as that at Harvard in 1916, had included a course in ethics. But before the 1980s, the subject had never really caught on. More books were written on business ethics between 1981 and 1986 than had been written in the previous twenty-five years together, and business schools could not ignore the sudden rise in public interest.[21]

Most of the swirling debate about ethics in business schools has revolved around the issues of whether it can be taught, what the purpose is in teaching it, where in the program the instruction should occur, and by what method.

As for *whether it's possible to teach ethics,* many have argued that ethics cannot be taught, that moral attitudes are already established by the time students reach graduate school. Courses, in their view, remain hopelessly theoretical, perhaps inculcating some cognitive information but not in any way altering behavior. One professor, citing the recent publication of thirty books on ethics, the founding of two new ethics journals, and the establishment of half a dozen research centers, pointed out how inefficient all these efforts were. All that mattered, he argued, was the attitude of the company employing the students after graduation: if the company wanted ethical behavior, the employees would behave ethically. One survey at the time, however, indicated that businesspeople themselves were more sanguine about the courses: only 11 percent of those questioned believed that effective teaching of ethics was impossible.[22]

The purpose of teaching ethics is equally controversial. Even among those who believe that ethics can and should be taught in schools, the stated reasons for doing so have varied widely. Presumably everybody hopes that such instruction will result in behavior on a higher ethical plane, but the actual claims are much more abstract and general. Some say simply that ethics courses will help focus the students' minds, while others speak of heightening their awareness of ethical issues. One articulate professor has argued that, through teaching the students various ethical systems—utilitarianism, universalism, distributive justice, and personal liberty—a school can at least show the students what's the right thing to do, even though it cannot necessarily make them do it. A typical and fairly comprehensive purpose statement is the following one by a professor, who makes lofty claims for the course but never quite promises any behavior changes as a result:

> The general purpose of the teaching of ethics ought to be that of stimulating the moral imagination, developing skills in the recognition and analysis of moral issues, eliciting a sense of moral obligation and personal responsibility, and learning both to tolerate and to resist moral disagreement and ambiguity.[23]

With respect to *when in the business program to teach ethics,* every possible variation has had its advocates. Most schools simply remain within their traditional framework by instituting one or more courses on the subject. A few, such as Iona College, have declared an "Institute of Ethics," suggesting a somewhat greater intention to emphasize research. Several people have argued that ethics should not be considered a separate subject but should be integrated into all courses. Dean Lester Thurow of MIT has written that schools can accomplish much by changing the emphasis in their existing courses. Finance courses, for example, can point out that merely maximizing net worth is not a satisfactory objective, and business law courses can emphasize broader considerations than merely what is legal. Social philosopher Amitai Etzioni later made the same point, citing as bad examples marketing courses that teach that manipulating customers is ethical and finance courses that teach how to break implicit contracts. Finally, one school has made use of visiting lecturers with special experience in the ethical field: convicted business felons from a nearby penitentiary who come to tell the students ruefully about their white-collar transgressions.[24]

How to teach ethics, and exactly what should be taught, of course, also vary widely from one school to another. One professor argues that no special course content is required because humanities courses give students all the ethical instruction they need. Most schools, however, do use specifically business-related materials, relying on the traditional lecture, discussion, and case methods in teaching them. One professor has found success in using group dynamics to raise students from one stage of moral development to a higher one; another recommends a system model such as is commonly used in the training field; and, in Britain, Harley Management College claims to experience success using computer conferencing as a way of encouraging student interaction in applying theoretical principles to actual situations.[25]

Starting at the end of the 1980s, surveys of students' ethical attitudes and practices began appearing. Now that fairly large numbers of students were taking ethics courses, researchers could begin looking for their common characteristics and for evidence of any changes occurring as a result of the studies. Several surveys found that business students were less ethical than other students, especially law students, and one study found that students in 1987 were less ethical than those in 1981.

Although such studies frequently became newspaper headlines and tele-

vision talk-show topics, doubts about their real significance were often expressed. Generally the studies did not fully take into account the differences
among various kinds of ethical instruction, the ethical propensities of students before they took the courses, or the amount of actual experience the
students had had. Furthermore the survey samples were inevitably smaller
than desirable, and not enough time has elapsed for a truly meaningful longi-
tudinal study. Finally, the nature of the subject guarantees that survey results will always be only dubiously reliable: a person may say on a
questionnaire that a certain action is ethical or unethical, but no survey can
ascertain whether that person will actually choose the ethical action in a
real-life setting. In many ways, the teaching of business ethics seems to
be still at a fairly primitive stage, with methods altogether inadequate to
the tasks.[26]

Ethics thus has become a major concern in all business schools, but
because the subject is often taught within other courses rather than separately it often shows up less prominently in curricular listings. When it does,
it may be simply as "Ethics" or "Ethics in Business," or it may have a more
elaborate name, such as "Business, Law, and Ethics in Modern Society"
(Connecticut), "Ethical and Legal Considerations" (Nebraska), or "Legal,
Political, and Ethical Issues for Business" (Arizona State). However it is
incorporated into the curriculum, its presence is unquestionably far greater
now than in any previous era in the history of business schools.

"Soft," Hard-to-Measure Skills. The almost sudden resurgence of "soft"
skills—variously described as "management," "people," "relationship," "interpersonal," or "leadership" skills—caught many observers by surprise.
Although surveys and other kinds of studies had long shown that such skills
were the ones that corporations deemed most lacking in new MBAs, the
schools generally had remained locked in the traditional teaching areas such
as finance, marketing, and production. By 1985, however, major changes
were evident. That year, AACSB announced a ten-year project to develop
a course in leadership, and Harvard introduced a course called "The Social
Psychology of Management," dealing with family concerns, and another
called "Power and Influence," which dealt with company politics.[27]

By the spring of 1986, the clamor could be heard everywhere. *Fortune*
said that a mandate was emerging for business schools to increase their
emphasis on "people" skills, and *Business Week* noted that schools everywhere were adding large numbers of such courses. One dean noted a greater
concern nationwide with such people skills as leadership and negotiation,
and another—an economist by training—said that "The most important
thing people can know is how to get along with and motivate others." Even
quantitative-oriented schools such as Carnegie Mellon introduced several
"soft" courses, and MIT announced a $5 million research project to assess
how technology had affected management practices.[28]

Over the next two years the movement toward new and expanded soft courses grew sharply. Several people testified to the need. In an important article and a major book, Stanford's management behavior expert, Harold J. Leavitt, forcefully argued that "pathfinding"—consisting of vision, values, and determination—was the most needed characteristic for a successful businessperson. But instead of teaching it, he went on, schools persisted in concentrating on far less important technical skills. "We have," he wrote, "built a weird, almost unimaginable design for MBA-level education. We then lay it upon well-proportioned young men and women, distorting them (when we are unlucky enough to succeed) into critters with lopsided brains, icy hearts, and shrunken souls."[29]

Others made similar observations. Dean Palmer of Wharton said that American business needs leaders, not maximizers of shareholders' value. Economist Leonard Silk criticized the schools for continuing to teach problem solving when values, goals, and vision are what is most needed. A Canadian survey of executives in multinational corporations revealed that soft skills were valued above all others: the six most desired competencies identified were communication skills, leadership skills, interpersonal skills, adaptability and flexibility, ethical and moral standards, and management skills—a list that forms a sharp contrast with what schools always had been and, to a very large extent, still were teaching.[30]

Three MIT professors argued in a book written in 1989 that schools must teach teamwork, human relations, and labor relations, in addition to the traditional emphasis on technology, if this country is to regain its competitive superiority in the global marketplace. And a Moravian College professor similarly argued that "cultural skills"—meaning a systems perspective, teaching how various parts function and how they relate to society—occupy a place at least as important as technical skills in business, and that schools should keep that fact in mind when training people. At the Wharton School, he pointed out, seven of the eight core units, and four of the five major units, were technical; at Harvard, even though the catalog said the school had a systems approach, all courses listed still were technical. In early MBA programs, he maintained, it made sense to focus on technical skills, since the students had generally been educated in the liberal arts. But today, with most students coming to MBA schools after studying business as undergraduates, the need is for nontechnical training.[31]

The schools clearly were listening. Chicago instituted a "Leadership Exploration and Development" (LEAD) program, and the University of Denver accepted a ten million dollar gift to establish a six-week program to train its students in the social graces. Even in the operations management and quantitative methods fields, a change toward softness was evident. Two professors at the University of Virginia's Darden School discerned four recent trends in those fields:

(1) Pedagogy has become less mathematical and more managerial.

(2) In Operations Management, the proportion of attention devoted to manufacturing operations has decreased, and that to service operations has increased.

(3) Production and inventory systems courses are being supplanted by courses in service management, quality, technology, and strategy.

(4) In Quantitative Methods, less emphasis is being put on mathematical detail, and more on formulation, application, and interpretation.[32]

The trend has continued without diminishing. In Britain, when (in 1989) the Council for Management Education and Development undertook to identify the competencies a manager should be able to demonstrate, it produced a list of nine "areas of knowledge and skill." Just ten years earlier the list would undoubtedly have contained mostly technical subjects, but now it was almost exclusively "soft" and nontechnical:

1. Identification of the management task
2. Personal skills
3. Effective management
4. Information management
5. Environment of the manager
6. Managing people
7. Managing resources
8. Client/customer relations
9. Personal effectiveness[33]

Globalization and the resulting multicultural workforce, among other things, are serving to reinforce the need for people skills. Corporations' preference for people trained in these skills was made clear in a study commissioned by the Darden School. Corporate recruiters identified the three most important characteristics they seek in prospective employees as communication skills, interpersonal skills, and self-motivation or initiative.[34]

Deemphasis of Finance. Although finance students continue to outnumber all others at most business schools, a trend away from finance and toward manufacturing and operations has definitely been taking place.

Even before the stock market dip in October 1987, rumblings of discontent were already being heard. The wave of scandals—mostly insider trading—that had rocked Wall Street earlier in the decade had made many people critical of the new breed of MBA, steeped in financial manipulation but otherwise ignorant of, and indifferent to, business. The Wharton School attracted an especially large amount of attention because of the prominent names, some of them shady, among their alumni—notably Saul Steinberg, Laurence Tisch, Ronald Perelman, Michael Milken, and Donald Trump. Whether the scandals deterred students from financial careers is uncertain. The *Wall Street Journal* reported in January 1987 that students were not changing their career plans, but in July another publication reported that changes—away from "balance sheet wizardry" and toward broader management skills—were in fact beginning to be evident. Apparently they were. In the spring, UCLA's Center on Futures Research had had to close down because of a lack of funding. Concern about "management by balance sheet" had been heard before, but this time it seemed to be growing ominous.[35]

After the October crash, changes did inevitably set in. The *Wall Street Journal,* hardly a week afterward, reported signs that some students were changing to different career plans, and two weeks later *Fortune* criticized the schools (mainly Harvard) for having lost their initial purpose: they had originally set out to build CEOs for American industry, but now they only trained people to get rich trading stock. The alumni, one alumnus said, are "not captains of industry but well paid lieutenants of Wall Street."[36]

By 1988 it was clear that a movement away from studies and careers in finance had indeed begun. A report in February said that recruitment by investment banks was already down 50 percent, and that no more than 20 percent of graduating students, as opposed to 30 percent the year before, were planning on investment banking careers. In March and again in April the *Wall Street Journal* reported a decline in student interest in Wall Street and investment banking, and by May *Industry Week* was wondering if manufacturing companies were ready to accept the larger number of new MBAs who were suddenly expressing interest in that kind of work. Consulting, manufacturing, and entrepreneurship were up everywhere, while banking and finance were sharply down—from 25 percent to 17 percent at Wharton, from 30 percent to 11 percent at Harvard, and similarly in other schools. The one recorded exception was Duke University's Fuqua School, where for some reason 17 percent more students expressed an interest in Wall Street careers than had done so before the crash.[37]

The long-predicted rise in students' interest in manufacturing and marketing careers was slowly but definitely underway. MIT's Sloan School established a joint degree program in management and manufacturing in 1988, and Northwestern, Carnegie Mellon, and Stanford did the same later. Called an "MMM"—Master's in Management and Manufacturing"—Northwestern's degree combined courses from the engineering and business schools in an effort to avoid the narrowness that could accompany study in one school alone. Big marketing firms, like Heinz, Clorox, Pepsico, and Kraft General Foods, did report a sharp increase in MBA interest, but manufacturing seems to have been the biggest beneficiary of the decline of finance.[38]

Ad Hoc Programs. In a lesser trend, business schools began addressing some much more specific topics than before. In some respects this change marked a reversal of the earlier change, when schools gave up their programs in meat-packing operations, the printing industry, mine technology, and baking. After three or four decades of general functional courses in finance, marketing, production, and management, businesses seem to have become impatient and to have demanded a more specific kind of education. Some companies contracted with schools for entirely customized programs; others used in-house courses and thereby sent a signal to the schools about what was wanted. "Specific, real-world goals" and "projects tied to real issues" were phrases often heard.[39]

Among the specialized programs and courses that business schools began to offer were some attention-getters like "The Commercial Development of Space" (Stanford). Several schools offered the opportunity to study in courses titled "Restructuring," "Failures," and "Crisis Management," as those subjects became prominent in the 1980s. "Product Design," "Health Care Management," "Sports Management," "Agriculture Management," and even "Country Music Management" programs could be found, as well as a Center for the Study of the Communications Industry at Fordham. A number of schools, including Case Western University, focused on the management of nonprofit enterprises.[40]

The example of real estate offers an insight into the dilemma that schools found themselves in with regard to offering such specific courses. Courses in real estate began flourishing in the mid-1980s, and graduates were reported to be getting good positions with prosperous firms that were, apparently, pleased with the products the schools were turning out. At the same time, however, some professionals in the field expressed distrust for the programs, calling them "formula-laden" and claiming that their methodical approach destroyed creativity. Thus it has become clear that some factions in the business community want such courses and others do not—and business schools are accused of faddishness if they offer them and unresponsiveness if they do not.[41]

New Methods of Teaching

Along with the new subjects being taught have come new ways of presenting them. None of them actually is new, but all run counter to the directions that MBA schools had been following for the previous twenty years. Four main directions of change stand out: away from analysis and toward synthesis, away from academic learning and toward experiential, away from quantitative studies and toward management and leadership, and away from functional or departmental studies and toward interdisciplinary approaches.

Synthesis. The accusation that "MBA" means "management by analysis" has been occasionally heard before, but since the mid-1980s it has been almost constantly in evidence. Instead of teaching how to break problems down into their components, the argument goes, business schools should be teaching students how to combine various pieces of information and knowledge into far-reaching decisions. Several critics of earlier MBA programs cited Harold Geneen and Robert McNamara as typical of the defective products those programs turned out—management of a conglomerate by balance sheet and management of a war by body count. No one, of course, has devised any recipe for creating clear constructive thinking, but emphasis on breadth, including wide learning in the humanities and social sciences, has been often mentioned.[42]

Experiential. For three decades following the academic-minded foundation reports of 1959, MBA programs tended to stress classroom learning rather than experience. By the mid-1980s this emphasis had become the object of a fair amount of criticism. In 1984 Secretary of Commerce Malcolm Baldrige accused the schools of pointing their students in the wrong direction—"up in the ivory tower" rather than "down on the factory floor." The professors were singled out for special censure, due mainly to what most observers saw as their increasingly irrelevant research and the perception that most professors never got close enough to a real business to see what really went on there. The *Wall Street Journal* devoted an entire article to mocking the theoretical research papers presented at a conference of the Academy of Management in 1988. Quite naturally, the graduates that business schools turned out also came in for a share of ridicule. The dean at Cornell contrasted them with the graduates of other kinds of schools:

> You can't imagine a medical school offering a degree to a doctor who hadn't been in an operating room. And in education you have to go in and teach and be supervised. [But] in business school we are completely indifferent as to whether people can practice or not.[43]

Changes began to be evident quite early in the decade. Fieldwork programs in which students participate in actual business continued to grow, until nearly every school had some sort of real world component. At least fourteen such programs were in operation in Canada by 1985. In a real-world move that seemed at the time likely to start a trend but did not, Harvard Business School announced in 1985 that it would no longer use the GMAT as a criterion for admission; it wanted good managers, according to the announcement, and the test instead merely selected good students. Also in 1985 the *Wall Street Journal* reported that many companies had begun encouraging their employees to work for specialized certificates or diplomas rather than attend MBA schools, since the certificate programs were practical, as the MBA was not. By 1988 two professors could say that they clearly perceived changes occurring because of, among other things, the frequent call for more experiential techniques in the schools. By the mid-1990s the students in America's business schools were far more involved with real businesses than their counterparts a decade earlier had been, and the trend in that direction has continued to increase.[44]

Emphasis on People Rather than Mathematics. The deemphasis of financial and other mathematical subjects that was mentioned earlier has been more far-reaching than just a change in coursework. It constitutes a change in attitude which now permeates teaching throughout the schools. The name "number-crunchers" had been accusingly hurled at MBA graduates for some time, but it was heard more and more frequently in the 1980s, mostly as a result of financial scandals and the 1987 stock market plunge. The implication all along had been, and continued to be, that mathematical expertise was largely irrelevant to good management. A kind of confirmation of this view came in 1994 when the University of Southern California conducted a study showing that students who had the highest math scores on the GMAT were consistently the same ones who had the lowest scores on managerial aptitude tests. Even before that study, business schools had shown a clear shift away from the training of business technicians and toward concern with motivation and "corporate culture." The leadership programs described earlier were the big beneficiaries of this shift of emphasis. At the University of Chicago, for example, where mathematical rigor had long been the single most important feature of the MBA curriculum, now the Leadership Exploration and Development program commands considerably more space in the school's catalog.[45]

Interdisciplinary. No one who examines MBA catalogs today can fail to see the breaking down of traditional departmental walls. The teaching of single, separate subjects had characterized all business schools since the beginning, whether the subjects were viewed as academic disciplines (mathematics, psychology, languages, English) or as business functions (accounting, manufacturing, marketing, personnel). Occasional calls for the dismantling of these walls of separation had been heard over the years, but nothing much actually happened until the late 1980s.

By then, just about everybody suddenly seemed to agree that the abolition of separate departments and disciplines—so that students could see a business whole—was necessary and overdue. The new emphasis on strategy by such thinkers and practitioners as Harvard's eminent Michael Porter has contributed to the movement. Porter calls strategy "an integrative subject" because it involves finance, marketing, organizational behavior, production, and logistics. Instead of considering these subjects separately as business schools have done in the past, one must combine them so that a manager can see the company's situation more broadly. Stanford's Harold Leavitt used different terms but argued similarly that emphasis on separate subjects had stifled creativity and constricted vision. The "vision," "values," and "determination" categories into which he divided his "pathfinding" philosophy obviously cut across all curricular and functional lines.[46]

Schools have been working hard to put these ideas into practice. Prof. Leavitt has proposed establishing a close working relationship between students and faculty, a comprehensive examination each year to compel the students to look at the subjects integratedly rather than separately, and a required interdisciplinary research project by each student. The Wharton School has attracted much attention by instituting a new curricular model that replaces single-subject teaching with broad integrative courses and that also encourages cross-disciplinary research projects. A survey of many schools in late 1992 found that interdisciplinary studies and team-teaching by instructors from different subject areas have already become common. Such a movement, one distinguished observer says, not only strengthens the curriculum but "forces faculty members to think more broadly and talk to each other."[47]

New Philosophies

In the catalogs of business schools as well as in the constantly increasing literature on the subject of MBA education, one can easily perceive a major shift in the philosophy underlying the teaching of business. The shift, in a word, has been toward the active. Changed philosophies of the subject, of the teaching methods, of the role of schools in the business community, of the method of evaluating success, and of the place of education in a business career have evolved from the shift. All of these have made appearances in past decades, but their reemergence at this time indicates a new direction in which MBA education is pointing.

An Active Philosophy of the Subject. The concept of business as a static group of principles waiting to be discovered and analyzed is dead forever. In the early decades of the MBA, as shown in previous chapters, everyone had believed in the existence of great "laws of commerce" that students could discover by analyzing data. These laws were considered universal and immutable, and consequently the task of the businessperson was to oversee their workings in a particular firm—thus the name business "administration." The administrator's job consisted of evaluating the various options at each decision point—whether to expand an operation, increase inventory, market a new product—and then making the choice most in keeping with the laws of commerce.

Such a view of business was essentially passive—a successful path was there if people could only discover it. That view has entirely given way to an active view, in which the main task of a business executive is now not so much to evaluate options as to generate them. Instead of believing that timeless theories, once discovered, can be brought to bear on any situation, people no longer believe in timeless theories at all. The successful businessperson is the one who creates opportunities rather than discovers them, and this creation process involves seeing and exploiting specific openings rather than applying laws. Criticisms that America's business schools had too long been theory driven instead of market driven were heard often, and the schools have responded with a clear move toward a more active view of business.[48]

An Active Philosophy of Teaching Methods. The old teaching model, in which students reportedly spent all their time sitting in classrooms and tak-

ing notes while the professors lectured, was probably never quite as universal as legend portrayed it, but in any case it has by now come close to
vanishing altogether. Much more common now is for students to work, in
teams, on projects that either are real or that closely simulate reality.

Fieldwork programs, as previously noted, have become virtually universal, but other forms abound also. Some companies sponsor competitions in
which student teams from many business schools vie to design or market a
new project. Also, professors use students to assist in consulting work, an
arrangement that sometimes has led to ethical questions by mixing financial
and academic incentives. Some universities and companies have formed
close working relationships in which students participate in day-to-day decision making and operations—an arrangement that, again, has occasionally
raised ethical questions. Back in 1930, as noted in chapter 4, Abraham
Flexner had decried Harvard's involvement in an advertising campaign for
Pet Milk. "Is it a proper concern of Harvard University?" he had asked,
with the clear implication that it was not. But sixty years later the emphasis
has shifted. No longer is such activity seen as assistance to a company;
instead it is seen as education for students, and thus the clear answer today
is that this kind of activity is precisely what students should be exposed to,
because it provides an active element to their education. It involves them
rather than merely instructing them.[49]

An Active View of the Business School's Role. Closely related to these
trends is a clear movement to get business schools themselves more actively
involved in the business world. Close relations had been advocated ever
since business schools began early in the century, generally taking the form
of executives serving as visiting lecturers in the university and students
serving as interns in companies. Such arrangements have continued to the
present: executives (even labor leaders) in residence, as previously noted,
are standard fixtures in most business schools, and fieldwork programs of
all descriptions are everywhere.

But since the 1980s such cooperation has expanded far beyond anything
seen before and has also taken new forms. In-house MBA programs, designed for and located entirely within companies, used to make news; nowa-
days they are so common nobody gives them any notice. The Kellogg School
at Northwestern University has emphasized such arrangements, and Babson
College in Massachusetts has even built a separate building for "company"
programs. Although some schools (Harvard and Stanford, for example) have
regarded such programs as dubious because they see ethical problems with
them, nearly all others welcome any such opportunities. In New Jersey,
Seton Hall University has established an MBA program for AT&T, and
nearby Rutgers University operates one for Merrill Lynch. Pace University
in New York City may have more such programs than any other university
in the nation. They are common also in Great Britain—for example the
business school at Strathclyde operates a program for the Rosyth Royal

Dockyard. More than any other one theme, this call for schools to become involved with the real world of business has dominated the works of reformers since 1985. Such respected thinkers as Henry Mintzberg have decried the distance between schools and companies, and no doubt partly as a result of their criticisms the two have grown unprecedentedly closer.[50]

An Active View of Evaluation. Output studies began in earnest in the early 1980s, and they have grown in size and importance to the present. No longer can an MBA school point solely to the number of Ph.D.s on its faculty, the number of books in its library, or the number of computers in its laboratories as evidence of its high quality. The most important criteria now, to all its constituencies, are those showing the success of its graduates. For example, the infamous "rankings," which have grown so important that schools uniformly scramble to get onto the lists, now all consider output criteria, such as the graduates' starting salaries and the opinions of alumni, in reaching their decisions. Also, university catalogs, which once refused to mention salaries, now openly brag about the money their graduates earn. Even newspaper surveys of students, which used to focus on their age, undergraduate major, and family background, now concern themselves mainly with career plans and expectations. A 1989 article about Harvard MBAs in Canada, a subject that ten years earlier would have been mainly a report, focused instead on the question of whether these young executives were what Canadian business actually needed—again reflecting the shift to an interest in outcomes.[51]

AACSB's ten-year "Outcome Measurement Project" was completed during the late 1980s, reflecting the wide interest in active or "output" evaluation. It consisted of measurement instruments to evaluate both the subject knowledge that a student should have learned in school and the skills and personal characteristics that a good manager should possess. The original intention was that the test would be administered to all entrants and all graduates of all business schools, so that the schools could be evaluated by measuring the value added to a student's worth as a result of study there. The project never actually turned out as intended because many people objected, some citing oversimplified criteria and others a possible conflict of interest. The fact that the project was undertaken at all, however, especially with a very large commitment of time and money, demonstrates the strength of the movement toward evaluation by output rather than input criteria.[52]

Active Involvement Throughout Careers. Interest in the concept of "lifelong learning" began to appear prominently in the mid-1980s, reflecting a view that a business school should actively interact with its clients throughout their careers rather than just at the beginning. This is not the same thing as "executive education," which, as previous chapters have noted, had been a lively movement for some time by now. That movement—executive education—began years ago at the University of Chicago, and it has by now grown to be a big business especially at a few major schools, such as Wharton, Northwestern University's Kellogg School, Duke University's Fuqua School, and Columbia University. *The New York Times* noted a 356 percent increase in the number of general management programs for executives, and an 856 percent increase in functional management programs, between 1962 and 1987—involving a 1,100 percent increase in the number of participants. The quality of such programs is sometimes called into question, as in a nationwide study conducted by Vanderbilt University's Owen School, but no one can doubt their popularity.[53]

But the emphasis this time is different. In recognition of the fact that management knowledge is accumulating at an unprecedented rate, which means that the skills a student learns in MBA school are said to be obsolete in five to seven years, the business schools have begun thinking of management education as a lifelong affair, something that needs updating every few years. Whereas executive education programs mostly aim at providing MBA degrees for managers in midcareer, lifelong learning aims at supplementing earlier education by looking at recent developments. As far back as 1986, Dean H. J. Zoffer at the University of Pittsburgh (who incidentally had been one of the founders of AACSB's Outcomes Evaluation project) listed the creation of "career-long education," or "educational segmentation," as one of his six principal aims as dean. By 1988 it was already being cited as a major trend across the country, and it has increased steadily to the present. The MBA, suddenly, is no longer considered a terminal degree.[54]

The MBA and the Public

As scattered and disparate as this list of new MBA developments may seem to be (Ill. 13–1), it actually represents a rather amazing consensus: virtually everybody agrees that these are the things that need to be done. Four book-length reports in the late 1980s, all regarded by their authors and sponsors as "major," "milestone," "blockbuster," and so on, all said virtually the same things. The Business-Higher Education Forum produced in 1985 a report called *America's Business Schools: Priorities for Change;* Britain's premier management guru, Charles Handy, wrote *The Making of Managers* for the Manpower Services Commission of the British Institute of Management in 1987; in 1988 two professors from the Universities of California and Oklahoma compiled a report for AACSB, *Management Education and Development: Drift or Thrust into the 21st Century,* which attracted much media attention; and in 1987 three MIT scholars—Professors Dertouzos, Lester, and Solow—wrote, as previously noted, an impressive blueprint for improving American business and business education—*Made in America: Regaining the Productive Edge.* From four such diverse sources—the U.S. government, a British management organization, an academic association

Illustration 13-1:

SUMMARY OF TRENDS IN MBA SCHOOLS SINCE 1985

Curriculum

    globalism
    entrepreneurship
    quality management
    ethics
    soft skills
    manufacturing
    ad hoc programs

Teaching Methods

    synthesis
    experience
    emphasis on people
    interdisciplinary work

Philosophy of Educating for Business

    active conception of the subject
    active approach to methods
    active view of the role of schools
    active methods of evaluation
    active involvement in careers

in America, and three professors (two engineers and an economist)—came one message: Business education must become more active.

Thus it is apparently true that what looks at first like a state of disarray actually represents more unanimity of opinion than most past decades have shown. Although schools have chosen many different ways of attaining their goal, the goal itself is a matter of common agreement: to bring the MBA programs out of their ivory tower isolation and into the real world.

So far as public opinion is concerned, the results have been very positive. Even amid the economic malaise that settled in across the United States and the world in the late 1980s, the press reports were quite favorable. The Conference Board reported the results of a survey showing that more executives than ever before had MBAs and other advanced degrees, and a *Business Horizons* article by two professors said the same thing: among the people promoted to vice president or higher in American industry, the percentage with master's degrees (mostly in business) had risen from 18 percent to 25 percent in the nine years from 1967 to 1976 (and higher since), and in forty top companies nearly half the upper level executives had MBAs. By 1985, as these professors noted in amazement, an MBA had replaced a liberal arts master's degree as the mark of a well-educated person. A Harris Poll in 1986 confirmed this sudden rise to a position of prestige: of the executives surveyed, 81 percent said business schools were "pretty good" or "excellent," 79 percent said earning an MBA was the only way to get ahead in their companies, and, most impressively, 78 percent said they would advise their children to get an MBA. Whatever complaints these executives may have expressed about too much theory and too high expectations were drowned out by the positive attitudes they themselves held.[55]

Corporate hiring practices in the late 1980s showed that this attitude was more than just lip service. The Dillon, Read investment company bought an eight-page advertisement in the Harvard Business School newspaper to proclaim the advantage of working for the firm, and employers regularly engaged in elaborate pursuit of top students, including extensive and expensive entertaining. Recruiting, one observer noted, was truly a *big* business, and one of the principal duties of executives was to recruit new MBAs from the most prestigious schools. Even if no other reasons existed, the status value alone motivated companies: They found it "nice to have a couple of Harvard MBAs parked in our driveway."[56]

The positive tone is continuing up to the very present. Whether evaluating the contribution of young MBA holders to a company or advising aspiring young businesspeople about the value of the degree for their careers, observers of the business scene have been far more complimentary than critical. A journal from the chemical industry raved that today's innovative, multidisciplinary, global-minded MBAs know more about business operations than ever before and can handle all aspects of product development from conception all the way through design, manufacture, and marketing. An international business journal quoted major executives as calling the MBA degree "a big plus" or even "a prerequisite," and an entire book was devoted to *The MBA Advantage: Why It Pays to Get an MBA*. Even the widespread belief that young MBA holders are finding it hard to get a job—which, as the beginning of this chapter noted, has had some basis in fact—was challenged by *Business Week* in late 1994: U.S.-based multinational firms, especially in management consulting and investment banking, are leading the way in a rejuvenated and very active recruitment market. The nay-sayers once again are in the minority, and the chorus of acclaim is strong, as the MBA approaches the end of its first century.[57]

Epilogue and Prologue

During the next year,

Somebody will propose that MBA schools should cooperate more closely with businesses.

And somebody will accuse MBA schools of being too closely allied with businesses.

Somebody will denounce MBA schools for being too theoretical and abstract.

And somebody will denounce MBA schools for being too practical and unintellectual.

Somebody will declare that the new crop of MBA graduates are this country's best hope for the future.

And somebody will denounce MBA graduates for being too ambitious, disloyal, cocky, callous, and expensive.

Somebody will demand that business schools conduct more research.

And somebody will complain that business schools are too research driven.

Somebody will propose that business students should study the humanities in order to broaden their perspective.

And somebody will complain that the humanities, being vague and impractical, have failed to produce leaders and should be replaced by business studies.

Somebody will object that business has no place in a university.

And somebody will urge other departments of the university to become as practical, efficient, and goal oriented as the business schools.

Somebody will suggest surveying businesses to see what they really want.

And somebody will be foolish enough to undertake such a survey, with vast corporate and government funding. The results will show that businesses want people with strong communication and interpersonal skills, an ethical sense, a global perspective, and an understanding of more than just finance.

Consequently, somebody will announce that business schools should become more concerned with communication, interpersonal skills, personal development, ethics, globalism, and service to society.

And some business schools will reply by pointing out that they already teach these things. Others will reply by establishing, with vast corporate and government funding, centers for the study of each of them.

Finally, somebody will declare that the MBA degree is past its prime and about to wither into oblivion, pointing out not just that the job market is weak but that other countries, much more sensible than the United States, have never had any use for graduate study in business from the beginning.

And meanwhile, the MBA will continue to be one of the most popular degrees offered in universities in America and around the world.

*　*　*

If one looks at the history of the MBA in this way, it appears to consist of nothing more than an endless cycle of the same arguments and developments. The most recent comments and criticisms, as well as the most innovations by the schools, all have exact parallels in the past, often as far back as 1910 and 1915.

For example, astute readers with long memories will no doubt have noticed the resemblance between the comments of the Cornell Dean in 1988, quoted earlier in this chapter, and those of the president of the Boston Board of Trade in 1884, quoted in chapter 1. Both pointed out the ironic fact that whereas society would never permit physicians, lawyers, or ministers to practice their professions without adequate training, people entering into business are routinely expected to undertake their work without any certificate or experience. Both were ardently advocating more specific training for business careers.

Such cyclicality or repetition, of course, is entirely to be expected, because the MBA is a creature of two worlds. To the academic world it runs a constant risk of being too practical and unintellectual, while to the business world it is constantly in danger of being scorned by hard workers who believe that the rough-and-tumble of real life can never be taught in a school.

But if one looks beyond this obvious tossing back on forth on the practical-theoretical spectrum, the MBA has undeniably gone through major transformations during its first century. Its purposes and curricula today bear little resemblance to those of eighty years ago, and its rise to prominence in the world has no counterpart in the past. It has changed education, changed business, and changed society.

Whatever specific characteristics the MBA may take on in the future, it will surely remain what it has evolved into over the past few decades: the best existing example of "liberal education," combining history, literature, language, mathematics, statistics, psychology, sociology, philosophy, logic, science, and technology in a way that fosters creativity, innovation, and personal development and contributes to the welfare of society.

Its defects are easily laughed at, but a look at its history shows it growing constantly closer to one goal: finding the perfect training for young men and women of business.

Notes

CHAPTER 1. GETTING STARTED: BEFORE 1910

1. The early years of the Amos Tuck School are detailed in Robert H. Guest, *A Brief History of the Amos Tuck School* (1981), published by the Amos Tuck School Alumni Office; Mary Munter, *Tuck School History* (1990), published by the Trustees of Dartmouth College; Harlow S. Person, "Professional Training for Business," *The World's Work* 8 (May 1904): 4767–70; Person, "Education for Business," *Annals of the American Academy of Political and Social Science* 28 (July 1906): 101–14; Person, "The Amos Tuck School of Dartmouth College," *Journal of Political Economy* 21 (February 1913): 117–27; and Marjorie Siegel, "Graduate Business Education: It All Began at Dartmouth College," *Dun's Review* 115 (March 1980): 25, 27.

2. The two quotations are from an issue of the *Sunday Telegraph* (London) in 1974 and from James L. Hayes, "A New Generation," *Management Review* 66 (October 1977): 2–3.

3. Paciolo's work has been reprinted with translation and notes as *Paciolo on Accounting*, ed. R. G. Brown and K. S. Johnston (New York: McGraw-Hill, 1963). Bacon's statement occurs in *The Advancement of Learning*.

4. C. McFerron Gittinger, *Broadening Horizons: A History of the College of Business Administration at the University of South Carolina*. Columbia: University of South Carolina Press, 1974.

5. F. Hunt, "The Education of a Man of Business," *Hunt's Merchants' Magazine* 15 (October 1846): 381–84.

6. Watts's book was reprinted by the Harvard University Graduate School of Business in 1946.

7. Frederick G. Nichols, *Frederick G. Nichols' Memoirs, 1878–1954: The Early Years of Business Education* (St. Peter, Minn.: Delta Pi Epsilon, 1979), 8–16.

8. Quoted in Leverett S. Lyon, *Education for Business* (University of Chicago, 1922), 94.

9. Eliot, "Commercial Education," *Educational Review* 18 (December 1899): 417–24.

10. William J. Amos, "An Ideal Business College," *Proceedings of the National Education Association* 33 (1894): 971–76.

11. Senate Committee on Education and Labor, *Report of the Committee of the Senate upon the Relations between Labor and Capital* (Washington, D.C., 1885), vol. 2, 964 and 1115.

12. Ibid., vol 2, 1203 and 1324.

13. Eustace C. Fitz, *The High School in Relation to Business Life* (Boston: The New England Publishing Company, 1884).

14. Medill's testimony is in *Report of the Committee of the Senate,* vol. 2, *The New York Times* article is "Training for Workmen," 20 June 1885, 3. Another such article, "Every Man a Master," appeared two months later (17 August, p. 3).

15. Edmund J. James, "The Problem of Commercial Education," *Publications of*

the Michigan Political Science Association, vol 5, part 2, 7–39. Horace Greeley, *An Address on Success in Business* (New York: S. S. Packard, 1867), 30.

16. Edmund J. James, *Education of Business Men: An Address before the American Bankers' Association, Saratoga, N.Y., 3 September 1890,* 10.

17. James, *Education of Business Men,* 11–12; W. J. Ashley, "A Science of Commerce and Some Prolegomena," *Science Progress in the Twentieth Century: A Quarterly Journal of Scientific Thought,* 1 (July 1906): 3–11.

18. Reprinted in Andrew Carnegie, *The Empire of Business* (New York: Doubleday, 1902): 109–11.

19. Quoted in Lyon, *Education for Business,* 82.

20. Horace Greeley, *An Address on Success in Business* (New York: S. S. Packard, 1867): 27–28.

21. James, *Education of Business Men,* 12.

22. L. J. Nations, "Business before Culture: College Becomes an Institution of Higher Earnings," *North American Review* 229 (June 1930): 705–12.

23. John Lyly, *Love's Metamorphosis,* act 3.

24. Felix Nieto DelRio, "Commercial and Industrial Education in Chile," *Bulletin of the Pan American Union* 49 (August 1919): 177–80.

25. Edmund J. James, *Origin and Progress of Business Education in the United States: An Address at a Conference at the University of Illinois* (1913), quoted in Benjamin Haynes and Harry Jackson, *A History of Business Education in the United States* (Cincinnati: Southwestern, 1935), 89.

26. Quoted in "Famous Firsts: How Business Schools Began," *Business Week,* 19 October 1963, 114–16.

27. Greeley, *An Address on Success in Business,* 21.

28. Morris Bishop, *A History of Cornell* (Ithaca: Cornell University Press, 1962); University of Illinois catalog (1868), 195; Henry R. Towne, "The Engineer As an Economist," *Transactions of the American Society of Mechanical Engineers* 7 (1886): 428–32; and Robert E. Lee's report to the trustees, quoted in Leon C. Marshall, *The American Collegiate School of Business* (Chicago: University of Chicago Press, 1928), 3.

29. Information about Joseph Wharton and his bequest is taken from Joanna W. Lippincott, *Biographical Memoranda Concerning Joseph Wharton, 1826–1901* (Philadelphia: Lippincott, 1909), and from Steven A. Sass's fine history of the Wharton School, *The Pragmatic Imagination* (Philadelphia: University of Pennsylvania Press, 1982), chapter 1.

30. From the preface to J. K. Ingram, *A History of Political Economy* (New York: Macmillan, 1888).

31. Notes of the ABA's Committee on Finance and Economy, 1 February 1892, appended to James, *Education of Business Men.*

32. Edmund J. James, *The Education of Business Men in Europe* (New York: American Bankers Association, 1893), 142.

33. Ibid., 181.

34. In addition to other sources as noted, I have relied for some of the information on James on Evarts B. Greene's article in the *Dictionary of American Biography.*

35. Frank Vanderlip, "Trade Schools" (1906), reprinted in *Business and Education* (New York: Duffield, 1907), a collection of Vanderlip's writings. Other speeches and articles referred to here are also included in that volume.

36. "Coordination of Higher Education" (1905).

37. "Political Problems of Europe," (n.d.), 409–10.

38. A New College Degree" (1905), 27.

39. Frank Vanderlip, *The Ultimate Dependence of New England upon Foreign Trade: Address Delivered before the Commercial Club of Boston, 19 March 1903.*

40. "A New College Degree," 41.

41. Person's diagram is reprinted in an article by Willard S. Hotchkiss, "The Basic Elements and Their Proper Balance in the Curriculum of a Collegiate Business School," *Journal of Political Economy* 28 (February 1920): 89–107.

42. This formulation appears in his "Education for Business," *Annals of the American Academy of Political and Social Science* 28 (July 1906): 101–14, and in his "University Schools of Business and the Training of Employment Executives," *Annals of the American Academy* 65 (May 1916): 117–27.

43. Person, "The Amos Tuck School at Dartmouth College," 120.

44. The earlier sentiments were quoted by Frank Vanderlip in *Business and Education,* 20–21. The last quotation is reprinted in Jeffrey L. Cruikshank's magnificent history of the Harvard Business School's first thirty-seven years, *A Delicate Experiment* (Boston: Harvard Business School Press, 1987), 25.

45. Alfred D. Chandler, *The Visible Hand: The Managerial Revolution in American Business* (Cambridge: Harvard University Press, 1977).

46. Pollard, *A History of the Ohio State University,* (Columbus: Ohio State University Press, 1952): 154.

47. William A. Scott, "Training for Business at the University of Wisconsin," *Journal of Political Economy* 21 (February 1913): 127–35.

CHAPTER 2. 1910–1918: SEARCHING FOR A CURRICULUM

1. *New York Times,* 4 May 1915, 14, and 31 January 1916, 10.

2. *New York Times,* 29 October 1916, section 2, p. 1.

3. *New York Times,* 24 December 1916, section 3, p. 8.

4. *New York Times,* 23 September 1911, 10, and 7 October 1911, 12.

5. Quoted in C. Aubrey Smith, *Fifty Years of Education for Business at the University of Texas.* Austin: University of Texas Press, 1962), 12.

6. F. E. Farrington, "Commercial Education in Germany," *School and Society* 3 (4 March 1918): 325–32; I. L Kandel, "Commercial Education in England, *School and Society,* (15 April 1916), 541–49; *New York Times,* 20 July 1918, 9; and John T. Swift, "Business Education in Japan: A Long Sighted Policy Has Established Comprehensive Commercial Schools to Train Efficient Business Men on a Scientific Basis," *ASIA: Journal of the American Asiatic Association* 17 (April 1917): 128–31.

7. William A. Scott, "Training for Business at the University of Wisconsin," *Journal of Political Economy* 21 (February 1913): 127–35.

8. M. E. Pearson, "An Education for Business," *NEA Proceedings* 52 (1912): 1046–50.

9. Reprinted in several places, including the Southern Methodist University School of Business catalog for 1959–60.

10. *New York Times,* 25 May 1914, 6; 29 June 1914, 4; 7 June 1914, section 6, p.4; and 22 March 1917, 10.

11. *New York Times,* 30 March 1913, section 5, p. 13; 3 November 1911, 4; and 22 June 1913, section 7, p. 8.

12. *New York Times,* 9 June 1916, 9; and Leon C. Marshall, "The College of Commerce and Administration at the University of Chicago," *Journal of Political Economy* 21 (February 1913): 97–110.

13. *New York Times,* 20 July 1918, 9.

14. Raphael N. Hamilton, S.J., *The Story of Marquette University* (Milwaukee:

Marquette University Press, 1953); Earl Jay Glade, "The Present Status of Business Education in the United States and Some Recommendations," *NEA Proceedings* 53 (1914): 652–56.

15. A. Wellington Taylor, "The Businessman's Opportunity," *Nation* 106 (28 March 1918): 380–82.

16. Leon C. Marshall, *The American Collegiate School of Business* (Chicago: University of Chicago Press, 1928), chapter 1; Joseph Mayer, "Modern Business Education and Research," *The Scientific Monthly* 20 (March 1925): 257–69; and Glade, "The Present Status of Business Education," 654.

17. Edwin R. Seligman, "A University School of Business," *Columbia University Quarterly* 18 (June 1916): 241–52.

18. Marshall, *The American Collegiate School of Business,* 11–12.

19. Quoted in Sherwin Cody, *Commercial Tests and How to Use Them* (Yonkers-on-Hudson, N.Y.: World Book Co., 1919), 2.

20. Glen L. Swiggett, "Commercial Education in Preparation for Foreign Service," *NEA Proceedings* 57 (1918): 238–40.

21. William E. Hotchkiss, "The Northwestern University School of Commerce," *Journal of Political Economy* 21 (March 1913): 196–208.

22. Lyon, *Education for Business,* 6.

23. Jeffrey Cruikshank, *A Delicate Experiment,* (Boston: Harvard Business School Press, 1987): 79–81.

24. M. E. Pearson, "An Education for Business," *NEA Proceedings* 51 (1912): 1046–50.

25. Norris A. Brisco, "Discussion," in *Journal of Political Economy* 25 (January 1917): 111–12.

26. Leon C. Marshall, "A Balanced Curriculum in Business Education," *Journal of Political Economy* 25 (January 1917): 84–105.

27. Marshall, Ibid., 90–91.

28. Ibid., 101.

29. Person, "University Schools of Business and the Training of Employment Executives," 117–27.

30. Edward D. Jones, "Some Propositions Concerning University Instruction in Business Administration," *Journal of Political Economy* 21 (March 1913): 185–95.

Chapter 3. 1919–1922: Explosive Growth, Descriptive Era

1. Figures are from L. C. Marshall, *The American Collegiate School of Business,* chapter 1.

2. *New York Times,* 28 November 1920, section 2, p. 18; 1 February 1921, 10; and 28 March 1921, 10.

3. Henry Smith Pritchett, "Is There a Place for a Profession in Commerce?" *Engineering News* 435 (9 May 1901): 343.

4. A. Wellington Taylor, "The Businessman's Opportunity," *Nation* 106 (28 March 1918): 380; and "University Training for Business," *The Weekly Review* 2 (16 June 1920): 634–36.

5. For example, Harvey Alden Wooster, "University Schools of Business and a New Business Ethics," *Journal of Political Economy* 27 (January 1919): 47–63; and Benjamin C. Gruenberg, "Commercial Education," *School and Society* 12 (9 October 1920): 300–04. *See also* Jeffrey Cruikshank, *A Delicate Experiment* (Boston, Harvard Business School Press, 1987), 84.

6. W. Lough, "Reorganization of Instruction in University Schools of Business," *Journal of Political Economy* 29 (October 1921): 656.

7. *New York Times,* 11 May 1922, 6.

8. Taylor, "The Businessman's Opportunity," *Nation* 28 March 1918; Lord Balfour, *New York Times,* 20 July 1918, 9.

9. Glen L. Swiggett, "The New Education and the Nation's Business," *School and Society* 10 (23 August 1919): 211–19.

10. Wooster, "University Schools of Business and New Business Ethics"; Lough, "Reorganization of Instruction in the University Schools of Business."

11. Forrest A. Kingsbury, "Business Judgment and the Business Curriculum," *Journal of Political Economy,* 30 (June 1922): 375–87; Woolley, "How Our Colleges Teach Business," *Collier's,* 11 March 1922, 5–6.

12. Thorstein Veblen, *The Higher Learning in America* (New York: Sagamore Press, 1957), chapter 7.

13. Reported in a *New York Times* editorial, 26 November 1919, 12.

14. *New York Times,* 13 March 1921, section 10, p. 4.

15. *New York Times,* 30 May 1920, section 6, p. 10.

16. *New York Times,* 10 April 1922, 1.

17. *New York Times,* 27 March 1920, 19; 28 March 1920, 12; and 9 May 1920, section 6, p. 6.

18. *New York Times,* 19 February 1922, 23; *New York Times,* 8 October 1922, section 2, p. 13; Eleanor Rust Collier, *The Boston University College of Business Administration, 1913–1958* (Boston University, 1959); J. Theyskens, "A Jesuit Higher School of Commercial Finance," *Catholic World* 114 (January 1922): 532–35.

19. Willard Hotchkiss, "The Basic Elements and their Proper Balance in the Curriculum of a Collegiate Business School," *Journal of Political Economy* 28 (February 1920): 92.

20. *New York Times,* 13 June 1923, 21.

21. Sir William Ashley, *Commercial Education* (London: Williams and Moorgate): 163.

22. Ibid., 130.

23. Taylor, "The Businessman's Opportunity," 380.

24. Ralph E. Heilman, discussion of L. C. Marshall, "The Relation of the Collegiate School of Business to the Secondary School System," *Journal of Political Economy* 28 (February 1920): 187.

25. *New York Times,* 3 March 1923, 4; and J. T. Holdsworth, "Commercial Education after the War," *NEA Proceedings* 58 (1918): 236–38.

26. Z. Clark Dickinson, "Bureaux for Economic and 'Business' Research in American Universities," *The Economic Journal* 35 (September 1925): 488.

27. Cruikshank, *A Delicate Experiment,* 60; Horace Secrist, "Research in Collegiate Schools of Business," *Journal of Political Economy* 28 (May 1920): 355–60.

28. James E. Pollard, *History of the Ohio State University* (Columbus: Ohio State University Press, 1952): 159.

29. Cruikshank, *A Delicate Experiment,* 61; Dickinson, "Bureaux for Economic and 'Business' Research," 398–415; *New York Times,* 24 September 1922, 29.

30. *New York Times,* 29 March 1922, 33.

31. Herman Schneider, *Thirty Years of Educational Pioneering: The Philosophy of the Cooperative System and Its Practical Test* (Cincinnati: University of Cincinnati Press, 1935); Charles W. Gerstenberg, "Special Problems in Content and Presentation in Finance Instruction in Large Schools of Commerce," *Journal of Political Economy* 29 (March 1921): 400–409; J. T. Madden, "Coordination of Instruction in

Collegiate Schools of Business with Corporation Training Courses," *Journal of Political Economy* 29 (November 1921): 720.

32. *New York Times,* 19 August 1920, 8, and 20 August 1920, 8.

33. Ralph L. Power, "Degrees in Commerce and Business Administration," *Education* 41 (June 1921): 632–35; Benjamin C. Gruenberg, "Commercial Education," *School and Society,* 9 October 1920, 300–304.

34. "University Training for Business," *The Weekly Review,* 16 June 1920, 634–36; Holdsworth, "Commercial Education after the War," 236–38.

Chapter 4. 1923–1930: New Prominence, New Activities

1. Quoted by L. S. Lyon in the *Proceedings of the American Association of Collegiate Schools of Business* (1928), 33.

2. H. E. Hoagland, "An Era of Water-Tight Compartment Instruction in Business Subjects," *Proceedings of the American Association of Collegiate Schools of Business* (1928).

3. Quoted in Norman F. Kallaus, *Meeting a Need: A History of Business Education at the University of Iowa* (Iowa City: College of Business Administration, University of Iowa, 1977), 5.

4. Leon C. Marshall, "The Collegiate School of Business at Erehwon," *Journal of Political Economy* 34 (June 1926): 289–326.

5. James Bossard and Frederic Dewhurst, *University Education for Business* (Philadelphia: University of Pennsylvania Press, 1931), 254; *New York Times,* 11 April 1926, section 2, p. 16; 27 January 1924, section 2, p. 2; 10 November 1929, section 2, p. 3; 9 February 1930, section 2, p. 2; 7 May 1929, 9; 27 May 1930, 47.

6. Bossard and Dewhurst, *University Education,* 254–55; the Universities of Georgia, Cincinnati, and Oregon catalogs; *New York Times,* 31 May 1924, 24; 18 January 1926, 23; 13 February 1930, 14.

7. *New York Times,* 2 June 1924, 1; 18 June 1924, 7; 19 September 1924, 18; and 23 November 1924, section 2, 4.

8. *New York Times,* 13 May 1923, section 2, p. 3; 20 April 1924, section 9, p. 20; 18 September 1924, 35; 31 January 1926, section 2, p. 3; 13 September 1923, 9; 24 May 1924, 20; 14 February 1930, 16; and 12 September 1926, section 2, p. 1.

9. *New York Times,* 12 January 1930, section 2, p. 20; 6 July 1930, section 2, 11; 9 July 1930, 39; 2 September 1928, section 2, p. 20; 23 September 1929, 55; 15 March 1925, section 11, p. 1; 16 January 1927, 9; 21 November 1928, 17.

10. Melvin T. Copeland, *And Mark an Era: The Story of the Harvard Business School* (Boston: Little, Brown, 1958): 175.

11. Jeffrey Cruikshank, *A Delicate Experiment* (Boston: Harvard Business School Press, 1987), 155; and Wallace B. Donham, *Administration and Blind Spots* (Boston: Harvard Graduate School of Business Administration, 1952), 13–14.

12. Elton Mayo, "The Irrational Factor in Human Behavior: The 'Night-Mind' in Industry," *Annals of the American Academy* 110 (November 1923): 117.

13. *New York Times,* 7 March 1927, 9; 2 January 1927, section 2, p. 14; and 1 July 1923, section 2, p. 3.

14. *New York Times,* 19 December 1923, 19, and 6 April 1923, 2.

15. A *London Evening News* interview, commented on in a *New York Times* editorial, 9 August 1924, 10.

16. *New York Times,* 5 December 1928, 8, and 7 December 1924, section 1, p. 17.

17. *New York Times,* 18 October 1924, 17; 7 April 1929, section 3, p. 5; and 14 August 1925, 12.

18. Richard J. Walsh, "The Doom of the Self-Made Man," "Carving Out a New Profession: Ways and Means of Professionalizing Business," and "Tools for To-Morrow: Further Facts about Professionalizing Business," in *Century Magazine* 109 (December 1924 and January and February 1925): 253–58, 386–92, 516–23.

19. Eliot G. Mears, "The Teaching of Commerce and Economics," *American Economic Review* 13 (December 1923): 648–51.

20. *New York Times,* 24 March 1925, 27; 13 October 1929, section 3, p. 4; 22 February 1924, 17; 24 February 1924, section 2, p. 7; 22 June 1924, section 2, p. 5; 7 September 1924, section 2, p. 3; 29 September 1924, 17; and 10 June 1927, 13.

21. *New York Times,* 2 March 1930, 28; 20 April 1930, section 1, p. 2; and 29 April 1930, 16.

22. Thurman W. Van Metre, *A History of the Graduate School of Business, Columbia University* (New York: Columbia University Press, 1954), 67; Frederic F. Van de Water, "Industry Goes to School," *The World's Work* 58 (January 1929): 74–79.

23. Frank T. Stockton, *Four Chapters in the History of the School of Business at the University of Kansas* (Lawrence: Center for Research in Business, University of Kansas, 1964); and catalogs for the University of Kansas.

24. John Jay Chapman, "Harvard and Education," *The Harvard Graduates' Magazine* 33 (September 1924): 37–45.

25. C. E. Ayres, "The College of Money-Changing: (I) Is Commerce Education?" and (II) Is Business a Profession?," *The New Republic,* 28 January and 4 February 1925, 250–52 and 280–83.

26. "Arlington J. Stone," "The Dawn of a New Science," *American Mercury* 14 (August 1928): 446–55.

27. Abraham Flexner, *Universities: American, English, German* (Oxford: Oxford University Press, 1930).

28. L. J. Nations, "Business Before Culture: College Becomes an Institution of Higher Earnings," *North American Review* 229 (January 1930): 705–12.

29. *New York Times,* 13 January, 18 January, and 20 January, 1925, pages 20, 28, and 14.

30. *New York Times,* 17 May 1925, section 8, p. 10.

31. *New York Times,* 23 April 1929, 48.

32. *New York Times,* 13 December 1925, section 2, p. 2; 15 January 1927, 14; 24 March 1929, section 2, p. 6; and 21 September 1930, Section 2, p. 2.

33. Jaromie Wiesner and Karol Ficek, "Education for Business in Czechoslovakia," *Journal of Political Economy* 34 (April 1926): 141–80; August Wilhelm Fehling, "Education for Business in Germany," *Journal of Political Economy* 34 (October 1926): 545–96; E. C. Longobardi, "Higher Commercial Education in Italy," *Journal of Political Economy* 35 (February 1927): 39–90; and J. G. Smith, Education for Business in Great Britain," *Journal of Political Economy* 36 (February 1928): 1–52.

34. "Collegiate Schools of Business," *School and Society* 18 (14 July 1923), 41; *New York Times,* 27 December 1929, 8, and 7 March 1929, 14.

35. Information about AACSB meetings is taken from the annual *Proceedings* and from the fiftieth anniversary history, *The American Association of Collegiate Schools of Business, 1916–1966* (Homewood, Ill.: Richard D. Irwin, 1966), chapter 6.

CHAPTER 5. 1930–1940: PHILOSOPHER OF BUSINESS AND SOCIETY

1. Eleanor Rust Collier, *The Boston University College of Business Administration, 1913–1958.* (Boston University, 1959).

2. *New York Times,* 6 July 1930, section 2, p. 11; 12 October 1930, section 1, p. 21; and 12 May 1930, 35.

3. *New York Times,* 21 February 1930, 27; 14 April 1930, 30; and 27 May 1930, 47.

4. *New York Times,* 15 February 1932, 31; 3 April 1932, section 2, p. 16; 24–25 March 1933, pp. 18 and 8; 31 October 1932, 3; 14 November 1932, 33; and 24 January 1933, 72.

5. *New York Times,* 24 April 1933, 28; 11 May 1933, 16; and 28 August 1933, 20.

6. *New York Times,* 27 December 1931, section 1, p. 26.

7. *New York Times,* 10 October 1931, 8.

8. *New York Times,* 28 March 1931, pp. 1 and 7.

9. *New York Times,* 7 August 1932, section 4, p. 1.

10. *New York Times,* 26 June 1932, section 9, p. 8; 29 November 1936, section 3, p. 1; and 7 May 1933, section 1, p. 21.

11. *New York Times,* 1 May 1934, 18, and 18 November 1934, section 2, p. 3.

12. *New York Times,* 8 July 1934, section 8, p. 16.

13. Herbert L. Towle, "Business Cycles and Business Men," *Scribner's Magazine* 99 (June 1936): 365–67.

14. *New York Times,* 2 July 1933, section 4, p. 7.

15. *New York Times,* 16 December 1934, section 1, p. 6.

16. *New York Times,* 5 October 1931, 15; 15 February 1932, 31; 24–25 March, 1933, pp. 18 and 8; 13 December 1933, 8; 30 September 1934, section 2, p. 2; 11 January 1935, 40; 9 and 10 May, 1936, pp. 6 and 21; 20 February 1937, 21; 26 April 1937, 33; 26 March 1938, 34; 11 March 1939, 12; and 6 May 1939, 4.

17. *New York Times,* 15 October 1931, section 2, 5; 17 September 1933, section 2, p. 3; 9 September 1934, section 2, p. 3; and 6 October 1935, 25.

18. *New York Times,* 29 November 1936, section 3, p. 9; 26 November 1939, section 2, p. 5; and 14 February 1937, section 2, p. 6.

19. *New York Times,* 14 January 1931, 42; 30 August 1936, section 2, p. 8; 17 October 1937, section 2, p. 4; and 12 February 1940, 24.

20. *New York Times,* 1 March 1931, 3; 24 June 1931, 31; 2 July 1932, 49; 24 April 1933, 28; 16 August 1938, 21; 17 June 1940, 30; 2 August 1931, section 2, p. 15; and 6 September 1931, section 2, p. 6.

21. *New York Times,* 9 February 1930, section 2, p. 2; 6 September 1931, section 2, p. 2; 11 June 1936, 28; 14 February 1927, section 2, p. 6; and 15 July 1934, section 2, p. 2.

22. *New York Times,* 11 September 1932, section 8, p. 7.

23. *New York Times,* 23 September 1934, section 2, p. 2; and Jeffrey Cruikshank, *A Delicate Experiment* (Boston: Harvard Business School Press, 1987), 188.

24. "Harvard and Yale to Give Joint Course in Law and Business," *School and Society* 37 (25 February 1933): 245; and Cruikshank, *A Delicate Experiment,* 192.

25. Benjamin M. Anderson, "Education for Business and Banking," *Education* 60 (March 1940), 396–402.

26. Wallace B. Donham, "The Failure of Business Leadership and the Responsibility of the Universities," *Harvard Business Review* 11 (July 1933): 418–35.

CHAPTER 6. 1940–1945: WAR

1. Information about these programs is taken from college catalogs. A systematic description can be found in Malcolm M. Willey, "The College Training Programs of the Armed Services," *Annals of the American Academy of Political and Social Science* 231 (January 1944): 14–28.

2. *New York Times,* 30 June 1941, 15; 23 June 1941, 30; 7 July 1941, 28; and 8 September 1941, 28.

3. Besides the college catalogs, *see The New York Times* for 6 July 1943, 25, and 24 July 1945, 14.

4. *New York Times,* 11 November 1942, 22; 26 December 1942, 16; and 25 March 1942, 25.

5. *A Delicate Experiment: The Harvard Business School 1908–1945* (Boston: Harvard Business School Press, 1987): 266.

6. *New York Times,* 17 September 1944, 36.

7. Russell A. Stevenson, "Training for Business," *Annals of the American Academy of Political and Social Science* 231 (January 1944): 98–99; *New York Times,* 17 October 1943, 5; 13 September 1943, 17; MIT President's Report, 1947.

8. Robert D. Calkins, "A Challenge to Business Education," *Harvard Business Review* 23 (winter 1944): 174–86.

9. AACSB *Proceedings* (1944); and Alvan E. Duerr, "A Business Point of View on Education," *Education* 62 (June 1942): 592–96.

10. *New York Times,* 12 August 1941, 17; AACSB *Proceedings* (1944) (Donham); MIT President's Report (1943); AACSB *Proceedings,* 1944 (Stevenson); and Cruikshank, *A Delicate Experiment,* 266–69.

11. AACSB *Proceedings* 1944; and Meg Hunter Naylor, *Thunderbird American Graduate School of International Management, 1946–1986* (Glendale, Arizona: American Graduate School of International Management, 1986).

12. AACSB *Proceedings* 1944 (Donham and Stevenson); *New York Times,* 17 October 1943, 5; and 17 September 1944, 36).

13. Thurman W. Van Metre, *A History of the Graduate School of Business—Columbia University* (New York: Columbia University Press, 1954), 77; and *New York Times,* 19 October 1941, section 2, p. 7.

14. "Business Humanist," *Time,* 25 May 1942, 36–37; *New York Times,* 15 May 1942, 18.

CHAPTER 7. 1945–1950: REGROUPING, RETHINKING

1. *New York Times,* 31 January 1946, 26; AACSB *Proceedings* (1946) (McClung); *Statistical Abstract of the United States, Historical Series.*

2. AACSB *Proceedings* (1946) (McClung); *New York Times,* 28 November 1947, 38; USOE/NCES Earned Degree Series.

3. *New York Times,* 21 November 1948, section 3, p. 6; and 30 November 1948, 20.

4. *New York Times,* 7 September 1947, section 2, pp. 1 and 3.

5. *New York Times,* 10 June 1949, 1, 18, and 26.

6. AACSB *Proceedings* (1946) McClung.

7. *New York Times,* 31 January 1946, 26, and 3 February 1946, section 4, p. 9.

8. *New York Times,* 23 June 1950, 42.

9. *New York Times,* 26 February 1949, 12; 5 May 1948, 37; 12 December 1948, section 4, p. 9; 30 May 1949, 21; and 28 August 1949, section 4, p. 9.

10. AACSB *Proceedings* (1946), McClung and Calkins.

11. AACSB *Proceedings* (1946), Taylor; *New York Times,* 11 May 1950, 25, and 5 November 1950, section 3, p. 9.

12. *New York Times,* 25 October 1948, 36; *Business Week,* 18 September 1948, 132; *New York Times,* 17 July 1951, 38.

CHAPTER 8. 1950–1959: GROWTH, CONFORMITY, AND GENERALISM—THE MBA TAKES OFF

1. Statistics, which are subject to all the usual cautions, are derived from Robert A. Gordon and James Edwin Howell, *Higher Education for Business* (New York: Columbia University Press, 1959): 21.

2. "New Look for B-School," *Business Week,* 25 June 1955, 64, 66.

3. David L. Bryant, "The Humanities: Basis for Business," *Office Executive* 33 (May 1958): 19–21.

4. *New York Times,* 26 May 1953, 23; *Wall Street Journal,* 9 July 1957, 1.

5. Colin Brooks, "Back to School with Tomorrow's Leaders," *The Director* 30 (January 1978): 40–41; Eileen Mackenzie, "Training Managers for Brazil's Boom," *International Management* 26 (July 1971): 20–24.

6. "Popularity Swamps the B-Schools," *Business Week* 15 December 1956, 193–94; USOE/NCES Earned Degree Series; "Even MBAs Feel the Pinch," *Business Week,* 21 June 1958, 60.

7. Peter F. Drucker, "The Graduate Business School," *Fortune* 42 (August 1950): 92–116.

8. Thomas H. Carroll, "Education for Business: A Dynamic Concept and Process," *Accounting Review* 23 (January 1958): 3–4; "Can You Teach Management?" *Business Week* 19 April 1952, 126–30.

9. *New York Times,* 17 July 1951, 38; "Popularity Swamps the B-Schools," *Business Week,* 15 December 1956, 193–94; Bryant, "The Humanities: Basis for Business," 19–21.

10. Thomas G. Gutteridge, "MBA Recruitment and Utilization: A Comparison of Two Perspectives," *Personnel Journal* 52 (April 1953): 193–303; "The Pay-Off Is Confidence," *Business Week,* 18 June 1955, 150–51.

11. *New York Times,* 1 December 1956, 17, and 5 December 1956, 46.

12. "Should a Businessman Be Educated?," *Fortune* 47 (April 1953): 113–14; Robert E. Wilson, "A Businessman Looks at Higher Education," *Vital Speeches,* 15 January 1954, 213–16.

13. Quoted in Charles A. Nelson, "Liberal Arts in Management," *Harvard Business Review* 36 (May-June 1958): 91–99.

14. Nelson, "Liberal Arts in Management"; Julius E. Eitington, "Liberal Learning for Enlightened Leadership," *Personnel Administration* 21 (July 1958): 8–19.

15. "Businessman, Meet Educator," *Business Week,* 21 November 1953, 129–32; Carroll, "Education for Business," 4.

16. *Wall Street Journal,* 17 March 1958, 1.

CHAPTER 9. 1959–1967: MIDCOURSE DEFLECTION—THE FOUNDATION REPORTS

1. Information and ideas in this chapter are greatly influenced by Steven Schlossman, Michael Sedlak, and Harold Wechsler, *The "New Look": The Ford Foundation and the Revolution in Business Education* (Los Angeles: Graduate Management

Admission Council, 1987); John J. Clark and Blaise J. Opulente, *The Impact of the Foundation Reports on Business Education* (Jamaica, N.Y.: St. John's University Press, 1963); and Jack N. Berhman and Richard I. Levin, "Are Business Schools Doing Their Job?" *Harvard Business Review* 62 (January–February 1984): 140–47.

2. Robert A. Gordon and James E. Howell, *Higher Education for Business* (New York: Columbia University Press, 1959), 136; and Frank C. Pierson, *The Education of American Businessmen* (New York: McGraw-Hill, 1959), x and 55.

3. Pierson, *The Education of American Businessmen,* 219; Gordon and Howell, *Higher Education for Business,* 139–40.

4. Pierson, *The Education of American Businessmen,* 270–73; Gordon and Howell, *Higher Education for Business,* 341–46.

5. Pierson, *The Education of American Businessmen,* 311–13; Gordon and Howell, *Higher Education for Business,* 380–81.

6. Pierson, *The Education of American Businessmen,* chapter 10, and Gordon and Howell, *Higher Education for Business,* chapter 11.

7. "They Prescribe More Education, Less Business," *Business Week,* 31 October 1959, 84–87ff.; *New York Times,* November 2, 1959, 61; "Deans' Club Peps Up," *Business Week,* 16 May 1964, 116–18; Peter Dubno and Walter Weintraub, "The Entrepreneurial Spirit: Who Nurtures It?" *Business Topics* 14 (summer 1966): 38–44.

8. John S. Fielden, "Thinking Ahead," *Harvard Business Review* 37 (November 1959): 35–36ff.

9. John G. B. Hutchins, "Education for Business Administration," *Administrative Science Quarterly* 5 (summer 1960): 279–85.

10. Leonard S. Silk, *The Education of Businessmen* (New York: Committee for Economic Development, 1960).

11. "Report of the Committee on the Study of the Ford and Carnegie Foundation Reports," *Accounting Review* 36 (April 1961): 191–96; Alfred L. Seelye, "The Role of Business Schools in a Changing Environment," *Accounting Review* 38 (April 1963): 302–9.

12. Richard L. Kozelka, *Professional Education for Business* (Minneapolis: School of Business Administration of the University of Minnesota, 1954).

13. John J. Clark and Blaise J. Opulente, *The Impact of the Foundation Reports on Business Education.* Jamaica, N.Y.: St. John's University Press, 1963; and *Wall Street Journal,* 20 March 1961, 10.

14. Jack N. Berhman and Richard I. Levin, "Are Business Schools Doing Their Job?," *Harvard Business Review* 62 (January–February 1984): 141.

15. "Further Education for Commerce," *Personnel Management* 41 (June 1959): 65–66.

16. Lord Franks, *Britain's Business Schools* (London: British Institute of Management, 1963).

17. Courtney C. Brown, "Knowledge of What?" *Saturday Review,* 17 January 1959, 52, 79, and "Needed: New Tools—New Methods," *Saturday Review,* 14 November 1959, 44–45; and *New York Times,* 9 March 1959, 31.

18. Albert Porter, "Books and the Bramble Bush," *Advanced Management/Office Executive* 1 (December 1962): 20–21.

19. Billy E. Goetz and Warren G. Bennis, "What We Know about Learning and Training," *Personnel Administration* 25 (March 1962): 20–29. 63.

20. "Changes at the Source," *Time,* 7 May 1965, 92, 94; "They Teach Business How to Make Decisions," *Business Week,* 18 September 1965, 72, 77; M. J. Rathbone, "What Kind of Managers for Tomorrow's World?," *Vital Speeches,* 1 April 1965.

21. Monis S. Viteles, "'Human Relations' and 'The Humanities' in the Education of Business Leaders," *Personnel Psychology* 12 (spring 1959): 1–28.

22. Leland Hazard, "Looking Ahead," *Harvard Business Review* 38 (November–December 1960): 39–40ff.; Joseph L. Vaughan, "Literature As Case History for Business," *Advanced Management* 25 (February 1960): 16–19.

23. William M. Kephart, James. E. MacNulty, and Earl J. McGrath, *Liberal Education and Business* (New York: Columbia Teachers College, 1963), 50; "Deans' Club Peps Up," *Business Week,* 16 May 1964, 116–18.

24. *New York Times,* 30 January 1959, 35; K. J. Cohen et al., "The Carnegie Tech Management Game," *Journal of Business* 32 (October 1960): 320–21; Walter S. Wikstrom, "The Serious Business of Business Games," *Management Record* 22 (February 1960): 6–8ff.; and James L. McKenney, "An Evaluation of a Business Game in an MBA Curriculum," *Journal of Business* 35 (July 1962): 278–86.

25. Hans B. Thorelli et al., "The International Operations Simulation at the University of Chicago," *Journal of Business* 35 (July 1962): 187–97.

26. *New York Times,* 13 May 1959, 34; "American University Establishes Center for International Business," *International Commerce,* 29 October 1962, 2; "Newest in B-Schools Spreads Gospel Abroad," *Business Week,* 14 July 1962, 62; "Tailoring the B-School to the New Business World," *Business Week,* 19 January 1963, 73–74ff.; "B-Schools Seek a Wider World," *Business Week,* 14 December 1963, 124–25.

27. "Hunting for Action—in Small Business," *Business Week,* 9 April 1966, 82–84; Richard Nason, "Harvardmen vs. Big Business," *Dun's Review and Modern Industry* 83 (January 1964): 41–42ff.; Richard M. Cyert and William R. Dill, "The Future of Business Education," *Journal of Business* 37 (July 1964): 221–37.

28. John Costello, "The West Points of Capitalism," *Nation's Business* 56 (June 1968): 70–71; Cyert and Dill, "The Future of Business Education," *Journal of Business* 37 (July 1964): 221–37; *New York Times,* 21 October 1963, 37; "Changes at the Source," *Time,* 7 May 1965, 92–94; "Stumping the Deans," *Business Week,* 8 May 1965, 106ff.

29. "Bared by a B-School," *Business Week,* 14 March 1964, 90ff.; "Where Experts Are Worlds Apart," *Business Week,* 7 November 1964, 74ff.; *New York Times,* 12 October 1966, 2; Dause L. Bibby, "Whose Business Is Business Education?," *Credit and Financial Management* 65 (July 1963): 12ff.; and William H. Whyte, *The Organization Man* (New York: Simon and Schuster, 1956): 107.

30. Frederick R. Kappel, "Business Schools and Future Business Leaders," *Public Utilities Fortnightly,* 25 April 1963, 55–56.

31. "B-School Grads Get Increasing Share of Executive Posts Open in Industry," *Business Week,* 3 October 1959, 63; Raymond L. Hilgert and Jerry D. Young, "Part Time MBA: A Survey and Its Implications for Management," *Personnel Journal* 43 (November 1964): 561ff.; and *Wall Street Journal,* 3 January 1962, 1; 11 April 1963, 1; and 20 April 1965, 1.

32. "The B-School," and "Executive Finishing Schools," *Forbes,* 15 June 1962, 42–45; "Education: Purdue vs. Harvard," *Forbes,* 15 October 1963, 47–48; and *New York Times,* 16 October 1966, section 3, p. 43; 6 February 1962, 32; and 14 December 1964, 43.

33. "Staff Tries School Ties," *International Commerce,* 18 May 1964, 7; *New York Times,* 5 March 1966, 5; and 19 November 1966, 76; and Charles Z. Wilson, "The Future of Business Education: Some Further Comments," *Journal of Business* 39 (January 1966): 74–75.

34. "Harvard in Europe," *Time,* 19 October 1959, 104; *Wall Street Journal,* 29 September 1959, 4; "Wanted—Business Schools," *Economist,* 21 March 1959, 1059; "Educating the Managers," *Economist,* 20 August 1960, 717; "Vague Advance," *Economist,* 2 April 1960, 25–26; *Wall Street Journal,* 11 November 1962, 8; "Nouvelle Vague in Business," *Economist,* 30 March 1963, 1284; "Peru Gets B-School,"

Business Week, 15 June 1963, 174; "Search for Talent," *Time,* 13 December 1963, 91; "17 Countries Send Executives to U. S. Management Course," *International Commerce,* 19 August 1963, 3; "Transplanting Harvard," *Economist,* 19 October 1963, 261–62; Roy Hill, "Bombay's Down-to-Earth Business School," *International Management* 28 (October 1973): 61–63; "Britain's Business Schools," *Economist,* 15 January 1966, 198–202; John G. Hutchinson, "Europe's Business Schools: A Good Start, But . . . ," *Columbia Journal of World Business* 1 (fall 1966): 59–65; "Mentors for Britain's Flagging Management," *Business Week,* 15 October 1966, 190–91ff.; and Leland Hazard, "Looking Around," *Harvard Business Review* 38 (November–December 1960): 39–40ff.

35. Madison Smartt Bell, *History of the Owen School from Its Early Origins to 1984* (Nashville: Vanderbilt University Press, 1985): 8–9; Bryan J. Nichols, "Education for Management Leadership," *Vital Speeches,* 15 December 1961, 154ff.; Committee for Economic Development, *Educating Tomorrow's Managers—The Business School and the Business Community* (New York: 1964); "Ringing a Bell for B-School Support," *Business Week* 7 November 1964, 172; "Changes at the Source," *Time,* 7 May 1965, 92ff.

CHAPTER 10. 1967–1971: WAR AND PROTEST—MBA ON THE DEFENSIVE

1. Jacques Barzun, *The American University: How It Runs, Where It is Going* (New York: Harper and Row, 1968).

2. James Ridgeway, *The Closed Corporation: American Universities in Crisis* (New York: Random House, 1968), 129.

3. *Wall Street Journal,* 16 January 1967, 28; "Is Hall of Fame a B-School Bust?" *Business Week,* 27 September 1969, 132.

4. "Top Students Sell Business Short," *Business Week,* 9 September 1967, 134–36ff.; *Wall Street Journal,* 1 April 1969, 1.

5. W. George Pinnell, "The Obligations of Education for Business," *Business Horizons* 10 (spring 1967): 5–14; "Milestones, 1829–1982," The Indiana University School of Business, n.d.; Oscar L. Dunn, "Business: Where the Action Is," *Business Horizons* 10 (spring 1967): 39–44.

6. Jeffrey St. John., "Business Isn't Really Selling Them," *Nation's Business,* 55 (August 1967): 83.

7. "Students Still Choose Business: What the Facts Show," *U. S. News and World Report,* 19 February 1968, 98–100; "Business As Usual," *Nation's Business* 57 (August 1969): 42–45.

8. Nathan A. Baily, "The Role of Business and Business Schools in Raising Ethical Standards in Business," *MSU Business Topics* 16 (spring 1968): 29–32; C. Stewart Sheppard, ed., *The First Twenty Years: The Darden School at Virginia* (Charlottesville: The Darden School, 1975), 145; Jeffrey L. Cruikshank, *A Delicate Experiment* (Boston: Harvard Business School Press, 1967), 192.

9. "Double-Barrelled Experts," *Forbes,* 15 March 1969, 66; "New Dean, New Era for Harvard B-School," *Business Week,* 24 January 1970, 58–60ff.; *Wall Street Journal,* 23 September 1970, 13.

10. *Wall Street Journal,* 21 December 1967, 1; *New York Times Magazine,* 10 November 1968, 25ff.; *New York Times,* 29 September 1968, 57, and 17 November 1968, 62.

11. *New York Times,* 18 January 1970, section 3, 5; *Wall Street Journal,* 27 July 1970, 17; *New York Times,* 25 October 1970, section 3, p. 3.

12. *Wall Street Journal,* 12 June 1968, 16.

13. *Wall Street Journal,* 22 August 1968, 1.

14. Richard N. Farmer and Barry Richman, "Subsystem Optimization in American Business Schools," *Management International Review* vol. 7, nos. 4–5 (1967): 143–54.

15. *New York Times,* 13 December 1970, section 3, p. 2.

16. "B-School Throws Away the Book," *Business Week,* 22 April 1967, 104–6ff.; *Wall Street Journal,* 9 April 1968, 1.

17. *Wall Street Journal,* 2 January 1971, 1.

18. "How Students Are Helping Ghetto Businessmen," *Management Review* 58 (July 1969): 59–62 (condensed from the Stanford Graduate School of Business Bulletin).

19. "How Business Schools Welcome the World," *Business Week,* 9 December 1967, 118–19ff.; *Wall Street Journal,* 29 January 1970, 1.

20. W. George Pinnell, "The Obligations of Education for Business," *Business Horizons* 10 (spring 1967): 5–14; Preston P. LeBreton, ed., *The Dynamic World of Education for Business* (Cincinnati, Ohio: Southwestern, 1969).

21. Thomas L. Wheelen, "Graduate Business Education for Personnel Management Executives," *Personnel Journal,* 49 (November 1970): 932–34; Leonard Sayles, "Whatever Happened to Management?—or Why the Dull Stepchild?" *Business Horizons* 13 (April 1970): 25–34.

22. Quoted in Sheldon Zalaznick, "The MBA: The Man, the Myth, and the Method," *Fortune,* May 1968, 168–71ff.

23. "Is Industry/B-School Marriage Pffft?," *Iron Age,* 27 March 1969: 25; James S. Hekimian, "Closing the Gap Between Business and the Schools," *Financial Executive* 37 (September 1969): 52–54.

24. "Business Schools on Course," *Economist,* 18 March 1967, 1048–49; Alastair Mant, *The Experienced Manager—A Major Resource* (London: British Institute of Management, 1969); Harold Rose, *Management Education in the 1970s* (London: National Economic Development Office, 1970); "Back to School," *Economist,* 27 June 1970, 60.

25. "What's Wrong with Business Education?" *Economist,* (21 November 1970): 72, 74.

26. "How the World Looks to Top Harvard MBAs," *Forbes,* 15 June 1968: 43–48; *Wall Street Journal,* 1 October 1968, 1; 1 April 1969, 1; 13 July 1970, 1; 21 July 1970, 1; 20 October 1970, 1.

27. Richard T. Hise and John K. Ryans, Jr., "Industry Image: Its Role in MBA Recruitment," *Personnel Journal* 48 (May 1969): 359–68; "Where Are All the B-School Grads Going?," *Iron Age,* 13 November 1969: 25; "New Dean, New Era for Harvard B-School," *Business Week,* 24 January 1970, 58–60ff.

28. T. G. P. Rogers, Peter Williams, and Jan Dauman, "First Catch Your MBA," *Personnel Management* 2 (November 1970): 36–38.

29. "Business Graduates: The Itinerant Managers," *Economist,* 3 October 1970, 70; "New Dean, New Era for Harvard B-School," *Business Week,* 24 January 1970, 58–60ff.; *Wall Street Journal,* 23 September 1970, 13.

30. James W. Kelley, "Management Grades the Graduate Business School," *Personnel* 46 (September 1969): 16–26; "How to Rise Fast: By Degrees," *Newsweek,* 25 December 1967, 60–62; "Big Men on Campus," *Newsweek,* 27 February 1967, 74–76; *Wall Street Journal,* 11 July 1967, 1; *New York Times,* 28 July 1968, section 3, p. 11.

31. John Kneen, "Recruiting MBAs: The Line Executive's Role," *Management*

Review 58 (October 1969): 65–69; "Bridging the International Management Gap," *Sales Management,* 1 February 1969: 50–53.

32. Alfred N. Page and Richard R. West, "Evaluating Student Performance in Graduate Schools of Business," *Journal of Business* 42 (January 1969): 36–41; *New York Times Magazine,* 10 November 1968, 25ff.; "Price Tag on MBAs Gets Higher," *Business Week,* 11 October 1969, 163.

33. John T. Wheeler, "Doctorates in Business Administration: A Demand and Supply Analysis," *California Management Review* 10 (fall 1967): 35–50.

34. Alvin A. Butkus, "Should Executives Go Back to School?" *Dun's* 96 (September 1970): 36–38; "Budget Cutters Worry B-Schools," *Business Week,* 26 December 1970, 15; *Wall Street Journal,* 20 March 1970, 1.

CHAPTER 11. 1971–1979: THE GOLDEN AGE OF INNOVATION

1. "The Booming Business Schools," *Dun's Review* 108 (July 1976): 20–21; Stephen Singular, "The Business Schools: A Bull Market in Applicants," *MBA* 9 (May 1975): 34–36; "The Worrisome Boom in Second-Rate B-Schools," *Business Week,* 6 March 1978, 82, 86.

2. "Student Tastes Shift to the Executive Suite," *Nation's Business* 59 (May 1971): 132–33.

3. Stephen Singular "The Business Schools: A Bull Market in Applicants," *MBA* 9 (May 1975): 34–36; *New York Times,* 26 November 1976, 1.

4. J. E. Steele and L. B. Ward, "MBAs: Mobile, Well Situated, Well Paid," *Harvard Business Review* 52 (January 1974): 99–110; Steven A. Sass, *The Pragmatic Imagination: A History of the Wharton School, 1881–1981* (Philadelphia: University of Pennsylvania Press, 1982), 314; M. P. Ostereicher, "Female Enrollment: Explosive Growth," *MBA* 11 (September 1977): 40–41; *New York Times,* 25 May 1975, section 3, p. 7; Doreen Sanders, "Here Come the Women—and It's About Time," *Business Quarterly* 49 (spring 1984): 136ff.; *New York Times,* 11 February 1974, 53; "Upswing in the MBA Market," *Nation's Business,* 62 (May 1974): 34–35.

5. "Upswing in the MBA Market," *Nation's Business* 62 (May 1974): 34–35; W. L. Jones and S. H. Schoen, "The New Minority Managers: How Far, How Fast?," *MBA* 11 (January 1977): 47–49; *New York Times,* 14 May 1978, 26; *Wall Street Journal,* 23 April 1973, 6.

6. J. E. Steele and L. B. Ward, "MBAs: Mobile, Well Situated, Well Paid," *Harvard Business Review* 52 (January 1974): 99–110; "Upswing in the MBA Market," *Nation's Business* 62 (May 1974): 34–35; *Wall Street Journal,* 15 October 1974, 1; "The Job Market Starts a B-School Stampede," *Business Week,* 2 June 1975, 50–51; "The Booming Business Schools," *Dun's Review* 108 (July 1976): 20–21; *New York Times,* 30 April 1978, section 12, p. 8.

7. *New York Times,* 30 April 1978, section 12, p. 8, and 29 March 1978, section 4, p. 11. All statistics are from USOE sources.

8. "Training MBAs for the Public Sector," *Business Week,* 10 June 1972, 82–84; *Wall Street Journal,* 20 October 1973, 1; Iain Carson, "Inside Harvard Business School," *International Management* 26 (August 1971): 20–21ff.; "Closed Loop," *MBA* 8 (1974); "The Frantic Competition for MBAs," *Business Week,* 6 July 1974, 58–59ff.; George J. Berkwitt, "MBAs—the New Militants," *Dun's* 101 (January 1973): 48–50; "Closed Loop," *MBA* 12 (1978).

9. *New York Times,* 1 October 1975, 1, 57; 13 September 1976, 43; 30 April 1978, section 12, p. 8; *Wall Street Journal,* 5 January 1976, 8; Lee Smith, "Yale's B-School with a Difference," *Dun's Review* 107 (February 1976): 63–65.

10. "A B-School for Entrepreneurs of Change," *Business Week*, 25 April 1970, 82, 86; Madison Smartt Bell, *History of the Owen School from Its Early Origins to 1984* (Nashville: Vanderbilt University Press, 1985): 44–58.

11. *New York Times*, 21 November 1976, section 3, p. 7; James R. Emshoff, "The Busch Center: An Organization Designed to Assure Quality Academic Research on Real-World Problems," *Interfaces* 7 (February 1977): 68–73.

12. "Making a B-School More Relevant," *Business Week*, 5 December 1970, 58–60.

13. Zane Knauss, "And Now . . . The TV-MBA," *MBA* 9 (July-August 1975): 32–33.

14. "Closed Loop," *MBA* 9 (September 1975); "My Son, the MBA," *Forbes*, 1 March 1977, 41–44.

15. "The Selling of Pace," *Dun's Review* 104 (August 1974): 71.

16. "B-School Students Run a Real Company," *Business Week*, 1 May 1971, 100, 102; "When B-Schoolers Act as Company Consultants," *Business Week*, 28 July 1975, 36–37.

17. David Oates, "The School That Puts Practice Before Theory," *Institutional Management* 29 (January 1979): 26–28.

18. Alexander G. Floyd, "The Modular Curriculum," *MBA* 8 (May 1974): 33–34.

19. "Closed Loop," *MBA* 9 (January, March, and December 1975).

20. Howard L. Fromkin, "The Behavioral Science Laboratories at Purdue's Krannert School," *Administrative Science Quarterly* 14 (June 1969): 171–77; "Machiavellian Tactics for B-School Students," *Business Week*, 13 October 1975, 86.

21. *New York Times*, 3 June 1973, 24; 1 April 1975, 1; 6 April 1975, section 4, p. 8; and 8 April 1973, section 3, p. 4.

22. "Closed Loop," *MBA* 9 (October 1977); *New York Times*, 21 November 1976, section 3, p. 7; Meg Hunter Naylor, *The Thunderbird American Graduate School of International Management, 1946–1986* (Glendale, Ariz.: American Graduate School of International Management, 1986); "A Year Abroad for Future MBAs," *Business Week*, 12 May 1973, 47.

23. Jesse S. Tarleton, "Recommended Courses in International Business for Graduate Business Students," *Journal of Business* 50 (October 1977): 438–47.

24. "Small Business Goes to Harvard," *Business Week*, 2 September 1972, 42–43.

25. *Wall Street Journal*, 15 April 1975, 1, and 31 January 1978, 1.

26. Alvin A. Butkus, "Should Executives Go Back to School?," *Dun's* 96 (September 1970): 36–38; "Budget Cutters Worry B-Schools," *Business Week*, 26 December 1970, 15; and Michael McGill, *American Business and the Quick Fix* (New York: Henry Holt, 1988): 14–15.

27. *Wall Street Journal*, 21 December 1976, 1; "Could You Qualify as a Master of Management?," *Industry Week*, 19 May 1975, 48–49ff.

28. "Where the Boss Gets an MBA on the Job," *Business Week*, 8 May 1971, 86–87; *New York Times*, 8 July 1972, 31; Iain Carson, "A New Concept to Train Managers," *International Management* 28 (May 1973): 32–35; *New York Times*, 17 February 1974, 117; Norman Sklarewitz, "Impresarios Go to School," *MBA* 11 (April, 1974): 32–33ff.

29. Arnold L. Paolasini, "Schools of Accounting: The Way of the Future," *Management Accounting* 59 (March 1978): 15–18.

30. "CPAs Get Their Own School," *Business Week*, 17 May 1976, 136ff.; D. F. Fetyko, "Who Shall Train Us?," *Management Accounting* 57 (January 1976): 13–14ff.; C. R. Grimstead, "New Schools of Accounting—Necessary," *CPA Journal* 46 (October 1976): 21–24; J. Marion Posey, "Professional Schools of Accounting: A Promising Alternative," *Management Accounting* 57 (January 1976): 15–17; and

W. G. Bremser et al., "The Feasibility of Professional Schools: An Empirical Study,' *Accounting Review* 52 (April 1977): 465.

31. "Closed Loop," *MBA* 12 (February 1968); J. E. Steele and L. B. Ward, "MBAs: Mobile, Well Situated, Well Paid," *Harvard Business Review* 52 (January 1974): 101; *Wall Street Journal*, 27 June 1972, 1; James L. Hayes, "A New Generation," *Management Review* 66 (October 1977): 2–3; "What They Taught Me at Business School," *Industrial Management* 4 (November 1974): 16–17ff.

32. Jacqueline A. Thompson, "Recruiting: The Best Year in a Decade," *MBA* 8 (March 1974): 42–44; "The Scramble for MBAs," *Dun's* 105 (June 1975): 87–88.

33. "Training MBAs for the Public Sector," *Business Week*, 10 June 1972, 82–84; David Oates, "Stanford Stresses Urban Management," *International Management* 28 (May 1973): 36–37ff.

34. Philip L. Zweig, "White House MBAs: Budget Cutting Begins at Home," *MBA* 11 (May 1977): 25–30.

35. "B-Schools Scramble for Perot's Cash," *Business Week*, 11 September 1971, 47–48; *New York Times*, 11 June 1972, 62; H. Justin Davidson, "How Businessmen Can Help Schools of Business," *Nation's Business* 63 (October 1975): 73–74; Wallace L. Jones and Sterling H. Schoen, "The New Minority Managers: How Far, How Fast?" *MBA* 11 (January 1977): 47–49.

36. *New York Times*, 13 February 1972, section 3, p. 3.; 2 October 1972, section 3, p. 7; 21 November 1976, section 3, p. 7; 14 December 1977, section 4, p. 13; *Wall Street Journal*, 30 October 1973, 1; Paula Gantz, "Life in Philadelphia," *MBA* 11 (November 1977): 56; Judson Gooding, "MBA, Harvard, '78: Sweeney's Way," *Across the Board* 15 (June 1978): 17–25; Alexander Ross, "The Case for Harvard B-School," *Canadian Business* 51 (March 1978): 38–40ff.

37. Roger M. Atherton, Jr., "B-School Survey: The Nationals vs. the Regionals," *MBA* 9 (October 1975): 30–33; *New York Times*, 9 June 1978, section 4, p. 4.

38. *New York Times*, 1 March 1978, section 4, p. 13; 30 April 1978, section 12, p. 8; and 23 May 1978, section 4, p. 1.

39. Rebecca Z. Margulies and Peter M. Blau, "America's Leading Professional Schools," *Change* 5 (November 1973): 21–27.

40. William R. Henry and E. Earl Busch, "Institutional Contributions to Scholarly Journals of Business," *Journal of Business* 47 (January 1974): 56–61; *New York Times*, 31 March 1974, section 3, p. 15.

41. *Wall Street Journal*, 3 June 1974, 25; *New York Times*, 18 July 1974, 36.

42. "The Fifteen Top Rated Graduate Business Schools in the United States," *MBA* 8 (December 1974): 21–25; "Stanford Beats Harvard," *Forbes*, 1 February 1975, 48.

43. "The MBA Survey of the Graduate Business Schools: The Top 15," *MBA* 9 (December 1975): 33–34ff.; *New York Times*, 14 December 1975, section 3, p. 15.

44. George Brooker and Philip Shinoda, "Peer Ratings of Graduate Programs for Business," *Journal of Business* 49 (April 1976): 83ff.

45. Joel Stern, "Why Case Study Is Not Enough," *MBA* 10 (October 1976): 46–47.

46. "Graduate Business Schools: The Top 10," *MBA* 10 (December 1976): 42ff.; *Wall Street Journal*, 27 January 1977, 1.

47. *New York Times*, 14 December 1977, section 4, p. 13; 9 January 1978, 31; 7 February 1978, 22.

48. Iain Carson, "Business School with Big Ambitions," *International Management* 26 (May 1971): 28–32; David Oates, "How Henley Broadens the Mind," *International Management* 26 (March 1971): 14–16; "Business Schools: Post-Owen," *Economist*, 24 July 1971: 72, 74; "The Big Boom in European B-Schools, *Business*

Week, 20 November 1971, 64ff.; "Picking the Capitalist Brain," *Business Week,* 27 March 1971, 40–41.

49. Norman Sklarewitz, "Business Schools Under Siege," *MBA* 11 (November 1977): 44; Rhoda Besuch, "Sabras Go to B-School," *MBA* 12 (August-September 1978): 44, 47; "Business Schools: Goodbye, America," *Economist,* 12 August 1972, 68, 70.

50. *New York Times,* 1 October 1972, section 3, p. 7; Susanne Lawrence, "Professor Ball: Man of the Moment," *Personnel Management* 4 (November 1972): 18–19.

51. Iain Carson, "A New Concept to Train Managers," *Industrial Management* 28 (May 1973): 32–35; Roy Hill, "Bombay's Down-to-Earth Business School," *International Management* 28 (October 1973): 61–63; David Oates, "The School That Puts Practice before Theory," *International Management* 29 (January 1974): 26–28; Peter Hobday, "Oasis in Manchester," *The Director: Journal of the Institute of Directors* 28 (November 1975): 203–4.

52. *Wall Street Journal,* 24 August 1976, 38.

53. *New York Times,* 8 January 1973, 78.

54. "Wharton Copes with Its Identity Crisis," *Business Week,* 23 July 1973, 49ff.

55. Thomas J. Von der Embse, D. Wayne Delozier, and Joseph F. Castellano, "Three Views of the Ideal MBA," *Business Horizons* 16 (December 1973): 85–91; Barry Render and Ralph M. Stair Jr., "Future Managers Need DP Training," *Infosystems* 22 (October 1975): 41–42.

56. C. Stewart Sheppard, ed., *The First Twenty Years: The Darden School at Virginia* (Charlottesville: The Darden School, 1975), last chapter.

57. C. Jackson Grayson, "The Business of Business Schools," *Wharton Magazine* 2 (spring 1977): 46–51.

58. Kermit O. Hanson, "The Defense," *Wharton Magazine* 2 (spring 1977): 63–64.

59. *New York Times,* 5 July 1978, section 4, p. 8; John J. Rasmussen and Thomas George, "After 25 Years: A Survey of Operations Research Alumni, Case Western University," *Interfaces* 8 (May 1978): 48–52.

60. "What Do You Want?" *Economist,* 9 January 1971, 71, 75.

61. Donald C. Hambrick, "What Should an MBA Program Be?," *MSU Business Topics* 23 (spring 1975): 41–47.

62. Paul J. Gordon, "The Unfinished Business of Business Education," *Conference Board Record* 13 (January 1976): 60–64.

63. "The Worrisome Boom in Second-Rate B-Schools, *Business Week,* 6 March 1978, 82, 86.

64. Robert C. Turner, "Enrollment Prospects for Collegiate Schools of Business," *Business Horizons* 19 (October 1966): 55–64; *Wall Street Journal,* 27 December 1978, 1; Richard J. Agnello and Joseph W. Hunt, Jr., "The Part-time MBA: It May Be a Better Investment Than Full-time," *MBA* 11 (October 1977): 26–30.

65. Robert Lamb, "A New Crop of MBAs Goes Looking for that 'Fast Track,'" *Fortune* 95 (June 1977): 160–65ff.

66. Pat Pfeiffer and Stanley J. Shapiro, "Male and Female MBA Candidates: Are there Personality Differences?," *Business Quarterly* 43 (spring 1978): 77–80; G. N. Punj and R. Staelin, "The Choice Process for Graduate Business Schools," *Journal of Marketing Research* 15 (November 1978): 588–98.

67. *Wall Street Journal,* 14 October 1975, 1, and 15 April 1975, 1.

68. *Wall Street Journal,* 17 September 1976, 27; "My Son, the MBA," *Forbes,* 1 March 1977, 41–44; *New York Times,* 23 May 1978, section 4, p. 1; Wyndham Robertson, "Women MBAs, Harvard, '73—How They're Doing," *Fortune,* 28 August 1978, 50–54ff.

69. M. W. Rader, "An Analysis of a Small, Closely Observed Labor Market:

Starting Salaries for University of Chicago MBAs," *Journal of Business* 51 (1 April 1978): 263–97.

70. Jacqueline A. Thompson, "Recruiting: The Best Year in a Decade," *MBA* 8 (March 1974): 42–44; "Upswing in the MBA Market," *Nation's Business* 62 (May 1974): 34–35; "A Cold Market for New MBAs," *Business Week,* 23 November 1974, 118.

71. *Wall Street Journal,* 15 October 1977, 1, and 9 April 1974, 1; "The Scramble for MBAs," *Dun's* 105 (June 1975): 87–88; "The Job Market Starts a B-School Stampede," *Business Week,* 2 June 1975, 50–51; "Glad Hands Greet MBAs this Spring," *Business Week,* 7 June 1976, 27–28; *New York Times,* 3 March 1976, 33, and 5 June 1977, section 3, p. 15; "In Hotter Pursuit of MBAs," *Business Week,* 7 February 1977, 98; *New York Times,* 23 May 1978, section 4, p. 1; and Phyllis Berman, "An Offer You Can't Refuse," *Forbes,* 13 November 1978, 110.

72. "The Job Market Starts a B-School Stampede," *Business Week,* 2 June 1975, 50–51; Stephen Singular, "The Business Schools: A Bull Market in Applicants," *MBA* 9 (May 1975): 34–36; *New York Times,* 20 July 1975, section 3, p. 13, and 3 March 1976, 33; *Wall Street Journal,* 23 September 1976, 1.

73. "The Job Market Starts a B-School Stampede," 50–51; and *New York Times,* 10 August 1975, section 3, p. 12.

74. J. Sterling Livingston, "The Myth of the Well Educated Manager," *Harvard Business Review* 49 (January-February 1971): 79–89; "Bunk?," *Economist,* 30 January 1971, 76.

75. Michael Simmons, "The Business Schools Pause for Thought," *The Director* 27 (December 1974): 506–9; "What They Taught Me at Business School," *Industrial Management* 4 (November 1974): 16–17ff.

76. "Business Schools: Criticism Crystallized," *Economist,* 3 July 1971, 67.

77. *Wall Street Journal,* 8 February 1977, 1; Carol J. Mammana, "Harris Bank Flap," *MBA* 11 (April 1977): 49.

78. Simmons, "The Business Schools Pause for Thought," *The Director* 27 (December 1974): 509; Lee Smith, "Yale's B-School with a Difference," *Dun's Review* 107 (February 1976): 63–65; H. Justin Davidson, "How Businessmen Can Help Schools of Business," *Nation's Business* 63 (October 1979): 73–74; *New York Times,* 7 January 1976, 26, and 28 March 1976, section 4, p. 16.

79. "Arlington J. Stone," "The Dawn of a New Science," *American Mercury* 14 (August 1928): 446.

80. "Troubles That Toppled a B-School Dean," *Business Week,* 17 May 1975, 28; *Wall Street Journal,* 29 October 1975, 1; "The Worrisome Boom in Second Rate B-Schools," *Business Week,* 6 March 1978, 82, 86.

81. "A New Degree of Demand for MBAs," *Nation's Business* 61 (July 1973): 34; John E. Steele and Lewis B. Ward, "MBAs: Mobile, Well Situated, Well Paid," *Harvard Business Review* 51 (January 1974): 99–110.

82. "My Son, the MBA," *Forbes,* 1 March 1977, 41–44; Christopher Scanlan, "Will the MBA Balloon Burst If the Feds Cut Student Loans?" *MBA* 11 (October 1977): 17–25.

83. "Closed Loop," *MBA* 12 (February 1978); "An Uneven Flow of Management Talent," *Business Week,* 20 February 1978, 68–70; *New York Times,* 30 April 1978, section 12, p. 8; Girash N. Punj and Richard Staelin, "The Choice Process for Graduate Business Schools," *Journal of Marketing Research* 15 (November 1978): 588–98; *New York Times,* 5 July 1978, section 4, p. 8.

84. Robert C. Turner, "Enrollment Prospects for Collegiate Schools of Business," *Business Horizons* 19 (October 1976): 53–64.

CHAPTER 12. 1979–1984: THE CRITICS TURN IT ON

1. *Consultants News,* quoted in "The Swing to Practicality in the Business Schools," *Business Week,* 23 July 1979, 190ff.; William C. Giaque and R. E. D.

Woolsey, "A Totally New Direction for Management Education: A Modest Proposal," *Interfaces* 11 (August 1981): 30–34; K. Larry Hastie, "A Perspective on Management Education," *Financial Management* 11 (winter 1982): 55–62; *New York Times,* 28 July 1982, section 4, p. 15; Bro Uttal, "The Animals of Silicon Valley," *Fortune,* 12 January 1981, 94.

2. Hyman G. Rickover, "Getting the Job Done Right," *New York Times,* 25 November 1981, 23.

3. "Don't Blame the System, Blame the Managers," *Dun's Review* 116 (September 1980): 82–88.

4. *New York Times,* 21 August 1980, section 4, p. 2.

5. Andrew Weiner, "Why MBAs Fizzle on the Firing Line," *Canadian Business* 54 (February 1981): 108–14.

6. Robert H. Hayes and William J. Abernethy, "Managing Our Way to Economic Decline," *Harvard Business Review* 58 (July-August 1980): 67–77.

7. *New York Times,* 30 May 1982, section 3, p. 1; Jim Fisk and Robert Barron (pseuds.), "A Rational Publishing Business—the MBA Way," *Publisher's Weekly,* 2 July 1982, 26–28; George Leonard, "The Great School Reform Hoax," *Esquire* 101 (April 1984): 50.

8. John Thackray, "The Business School Backlash," *Management Today* 70 (August 1981): 58–61; Nicholas Newman, "The MBA Credibility Gap," *Management Today* 70, (December 1981): 46–49ff.

9. George Bickerstaffe, "Crisis of Confidence in the Business Schools," *International Management,* 1 August 1981, 19ff.; "Japan Gives the B-School an A—for Contacts," *Business Schools,* 19 October 1981, 132ff.

10. Steven Muller, quoted in Robert R. Rehder, "American Business Education—Is It Too Late to Change?," *Sloan Management Review* 23 (winter 1982): 64–71; Edward J. Mandt, "The Failure of Business Education—and What to Do About It," *Management Review* 71 (August 1982): 47–52; *New York Times,* 31 August 1982, 21; and Philip Sadler, quoted in "It's Time to Get Back to Basics, Managers Are Warned," *Personnel Management* 16 (April 1984): 10.

11. *New York Times,* 30 April 1979, 14, and 28 January 1980, section 4, p. 1; George Bickerstaffe, "Crisis of Confidence in the Business Schools," *International Management* 26 (August 1981): 19ff.

12. "What Are They Teaching in the B-Schools?" *Business Week,* 10 November 1980, 61ff.; Duane Windsor and Francis D. Tuggle, "Redesigning the MBA Curriculum," *Interfaces* 12 (August 1982): 72–78; *New York Times,* 20 July 1982, section 1, p. 19; and 25 April 1982, section 12, p. 54.

13. "Wntd: Mgt Intrns (MBA Not Req'd)," *Management Review* 68 (June 1979): 5; "Reevaluating the Costly MBA," *Management Review* 69 (August 1980): 6.

14. Fixing the Blame for MBAs' High Salaries," *Management Review* 70 (November 1981): 54; *New York Times,* 10 February 1982, section 4, p. 21.

15. *Wall Street Journal,* 12 September 1980, 23; "What Are They Teaching in the B-Schools?," *Business Week,* 10 November 1980, 61ff.; *New York Times,* 4 January 1981, 1; Judd Alexander, "Do We Want Cookie-Cutter Training for Executives?" *Industry Week,* 24 August 1981, 13.

16. Susan Fraker, "Tough Times for MBAs," *Fortune,* 12 December 1983, 64–72; John S. McClenahan, "New Marching Orders for MBAs," *Industry Week,* 8 August 1983, 49–51; "Harvard Business School: The Hardest Case Study Is Itself," *Economist,* 27 October 1984, 81–82; Jack N. Behrman and Richard I. Levin, "Are Business Schools Doing Their Job?" *Harvard Business Review* 62 (January-February 1984) 140–47.

17. Nicholas Newman, "The MBA Credibility Gap," *Management Today* 70 (December 1981) 46–49ff.; John Thackray, "The Business School Backlash," *Management Today* 70 (August 1981): 58–61.

18. John A. Byrne, "The MBA Mills," *Forbes*, 19 November 1984), 316–18ff.

19. Maria Fisher, "What's an MBA Really Worth?," *Forbes*, 19 December 1983, 176.

20. "Arabs at Western Business Schools: The Backlash Begins," *International Management* 37 (April 1982): 31ff.

21. "Demand Is Soaring for MBA Graduates," *Business Week*, 15 January 1979, 42; *New York Times*, 14 October 1979, section 12, p. 74; *Wall Street Journal*, 2 November 1979, 48.

22. Lynn Adkins, "Glut Coming in MBAs?," *Dun's Review* 115 (March 1980): 104–6; Robert Runde, "A Two-Tier Market for Lawyers and MBAs," *Money* 9 (May 1980): 80–82; "Reevaluating the Costly MBA," *Management Review* 69 (August 1980): 6.

23. "The MBA Glut Is Now Hitting the Top Ten," *Business Week*, 15 March 1982, 30–31; Walter Kiechel III, "Bunch and Crunch on the Fast Track," *Fortune*, 3 May 1982, 313–14; *New York Times*, 30 June 1982, section 4, p. 17.

24. *New York Times*, 27 October 1980, section 4, p. 19; R. S. Stainton, "MBA Can Mean Management By Action," *Interfaces*, 11 October 1981), 1–7.

25. *Wall Street Journal*, 13 May 1980, 1; *New York Times*, 16 July 1980, section 4, p. 17; Thomas R. Horton, "Masters of Management," *Management Review* 71 (October 1982): 2–3; *New York Times*, 31 July 1984, section 3, pp. 1, 11.

26. "Recruiting for Retailing," *Stores* 64 (April 1983): 66–67; Shirley S. Kenny, "Humanities and Business: Educational Reform for Corporate Success," *Business and Society Review* 48 (winter 1984): 23–26.

27. Bruce A. Jacobs, "Shop Floor MBAs," *Industry Week*, 14 November 1982, 87, 90.

28. William C. Giaque, "Taking the Classroom into Reality: A Field Consulting Experience for MBAs," *Interfaces* 20 (August 1980): 1–10; "On the Job Training for Fledgling MBAs," *Management Review* 70 (November 1981): 40–41; *New York Times*, 16 September 1982, section 4, p. 7; "Europe Puts the Business Back into Business Schools," *Economist*, 14 April 1984, 89–90.

29. "Holding Class in the Boardroom," *Chemical Week*, 16 April 1980, 57; "MBA Students Assist New Jersey Exporters," *Business America*, 7 February 1983, 19; *Wall Street Journal*, 23 August 1984, 2, and 5 April 1984, 1.

30. *New York Times*, 17 January 1982, section 3, 2; Nicholas Newman, "The MBA Credibility Gap," *Management Today* 70 (December 1981): 46–49ff.

31. *New York Times*, 9 October 1979, section 4, p. 2; 23 March 1980, section 3, p. 7; 17 March 1983, section 4, p. 2; 20 February 1980, section 4, p. 1; 19 July 1980, section 4, p. 12; Marilyn Wellemeyer, "Executives on Campus," *Fortune*, 18 April 1983: 137ff.; *New York Times*, 14 November 1982, section 12, p. 56.

32. "The Swing to Practicality in the Business Schools," *Business Week*, 23 July 1979, 190ff.; *New York Times*, 18 March 1979, section 3, p. 1.

33. *Wall Street Journal*, 26 January 1981, 1; "Hard Times Push B-Schools into Basics," *Business Week*, 30 August 1982, 23–24; John A. Byrne, "Nuts and Bolts Bosses," *Forbes*, 26 September 1983, 128, 132; Susan Fraker, "Tough Times for MBAs," *Fortune*, 12 December 1982, 64–72.

34. "A Business School Dean Manages Change and 'Herds the Cats,'" *International Management* 38 (August 1983): 25–26; Karen Greenberg, "B-Schools Show New Interest in Manufacturing," *Advanced Management Journal* 49 (spring 1984): 53.

35. "A Better Crop for B-Schools," *Business Week*, 14 September 1981, 11; *Wall Street Journal*, 14 May 1981, 1; Herbert L. Schuette, "Educating Executives: Computers Bring the Factory to the Classroom," *Management Review* 73 (March 1984):

15–21; Karen Greenberg, "B-Schoolers Show New Interest in Manufacturing," *Advanced Management Journal* 49 (spring 1984): 53; *Wall Street Journal,* 10 February 1984, 26.

36. Michael Thoryn, "Small Business Survival Courses," *Nation's Business* 70 (July 1982): 17–68; *New York Times,* 17 November 1982, section 4, p. 19.

37. *Wall Street Journal,* 7 May 1984, 35; Sharon Nelton, "Molding Managers for the Tests of Tomorrow," *Nation's Business* 72 (April 1984): 30–31ff.; "B-Schools Try to Churn Out Entrepreneurs," *Business Week,* 5 March 1984, 102.

38. "A Business School Dean Manages Change and 'Herds the Cats,'" *International Management* 38 (August 1983): 25–26; *New York Times,* 16 September 1984, section 3, p. 15, and 16 September 1982, section 4, p. 7; "B-Schools Try to Churn Out Entrepreneurs," *Business Week,* 5 March 1984, 102; Bryan W. Clark, Charles H. Davis, and Verne C. Harnish, "Do Courses in Entrepreneurship Aid in New Venture Creation?," *Journal of Small Business* 22 (April 1984): 26–31.

39. *Wall Street Journal,* 31 May 1979, 1; *New York Times,* 6 April 1983, section 4, p. 21; *Wall Street Journal,* 15 November 1984, 1.

40. *New York Times* 25 April 1982, section 12, p. 54; 6 September 1984, section 3, p. 15; *Wall Street Journal,* 12 March 1981, 33; *New York Times,* 20 February 1983, section 3, p. 27; 3 October 1982, section 3, p. 21.

41. *Wall Street Journal,* 20 October 1982, 1; *New York Times,* 27 June 1982, section 3, p. 8.

42. J. A. Byrne, "Some Thoughts from the Best and Brightest MBAs," *Forbes,* 3 June 1985: p. 215ff.; Samuel I. Doctors, "Experiential Learning/Social Problem-Solving Programs in Graduate Schools of Business," *Review of Black Political Economy* 10 (winter 1980): 209–18; *New York Times,* 1 February 1981, section 3, p. 6.

43. Sharon Nelton, "Molding Managers for the Tests of Tomorrow," *Nation's Business* 72 (April 1984): 30–31ff.; "A Business School Dean Manages Change and 'Herds the Cats,'" *International Management* 38 (August 1983): 25–26; "Are MBAs More Than Quantitative Robots?," *Business and Society Review* 44 (winter 1983): 4–12.

44. "Are MBAs More than Quantitative Robots?" 4–12.

45. *New York Times,* 6 July 1980, 23; 19 March 1980, section 4, p. 17; 30 August 1981, section 12, p.23.

46. George K. Saul, "Business Ethics: Where Are We Going?" *Academy of Management Review* 6 (April 1981): 269–76.

47. Bowen H. McCoy, "Applying the Art of Action-Oriented Decision Making to the Knotty Issues of Everyday Business Life," *Management Review* 72 (July 1983): 20–24; *Wall Street Journal,* 6 August 1979, 10.

48. *New York Times,* 21 November 1984, section 4, p. 14; 19 August 1984, section 3, p. 12; George K. Saul, "Business Ethics: Where Are We Going?," *Academy of Management Review* 6 (April 1981): 269–76.

49. *Wall Street Journal,* 30 September 1984, 1; "Fixing the Blame for MBAs' High Salaries," *Management Review* 70 (November 1981): 54.

50. George Bickerstaffe, "Crisis of Confidence in the Business Schools," *International Management* 36 (August 1981): 19ff.; Thomas D. Weldon and Norman R. Weldon, "Meeting Expectations: New MBAs and Their Employers," *Business Horizons* 24 (November-December 1981): 30–31; William D. Wooldredge, "Fast Track Programs for MBAs: Do They Really Work?," *Management Review* 68 (April 1979): 9–13.

51. Nancy Darsey and Jean Dorrell, "The Demography and Professional Status of the ABC Members, 1985 Compared with 1968," *Bulletin of the Association for Business Communication* 50 (June 1987): 2; Shirley S. Kenny, "Humanities and Busi-

ness: Educational Reform for Corporate Success," *Business and Society Review* 48 (winter 1984): 23–26.

52. *Wall Street Journal,* 18 October 1983, 1; *New York Times,* 2 September 1981, section 4, p. 13; 23 May 1982, section 3, p. 19.

53. Gordon Wills, "Marketing a Business School to Industry," *Industrial Marketing Management* 11 (October 1982): 303–10.

54. "A Plan to Rate B-Schools by Testing Skills," *Business Week,* 19 November 1979, 171ff.; George Bickerstaffe, "Crisis of Confidence in the Business Schools," *International Management* 36 (August 1981), 19ff.

55. "A Plan to Rate B-Schools by Testing Skills," *Business Week,* 19 November 1979, 171ff.; Robert H. Rehder, "American Business Education: Is It Too Late to Change?," *Sloan Management Review* 23 (winter 1982): 63–71.

56. *New York Times,* 8 April 1982, 1; 13 April 1982, section 3, p. 1; Robert H. Rehder, "The Creative MBA: A New Proposal for Balancing the Science and Art of Management," *Business Horizons* 26 (November-December 1983): 52–54.

57. Mistal Schiff, "The Business School Establishment vs. the Accounting Profession," *Journal of Accountancy* 149 (April 1980): 84–88; Barry Render and Ralph M. Stair, "Information Processing Skills for Future Managers," *Journal of Systems Management* 31 (May 1980): 12–14; Fred D. Reynolds, "How to Make a Marketing-Research Professional," *Journal of Advertising Research* 21 (April 1981): 19–21; Gary L. Benson, "On the Campus: How Well Do Business Schools Prepare Graduates for the Business World?" *Personnel* 60 (July–August 1983): 61–65.

58. "Demand Is Soaring for MBA Graduates," *Business Week,* 15 January 1979, 42; *Wall Street Journal,* 26 June 1979, 1; Max B. E. Clarkson, "Managerial Education: A Parasitical Reliance on Imported Skills," *Canadian Business Review* 6 (spring 1979): 19–24.

59. *Wall Street Journal,* 11 February 1980, 1; 15 April 1980, 1; 25 September 1980, 35; *New York Times,* 18 May 1980. section 3, p. 1; 21 September 1980, section 3, p. 21; Margaret Price, "Consulting Firms Lure Top MBA Graduates," *Industry Week,* 13 October 1980, 46–48; "Who Says College Doesn't Pay?" *Sales and Marketing Management,* 7 July 1980, 8.

60. *New York Times,* 28 September 1981, 31; John Thackray, "The Business School Backlash," *Management Today* 70 (August 1981): 58–61; *Wall Street Journal,* 16 April 1981, 29; 15 December 1981, 1.

61. "Job Offers Are Chasing the New MBAs Again," *Business Week,* 9 April 1984, 32–33; "A New B-School Mission: Teaching High-Tech Savvy," *Business Week,* 19 November 1974, 170ff.

62. *Wall Street Journal,* 17 April 1979, 1; USOE/NCES figures; N. Alexander, "Outlook for MBAs," *Black Enterprise* 13 (December 1982): 22; "Your Second Chance at an MBA," *Business Week,* 26 March 1984, 138–39; *New York Times,* 14 November 1984, section 4, 17; "British Business Schools: Packing Them In," *Economist,* 12 May 1984, p. 78.

63. *Wall Street Journal,* 26 January 1981, 1; 25 February 1981, 1; *New York Times,* 27 September 1981, section 3, p. 1.

64. "Faculty Shortage Is Plaguing B-Schools," *Industry Week,* 19 April 1982, 114ff.; *Wall Street Journal,* 17 June 1982, 1; *New York Times,* 28 July 1981, section 4, p. 15.

65. Robert M. Donnelly, "How to Manage the MBA," *Advanced Management Journal* 47 (summer 1982): 43–45; J. D. Hunger and T. L. Wheelen, "A Recruiter's Question: How Does the Bachelor's Degree in Business Compare to the MBA?," *Human Resources Management* 19 (February 1980): 2–15; *Wall Street Journal,* 5 June 1979, 1; Kevan Pearson, "Graduates: The Human Investment," *Management*

Today 69 (May 1980): 118ff.; Diane Wilson, "Blood, Sweat, and Two Years," *Canadian Business* 54 (October 1981): 48–60.

66. Dick Wasserman, "How Do MBAs Fare in Advertising?," *Advertising Age,* 28 July 1980, 52; Walter J. Salmon, "Don't Shy Away from the MBA," *Progressive Grocer* 59 (June 1980): 7–8; *New York Times,* 18 July 1984, section 4, p. 23.

67. "Do Business Schools Teach Absolute Rot?," *Business and Society Review* 40 (winter 1981–82): 61–65; "Are MBAs More than Quantitative Robots?," *Business and Society Review* 44 (winter 1983): 4–12; Sharon Nelton, "Molding Managers for the Tests of Tomorrow," *Nation's Business* 72 (April 1984): 30–31ff.; Martin J. Gannon and Peter Arlow, "The Mystique of the MBA Degree," *Business Horizons* 28 (January-February 1985): 20–25; "A Distinguished Tradition," *The Accountant,* 6 March 1980, 338.

68. "Boosting the Careers of B-School Grads," *Business Week,* 11 October 1982, 72; J. Scott Armstrong, "The Ombudsman: Learner Responsibility in Management Education, or Ventures into Forbidden Research," *Interfaces* 13 (April 1983): 26–38.

69. *New York Times,* 16 July 1980, section 4, p. 17; Lynn Adkins, "Glut Coming in MBAs?," *Dun's Review* 115 (March 1980): 104–6; *Wall Street Journal,* 13 May 1980, 1; Thomas R. Horton, "Masters of Management," *Management Review* 71 (October 1982) p. 23; *New York Times,* 31 January 1984, section 3, p. 1ff.

70. *New York Times,* 11 June 1980, section 4, p. 17; 11 September 1979, section 4, p. 5; *Wall Street Journal,* 10 March 1981, 18.

71. John Thackray, "The Business School Backlash," *Management Today* 70 (August 1981): 58–61; Duane Windsor and Francis D. Tuggle, "Redesigning the MBA Curriculum," *Interfaces* 12 (August 1982): 72–78; Robert Dries, "Where the Profs Are Sales Pros," *Sales and Marketing Management,* 16 May 1983, 51–62.

72. *New York Times,* 20 March 1977, section 3, p. 7.

73. Lawrence J. Moore and Bernard W. Taylor III, "A Study of Institutional Publications in Business-Related Academic Journals, 1972–1978," *Quarterly Review of Economics and Business* 20 (spring 1980): 87–97; William R. Henry and E. Earl Burch, "Institutional Contributions to Scholarly Journals of Business" *Journal of Business* 47 (January 1974): 56–66.

74. K. Larry Hastie, "A Perspective on Management Education," *Financial Management* 11 (winter 1982): 55–62; J. Scott Armstrong, "Unintelligible Management Research and Academic Prestige," *Interfaces* 10 (April 1980): 80–86.

Chapter 13. Since 1984: The Active MBA

1. Steven Prokesch, "Classes for Execs: A Quick Buck for B-Schools?" *Business Week,* 11 February 1985, 56; *Wall Street Journal,* 28 March 1985, 35.

2. John A. Byrne, "MBAs Are Hotter than Ever," *Business Week,* 9 March 1987, 46, 48; *Wall Street Journal,* 6 May 1986, 1; *New York Times,* 21 September 1986, section 3, p. 1; *Des Moines Sunday Register,* 23 October 1988, 1, 4A; *Iowa City Press Citizen,* 19 October 1988, 1B; *Wall Street Journal,* 15 March 1988, p. 1.

3. Dana Wechsler Linden, "Another Boom Ends," *Forbes,* 20 January 1992, 76–80; Cyndee Miller, "MBA Boom Goes Bust: Grads Face Increasingly Bleak Market As Darling Degree of the '80s Loses Its Allure," *Marketing News,* 2 March 1992, 1, 22; Lori Bongiorno, "B-Schools Are Taking a Crash Course in Hoopla," *Business Week,* 19 April 1993, 38.

4. *Newsline* (AACSB) 23 (winter 1993): 1–4; *Wall Street Journal,* 6 April 1994,B-1.

5. "Run Schools Like Businesses," *Economist,* 3 January 1987, 49; "CMED

Group Proposes End to Business School Subsidy," *Personnel Management* 21 (June 1989): 7–8; "Moore or Less?" *Economist,* 21 February 1987, 69–70.

6. Anthony P. Carnevale, "Management Training Today and Tomorrow," *Training and Development Journal* 42 (December 1988): 18–29; Frederick Maidment, "Educating Execs: B-Schools Want the Job," *Management World* 15 (June 1986): 44; *New York Times,* 28 January 1985, section 1, p. 10; Mary Brandenburg, "Business Skills and How to Master Them," *Accountancy* 103 (January 1989): 70–71.

7. *New York Times,* 22 December 1987, section 4, p. 17; 8 February 1988, section 4, p. 8; *Wall Street Journal,* 19 February 1987, 32; "Hungarians Embrace Western Management," *International Management* 43 (May 1988): 10, 15; Monica Roman, "From the Halls of U.S. Business Schools to the Mills of Hungary," *Business Week,* 17 August 1991, 26; *Wall Street Journal,* 22 November 1988, A-1; *New York Times,* 2 May 1988, section 4, p. 1; "Friday Night MBAs," *Economist,* 4 October 1986, 66–67; George Bickerstaffe, "Lessons of the Masters," *International Management* 49 (April 1994): 54–55; "Who Needs MBAs?," *Economist,* 4 June 1988, 62–63; "Report Calls for Launch of New Diploma," *Personnel Management* 19 (June 1987): 17; Leo Murray, "Can Business Schools Solve Their Identity Crisis?" *Personnel Management* 21 (August 1989): 4; "Cap, Gown, and Pinstripe," *Newsweek,* 18 September 1989, 46; Dudley Fernando, "The Chalk and Cheese MBAs," *Gulf News* (Qatar), 14 September 1989, 15; "Cambridge's Co-op MBAs," *Industry Week,* 2 September 1991, 30–31.

8. *New York Times,* 13 December 1987, section 1, p. 35.

9. "For Women, the Bloom Might Be Off the MBA," *Business Week,* 14 March 1988, 39; *Wall Street Journal,* 16 December 1986, 1; P. E. Stephan, "The Career Prospects of Female MBAs," *Business* 37 (January-March 1987): 37–41.

10. *Wall Street Journal,* 31 December 1985, 1; *New York Times,* 25 August 1991, section 3, p. 25; *USA Today,* 19 October 1994, section B, p. 2; *American Banker,* 15 August 1991, 8.

11. Donald M. Pattillo, "A Cooperative Approach to International Business Training," *Business America,* 31 March 1986, inside front cover; *Washington Times,* 13 June 1990, section C, p. 1; T. S. Chan, "Developing International Managers," *Journal of Management Development* 13 (1994): 38–46; John Lorinc, "The World's Their Oyster," *Canadian Banker* 66 (April 1993): 54–58.

12. *Wall Street Journal,* 22 May 1986, 1; 18 November 1986, 1; *New York Times,* 19 May 1987, section 4, p. 29; 2 March 1988, section 4, p. 2; "U.S. University to Teach Western Business Skills to Soviet Execs," *Business America,* 28 August 1989, 14; "U.S., Chinese Governments Extend SUNY-Buffalo Chinese MBA Program," *Business America,* 16 January 1989, 17; Anat Arkin, "How International Are Britain's Business Schools?," *Personnel Management* 23 (November 1991): 28–31; Heinz Weirich, "Training Managers for the Global Market," *Business* 40 (July–September 1990): 40–43; Michael Blanden, "Master of None," *Banker* 141 (January 1991): 24, 26; S. Tamer Cavusgil, *Internationalizing Business Education: Meeting the Challenge* (East Lansing: Michigan State University, 1993).

13. *Wall Street Journal,* 4 April 1985, 1; *New York Times,* 27 August 1985, section 3, p. 1; Robert Ronstadt, "The Educated Entrepreneurs: A New Era of Entrepreneurial Education Is Beginning," *American Journal of Small Business* 10 (summer 1985): 7–23.

14. *New York Times,* 27 August 1985, section 3, p. 1; *New York Times Magazine,* 8 June 1986, 84; Ronstadt, "The Educated Entrepreneurs," *American Journal of Small Business* 10 (summer 1985): 10–11.

15. *Wall Street Journal,* 4 April 1985, 1; *New York Times Magazine,* 8 June 1986, 84; *Wall Street Journal,* 18 November 1986, 1; *New York Times,* 24 March 1987,

section 4, p. 27; Leonard H. Chusimir, "Entrepreneurship and MBA Degrees: How Well Do They Know Each Other?" *Journal of Small Business Management* 26 (July 1988): 71–74.

16. Andrew Wallenstein, "Can You Teach Entrepreneurship?," *Business Week*, 27 October 1993, 139–43; Carol Oliver, "Intrapreneurship and Entrepreneurship Amongst MBA Graduates," *Management Decision* 29 (1991): 8–11.

17. Alex McDonald, "Teaching the UK to Learn from Japan," *Management Today* 74 (January 1985): 19; *New York Times*, 5 July 1988, section 4, p. 9.

18. Robert J. Samuelson, Armand Feigenbaum, Kaes Van Ham, and W. Edwards Deming, all quoted in Lloyd Dobyns, *Quality or Else: The Revolution in World Business* (Boston: Houghton Mifflin, 1991).

19. "TQM Research Gets funding Boost," *Newsline* (AACSB) 23 (fall 1992): 15; J. C. Mason, "Business Schools: Striving to Meet Customer Demand," *Management Review* 81 (September 1992): 10–14; J. H. Foggin, "Meeting Customer Needs," *Survey of Business* 28 (summer 1992): 6–9; Michael Barrier, "Business Schools, TQM, and You," *Nation's Business* 81 (July 1993): 60–61.

20. J. H. Sheridan, "A New Breed of MBA," *Industry Week*, 4 October 1993, 11–16.

21. *New York Times*, 24 August 1986, section 4, p. 7.

22. *New York Times*, 24 August 1986, section 4, p. 7; *Wall Street Journal*, 27 April 1987, 24; 22 March 1988, 37. *See also* "Is Greed America's New Creed?" *Business and Society Review* 61 (spring 1987): 4–8.

23. Kirk O. Hanson, "What Good Are Ethics Courses?" *Across the Board* 24 (September 1987): 10–11; V. K. Strong, "There Is Relevance in the Classroom: Analysis of Present Methods of Teaching Business Ethics," *Journal of Business Ethics* 9 (July 1990): 603–7; Larue Tone Hosmer, "Adding Ethics to the Business Curriculum," *Business Horizons* 31 (July–August 1988): 9–15; Ronald R. Sims, "Increasing Applied Business Ethics Courses in Business School Curricula," *Journal of Business Ethics* 10 (March 1991): 211–19.

24. *New York Times*, 6 September 1987, section 22, p. 29; 14 June 1987, section 4, p. 25; "White-Collar Criminals Teach Business Ethics to MBA Students," *Newsline* (AACSB) 23 (fall 1992): 16.

25. Thomas M. Mulligan, "The Two Cultures in Business Education," *Academy of Management Review* 12 (October 1987): 593–99; Donald R. Nelson, "Promoting Moral Growth Through Intra-Group Participation," *Journal of Business Ethics* 9 (September 1990): 731–39; Jai Ghorpade, "Ethics in MBA Programs: The Rhetoric, the Reality, and a Plan of Action," *Journal of Business Ethics* 10 (December 1991): 891–905; Philip Stiles, "Teaching Business Ethics: An Open Learning Approach," *Management Education and Development* 24 (autumn 1993): 246–61.

26. Michael S. Lane, "Ethics in Education: A Comparative Study," *Journal of Business Ethics* 8 (December 1989): 943–49; Donald L. McCabe, "Context, Values, and Moral Dilemmas: Comparing the Choices of Business and Law School Students," *Journal of Business Ethics* 10 (December 1991): 951–60; Donald L. McCabe, "The Effects of Professional Education on Values and the Resolution of Ethical Dilemmas: Business School vs. Law School Students," *Journal of Business Ethics* 13 (September 1994): 693–700; G. M. Zinkhan, "MBAs' Changing Attitude Toward Marketing Dilemmas, 1981–1987," *Journal of Business Ethics* 8 (December 1989): 963–74; James Weber, "Measuring the Impact of Teaching Ethics to Future Managers: A Review, Assessment, and Recommendation," *Journal of Business Ethics* 9 (March 1990): 183–90.

27. George L. Benson, "On the Campus: How Well Do Business Schools Prepare Graduates for the Business World?," *Personnel* 60 (July–August 1983): 61–65; *New*

York Times, 20 October 1985, section 3, p. 1; 16 October 1985, section 3, p. 1; Barbara Buell, "Learning How to Play the Corporate Power Game," *Business Week,* 26 August 1985, 54, 56.

28. Curtis W. Tarr, "How to Humanize MBAs," *Fortune,* 31 March 1986, 153–54; John A. Byrne, "The Battle of the B-Schools Is Getting Bloodier," *Business Week,* 24 March 1986, 61ff.

29. Harold J. Leavitt, "Educating Our MBAs: On Teaching What We Haven't Taught," *California Management Review* 31 (spring 1989): 38–50; and *Corporate Pathfinders: Building Vision and Values into Organizations* (Homewood, Ill.: Dow Jones Irwin, 1986).

30. Russell Palmer, "Forget Managers; What We Need Are Leaders," *Business Month* 133 (January 1989): 69–70; Leonard Silk, "What America Needs Is a New Improved MBA," *Business Month* 134 (September, 1989): 9–11; Paul W. Beamish, "International Business Education: A Corporate View," *Journal of International Business Studies* 20 (fall 1989): 553–64.

31. Anne Ritter, "MBA and Business: The End of the Affair," *Personnel* 66 (November 1989): 6; Michael L. Dertouzos, Richard K. Lester, and Robert M. Solow, *Made in America: Regaining the Productive Edge* (Cambridge: MIT Press, 1989); William F. Roth Jr., "Today's MBA: A Lot to Learn," *Personnel* 66 (May 1989): 46–51.

32. *New York Times,* 7 January 1990, section 4A, p. 7; David Greising, "Chicago's B-School Goes Touchy-Feely," *Business Week,* 27 November 1989, 140; R. L. Carraway and J. R. Freeland, "MBA Training in Operations Management and Quantitative Methods," *Interfaces* 19 (July–August 1989): 75–88.

33. Derek Hornby and Raymond Thomas, "Towards a Better Standard of Management?" *Personnel Management* 21 (January 1989): 52–55.

34. Noritake Kobayashi, "The Renaissance of U. S. Business Education," *Tokyo Business Today* 59 (July 1991): 33; Karen D. Down, "What Corporations Seek in MBA Hires: A Survey," *Selections* 10 (winter 1994): 34–39.

35. Richard Greene, "Their Eyes Are on the Main Chance," *Forbes,* 9 March 1987, 69ff.; *Wall Street Journal,* 28 January 1987, 31; Andrea Gabor, "What They Don't Teach You at Business School," *U. S. News and World Report,* 13 July 1987, 44–46; *Wall Street Journal,* 21 May 1987, 1.

36. *Wall Street Journal,* 23 October 1987, 29; 29 October 1987, 30; Walter Kiechel III, "New Debate about Harvard Business School," *Fortune,* 9 November 1987, 34ff.

37. Richard Kemp, "The Bleak Outlook for New MBAs," *Institutional Investor* 22 (February 1988): 144–45; Wall Street Journal, 10 March 1988, 27; 12 April 1988, 1; Stanley Modic, "Black Monday Has MBAs Eyeing Industry," *Industry Week,* 2 May 1988, 9; Peter Nulty, "Where the 1988 MBAs Are Going," *Fortune,* 29 August 1988, 48–51; *Wall Street Journal,* 6 December 1988, A1; 25 October 1988, 1.

38. Brian S. Moskal, "Engineers Can Grab a Lifeline," *Industry Week,* 19 March 1990, 40; "Move Over MBAs, Here Come MMMs," *Fortune,* 18 January 1990: 16; Bruce Nussbaum, "Re-Making the Harvard B-School," *Business Week,* 24 March 1986, 54–59; Laura Zinn, "Takeovers Are Out, Soap Powder Is In," *Business Week,* 6 May 1991, 82–83; Patricia Hamilton, "Training World-Class Manufacturers," *D&B Reports* 43 (January–February 1994): 26ff.

39. Lori Bongiorno, "Corporate America's New Lesson Plan," *Business Week,* 25 October 1993, 102–4.

40. *Wall Street Journal,* 29 April 1986, 1; 10 August 1985, 13; 15 December 1986, 29; *New York Times,* 30 November 1985, 1; *Wall Street Journal,* 27 April 1987, 27; Keith Girard, "At Last, MBAs Learn to Manage," *Business Month,* 133 (May 1989): 13–14; *Wall Street Journal,* 7 May 1986, 37; Dennis Young, "Nonprofit Management

Education Comes of Age: A Progress Report," *Nonprofit World* 8 (November–December 1990): 17–19.

41. *Wall Street Journal,* 8 November 1985, 35.

42. Harold J. Leavitt, "Educating Our MBAs: On Teaching What We Haven't Taught," *California Management Review* 31 (spring 1989): 38–50; Henry Mintzberg, *Mintzberg on Management* (New York: Free Press, 1989); Edgar H. Schein, *Management Education: Some Troublesome Realities and Possible Remedies,* Working Paper #WP1899–97, (MIT Sloan School of Management, 1987).

43. Baldrige, quoted by Earl F. Cheit, "Business Schools and Their Critics," *California Management Review* 27 (spring 1985): 48; Henry Mintzberg, *Mintzberg on Management* (New York: Free Press, 1987); *Wall Street Journal,* 15 August 1988, 17; Curtis Tarr, quoted by John A. Byrne, "Where the Schools Aren't Doing Their Homework," *Business Week,* 28 November 1988, 84ff.

44. Sandra Bernstein, "Invest in the Future: Hire an MBA Student," *Canadian Business* 58 (July 1985): 115–17; Anne McGrath, "GMAT Flunks Out at Harvard," *Forbes,* 23 September 1985, 199–200; *Wall Street Journal,* 10 September 1985, 33; Bernard Keys and Joseph Wolfe, "Management Education and Development: Current Issues and Emerging Trends," *Journal of Management* 14 (June 1988): 205–29.

45. Michael McGill, *American Business and the Quick Fix* (New York: Holt, 1988); Helen J. Muller et al., "Have the Business Schools Let Down U.S. Corporations?" *Management Review* 30 (October 1988): 24–31; "Management Material," *CA Magazine* 127 (December 1994): 9.

46. John Thackray, "Guru on the Riverbank," *Management Today* 78 (August 1989): 53–56; Harold J. Leavitt, "Educating Our MBAs: On Teaching What We Haven't Taught," *California Management Review* 31 (spring 1989): 38–50.

47. Harold J. Leavitt, "Socializing Our MBAs: Total Immersion? Managed Cultures? Brainwashing?" *California Management Review* 33 (summer 1991): 127–43; "Wharton Business School: A New MBA," *Economist* 14 December 1991, 72–74; J. C. Mason, "Business Schools: Striving to Meet Customer Demand," *Management Review* 81 (September 1992): 10–14; David H. Blake, quoted in the *New York Times,* 6 March 1990, section D, p. 16.

48. Harold J. Leavitt, "Educating Our MBAs," *California Management Review* 62 (September 1989): 68ff.; Joel M. Stern, "In Defense of MBAs," *Fortune,* 19 August 1985, 233ff.; B. G. Yovovich, "MBA Programs See a Change in Course," *Business Marketing* 79 (March 1994): 27; Michael Osbaldeston and Alan Warner, "In Search of Excellence in Business Schools," *Personnel Management* 17 (March 1985): 30–34; William A. Stoever, "Management Teaching Isn't *Fun* Any More," *Business Horizons* 30 (January–February 1987): 85–87.

49. *Wall Street Journal,* 25 November 1986, 31; Abraham Flexner, *Universities: American, English, German* (Oxford University Press, 1930): 168.

50. *Wall Street Journal,* 28 October 1986, 1; "When Companies Tell B-Schools What to Teach," *Business Week,* 10 February 1986, 60–61; Gordon Anderson, "MBAs Tailored to Suit the Company Shape," *Personnel Management* 21 (December 1989): 71–73; Henry Mintzberg, *Mintzberg on Management* (New York: Free Press, 1989).

51. *Wall Street Journal,* 31 May 1988, 1; John Lorinc, "Class Action," *Canadian Business* 62 (September 1989): 68ff.

52. "Ten-Year Effort Produces Outcome Measurement Tools," *Newsline* (AACSB) 17 (June–August 1987): 1–4; "The Outcome Measurement Project: Details and Directions," *Newsline* (AACSB) 17 (June–August 1987): 5; J. David Reitzel, "Editorial," *American Business Law Journal* 25 (winter 1988), xiii–xxii; letter, Karen S. Martinez (AACSB) to author, 11 June 1991.

53. George S. Odiorne, The Executive MBA: A New Way to Develop Talent," *Personnel* 62 (November 1985): 38–43; Steven Prokesch, "Classes for Execs: A Quick Buck for B-Schools?," *Business Week,* 11 February 1985, 56; *New York Times,* 4 January 1987, section 12, p. 72; Lynda Phillips-Madison and Paula R. Sloan, "EMBA Buyers, Beware,' *Management Review* 76 (November 1987): 52–54.

54. H. J. Zoffer, "How One Dean Would Change the Business Schools," *Management Review* 75 (May 1986): 60–61; Bernard Keys and Joseph Wolfe, "Management Education and Development: Current Issues and Emerging Trends," *Journal of Management* 14 (June 1988): 205–29; *New York Times,* 4 January 1987, section 12, p. 72.

55. *New York Times,* 17 September 1985, section 4, 5; M. J. Gannon and Peter Arlow, "The Mystique of the MBA Degree," *Business Horizons* 28 (January–February 1985): 20–25; "BW/Harris Poll: How Execs Rate a B-School Education," *Business Week,* 24 March 1986, 64.

56. *Wall Street Journal,* 3 December 1985, 1; Beth Selby, "Recruiting Rites at the Harvard B-School," *Institutional Investor* 20 (March 1986): 78ff.; Craig Mellow, "And a Harvard MBA Shall Lead Us," *Across the Board* 23 (April 1986): 12–19.

57. Gail Dutton, "MBAs: On Target," *Chemical Marketing Reporter,* 24 October 1994, SR-12; Mel Mandell, "A Matter of Degree," *World Trade* 7 (September 1994): 80–84; Ronald Yeaple, *The MBA Advantage: Why It Pays to Get an MBA* (Holbrook, Mass: B. Adams, 1994); Lori Bongiorno, "Is There an MBA Glut? If You Answered No, You Pass," *Business Week,* 24 October 1994, 71–72.

Annotated Bibliography

Three types of sources have provided most of the information in this history: catalogs of colleges and universities, histories of colleges or at least of their business schools, and thousands of secondary sources—magazines and newspaper articles about MBA schools, and books about business and about business education.

Following is a briefly annotated list of some of the best known, most valuable, or most provocative writings on the history of business education.

American Association of Collegiate Schools of Business, 1916–1966. Homewood, Ill: R. D. Irwin, 1966. [The 50th anniversary official history of the influential AACSB.]

Behrman, Jack N., and Richard I. Levin. "Are Business Schools Doing Their Job?" *Harvard Business Review* 62 (January–February 1984): 140–47. [Powerful plea for business schools to break from their previous research-dominated mold.]

Bossard, James, and Francis Dewhurst. *University Education for Business.* Philadelphia: University of Pennsylvania Press, 1931. [A survey of the status of business education after three decades.]

Chandler, Alfred D. *The Visible Hand: The Managerial Revolution in American Business.* Cambridge: Harvard University Press, 1977. [The rise of the concept of "management," with observations on the training it requires.]

Copeland, Melvin T. *And Mark an Era: The Story of the Harvard Business School.* Boston: Little, Brown, 1958. [The first history of HBS, by one of its earliest faculty members.]

Cruikshank, Jeffrey L. *A Delicate Experiment.* Boston: Harvard Business School Press, 1987. [A beautifully illustrated, fascinating, and immensely informative history of the Harvard Business School from the beginnings to World War II.]

Donham, Wallace B. "The Failure of Business Leadership and the Responsibility of the Universities." *Harvard Business Review* 11 (July 1933), 418–35. [A deep and thought-provoking analysis of business's rise in prominence and its consequent duties to society.]

Drucker, Peter F. "The Graduate Business School." *Fortune* 42 (August 1950): 92–116. [Trenchant, and generally favorable, views by the famed management authority, at the time when the MBA was beginning its ascent.]

Flexner, Abraham. *Universities: American, English, German.* Oxford: Oxford University Press, 1930. [A classicist's denunciation of the rise of business studies in college.]

Gordon, Robert A., and James E. Howell. *Higher Education for Business.* New York: Columbia University Press, 1959. [One of the two infamous "foundation reports." See chapter 9.]

Hayes, Robert H., and William J. Abernethy. "Managing Our Way to Economic Decline." *Harvard Business Review* 58 (July–August 1980): 67–77. [One of the most influential articles of the past two decades. The failure of business education is seen as a main reason for America's loss of competitiveness.]

319

Hunter Naylor, Meg. *Thunderbird American Graduate School of International Management*. Glendale, Ariz.: American Graduate School of International Management, 1986. [Interesting history of a school founded with a specific focus.]

Kozelka, Richard L. *Professional Education for Business*. Minneapolis: School of Business Administration of the University of Minnesota, 1954. [A superb self-study of collegiate business education by a thoughtful dean. Commissioned by the AACSB, it represented the best thinking of business educators about the state of their profession in the mid-1950s.]

Lyon, Levrett S. *Education for Business*. Chicago: University of Chicago Press, 1922. [A general survey of the state of business education at the time of the first wave of growth.]

Marshall, Leon C. *The American Collegiate School of Business*. Chicago: University of Chicago Press, 1928. [A collection of writings about business education, already somewhat outdated at the time but still interesting.]

———. "The College of Commerce and Administration at the University of Chicago." *Journal of Political Economy* 21 (February 1913): 97–110. [Description of a curriculum that reflected a heavy sense of the social responsibility of business—a social scientist's early efforts to steer business education away from mere profit-making.]

———. "The Collegiate School of Business at Erewhon." *Journal of Political Economy* 34 (June 1926): 289–326. [An attempt to design a perfect business school—notable mainly because it shows how tradition-bound the early theorists were and how little they were able to formulate new concepts.]

McGill, Michael. *American Business and the Quick Fix*. New York: Holt 1988. [A joyful romp through the fads and fancies of the 1970s and 1980s.]

Mencken, H. L. See Stone.

Nations, L. J. "Business Before Culture: College Becomes an Institution of Higher Earnings." *North American Review* 229 (January 1930), 705–12. [An economist's apprehensive look at the rise of collegiate business studies.]

Pierson, Frank C. *The Education of American Businessmen*. New York: McGraw-Hill, 1959. [One of the two infamous "foundation reports." See chapter 9.]

Porter, Lyman W., and Lawrence E. McKibbin. *Management Education and Development: Drift or Thrust into the 21st Century?* New York: McGraw-Hill, 1988. [Despite the publicity that accompanied its publication, a rather bland rehashing of old issues surrounding management education.]

Rickover, Hyman G. "Getting the Job Done Right." *New York Times*, 25 November 1981, 23. [Stern denunciation of the idea that "management science" even exists.]

Ridgeway, James. *The Closed Corporation: American Universities in Crisis*. New York: Random House, 1968. [Investigative journalism exposing the close links between universities and government, especially with reference to the Vietnam War.]

Sass, Steven A. *The Pragmatic Imagination*. Philadelphia: University of Pennsylvania Press, 1982. [A fine history of the pioneering Wharton School.]

Sheppard, C. Stuart, ed. *The First Twenty Years: The Darden School at the University of Virginia*. Charlottesville: The Darden School, 1975. [Interesting and thoughtful history of a later-starting school that became very prominent.]

Stone, Arlington J. [Pseud. for H. L. Mencken]. "The Dawn of A New Science."

American Mercury 14 (August 1928): 446–55. [Riotously funny denunciation of education for business.]

Veblen, Thorstein. *The Higher Learning in America* (1918). New York: Sagamore Press, 1957. [A classicist's denunciation of business education. Cranky and enjoyable, but not influential.]

Index